Finance, Economics, and Mathematics

Finance, Economics, and Mathematics

OLDRICH ALFONS VASICEK

WILEY

Published by John Wiley & Sons, Inc., Hoboken, New Jersey.

Published simultaneously in Canada.

For general information on our other products and services or for technical support, please contact our Customer Care Department within the United States at (800) 762-2974, outside the United States at (317) 572-3993 or fax (317) 572-4002.

Wiley publishes in a variety of print and electronic formats and by print-on-demand. Some material included with standard print versions of this book may not be included in e-books or in print-on-demand. If this book refers to media such as a CD or DVD that is not included in the version you purchased, you may download this material at http://booksupport.wiley.com. For more information about Wiley products, visit www.wiley.com.

Library of Congress Cataloging-in-Publication Data

Vasicek, Oldrich Alfons, 1941- author.
[Essays. Selections]
Finance, economics, and mathematics / Oldrich Alfons Vasicek.
pages cm
Includes index.
ISBN 978-1-119-12220-3 (cloth), ISBN 978-1-119-18620-5 (epub), ISBN 978-1-119-18621-2 (ePDF)
1. Finance. 2. Economics. 3. Finance, Mathematical. I. Title.
HG173.V36 2015
332–dc23
2015026777

Cover Design: Wiley
Cover Image: Tech background © RomanOkopny / iStockphoto

10 9 8 7 6 5 4 3 2 1

MIX
Paper from responsible sources
FSC
www.fsc.org
FSC® C013604

Contents

Foreword

About a half century ago began a remarkable intellectual revolution which transformed the field of finance from a collection of anecdotes and accounting identities into a scientific discipline with general principles and rigorous empirical assessments of its hypotheses. In the ensuing decades, finance science was both shaped, and shaped by, the extraordinary transformation of the practice of finance.

Oldrich Vasicek was one of the pioneer scientists to provide foundational contributions in the pricing and risk measurement of fixed income securities–default-free bonds that form the term structure of interest rates, and credit-risky bonds and loans–and to implement them in practice. Here we have the collection of the original papers and articles of his intellectual history of thought–with the content of the models still applicable today.

Whether a master researcher, experienced finance professional or novice student of finance, you are in for a treat.

Bon appétit!

Robert C. Merton
Distinguished Professor of Finance
MIT Sloan School of Management
1997 Nobel Memorial Prize in Economic Sciences

Preface

This book is a selection of my published and unpublished papers written between 1968, when I came to the United States, and 2014. The ideas for them came to me at different times and in different circumstances. I have worked as a theoretical mathematician in the Czech Academy of Sciences, as a vice-president in a large U.S. bank, as an external consultant in a small investment technology software developer, as a full-time professor and a visiting professor at several universities. I have been a founding partner and a managing director in a startup, a special adviser for a large bond rating firm and, since 2010, an independent researcher not associated with any institution.

I cannot say which was the most satisfying. It has all been fun, and still is. I have met, and in many cases worked with, many extremely interesting and capable people. These meetings, discussions, and collaboration have meant a lot to me.

I have usually worked somewhat outside the organizational structure. I have never had a subordinate, which was exactly as I wanted it. And I have been very fortunate that I rarely found much discrepancy between what I wanted to work on, and between what seemed to be needed at the time.

I have enjoyed collaborating with other people. A number of the papers in this collection are joint works. I would like to take this opportunity to thank my coauthors: Gifford Fong, my one-time employer and long-time friend, with whom I wrote six of the papers here; John McQuown, who hired me to Wells Fargo Bank on my arrival to the USA, with whom, along with Stephen Kealhofer, we founded the KMV Corporation years later, and with whom I have been friends the whole time; my colleague at the University of Rochester, the late Professor Julian Keilson; and the tireless and resourceful Professor Helyette Geman, who arranged my pleasant stay at ESSEC. I appreciate their input, insights, and joint work.

I would like to express my thanks and appreciation to many people. There are some, however, that I cannot but mention specifically: my father, JUDr. Oldřich Vašíček, who encouraged and supported my interest in mathematics from early childhood; the late Professor Alois Apfelbeck, much feared for his first-year analysis class, who singlehandedly, and successfully, opposed the Party authorities from expelling me from the university;

John McQuown, who introduced me to finance; Professor Richard Roll, whose critique of an earlier draft of my 1977 paper made me to rewrite it for much improvement; and Professor Robert Merton, one of the smartest yet gracious people I know. To these and many other people who helped me by advice, debate, collaboration, or example, I wish to give my gratitude.

Oldrich Alfons Vasicek
August 2014

PART

One

Efforts and Opinions

"A lot of attention goes to the pricing of various complicated debt instruments because those instruments are becoming more common. That's needed short-term. I think long-term it's important to understand the more basic problem we were talking about before — what exactly goes into the pricing of the straight debt of a firm. That's the economics of credit, not the valuation of assorted derivatives. There is too much mathematics and too little economics in finance nowadays. That may sound funny coming from a mathematician, but nevertheless that's my opinion. We must not forget that the subject of finance is economic decisions". *(page 15)*

CHAPTER 1

Introduction to Part I

The past fifty years or so have been a time of great bloom in the field of finance. This period has seen the birth of concepts such as variance as a quantitative definition of risk, portfolio diversification as a means of controlling risk, portfolio optimization in the mean/variance framework, expected utility maximization as an investment and consumption decision making criterion. These notions were applied in the development of Capital Asset Pricing Model to describe the market equilibrium, to the concepts of systematic and specific risks and the introduction of asset beta. We have witnessed the revolution brought by the theory of options pricing. We have seen the appearance of the general principle of asset pricing as the present value of the cash flows expected under the risk-neutral probability measure. We have seen the development of the theory of the term structure of interest rates and the pricing of interest rate derivatives.

These theoretical developments have been accompanied by equally exciting changes in investment practices and indeed in the nature of capital markets. Few of us can still envision investment decision making without quantitative risk measurement, without hedging techniques, without deep and efficient markets for futures and options, without swaps and interest rate derivatives, and without computer models to price such instruments. And yet, these are all very recent developments. It has not been much longer than some thirty years ago that the very notion of an index fund was greeted with disbelief, if not outright ridicule!

I had the great fortune to be cast right into the middle of such developments when I joined the Management Science Department of Wells Fargo Bank in 1969. The annual conferences organized by Wells Fargo in the early seventies brought together people such as Franco Modigliani, Merton Miller, Jack Treynor, William Sharpe, Fisher Black, Myron Scholes, Robert Merton, Richard Roll and many others. The second half of the twentieth century was

---

Risk, 72-73, December 2002

in my eyes as exciting in the field of finance as the first half must have been in physics.

I have worked on a variety of projects at Wells Fargo and later at the University of Rochester and the University of California at Berkeley, but one thing that bothered me for quite a while in the mid-seventies was the absence of solid results on the pricing of bonds. At that time, the CAPM was already in existence, and people had tried to apply it to bonds by measuring their betas to determine the yield, but that did not really lead anywhere. The options pricing theory had also been freshly developed by then, but it did not seem very feasible to apply a theory of pricing derivative assets to assets as primary as government bonds. What would be the underlying?

And yet, it was obvious that there must be some conditions that govern interest rate behavior in efficient markets. You cannot have, for instance, a fixed-income market in which the yield curves are always flat and move up and down in some random fashion through time, because then a barbell portfolio would always outperform a bullet portfolio of the same duration, and therefore it would be possible to set up a profitable riskless arbitrage. But what are these conditions?

The clue came from comparing the return to maturity on a term bond to that of a repeated investment in a shorter bond. The common denominator between bonds of any maturity would be a rollover of the very short bond, and thus it seemed natural to postulate that the pricing of a bond should be a function of the short rate over its term. And once the idea of describing the short rate by a Markov process came to me, it became obvious: the future behavior of the short rate is determined by its current value and therefore the price of the bond must be a function of the short rate! From then on, it's mathematics: in order to exclude riskless arbitrage, this function must be such that the expected excess return on each bond is proportional to its risk, which gives rise to a partial differential equation. The boundary condition of this equation is the maturity value, and the solution is the bond price. This was my 1977 paper. (Curiously, the thing that became known as the Vasicek model was just an example that I put in that paper to illustrate the general theory on a specific case. Well, you never know.)

Since then, it was like opening Pandora's box. Great many papers followed, extending the model in various ways—multiple factors, non-Markov risk sources, development of various specific models for practical use. One paper I have a great respect for is the Cox, Ingersoll and Ross article (for some reason, they did not publish the paper until 1985, although they did the work many years earlier), because it is about more than interest rates: it is about an equilibrium in the bond market.

A big shift came in 1986 with the publication of the Ho and Lee paper. This article presented a simple interest rate model, which was just a special case of my theory. The shift was in the interpretation: Ho and Lee assumed that the current bond prices were given (equal to the actual observed prices) and concerned themselves with pricing interest rate derivatives. This, of course, allows very useful applications for valuation of various instruments from simple callable bonds to the most complex swaptions.

The Ho and Lee paper engendered a great development effort in that direction, including the 1992 paper by Heath, Jarrow, and Morton, which formalized this approach. This direction was in fact taken further: There are models that assume as given not only the current bond prices, but also prices of caps and floors or even more. These models, used then to value other derivatives, have the great virtue of fitting the current market pricing of the more primary assets.

While I appreciate the usefulness of these models, I somewhat regret the direction away from the economics. To ask how derivatives are priced given the pricing of bonds seems to me assuming away the more interesting question: How are bonds priced? I personally hope to see a return to efforts to understand the economics, rather just to aid trading.

A similar situation has arisen in default risk measurement and pricing, another subject dear to my heart. The so-called reduced-form models, which have been advocated for the purpose of credit risk analysis, assume that corporate debt prices are given and use these prices to value debt derivatives. Again, to me it seems that the more interesting question is how to price corporate debt. Fortunately, this is possible given the legacy of Merton, Black, and Scholes, since corporate liabilities are derivatives of the firm's asset value, and a structural model of the firm can price its debt (and debt derivatives) from equity prices.

As appreciative as I am of the past in the field of finance, I am equally enthusiastic about its future. There will be no lack of problems to address, and there will be no lack of talent to solve them. Indeed, it is the professionals in this area of endeavor that are its greatest assets, and I am grateful to have worked with, and learned from, so many of them.

CHAPTER 2

Lifetime Achievement Award

By Dwight Cass

In the late 1960s, Wells Fargo Bank in San Francisco assembled a team of uniquely gifted thinkers who would go on to push the boundaries of financial theory. Working alongside William Sharpe, Myron Scholes, Fisher Black, and Robert Merton at the time was Oldrich Vasicek, who is *Risk's* lifetime achievement award recipient. Like his Wells Fargo colleagues, Vasicek has had a profound effect on both financial theory and practice. His equilibrium model of the term structure of interest rates is widely acknowledged as the landmark work in the field, and many credit it for setting off the series of modeling innovations that paved the way for the rapid growth of the interest rate derivatives market. Ten years later, he developed a groundbreaking credit portfolio risk model that paved the way for the approaches incorporated in the Basel II capital Accord.

Among market practitioners, he is perhaps best known for co-founding KMV, the San Francisco credit analysis firm, and for using Scholes, Black, and Merton's insights on option pricing to develop the expected default frequency (EDF) credit pricing system—a so-called Merton model approach—at the heart of KMV's product line. The company has been extremely successful, with KMV claiming more than 70 percent of the world's largest financial institutions as clients. It is hard to find a major credit derivatives dealer or loan house that does not use it. The success of

Risk, 44-45, January 2002

the approach has prompted other companies, including Moody's Investors Service and JPMorgan Chase, to add a Merton model-based default probability estimator to their offerings.

This combination of theoretical and business accomplishments alone might be enough to warrant *Risk's* lifetime achievement award. But 60-year-old Vasicek has shown no interest in resting on his laurels to free more time for his enthusiasms, which range from playing classical flute music to windsurfing in the cold, windy waters surrounding San Francisco. He continues to tackle new challenges, such as the tricky problem of modeling spot and derivatives price behavior of nonstorable commodities such as electricity and telecoms bandwidth (on which he co-authored a technical article with Hélyette Geman published in the August 2001 issue of *Risk*). And, according to his colleagues at KMV, he remains the driving force behind the evolution of that firm's product line.

Vasicek did not originally intend to pursue a career as a financial theorist. He trained in his native Czechoslovakia as a mathematician, earning a PhD with honors in probability theory from Charles University in 1968. The first event that placed him on the road to his career in finance was the Soviet invasion in August of that year. Vasicek had been at the Czechoslovak Academy of Science in Prague, working in pure mathematics, when the Soviet tanks rolled in. He and his wife left for Vienna a few days later.

He made his way to San Francisco and began applying for jobs as a mathematician. He was interviewed for several positions—including a job at Stanford University's marine biology department doing spectral analyses of dolphins' songs. But fate lent a hand again, and he was interviewed by John (Mac) McQuown, head of Wells Fargo's Management Science Department, who was looking to hire several mathematicians. "I'm a mathematician by profession, and only went into finance because my first job here was in a bank," Vasicek jokes.

McQuown's group already included Scholes, Merton, and Black. Also, Sharpe was consulting for the bank. This was before the Black-Scholes option pricing model had been published. "Mac hired these guys before they were famous," Vasicek says. Wells Fargo was one of the first banks to embrace Sharpe's capital asset pricing model (CAPM), and McQuown's group was looking at ways to apply it. Vasicek worked on this project and on index fund construction.

McQuown, who would later launch KMV with Vasicek and Stephen Kealhofer, said Vasicek's talents quickly became obvious. "I vividly remember Fischer Black saying to me, on a couple of occasions, that when he had a really intractable mathematical problem, he would go to Oldrich," he says.

Myron Scholes, the Nobel laureate in economics who is now a finance professor at Stanford University in Palo Alto, California, says: "He's got tremendous mathematical and engineering abilities, and is also a very good listener. He articulates his views and holds to his path if he thinks he is right, but he's willing to appreciate other people's views, which makes him a good scientist." Indeed, in an arena where oversized egos are often the norm, many of Vasicek's past and current colleagues praise his tolerance and humility. "He has ideas that seem quite simple in retrospect, so much so that they're quickly borrowed by everyone else. But they reflect a deep and powerful mind." says Kealhofer. "He has a wonderful old world/new world charm—a mixture of Prague and San Francisco," he adds.

In 1974, Vasicek left Wells Fargo to teach at the University of Rochester (New York) Graduate School of Management, where he would stay for two years. During this period, his attention turned to the problem of interest rate behavior, which he would continue to pursue when he returned to California as a visiting professor at UC Berkeley's business school. "The pricing of bonds and behavior of interest rates was an open question at that point," Vasicek says. "The work on the CAPM was exciting, but the research that had been done wasn't applicable to bonds."

Vasicek realized that arbitrage would link bond prices up and down the term structure, so, for example, there had to be a relationship between investing in a one-year bond twice in succession and investing in a two-year bond straight off. He found the common denominator to be the short-term interest rate. "If you postulate that the pricing of a long bond is a function of the short rate over the term of the bond, or more accurately, of your probabilistic description of the short rate's behavior over the term of the term bond, you have a common variable for the pricing of bonds," he notes. "In other words, you have a state variable for the pricing of bonds with all terms from the current value of the short rate—that was the point at which the idea really broke for me at the time," he says.

INSPIRATION

Vasicek's paper, titled "An Equilibrium Characterization of the Term Structure," was published in the *Journal of Financial Economics* in 1977. It was either the basis for, or inspired many of the theoretical advances that came in the years that followed. Among these was the influential 1985 Cox-Ingersoll-Ross model. One of that model's authors, Stephen Ross, professor of finance and economics at MIT's Sloan School of Management in Boston, says of Vasicek's work: "It is a wonderfully simple, empirically amenable model. It guides us in a lot of our intuitions about the subject." McQuown argues that Vasicek's model was the critical catalyst that spurred development of the interest rate derivatives market. "The interest rate swap market relies on that model," he says. "If it wasn't for Oldrich's contribution, the interest rate swap market may have taken longer to develop. I dare say the problem would have been solved sometime, but Oldrich solved it first."

"It was like opening a Pandora's box as far as academic research goes," Vasicek says. But, he notes with some modesty that he had not actually aimed to redefine how the world viewed interest rate products. "But what's kind of funny is that my paper focused on the theory," he says. "What has become known as the Vasicek model was just an example. I developed the theory and I wanted to illustrate it on a particular type of process and go through the calculation and determine the final equation. But it's the example I used that's been remembered."

The shift in his emphasis to credit risk came when McQuown recruited Vasicek for an ill-fated scheme in the early 1980s. "I persuaded him to join me in a venture that ultimately went down the tubes called Diversified Corporate Loans in 1983. We wanted to create a pool of credit from major US banks where the banks could swap qualified loans into a pool in return for a pool interest." The idea was to give the banks liquidity and portfolio diversification, but to do so, the firm needed a way to value credit risk, to aid the participating banks in valuing the loans they put into the pool, and the pool itself.

"So," Vasicek says, "I started to work on credit. Up to then, credit was strictly a judgment call. So I developed an application of option pricing theory—the Black-Scholes and Merton work." Kealhofer says: "He laid down the theoretical footprint in a short time that we've been using for 17 years now. He laid the groundwork for both the basic credit technology and the portfolio technology. We've been laboring in those two veins ever since."

When DCL went out of business in 1989, Kealhofer (who had joined several years before), McQuown and Vasicek launched KMV to further develop and market the credit evaluation tool. Myron Scholes says: "It set the stage for using more modern technology than the rating agencies have used, and it led to more people thinking about using option technology to do credit pricing. Others had used the option framework to price debt. But his work at KMV took the lead in developing something that was usable by a vast number of people." Indeed, having a widely available set of reliable credit pricing tools was a necessary precondition for the development of the credit derivatives market, Scholes notes.

PIONEERING

MIT's Ross says: "Vasicek's work on credit risk is a different kind of pioneering. It's a demonstration of how one can take high-quality academic work and turn it into a solid business without compromising the academic stuff or the understanding of the needs of the marketplace. Marrying those two is never easy."

Vasicek says the launch of competing Merton-model products—JPMorgan Chase's being the most recent, the specifications of which were published in the November 2001 issue of *Risk*—is good for the markets. "I'm glad that people are becoming interested, because any effort in this direction will make the market for these securities more liquid and more efficient," he says. "There has been a bit of confusion about what a Merton model is. I guess people keep forgetting it is not a formula, it is a framework. It is a structure that allows you to get a specific mathematical solution to the value of a firm. But it would depend on the assumptions you make about the firm's financial structure and the capital statements and the payments the firm is making—coupons, dividends, and the nature of the debt, convertibility and optionality. It's a very complicated thing. We give a lot of attention to how we characterize the firm, on top of the mathematical problem, then it's a fair amount of work."

As co-head of KMV's research group, Vasicek continues to guide development of the firm's products. "We just rolled out a new method of calculating a loss on credit instruments that uses the empirical distribution of default risk," Kealhofer says. "That was suggested by Oldrich." As factors such as the Basel Accord and the rapid growth of the credit derivatives and synthetic collateralized debt obligation markets have kept the credit risk modeling arms race in full swing, and new pricing challenges such as those in the electricity and bandwidth markets have arisen, Vasicek's work has remained at the vital crux between theory and practice.

CHAPTER 3

One-on-One Interview with Oldrich Alfons Vasicek

By Nina Mehta

Oldrich Alfons Vasicek, a mathematician, is one of the leading lights in modern finance. His 1977 paper, "An Equilibrium Characterization of the Term Structure," described the behavior of interest rates across maturities and paved the way for the development of the interest rate derivatives market. He is one of the co-founders of KMV Corp., the granddaddy of credit risk modeling firms, which Moody's Investors Service bought in 2002 (and renamed Moody's KMV). Throughout his career Vasicek has been at the forefront of credit risk modeling. Earlier this year he increased his stockpile of awards when he was named the 2004 IAFE/SunGard Financial Engineer of the Year. The author of more than 30 papers in mathematical and finance journals, Vasicek received a PhD in probability theory from Charles University in Prague, in what is now the Czech Republic, in 1968. This interview was conducted in February.

FEN: You've worked on models to value credit risk for a large part of your career, but you said recently that valuing the plain debt of a single issuer is more challenging. Why?

Oldrich Vasicek: It's a very basic question we need to ask and answer with a higher priority than asking how the derivatives are priced. Derivatives are secondary instruments. I'm not a great fan of so-called reduced-form models, which assume you know how to price debt—namely, that you observe the market prices of plain debt of various maturities—and once you have that, you price the credit default swaps and other options.

Financial Engineering News, May 2005

We need to understand how the more primary instruments are priced. In theory, we have the methodology available to do so—the Merton-Black-Scholes approach to valuing corporate liabilities. A company's debt is, after all, an option on the company's assets. If we know the terms of the option—that is, the financial structure of the firm—and we know the market value of the firm's assets, which we can infer from the stock price, then the derivative asset pricing theory should enable us to come up with the value of the debt. That approach been around for 30 years, but applying it is not a trivial problem because the firm's liability structure is usually very complex. There are various contingencies that are hard to describe and analyze mathematically.

FEN: Has this problem become more pressing in recent years because companies can now issue complex hybrid instruments across the debt-equity range?

Vasicek: It's always been a problem. A perfectly theoretically and practically complete solution has never really been available. It is more difficult because of new instruments constantly being invented and brought into practice. Financing now includes much more complex instruments than what was in use 20 years ago.

FEN: Credit models have become more and more sophisticated as the market has grown up around them. In your view, is there some area of insufficiency in credit risk valuation?

Vasicek: I'm not sure whether the existing approaches to credit valuation actually take into account correctly the possibility of very atypical catastrophic events that have not happened for the last 50 years, but that may be lurking in the future—such as a general collapse of the whole economy or a Great Depression or something of that nature. Empirical works that measure the default probabilities of various classes of credit risk typically use data that don't cover the occurrence of any such events. People may be a little too optimistic in measuring the probabilities of default if inferences are based just on data covering periods of relative calm.

FEN: So model prices for debt instruments don't correctly include the possibility of extreme events occurring?

Vasicek: No. Look at it this way: To protect himself against extreme losses, a lender may buy a way-out-of-the-money put on the company's stock. But if there is a general economic collapse, chances are that the issuers of the put will be unable to honor their obligation, since they will themselves be bankrupt.

On the other hand, I think that the market pricing of debt actually does take these kinds of things into account—that would explain the discrepancy between the probabilities of default, particularly on high-quality credits, and the actual pricing of debt for those companies. Typically, for high-quality corporate credits the spread over the riskless rate is higher than the measured probability of default. Part of the possible explanation is that the bond market incorporates the possibility of extreme events occurring in the future, while models do not.

FEN: You're talking about high-quality debt because there are fewer other reasons that would explain the excess spread?

Vasicek: Yes. The same thing would be true for low-quality debt, but it would add a relatively smaller amount to the risk premia.

FEN: I know you've cut back your work in the credit area in the last few years, but let me ask you where you think credit modeling is heading. What kinds of questions should credit modelers try to address?

Vasicek: A lot of attention goes to the pricing of various complicated debt instruments because those instruments are becoming more common. That's needed short-term. I think long-term it's important to understand the more basic problem we were talking about before—what exactly goes into the pricing of the straight debt of a firm. That's the economics of credit, not the valuation of assorted derivatives. There is too much mathematics and too little economics in finance nowadays. That may sound funny coming from a mathematician, but nevertheless that's my opinion. We must not forget that the subject of finance is economic decisions.

FEN: You have a paper that's just coming out in the *Journal of Financial Economics* called "The Economics of Interest Rates." That's an example of what you're talking about, since you're focusing on the economics rather than the behavior of interest rates, which is where you initially made your name in finance. What does the paper say, and why is it interesting?

Vasicek: The area we somehow lost sight of, and should return to now, is economics. Twenty or thirty years ago it was the focus of a large portion of the work in finance. A prime example of an early work that went in that direction is the Cox-Ingersoll-Ross paper that was published in 1985. You can view this recent paper of mine as a generalization of that approach.

What Cox, Ross, and Ingersoll did at the time is they said, Where do interest rates come from? They had a formal description of the economic opportunities in a society on the one hand, and, on the other hand, a quantitative description of the preferences of the participants—preferences for current versus future consumption, the degree of risk aversion, and so on. If you then impose the market clearing conditions that ensure the existence of an equilibrium, you can see how the prices of various assets and in particular the prices of bonds—that is, the determination of interest rates—would happen in that economy.

But they assumed that everybody's preferences are the same, that you have homogenous investors in the economy, which is a limiting factor in the analysis. For one thing, there would be no borrowing or lending in that economy and the bond market wouldn't exist, because if everybody had the same preferences, everybody would hold the same investment portfolio. Besides, in reality, investors do have different preferences. So I have attempted to extend the general equilibrium models by incorporating heterogeneous preferences among investors. I'd been working on this problem for three or four years, but the actual breakthrough that allowed me to come up with the solution occurred about a year ago.

FEN: What was the breakthrough?

Vasicek: The main difficulty in dealing with heterogeneous investors is that the society's average, or aggregate, attitude toward risk and toward present versus future consumption shifts through time. This is because the investors' wealth levels change due to their different investment portfolios, and that gives different weights to their individual preferences. It turned out that the behavior of the individual wealth levels is driven by a single stochastic process, which gives you a mathematically tractable way of characterizing the development of the aggregate preferences.

FEN: Let me go back to an earlier point in your career. What exactly were you hired to do at Wells Fargo?

Vasicek: The Management Sciences Department of Wells Fargo was trying to look at the implications of newfangled theories such as the Capital Asset Pricing Model in the banking and investment practice. I was hired to be part of that because these models are highly quantitative and a mathematical background is definitely useful, even though they are essentially economic theories. CAPM was just making it into existence at that time. In fact, it was very slow in getting accepted. When I started at Wells Fargo in early 1969, most people in the bank still thought it was nonsense to measure risk by the variance of returns.

FEN: You went on to do other research, and in 1977 you published "An Equilibrium Characterization of the Term Structure." Were you already thinking about interest rates at Wells Fargo?

Vasicek: No. It was when I was at the University of Rochester in New York, and then when I came back to California in 1976 and was teaching part-time at the University of California at Berkeley and doing part-time consulting for Wells Fargo that I got most of that work done.

FEN: What drew you to the term structure of interest rates?

Vasicek: At the time, there was very little available on the pricing of riskless debt and on interest rates in general. There was CAPM, which addressed the risk-return relationship of financial assets, but that was mostly applied to equities. There was the option-pricing theory for the pricing of derivative assets. But there was not much available on interest rates—how they behave, why they behave that way, what the relationships are among interest rates of various maturities. Some empirical work was available, but there was no theory of the term structure, so there was a void or gap. I was bothered by the gap, so I started to look into that.

FEN: And bridged that gap. In 1983, you and John McQuown formed Diversified Corporate Loans, a high-minded but relatively short-lived venture. At that time mortgages were resold but commercial loans stayed put on the balance sheet. You were essentially trying to restructure a traditional business.

Vasicek: Right. For some larger loans there were multiple lenders and there was some packaging and selling of loans, but that was not enough. We wanted to give banks an opportunity to diversify their portfolios.

FEN: McQuown came up with the idea of pooling loans, right? Did he have to sell you on the concept?

Vasicek: It was his idea but it made immediate sense to me. It was a meaningful thing. If you have an equities market where securities are efficiently and easily traded, any institutional investor can get a reasonably diversified portfolio. But it is much harder to get a well-diversified portfolio in a less-liquid market like bank loans because you do not have access through origination to the whole market. It's not good if a portfolio is concentrated in a specific industry or geographical region. Short of an efficient and extensive bond exchange, like a stock exchange—which was then and still is a ways away—the next means of allowing banks to diversify their loan portfolios would be for them to sell off a part of their portfolios to a pool and get back a share of the pool. That's what we were trying to do.

FEN: But banks were reluctant to do that because they thought it would hurt their relationship with borrowers. Was that surprising to you at the time?

Vasicek: I was not involved in visits to banks. I was trying to get a first crack on the valuation of the debt, trying to come up with what was later extended into the KMV approach. It was obvious that a condition for such pooling of loans across banks would be having a reasonable understanding of the value of those loans. These were privately held instruments by the originating bank. There was no secondary market.

What was needed was some measure of the default risk for the pricing of these loans. I was spending my time trying to come up with a theoretical methodology for doing so.

FEN: The modeling you did at KMV Corporation was a continuation of what you were doing at DCL.

Vasicek: Yes, it was a continuation of that same effort. The early experience of the Black-Scholes-Merton approach to valuing debt had been so successful in actually giving an early warning of bankruptcies that when DCL closed, we thought a credit risk valuation methodology might have some value of its own.

FEN: When you, McQuown, and Stephen Kealhofer formed KMV, was there an end point? How did you expect the market to evolve?

Vasicek: It seemed to me that the approach made sense. If you develop something that makes sense, there should be an interest in it. KMV was a collective effort. I did my part on the theory of credit valuation. Steve made the approach applicable to real firms and real data. Mac kept track of the conceptual goal of these efforts and went to banks like a missionary to the native tribes to convince them that these crazy things could actually have some value for them.

FEN: KMV's EDF (expected default frequency) measures and quantitative models have long been considered a counterbalance to the more qualitative models used by rating agencies. As rating agencies began buying credit risk modeling firms, there have been grumblings that there's been a reduction in terms of the different approaches to credit valuation. Is there any validity to that?

Vasicek: I don't think that happened. Moody's has consciously kept a separation between the tradition of letter-rating methodologies and the KMV approach in order to have independent viewpoints on credit valuation. If anything, there have been lots of new models coming out in the industry.

FEN: What do you think credit rating agencies and modelers learned from Enron, Worldcom, and other bankruptcies?

Vasicek: The Enron case demonstrates the power of market-price-based measures of risk. The KMV model was giving warning signals before concerns found their way into ratings and bond market prices. Ratings often don't pay sufficient attention to market prices—by prices, I don't mean just the value of the stock but also its behavior, its volatility. If there's a lesson from the Enron case, it is that measures such as stock price volatility should be more explicitly incorporated into the criteria for forming letter ratings.

FEN: I read something interesting a couple of days ago. CreditSights, an independent credit analysis and research firm, recently looked at

Venezuelan and Brazilian sovereign debt and pointed out that Brazilian debt had higher ratings than Venezuelan debt. However, Venezuelan debt looked stronger, based on 13 out of 15 quantitative indicators. CreditSights observed that subjective factors often wind up trumping quantitative factors in assessing the credit quality of sovereign debt. What do you think?

Vasicek: I do not know of any theoretically satisfying model for sovereign debt, frankly. So far, we've been talking about corporate debt for publicly held corporations. For those kinds of debt instruments we may not have perfectly worked out models, but we do have an approach—the derivative asset-pricing model. For sovereign debt, what's available right now is a combination of empirical statistical-type models and subjective judgment. There's no self-contained theory or model that exists for the valuation of sovereign debt.

CHAPTER 4

Credit Superquant

By Robert Hunter

Oldrich Alfons Vasicek is perhaps the most unlikely member of the Derivatives Hall of Fame. That he ended up studying derivatives at all can be chalked up to pure happenstance. Had events occurred differently in his early years, Vasicek might well have spent his career studying nuclear physics or marine biology rather than default probabilities. The derivatives world is fortunate things turned out the way they did.

Vasicek, now 58, was born in Prague, Czechoslovakia, and was drawn to mathematics at an early age. His father, a lawyer, had suffered through the vastly different but equally onerous political systems of Nazism and Communism, and believed his children should choose careers in the physical sciences, which were less vulnerable to political crosscurrents.

At his father's urging, Oldrich studied nuclear physics at the Czech Technical University, but never lost his passion for mathematics. When the university introduced a new degree program in pure mathematics for selected students, Oldrich jumped at the chance. In 1964, he earned a master's degree in math.

Immediately after graduating, he enrolled at Charles University in Prague to pursue a PhD in probability theory. He earned his diploma four years later, just as Soviet tanks rolled into Prague to restore order to an unraveling government. Within five days of the invasion, Vasicek and his wife, a physician, boarded a train leaving the country.

Vasicek made his way to San Francisco in late 1968 and started to look for a job. Stanford University's biology department was looking for a mathematician to do spectral analysis of dolphins' sounds, but passed on Vasicek.

Derivatives Strategy, March 2000

Wells Fargo Bank, which needed a research analyst in its management science department, quickly nabbed Vasicek for the post in January 1969. In the coming decade, the derivatives explosion would reshape finance. Vasicek, still a financial neophyte, would be at the epicenter of the changes.

GOOD COMPANY

In the early 1970s, Wells Fargo's Management Science Department began organizing annual conferences that brought select academicians together with half a dozen bankers to discuss various cutting-edge topics in finance. The 1970 affair featured two young turks named Fischer Black and Myron Scholes, who had just begun thinking about the problem of valuing equity options. Their effect on Vasicek was immediate. "It was like being in heaven, being exposed to all of these new ideas and these people," he recalls. Later conferences brought Merton Miller, Franco Modigliani, and Robert Merton, who introduced his continuous time equation before it was published.

The conferences awakened in Vasicek a passion for finance he never knew he had. By the early 1970s, he was working with Black, Scholes, William Sharpe, and others to develop for Wells Fargo a radical new investment vehicle known as an index fund. "You cannot imagine how revolutionary an idea it was at the time," Vasicek recalls. "The basic plan was to form a capitalization-weighted stock market fund. The whole bank went up in arms. The security analyst division was aghast. They said, 'You mean you want to buy all the dogs along with the good stocks? You're not going to do fundamental analysis of stocks to see which ones are good and which are bad?' We said, 'No, the market's already doing that.'" After two years of in-fighting, the team was encouraged to resign. "The bank just couldn't comprehend the idea, because nobody else was doing this," Vasicek says.

Vasicek headed east to take a teaching job at the University of Rochester. After two upstate New York winters, he went back to California, this time as a visiting professor at the University of California at Berkeley. In 1977, he wrote a paper that would change the face of finance. In "An Equilibrium Characterization of the Term Structure," published in the *Journal of Financial Economics*, Vasicek first traced the relationship between the term structure of interest rates and the pricing of bonds. The paper examined how interest rates affect prices of riskless bonds, such as Treasuries. It asked how bonds of different maturities are related to each other, what kind of stochastic processes derived them, and what kind of conditions have to hold across the whole bond market, for all maturities, so that it stays in equilibrium.

"That was, at the time, kind of a novel thing," Vasicek says modestly. "When I was working on it, the theory available for stocks was the Capital

Asset Pricing Model. Somehow, it wasn't perceived as being applicable to bonds—they didn't seem to have any beta. The bond question was hard to get hold of. Then the idea that illuminated my thinking was the consideration that the pricing of longer bonds must in some way be related to what the short rate would do over the tenure of the bond. Now it seems fairly obvious, but it surely wasn't at the time."

The basic assumption of the theory was that the pricing of, say, a five-year bond is a function of the short rate—or, more accurately, today's probability assessment of the behavior of the short rate—over the next five years. "This was something to build on," he says. "You simply need to specify what type of stochastic processes you're dealing with. The mathematical implementation was easy; the idea was the hardest part—that the short rate over that span is what should determine the price of the long bond."

The idea caught on instantly. Within a few years, dozens of articles were popping up in journals that took the concept further. Now, in one form or another, anybody who buys, sells, prices, or structures an interest rate derivative is using some version of Vasicek's model.

CREDIT IS DUE

Despite such success—or maybe because of it—Vasicek realized his heart wasn't in teaching. He needed to be on the front lines all the time, focusing his considerable mathematical powers on the furthest reaches of finance theory. In 1978, Vasicek left Berkeley to become a consultant, eventually ending up at Gifford Fong Associates, where he became a senior research associate in 1980, specializing in mathematical approaches to the newest exotic products in the rapidly growing derivatives markets.

After several years in that role, he left to become a partner in a new company, Diversified Corporate Finance, together with John McQuown, who had first hired Vasicek at Wells Fargo in 1969. The company was built with a groundbreaking mission: to pool bank loans to improve asset diversification. The concept was, by today's standards, quite simple: Banks would contribute their loans to a massive pool of diverse loans in exchange for a share of the entire pool. "They were entirely off-balance-sheet transactions," Vasicek says. "In effect, they were the first credit derivatives." But banks were afraid to take the plunge.

Meanwhile, Vasicek was working on some theoretical questions relating to credit. While at DCF, he created a proprietary credit valuation model to help banks evaluate the loans they were contributing to the pool and evaluate the pool itself. The model, later published under the title "Credit Valuation" in several publications, is based on the assumption that credit valuation should not be a subjective judgment of an individual credit analyst, but rather should be inferred objectively from the characteristics of the firm and the firm's share price.

"It sounds extremely natural now, valuing the debt of a company from knowing its equity and derivative asset pricing," says Vasicek. "We take it for granted. But in the mid-1980s they were absolutely laughing at us." The theoretical underpinning for the model went back to Black and Scholes, who argued in the 1970s that the stock of a firm is simply a call on the firm's assets. When Vasicek tried to apply that thinking to credit, he was met with tremendous resistance.

"Prospective clients said you value credit by knowing the corporate customer, working with him, analyzing, going to visit, having him visit you, studying the financial statements. It was a completely nonanalytical approach, based on the relationship with the client and on experience. We proposed that the stock market in effect does all that—that it's the aggregate judgment of hundreds of thousands of investors, with the bottom line of their evaluation expressed as the price at which they're willing to buy and sell the stock. If we could succeed in extracting the information from the stock and converting it to the valuation of the credit, we'd capitalize on all this information. In fact, unless the bank credit officer knows something that the market does not know, it should be a superior gauge. You'd have to know more than the aggregate of market participants to arrive at a superior valuation."

Vasicek was so sure of his revelation that DCF hired a retired former bank credit officer to soothe potential clients. To no avail: The company folded in 1989.

But Vasicek moved forward. After the failure of DCF, he cofounded KMV Corp. with McQuown and Steve Kealhofer, a former Berkeley professor who had also worked at DCF. The new firm beefed up its credit capabilities. In addition to portfolio risk management systems, KMV offers explicit default probabilities from one year to five years for 20,000 companies worldwide. Whereas most portfolio managers used agency ratings to gauge expected losses, KMV offered a quantitative measure—which, among other things, also helped banks price loans and make lending decisions. While Vasicek's pioneering use of quantitative methods in credit analysis would prove instrumental to the credit derivatives boom of the 1990s, demand for KMV's services was nonexistent in the beginning. It took two years for the company to sign up its first client, Bank of America.

Once Bank of America signed on, however, business snowballed. One client led to two, then five, then ten, and before long KMV could count 35 of the world's 50 biggest banks as clients. KMV now models portfolios with combined assets of several trillion dollars.

Nowadays, Vasicek is spending much of his time developing pricing mechanisms for credit derivatives. "You need to know the complete probability distribution of the potential losses in the underlying portfolio before you can fully structure or write, say, a collateralized bond obligation," he says.

Thanks to Oldrich Vasicek, this is no longer such a difficult proposition.

PART Two

Term Structure of Interest Rates

The price $P(t, s)$ at time t of a default-free zero-coupon bond with unit face value maturing at time s is given by the equation

$$P(t, s) = \mathrm{E}_t \exp\left(-\int_t^s r(\tau)\,\mathrm{d}\tau - \frac{1}{2}\int_t^s q^2(\tau)\mathrm{d}\tau + \int_t^s q(\tau)\mathrm{d}z(\tau) \right)$$

where $r(t)$ is the short interest rate, $z(t)$ is a Wiener process constituting a source of risk, and $q(t)$ is the market price of risk. (page 38)

CHAPTER 5

Introduction to Part II

Interest rates are a function of time and term (time to maturity). As a function of time, rates behave as stochastic processes. As a function of term, interest rates on a given date form a *yield curve*. Term structure models describe the behavior of interest rates of different maturities as a joint stochastic process.

Term structure models are a necessary tool for valuation and risk management of interest rate contingent claims—that is, securities or transactions whose payoff depends on future values of interest rates, such as callable or putable bonds, swaps, swaptions, caps, and floors. For instance, a bond will be called if its value on the call date is greater than the call price. To determine the current value of the bond, it is necessary to know the subsequent behavior of interest rates. The same is true for all debt securities subject to prepayment, such as mortgages with refinancing options.

The immediate acceptance and application of term structure models in banking and investment practice is due to the fact that there are few financial instruments whose value is not in some degree dependent on future interest rates. Even stock options such as calls and puts depend on the development of interest rates. Interest rate models enter into valuation of firms and their liabilities. Besides valuation, term structure models are necessary for interest rate risk measurement, management, and hedging.

Interest rates of different maturities behave as a joint stochastic process. Not all joint processes, however, can describe interest rate behavior in an efficient market. For instance, suppose that a term structure model postulates that rates of all maturities change in time by equal amounts, that is, that yield curves move by parallel shifts (which, empirically, appears to be a reasonable first-order approximation). It can be shown that in this case a portfolio consisting of a long bond and a short bond would always outperform a medium-term bond with the same Macaulay duration. In an efficient market, supply and demand would drive the price of the medium maturity bond down and the prices of the long and short bonds up. As this would cause the yield on the medium bond to increase and the yields on the long and short bonds to decrease, the yield curves would not stay parallel. This model therefore cannot describe interest rate behavior.

In order that riskless arbitrage opportunities are absent, the joint process of interest rate behavior must satisfy some conditions. Determining these conditions and finding processes that satisfy them is the purpose of *term structure theory*. Term structure *models* are specific applications of term structure theory.

The joint stochastic process is driven by sources of uncertainty. For continuous processes, the sources of uncertainty are often specified as Wiener processes. If the evolution of the yield curve can be represented by Markovian state variables, these variables are called *factors*.

A general theory of one-factor term structure models is given in the 1977 paper "An Equilibrium Characterization of the Term Structure" (Chapter 6). It is proven that the term structure is fully described by the specification of the behavior of the short rate and the market price of risk. This relationship is expressed by the fundamental bond pricing equation (18) in that chapter, which gives the price of a bond as a function of the short rate and the market price of risk over the term of the bond.

The bond pricing equation was derived as the solution to a partial differential equation under certain assumptions, but it is valid generally for *any* arbitrage-free term structure model. The equation is valid even in the case of multiple factors or multiple risk sources, if the products in the equation are interpreted as scalar products of vectors. Every term structure model is either a direct application of that equation, or it assumes that the equation is true for bonds and uses it to price interest rate derivatives (as in the Heath, Jarrow, Morton model).

The 1977 paper gives an example of a term structure model in which the short rate follows a mean reverting random walk (the Ornstein-Uhlenbeck process), and the market price of risk is constant. In this example, which has become known as the "Vasicek model," interest rates are Gaussian.

The difference between the forward rate and the expected spot rate has been traditionally called the liquidity premium. The unpublished memorandum written in 1979, "The Liquidity Premium" (Chapter 7), shows that the liquidity premium consists of two components: The first component, driven by the market price of risk, is equal to the expected integral over the span of the forward rate of the forward rate volatility multiplied by the market price of risk. The second component is equal to the negative of the expected aggregate over the forward rate span of the bond price volatility times the forward rate volatility. This component, which is present even if the market price of risk is zero, arises as a result of the nonlinear relationship between prices and rates.

A plot of bond yields on a given date as a function of term is called the yield curve. Since yield quotes are typically available only for selected maturities, it has been necessary to interpolate between these maturities, or differently stated, fitting a smooth curve to the discrete data. A favorite method for doing so had been the use of polynomial splines to the yields. The paper "Term Structure Modeling Using Exponential Splines" (Chapter 8), written in 1982 with H. Gifford Fong, proposes a different method, namely fitting exponential splines to the discount function. The advantages of using this type of splines are their desirable asymptotic properties, and their having both a sufficient flexibility to fit a wide variety of yield curves and a sufficient robustness to produce stable forward rate curves.

Heath, Jarrow, and Morton in their intricate 1992 paper proposed a framework for pricing interest rate derivatives based on the knowledge of the initial term structure and of the forward rate volatilities. By writing the dynamics of interest rates directly in terms of a process that is Wiener under the martingale measure, it is possible to price interest rate contingent claims without knowing the market price of risk. The 1994 memorandum "The Heath, Jarrow, Morton Model" (Chapter 9) provides a three-line derivation of the HJM model.

CHAPTER 6

An Equilibrium Characterization of the Term Structure

ABSTRACT

The paper derives a general form of the term structure of interest rates. The following assumptions are made: (A.1) The instantaneous (spot) interest rate follows a diffusion process; (A.2) the price of a discount bond depends only on the spot rate over its term; and (A.3) the market is efficient. Under these assumptions, it is shown by means of an arbitrage argument that the expected rate of return on any bond in excess of the spot rate is proportional to its standard deviation. This property is then used to derive a partial differential equation for bond prices. The solution to that equation is given in the form of a stochastic integral representation. An interpretation of the bond pricing formula is provided. The model is illustrated on a specific case.

INTRODUCTION

Although considerable attention has been paid to equilibrium conditions in capital markets and the pricing of capital assets, few results are directly applicable to description of the interest rate structure. The most notable exceptions are the works of Roll (1970, 1971), Merton (1973, 1974), and Long (1974). This paper gives an explicit characterization of the term structure of interest rates in an efficient market. The development of the model is based

---

Journal of Financial Economics 5, No. 2, 177–188, 1977; reprinted in *Vasicek and Beyond: Approaches to Building and Applying Interest Rate Models*, L. Hughston (ed.), London: Risk Publications, 1996; reprinted in *The Debt Market*, S.A. Ross (ed.), Glos, G.B.: Elgar Publishing Ltd., 2000; reprinted in *Options Markets*, G. M. Constantinides and A. G. Malliaris (eds.), Glos, G.B.: Elgar Publishing Ltd., 2000.
The author wishes to thank P. Boyle, M. Garman, M. Jensen, and the referees, R. Roll and S. Schaefer, for their helpful comments and suggestions.

on an arbitrage argument similar to that of Black and Scholes (1973) for option pricing. The model is formulated in continuous time, although some implications for discrete interest rate series are also noted.

NOTATION AND ASSUMPTIONS

Consider a market in which investors buy and issue default-free claims on a specified sum of money to be delivered at a given future date. Such claims will be called (discount) bonds. Let $P(t, s)$ denote the price at time t of a discount bond maturing at time s, $t \leqq s$, with unit maturity value,

$$P(s, s) = 1.$$

The yield to maturity $R(t, T)$ is the internal rate of return at time t on a bond with maturity date $s = t + T$,

$$R(t, T) = -\frac{1}{T} \log P(t, t + T), \quad T > 0. \tag{1}$$

The rates $R(t, T)$ considered as a function of T will be referred to as the term structure at time t.

The forward rate $F(t, s)$ will be defined by the equation

$$R(t, T) = \frac{1}{T} \int_t^{t+T} F(t, \tau)\,\mathrm{d}\tau. \tag{2}$$

In the form explicit for the forward rate, this equation can be written as

$$F(t, s) = \frac{\partial}{\partial s}[(s - t)R(t, s - t)]. \tag{3}$$

The forward rate can be interpreted as the marginal rate of return from committing a bond investment for an additional instant.

Define now the spot rate as the instantaneous borrowing and lending rate,

$$r(t) = R(t, 0) = \lim_{T \to 0} R(t, T). \tag{4}$$

A loan of amount W at the spot rate will thus increase in value by the increment

$$\mathrm{d}W = Wr(t)\mathrm{d}t. \tag{5}$$

This equation holds with certainty. At any time t, the current value $r(t)$ of the spot rate is the instantaneous rate of increase of the loan value. The subsequent values of the spot rate, however, are not necessarily certain. In fact, it will be assumed that $r(t)$ is a stochastic process, subject to two requirements:

First, $r(t)$ is a continuous function of time, that is, it does not change value by an instantaneous jump. Second, it is assumed that $r(t)$ follows a Markov process. Under this assumption, the future development of the spot rate given its present value is independent of the past development that has led to the present level. The following assumption is thus made:

(A.1) The spot rate follows a continuous Markov process.

The Markov property implies that the spot rate process is characterized by a single state variable, namely its current value. The probability distribution of the segment $\{r(\tau), \tau \geqq t\}$ is thus completely determined by the value of $r(t)$.

Processes that are Markov and continuous are called diffusion processes. They can be described [cf. Itô (1961), Gikhman and Skorokhod (1969)] by a stochastic differential equation of the form

$$dr = f(r,t)\,dt + \rho(r,t)\,dz, \tag{6}$$

where $z(t)$ is a Wiener process with incremental variance dt. The functions $f(r,t), \rho^2(r,t)$ are the instantaneous drift and variance, respectively, of the process $r(t)$.

It is natural to expect that the price of a discount bond will be determined solely by the spot interest rate over its term, or more accurately, by the current assessment of the development of the spot rate over the term of the bond. No particular form of such relationship is presumed. The second assumption will thus be stated as follows:

(A.2) The price $P(t,s)$ of a discount bond is determined by the assessment, at time t, of the segment $\{r(\tau), t \leqq \tau \leqq s\}$ of the spot rate process over the term of the bond.

It may be noted that the expectation hypothesis, the market segmentation hypothesis, and the liquidity preference hypothesis all conform to assumption (A.2), since they all postulate that

$$R(t,T) = E_t\left(\frac{1}{T}\int_t^{t+T} r(\tau)\,d\tau\right) + \bar{\pi}(t,T,r(t)),$$

with various specifications for the function $\bar{\pi}$.

Finally, it will be assumed that the following is true:

(A.3) The market is efficient; that is, there are no transactions costs, information is available to all investors simultaneously, and every investor acts rationally (prefers more wealth to less, and uses all available information).

Assumption (A.3) implies that investors have homogeneous expectations, and that no profitable riskless arbitrage is possible.

By assumption (A.1) the development of the spot rate process over an interval (t, s), $t \leqq s$, given its values prior to time t, depends only on the current value $r(t)$. Assumption (A.2) then implies that the price $P(t, s)$ is a function of $r(t)$,

$$P(t, s) = P(t, s, r(t)). \tag{7}$$

Thus, the value of the spot rate is the only state variable for the whole term structure. Expectations formed with the knowledge of the whole past development of rates of all maturities, including the present term structure, are equivalent to expectations conditional only on the present value of the spot rate.

Since there exists only one state variable, the instantaneous returns on bonds of different maturities are perfectly correlated. This means that the short bond and just one other bond completely span the whole of the term structure. It should be noted, however, that bond returns over a finite period are not correlated perfectly. Investors unwilling to revise the composition of their portfolio continuously will need a spectrum of maturities to fulfill their investment objectives.

THE TERM STRUCTURE EQUATION

It follows from Eqs. (6) and (7) by the Itô differentiation rule [cf., for instance, Itô (1961), Kushner (1967), Åström (1970)], that the bond price satisfies a stochastic differential equation

$$dP = P\mu(t, s)\,dt - P\sigma(t, s)\,dz, \tag{8}$$

where the parameters $\mu(t, s) = \mu(t, s, r(t))$, $\sigma(t, s) = \sigma(t, s, r(t))$ are given by

$$\mu(t, s, r) = \frac{1}{P(t, s, r)} \left[\frac{\partial}{\partial t} + f\frac{\partial}{\partial r} + \frac{1}{2}\rho^2 \frac{\partial^2}{\partial r^2} \right] P(t, s, r), \tag{9}$$

$$\sigma(t, s, r) = -\frac{1}{P(t, s, r)}\, \rho \frac{\partial}{\partial r} P(t, s, r). \tag{10}$$

The functions $\mu(t, s, r), \sigma^2(t, s, r)$ are the mean and variance, respectively, of the instantaneous rate of return at time t on a bond with maturity date s, given that the current spot rate is $r(t) = r$.

Now consider an investor who at time t issues an amount W_1 of a bond with maturity date s_1, and simultaneously buys an amount W_2 of a bond maturing at time s_2. The total worth $W = W_2 - W_1$ of the portfolio thus constructed changes over time according to the accumulation equation

$$dW = (W_2\mu(t,s_2) - W_1\mu(t,s_1))dt - (W_2\sigma(t,s_2) - W_1\sigma(t,s_1))\,dz \qquad (11)$$

[cf. Merton (1971)]. This equation follows from Eq. (8) by application of the Itô rule.

Suppose that the amounts W_1, W_2 are chosen to be proportional to $\sigma(t,s_2), \sigma(t,s_1)$, respectively,

$$W_1 = W\sigma(t,s_2)/(\sigma(t,s_1) - \sigma(t,s_2)),$$

$$W_2 = W\sigma(t,s_1)/(\sigma(t,s_1) - \sigma(t,s_2)).$$

Then the second term in Eq. (11) disappears, and the equation takes the form

$$dW = W(\mu(t,s_2)\sigma(t,s_1) - \mu(t,s_1)\sigma(t,s_2))(\sigma(t,s_1) - \sigma(t,s_2))^{-1}\,dt. \qquad (12)$$

The portfolio composed of such amounts of the two bonds is instantaneously riskless, since the stochastic element dz is not present in (12). It should therefore realize the same return as a loan at the spot rate described by Eq. (5). If not, the portfolio can be bought with funds borrowed at the spot rate, or otherwise sold and the proceeds lent out, to accomplish a riskless arbitrage.

As such arbitrage opportunities are ruled out by Assumption (A.3), comparison of Eqs. (5) and (12) yields

$$(\mu(t,s_2)\sigma(t,s_1) - \mu(t,s_1)\sigma(t,s_2))/(\sigma(t,s_1) - \sigma(t,s_2)) = r(t),$$

or equivalently,

$$\frac{\mu(t,s_1) - r(t)}{\sigma(t,s_1)} = \frac{\mu(t,s_2) - r(t)}{\sigma(t,s_2)}. \qquad (13)$$

Since Eq. (13) is valid for arbitrary maturity dates s_1, s_2, it follows that the ratio $(\mu(t,s) - r(t))/\sigma(t,s)$ is independent of s. Let $q(t,r)$ denote the common value of such ratio for a bond of any maturity date, given that the current spot rate is $r(t) = r$,

$$q(t,r) = \frac{\mu(t,s,r) - r}{\sigma(t,s,r)}, \quad s \geqq t. \qquad (14)$$

The quantity $q(t,r)$ can be called the market price of risk, as it specifies the increase in expected instantaneous rate of return on a bond per an additional unit of risk.

Eq. (14) will now be used to derive an equation for the price of a discount bond. Writing (14) as

$$\mu(t, s, r) - r = q(t, r)\sigma(t, s, r),$$

and substituting for μ, σ from Eqs. (9) and (10) yields, after rearrangement,

$$\frac{\partial P}{\partial t} + (f + pq)\frac{\partial P}{\partial r} + \frac{1}{2}\rho^2\frac{\partial^2 P}{\partial r^2} - rP = 0, \quad t \leqq s. \tag{15}$$

Eq. (15) is the basic equation for pricing of discount bonds in a market characterized by Assumptions (A.1), (A.2), and (A.3). It will be called the term structure equation.

The term structure equation is a partial differential equation for $P(t, s, r)$. Once the character of the spot rate process $r(t)$ is described and the market price of risk $q(t, r)$ specified, the bond prices are obtained by solving (15) subject to the boundary condition

$$P(s, s, r) = 1. \tag{16}$$

The term structure $R(t, T)$ of interest rates is then readily evaluated from the equation

$$R(t, T) = -\frac{1}{T}\log P(t, t + T, r(t)). \tag{17}$$

STOCHASTIC REPRESENTATION OF THE BOND PRICE

Solutions of partial differential equations of the parabolic or elliptic type, such as Eq. (15), can be represented in an integral form in terms of an underlying stochastic process [cf. Friedman (1975)]. Such representation for the bond price as a solution to the term structure equation (15) and its boundary condition is as follows:

$$P(t, s) = E_t \exp\left(-\int_t^s r(\tau)\,\mathrm{d}\tau - \frac{1}{2}\int_t^s q^2(\tau, r(\tau))\,\mathrm{d}\tau + \int_t^s q(\tau, r(\tau))\,\mathrm{d}z(\tau)\right),$$
$$t \leqq s. \tag{18}$$

To prove (18), define

$$V(u) = \exp\left(-\int_t^u r(\tau)\,\mathrm{d}\tau - \frac{1}{2}\int_t^u q^2(\tau, r(\tau))\mathrm{d}\tau + \int_t^u q(\tau, r(\tau))\,\mathrm{d}z(\tau)\right),$$

and apply Itô's differential rule to the process $P(u, s)V(u)$. Then

$$\begin{aligned}
\mathrm{d}(PV) &= V\mathrm{d}P + P\mathrm{d}V + \mathrm{d}P\,\mathrm{d}V \\
&= V\left(\frac{\partial P}{\partial t} + f\frac{\partial P}{\partial r} + \frac{1}{2}\rho^2\frac{\partial^2 P}{\partial r^2}\right)\mathrm{d}u + V\frac{\partial P}{\partial r}\rho\mathrm{d}z + PV\left(-r - \frac{1}{2}q^2\right)\mathrm{d}u \\
&\quad + PVq\mathrm{d}z + \frac{1}{2}PVq^2\mathrm{d}u + V\frac{\partial P}{\partial r}\rho q\,\mathrm{d}u \\
&= V\left(\frac{\partial P}{\partial t} + (f + \rho q)\frac{\partial P}{\partial r} + \frac{1}{2}\rho^2\frac{\partial^2 P}{\partial r^2} - rP\right)\mathrm{d}u + PVq\mathrm{d}z + V\frac{\partial P}{\partial r}\rho\,\mathrm{d}z \\
&= PVq\mathrm{d}z + V\frac{\partial P}{\partial r}\rho\,\mathrm{d}z,
\end{aligned}$$

by virtue of Eq. (15). Integrating from t to s and taking expectation yields

$$E_t(P(s, s)V(s) - P(t, s)V(t)) = 0,$$

and Eq. (18) follows.

In the special case when the expected instantaneous rates of return on bonds of all maturities are the same,

$$\mu(t, s) = r(t), \quad s \geqq t,$$

(this corresponds to $q = 0$), the bond price is given by

$$P(t, s) = E_t \exp\left(-\int_t^s r(\tau)\,\mathrm{d}\tau\right). \tag{19}$$

Eq. (18) can be given an interpretation in economic terms. Construct a portfolio consisting of the long bond (bond whose maturity approaches infinity) and lending or borrowing at the spot rate, with proportions $\lambda(t)$, $1 - \lambda(t)$, respectively, where

$$\lambda(t) = (\mu(t, \infty) - r(t))/\sigma^2(t, \infty).$$

The price $Q(t)$ of such portfolio follows the equation

$$\mathrm{d}Q = \lambda Q(\mu(t, \infty)\,\mathrm{d}t - \sigma(t, \infty)\mathrm{d}z) + (1 - \lambda)Qr\,\mathrm{d}t.$$

This equation can be integrated by evaluating the differential of log Q and noting that $\lambda(t)\sigma(t,\infty) = q(t, r(t))$. This yields

$$\mathrm{d}(\log Q) = \lambda\mu(t,\infty)\,\mathrm{d}t - \lambda\sigma(t,\infty)\mathrm{d}z + (1-\lambda)r\,\mathrm{d}t - \frac{1}{2}\lambda^2\sigma^2(t,\infty)\mathrm{d}t$$

$$= r\,\mathrm{d}t + \frac{1}{2}q^2\mathrm{d}t - q\mathrm{d}z,$$

and consequently

$$\frac{Q(t)}{Q(s)} = \exp\left(-\int_t^s r(\tau)\,\mathrm{d}\tau - \frac{1}{2}\int_t^s q^2(\tau, r(\tau))\mathrm{d}\tau + \int_t^s q(\tau, r(\tau))\mathrm{d}z(\tau)\right).$$

Thus, Eq. (18) can be written in the form

$$P(t,s) = E_t Q(t)/Q(s), \quad t \leqq s. \tag{20}$$

This means that a bond of any maturity is priced in such a way that the same portion of a certain well-defined combination of the long bond and the riskless asset (the portfolio Q) can be bought now for the amount of the bond price as is expected to be bought at the maturity date for the maturity value.

Equivalently, Eq. (20) states that the price of any bond measured in units of the value of such portfolio Q follows a martingale,

$$\frac{P(t,s)}{Q(t)} = E_t\frac{P(\tau,s)}{Q(\tau)}, \quad t \leqq \tau \leqq s.$$

Thus, if the present bond price is a certain fraction of the value of the portfolio Q, then the future value of the bond is expected to stay the same fraction of the value of that portfolio.

In empirical testing of the model, as well as for applications of the results, it is necessary to know the parameters f, ρ of the spot rate process, and the market price of risk q. The former two quantities can be obtained by statistical analysis of the (observable) process $r(t)$. Although the market price of risk can be estimated from the defining Eq. (14), it is desirable to have a more direct means of observing q empirically. The following equality can be employed:

$$\left.\frac{\partial R}{\partial T}\right|_{T=0} = \frac{1}{2}(f(t, r(t)) + \rho(t, r(t)) \cdot q(t, r(t))). \tag{21}$$

Once the parameters f, ρ are known, q could thus be determined from the slope at the origin of the yield curves. Eq. (21) can be proven by taking the second derivative with respect to s of (18) (Itô's differentiation rule is needed), and putting $s = t$. This yields

$$\left.\frac{\partial^2 P}{\partial s^2}\right|_{s=t} = r^2(t) - f(t, r(t)) - \rho(t, r(t)) \cdot q(t, r(t)). \tag{22}$$

But from (1),

$$\left.\frac{\partial^2 P}{\partial s^2}\right|_{s=t} = r^2(t) - 2\left.\frac{\partial R}{\partial T}\right|_{T=0}. \tag{23}$$

By comparison of (22), (23), Eq. (21) follows.

A SPECIFIC CASE

To illustrate the general model, the term structure of interest rates will now be obtained explicitly in the situation characterized by the following assumptions: First, that the market price of risk $q(t, r)$ is a constant,

$$q(t, r) = q,$$

independent of the calendar time and of the level of the spot rate. Second, that the spot rate $r(t)$ follows the so-called Ornstein-Uhlenbeck process,

$$\mathrm{d}r = \alpha(\gamma - r)\mathrm{d}t + \rho\,\mathrm{d}z, \tag{24}$$

with $\alpha > 0$, corresponding to the choice $f(t, r) = \alpha(\gamma - r), \rho(t, r) = \rho$ in Eq. (6). This description of the spot rate process has been proposed by Merton (1971).

The Ornstein-Uhlenbeck process with $\alpha > 0$ is sometimes called the elastic random walk. It is a Markov process with normally distributed increments. In contrast to the random walk (the Wiener process), which is an unstable process and after a long time will diverge to infinite values, the Ornstein-Uhlenbeck process possesses a stationary distribution. The instantaneous drift $\alpha(\gamma - r)$ represents a force that keeps pulling the process towards its long-term mean γ with magnitude proportional to the deviation of the process from the mean. The stochastic element, which has a constant instantaneous variance ρ^2, causes the process to fluctuate around the level γ in an erratic, but continuous, fashion. The conditional expectation and variance of the process given the current level are

$$E_t r(s) = \gamma + (r(t) - \gamma)\mathrm{e}^{-\alpha(s-t)}, \quad t \leqq s, \tag{25}$$

$$\mathrm{Var}_t r(s) = \frac{\rho^2}{2\alpha}(1 - \mathrm{e}^{-2\alpha(s-t)}), \quad t \leqq s, \tag{26}$$

respectively.

It is not claimed that the process given by Eq. (24) represents the best description of the spot rate behavior. In the absence of empirical results on the character of the spot rate process, this specification serves only as an example.

Under such assumptions, the solution of the term structure equation (15) subject to (16) [or alternatively, the representation (18)] is

$$P(t,s,r) = \exp\left[\frac{1}{\alpha}\left(1 - e^{-\alpha(s-t)}\right)(R(\infty) - r) - (s-t)R(\infty) - \frac{\rho^2}{4\alpha^3}\left(1 - e^{-\alpha(s-t)}\right)^2\right],$$
$$t \leqq s, \tag{27}$$

where

$$R(\infty) = \gamma + \rho q/\alpha - \frac{1}{2}\rho^2/\alpha^2. \tag{28}$$

The mean $\mu(t,s)$ and standard deviation $\sigma(t,s)$ of the instantaneous rate of return of a bond maturing at time s is, from Eqs. (9), (10),

$$\mu(t,s) = r(t) + \frac{\rho q}{\alpha}(1 - e^{-\alpha(s-t)}),$$
$$\sigma(t,s) = \frac{\rho}{\alpha}(1 - e^{-\alpha(s-t)}),$$

with $t \leqq s$. It is seen that the longer the term of the bond, the higher the variance of the instantaneous rate of return, with the expected return in excess of the spot rate being proportional to the standard deviation. For a very long bond (i.e., $s \to \infty$) the mean and standard deviation approach the limits

$$\mu(\infty) = r(t) + \rho q/\alpha,$$
$$\sigma(\infty) = \rho/\alpha.$$

The term structure of interest rates is then calculated from Eqs. (17) and (22). It takes the form

$$R(t,T) = R(\infty) + (r(t) - R(\infty))\frac{1}{\alpha T}(1 - e^{-\alpha T}) + \frac{\rho^2}{4\alpha^3 T}(1 - e^{-\alpha T})^2, \quad T \geqq 0, \tag{29}$$

Note that the yield on a very long bond, as $T \to \infty$, is $R(\infty)$, thus explaining the notation (28).

The yield curves given by (29) start at the current level $r(t)$ of the spot rate for $T = 0$, and approach a common asymptote $R(\infty)$ as $T \to \infty$. For values of $r(t)$ smaller or equal to

$$R(\infty) - \frac{1}{4}\rho^2/\alpha^2,$$

the yield curve is monotonically increasing. For values of $r(t)$ larger than that but below

$$R(\infty) + \frac{1}{2}\rho^2/\alpha^2,$$

it is a humped curve. When $r(t)$ is equal to or exceeds this last value, the yield curves are monotonically decreasing.

Eq. (29), together with the spot rate process (24), fully characterizes the behavior of interest rates under the specific assumptions of this section. It provides both the relationship, at a given time t, among rates of different maturities, and the behavior of interest rates, as well as bond prices, over time. The relationship between the rates $R(t, T_1), R(t, T_2)$ of two arbitrary maturities can be determined by eliminating $r(t)$ from Eq. (29) written for $T = T_1, T = T_2$. Moreover, Eq. (29) describes the development of the rate $R(t, T)$ of a given maturity over time. Since $r(t)$ is normally distributed by virtue of the properties of the Ornstein-Uhlenbeck process, and $R(t, T)$ is a linear function of $r(t)$, it follows that $R(t, T)$ is also normally distributed. The mean and variance of $R(\tau, T)$, given $R(t, T), t < \tau$, are obtained from Eq. (29) by use of Eqs. (25) and (26). The calculations are elementary and will not be done here. It will only be noted that Eqs. (24) and (29) imply that the discrete rate series,

$$R_n = R(nT, T), n = 0, 1, 2, \dots,$$

follows a first-order linear normal autoregressive process of the form

$$R_n = c + a(R_{n-1} - c) + \varepsilon_n, \tag{30}$$

with independent residuals ε_n [cf. Nelson (1972)]. The process in Eq. (30) is the discrete elastic random walk, fluctuating around its mean c. The parameters c, a, and $s^2 = E\varepsilon_n^2$ could be expressed in terms of γ, α, ρ, q. In particular, the constant a, which characterizes the degree to which the next term in the series $\{R_n\}$ is tied to the current value, is given by $a = \mathrm{e}^{-\alpha T}$.

Also, Eq. (29) can be used to ascertain the behavior of bond prices. The price $P(\tau, s)$, given its current value $P(t, s)$, $t \leqq s$, is lognormally distributed, with parameters of the distribution calculated using Eqs. (1), (25), (26), and (29).

The difference between the forward rates and expected spot rates, considered as a function of the term, is usually referred to as the liquidity premium [although, as Nelson (1972) argues, a more appropriate name would be the term premium]. Using Eqs. (3) and (25), the liquidity premium implied by the term structure (29) is given by

$$\begin{aligned}\pi(T) &= F(t, t+T) - E_t r(t+T) \\ &= \left(R(\infty) - \gamma + \frac{1}{2}\frac{\rho^2}{\alpha^2}\mathrm{e}^{-\alpha T}\right)(1 - \mathrm{e}^{-\alpha T}), \quad T \geqq 0.\end{aligned} \tag{31}$$

The liquidity premium (Eq. (31)) is a smooth function of the term T. It is similar in form to the shape of the curves used by McCulloch (1975) in fitting observed estimates of liquidity premia. Its values for $T = 0$ and $T = \infty$ are $\pi(0) = 0, \pi(\infty) = R(\infty) - \gamma$, respectively, the latter being the difference between the yield on the very long bond and the long-term mean of the spot rate. If $q \geqq \rho/\alpha$, $\pi(T)$ is a monotonically increasing function of T. For $0 < q < \rho/\alpha$, it has a humped shape, with maximum of $q^2/2$ occurring at

$$T = \frac{1}{\alpha} \log \left(\frac{\rho/\alpha}{\rho/\alpha - q} \right).$$

If the market price of risk $q \leqq 0$, then $\pi(T)$ is a monotonically decreasing function.

REFERENCES

Åström, K.J. (1970). *Introduction to Stochastic Control Theory*. New York: Academic Press.

Black, F., and M. Scholes. (1973). "The Pricing of Options and Corporate Liabilities." *Journal of Political Economy*, 81, 637–654.

Friedman, A. (1975). *Stochastic Differential Equations and Applications*. New York: Academic Press.

Gikhman, I.I., and A.V. Skorokhod. (1969). *Introduction to the Theory of Random Processes*. Philadelphia, PA: W. B. Saunders.

Itô, K. (1961). *Lectures on Stochastic Processes*. Bombay: Tata Institute.

Kushner, H.J. (1967). *Stochastic Stability and Control*. New York: Academic Press.

Long, J.B. (1974). "Stock Prices, Inflation, and the Term Structure of Interest Rates." *Journal of Financial Economics*, 1, 131–170.

McCulloch, J.H. (1975). "An Estimate of the Liquidity Premium." *Journal of Political Economy*, 83, 95–119.

Merton, R.C. (1971). "Optimum Consumption and Portfolio Rules in a Continuous-Time Model." *Journal of Economic Theory*, 3, 373–413.

Merton, R.C. (1973). "An Intertemporal Capital Asset Pricing Model." *Econometrica*, 41, 867–887.

Merton, R.C. (1974). "On the Pricing of Corporate Debt: The Risk Structure of Interest Rates." *Journal of Finance*, 29, 449–470.

Nelson, C.R. (1972). *The Term Structure of Interest Rates*. New York: Basic Books.

Roll, R. (1970). *The Behavior of Interest Rates: The Application of the Efficient Market Model to U.S. Treasury Bills*. New York: Basic Books.

Roll, R. (1971). "Investment Diversification and Bond Maturity." *Journal of Finance*, 26, 51–66.

CHAPTER 7

The Liquidity Premium

Let the price $P(u, v)$ at time u of a discount bond maturing at time v be described by the stochastic differential equation

$$\mathrm{d}P(u, v) = P(u, v)\mu(u, v)\mathrm{d}u - P(u, v)\sigma(u, v)\mathrm{d}z \tag{1}$$

where $z(u)$ is a Wiener process. As shown in Vasicek (1977) (Chapter 6 of this volume), the mean $\mu(u, v)$ and volatility $\sigma(u, v)$ of the instantaneous rate of return are related by

$$\mu(u, v) = r(u) + q(u)\sigma(u, v) \tag{2}$$

where $r(u)$ is the spot rate and $q(u)$ is the market price of risk. Eq. (1) can be written as

$$\frac{\mathrm{d}P(u, v)}{P(u, v)} = r(u)\mathrm{d}u + \sigma(u, v)q(u)\mathrm{d}u - \sigma(u, v)\mathrm{d}z. \tag{3}$$

Integrate Eq. (3) over u from t to s, $t \leq s$. We get

$$\log P(s, v) - \log P(t, v) + \frac{1}{2}\int_t^s \sigma^2(u, v)\mathrm{d}u = \int_t^s r(u)\mathrm{d}u + \int_t^s \sigma(u, v)q(u)\mathrm{d}u - \int_t^s \sigma(u, v)\mathrm{d}z(u) \tag{4}$$

Now differentiate this equation with respect to v. This produces

$$F(s, v) = F(t, v) - \int_t^s \psi(u, v)q(u)\mathrm{d}u + \int_t^s \psi(u, v)\sigma(u, v)\mathrm{d}u + \int_t^s \psi(u, v)\mathrm{d}z(u) \tag{5}$$

Unpublished memorandum, 1979

where

$$F(t,v) = -\frac{\partial}{\partial v}\log P(t,v) \tag{6}$$

is the forward rate, and

$$\psi(t,v) = \frac{\partial\sigma(t,v)}{\partial v} \tag{7}$$

is the volatility of the forward rate $F(t, v)$. The stochastic differential equation corresponding to the integral form (5) is

$$dF(t,v) = -\psi(t,v)q(t)\mathrm{d}t + \psi(t,v)\sigma(t,v)\mathrm{d}t + \psi(t,v)\mathrm{d}z(t). \tag{8}$$

We note that the drift of forward rates is fully determined by their volatilities and the pricing of risk.

The dynamic of the spot rate is described by

$$\mathrm{d}r(t) = \left.\frac{\partial F(t,s)}{\partial s}\right|_{s=t}\mathrm{d}t - \rho(t)q(t)\mathrm{d}t + \rho(t)\mathrm{d}z(t) \tag{9}$$

where $\rho(t) = \psi(t, t)$ is the volatility of the spot rate. The drift of the spot rate is equal to the slope of the forward rate curve at the origin, less the market price of risk multiplied by the volatility of the spot rate. This is consistent with equations (21) and (22) in Vasicek (1977).

Put $v = s$ in Eq. (5). Then

$$r(s) = F(t,s) - \int_t^s \psi(u,s)q(u)\mathrm{d}u + \int_t^s \psi(u,s)\sigma(u,s)\mathrm{d}u + \int_t^s \psi(u,s)\mathrm{d}z(u). \tag{10}$$

Taking the expectation as of time t yields the equation

$$E_t r(s) = F(t,s) - E_t\int_t^s \psi(u,s)q(u)\mathrm{d}u + E_t\int_t^s \psi(u,s)\sigma(u,s)\mathrm{d}u. \tag{11}$$

The liquidity premium (or term premium, as it should be called) $\pi(t, s)$ is given by

$$\pi(t,s) = F(t,s) - E_t r(s) = E_t\int_t^s \psi(u,s)q(u)\mathrm{d}u - E_t\int_t^s \psi(u,s)\sigma(u,s)\mathrm{d}u. \tag{12}$$

The liquidity premium in a term structure of interest rates has two components. The first component is driven by the market price of risk. It is equal to the expected integral over the span of the forward rate of the forward rate volatility multiplied by the market price of risk. There is, however, a second component, which is present even if the market price of risk is zero. This component, equal to the negative of the expected aggregate over the forward rate span of the bond price volatility times the forward rate volatility, arises as a result of the nonlinear relationship between prices and rates.

REFERENCES

Vasicek, Oldrich, A. (1977). "An Equilibrium Characterization of the Term Structure." *Journal of Financial Economics*, 5, 177–188.

CHAPTER 8

Term Structure Modeling Using Exponential Splines

By Oldrich A. Vasicek and H. Gifford Fong

INTRODUCTION

Term structure of interest rates provides a characterization of interest rates as a function of maturity. It facilitates the analysis of rates and yields such as discussed in Dobson, Sutch, and Vanderford [1976], and provides the basis for investigation of portfolio returns as for example in Fisher and Weil [1971]. Term structure can be used in pricing of fixed-income securities (cf., for instance, Houglet [1980]), and for valuation of futures contracts and contingent claims, as in Brennan and Schwartz [1977]. It finds applications in analysis of the effect of taxation on bond yields (cf. McCulloch [1975a] and Schaefer [1981]), estimation of liquidity premia (cf. McCulloch [1975b]), and assessment of the accuracy of market-implicit forecasts (Fama [1976]). Because of its numerous uses, estimation of the term structure has received considerable attention from researchers and practitioners alike.

A number of theoretical equilibrium models has been proposed in the recent past to describe the term structure of interest rates, such as Vasicek [1977] (Chapter 6 of this volume), Brennan and Schwartz [1979], Langetieg [1980], and Cox, Ingersoll, and Ross [1981]. These models postulate alternative assumptions about the nature of the stochastic process driving

Journal of Finance 37, No. 2, 339–348, 1982; reprinted in *Dynamic Asset-Pricing Models*, A.W. Lo (ed.), Cheltenham, G.B.: Edward Elgar Publishing Ltd., 2007.

interest rates, and deduct a characterization of the term structure implied by these assumptions in an efficiently operating market. The resulting spot rate curves have a specific functional form dependent only on a few parameters.

Unfortunately, the spot rate curves derived by these models (at least in the instances when it was possible to obtain explicit formulas) do not conform well to the observed data on bond yields and prices. Typically, actual yield curves exhibit more varied shapes than those justified by the equilibrium models. It is undoubtedly a question of time until a sufficiently rich theoretical model is proposed that provides a good fit to the data. For the time being, however, empirical fitting of the term structure is very much an unrelated task to investigations of equilibrium bond markets.

The objective in empirical estimation of the term structure is to fit a spot rate curve (or any other equivalent description of the term structure, such as the discount function) that (1) fits the data sufficiently well, and (2) is a sufficiently smooth function. The second requirement, being less quantifiable than the first, is less often stated. It is nevertheless at least as important as the first, particularly since it is possible to achieve an arbitrary good (or even perfect) fit if the empirical model is given enough degrees of freedom, with the consequence that the resulting term structure makes little sense. For a discussion of this point, see Langetieg and Smoot [1981].

A simple approach to estimation of the term structure is to postulate that bond payments occur only on a discrete set of specified dates, and assume no relationship among the discount factors corresponding to these dates (such as that they lie on a smooth curve). The discount factors can then be estimated as the coefficients in a regression with the bond payments on the given set of dates as the independent variables, and the bond price as the dependent variable. This approach has been taken by Carleton and Cooper [1976]. They include both U.S. Treasury and Federal Home Loan Bank securities in the estimation, with an adjustment for the default risk in the FHLB bonds. The resulting discount function is discrete rather than continuous, and the forward rates are found not to be smooth.

McCulloch [1971] introduced the methodology of fitting the discount function by polynomial splines. This produces estimates of the discount function as a continuous function of time. For cubic or higher order splines, the forward rates are a smooth function. Since the model is linear in the discount function, ordinary least-squares regression techniques can be used.

In addressing the effect of taxation, McCulloch [1975a] estimates the after-tax term structure of interest rates and the marginal income tax rate. Estimates of the tax rate were achieved by minimizing the standard error of the regression. This estimated tax rate is used to convert the after-tax term structure into a before-tax term structure. This procedure makes the estimated forward rates very sensitive to any estimation errors in the tax rate.

Moreover, because the tax effect is estimated by best fitting to minimize large errors, the inclusion of special securities such as flower bonds tends to prejudice the results.

Langetieg and Smoot [1981] discuss extensions of McCulloch's spline methodology. These include fitting cubic splines to the spot rates rather than the discount function, and varying the location of the spline knots. Nonlinear estimation procedures are required in these models.

This paper presents a different approach, which can be termed an *exponential spline fitting*. The methodology described here has been applied to historical price data on U.S. Treasury securities with satisfactory results. The technique produces forward rates that are a smooth continuous function of time. The model has desirable asymptotic properties for long maturities, and exhibits both a sufficient flexibility to fit a wide variety of shapes of the term structure, and a sufficient robustness to produce stable forward rate curves. An adjustment for the effect of taxes and for call features on U.S. Treasury bonds is included in the model.

In the next section, we provide a brief description of the basic concepts of the term structure, such as spot and forward rates, market-implicit forecasts, and the discount function. This provides some background for understanding some of the prior work, and of the model to be proposed in the last section.

CONCEPTS AND TERMS

The *spot interest rate* of a given maturity is defined as the yield on a pure discount bond of that maturity. The spot rates are the discount rates determining the present value of a unit payment at a given time in the future. Spot rates considered as a function of maturity are referred to as the *term structure of interest rates*.

Spot rates are not directly observable, since there are few pure discount bonds beyond maturities of one year. They have to be estimated from the yields on actual securities by means of a *term structure model*. Each actual coupon bond can be considered a package of discount bonds, namely one for each of the coupon payments and one for the principal payment. The price of such component discount bonds is equal to the amount of the payment discounted by the spot rate of the maturity corresponding to this payment. The price of the coupon bond is then the sum of the prices of these component discount bonds. The *yield to maturity* on a coupon bond is the internal rate of return on the bond payments, or the discount rate that would equate the present value of the payments to the bond price. It is seen that the yield is thus a mixture of spot rates of various maturities. In calculation of yield, each bond payment is discounted by the same rate, rather than by the spot rate corresponding to the maturity of that payment. Decomposing the actual yields on coupon bonds into the spot rates is the principal task of a term structure model.

Spot rates describe the term structure by specifying the current interest rate of any given maturity. The implications of the current spot rates for future rates can be described in terms of the *forward rates*. The forward rates are one-period future reinvestment rates, implied by the current term structure of spot rates.

Mathematically, if R_1, R_2, R_3 ... are the current spot rates, the forward rate F_t for period t is given by the equation

$$1 + F_t = \frac{(1 + R_t)^t}{(1 + R_{t-1})^{t-1}}, \qquad t = 1, 2, 3, \cdots. \tag{1}$$

This equation means that the forward rate for a given period in the future is the marginal rate of return from committing an investment in a discount bond for one more period. By definition, the forward rate for the first period is equal to the one period spot rate, $F_1 = R_1$.

The relationship of spot and forward rates described by Eq. (1) can be stated in the following equivalent form:

$$(1 + R_t)^t = (1 + F_1)(1 + F_2) \cdots (1 + F_t). \tag{2}$$

This equation shows that spot rates are obtained by compounding the forward rates over the term of the spot rate. Thus, the forward rate F_t can be interpreted as the interest rate over the period from $t - 1$ to t that is implicit in the current structure of spot rates.

Just as the forward rates are determined by the spot rates using Eq. (1), the spot rates can be obtained from the forward rates by Eq. (2). Thus, either the spot rates or the forward rates can be taken as alternative forms of describing the term structure. The choice depends on which of these two equivalent characterizations is more convenient for the given purpose. Spot rates describe interest rates over periods from the current date to a given future date. Forward rates describe interest rates over one-period intervals in the future.

There is a third way of characterizing the term structure, namely by means of the *discount function*. The discount function specifies the present value of a unit payment in the future. It is thus the price of a pure discount riskless bond of a given maturity. The discount function D_t is related to the spot rates by the equation

$$D_t = \frac{1}{(1 + R_t)^t} \tag{3}$$

and to the forward rates by the equation

$$D_t = \frac{1}{(1+F_1)(1+F_2)\ \cdots(1+F_t)}. \tag{4}$$

The discount function D_t considered in continuous time t is a smooth curve decreasing from the starting value $D_0 = 1$ for $t = 0$ (since the value of one dollar now is one dollar) to zero for longer and longer maturities. It typically has an exponential shape.

While the discount function is usually more difficult to interpret as a description of the structure of interest rates than either the spot rates or the forward rates, it is useful in the *estimation* of the term structure from bond prices. The reason is that bond prices can be expressed in a very simple way in terms of the discount function, namely the sum of the payments multiplied by their present value. In terms of the spot or forward rates, bond prices are a more complicated (nonlinear) function of the values of the rates to be estimated.

The concept of forward rates is closely related to that of the *market-implicit forecasts*. The market-implicit forecast $M_{t,s}$ of a rate of maturity s as of a given future date t is the rate that would equate the total return from an investment at the spot rate R_t for t periods reinvested at the rate $M_{t,s}$ for additional s periods, with the straight investment for $t + s$ periods at the current spot rate R_{t+s}. Mathematically, this can be written as follows:

$$(1+R_t)^t(1+M_{t,s})^s = (1+R_{t+s})^{t+s}. \tag{5}$$

The market-implicit forecasts can be viewed as a forecast of future spot rates by the aggregate of market participants. Suppose that the current one-year rate is 12 percent, and that there is a general agreement among investors that the one-year rate a year from now will be 13 percent. Then the current two-year spot rate will be 12.50 percent, since

$$(1+0.1250)^2 = (1+0.12)(1+0.13).$$

The two-year rate would be set in such a way that the two-year security has the same return as rolling over a one-year security for two years. There may not be such a general agreement as to the future rate, and in any case the forecast would not be directly observable. Knowing the current one-year and two-year spot rates, however, enables us to determine the future rate for the second year that would make the two-year bond equivalent in terms of total return to a rollover of one-year bond. This rate is the market-implicit forecast.

The market-implicit forecasts have a number of interesting properties. The first thing to note is that when a *futures contract* is available for a given future period, the rate on the futures contract is equal to the market-implicit forecast (up to a difference attributable to transaction costs). If this were not true, a riskless arbitrage can be set between a portfolio consisting of the futures contract and a security maturing at the execution date on one hand, and a security maturing at the maturity date of the contract on the other hand. Such riskless arbitrage opportunities should not exist in efficient financial markets.

Another feature of market-implicit forecasts is that the *holding period return* calculated using these forecasts is the same for any default-free security, regardless of its maturity. It is equal to the spot rate corresponding to the length of the holding period. Indeed, the total return over a holding period of length h on an issue with maturity s ($s > h$) is equal to

$$\frac{(1+R_s)^s}{(1+M_{h,s-h})^{s-h}}.$$

Recalling the definition of the market-implicit forecast in Eq. (5), the total return over the holding period is readily calculated as

$$\frac{(1+R_s)^s}{(1+M_{h,s-h})^{s-h}} = \frac{(1+R_s)^s(1+R_h)^h}{(1+R_s)^s} = (1+R_h)^h.$$

Thus, the holding period return is independent of the maturity of the security, and is given by the spot rate for the holding period.

This is a characterization of the market-implicit forecasts that can actually serve as their definition. No other set of forecasts would have the property in which the holding period returns over a given period are the same for securities of all maturities (including coupon bonds). In a sense, the market-implicit forecast is the most "neutral" forecast. It is the equilibrium expectation such that no maturities or payment schedules are ex-ante preferred to others.

The definition of the market-implicit forecasts as given by Eq. (5) is perhaps more intuitive if stated in terms of the forward rates. It is given by the following equation:

$$(1+M_{t,s})^s = (1+F_{t+1})(1+F_{t+2})\cdots(1+F_{t+s}). \tag{6}$$

Specifically, the market-implicit forecast of one-period rate is equal to the forward rate for that period,

$$M_{t,1} = F_t.$$

It is seen from Eq. (6) that the market-implicit forecast is obtained by compounding the forward rates over the period starting at the date of the forecasting horizon and extending for an interval corresponding to the term of the forecasted rate. In other words, the market-implicit forecast corresponds to the scenario of *no change in the forward rates*. The current spot rates then change by rolling along the forward rate series.

One last thing to mention about the market-implicit forecasts is that since it is a forecast of the future spot rates, we can also infer from it the corresponding forecast of yields, discount functions, and all other characterizations of the *future term structure*. The current and future term structures have the forward rates as the one common denominator, which makes the forward rates the basic building blocks of the structure of interest rates.

THE MODEL

In specification of the model proposed for estimation of the term structure, we will use the following notation:

- t time to payment (measured in half years)
- $D(t)$ the discount function, that is, the present value of a unit payment due in time t
- $R(t)$ spot rate of maturity t, expressed as the continuously compounded semiannual rate. The spot rates are related to the discount function by the equation

$$D(t) = e^{-tR(t)}$$

- $F(t)$ continuously compounded instantaneous forward rate at time t. The forward rates are related to the spot rate by the equation

$$F(t) = \frac{-d}{dt} \log D(t) = R(t) + t\frac{d}{dt}R(t).$$

- n number of bonds used in estimation of the term structure
- T_k time to maturity of the k-th bond, measured in half years
- C_k the semiannual coupon rate of the k-th bond, expressed as a fraction of the par value
- P_k price of the k-th bond, expressed as a fraction of the par value.

The basic model can be written in the following form:

$$P_k + A_k = D(T_k) + \sum_{j=1}^{L_k} C_k D(T_k - j + 1) - Q_k - W_k + \varepsilon_k \qquad k = 1, 2, \cdots, n \tag{7}$$

where

$$A_k = C_k(L_k - T_k)$$

is the accrued interest portion of the market value of the k-th bond,

$$L_k = [T_k] + 1$$

is the number of coupon payments to be received, Q_k is the price discount attributed to the effect of taxes, W_k is the price discount due to call features, and ε_k is a residual error with $E\varepsilon_k = 0$.

The model specified by Eq. (7) is expressed in terms of the discount function, rather than the spot or forward rates. The reason for this specification is that the price of a given bond is linear in the discount function, while it is nonlinear in either the spot or forward rates. Once the discount function is estimated, the spot and forward rates can easily be calculated.

An integral part of the model specification is a characterization of the structure of the residuals. We will postulate that the model be *homoscedastic in yields*, rather than in prices. This means that the variance of the residual error on yields is the same for all bonds. The reason for this requirement is that a given price increment, say \$1 per \$100 face value, has a very different effect on a short bond than on a long bond. Obviously, an error term in price on a three-month Treasury bill cannot have the same magnitude as that in price of a 20-year bond. It is, however, reasonable to assume that the magnitude of the error term would be the same for yields.

With this assumption, the residual variance in Eq. (7) is given as

$$E\varepsilon_k^2 = \sigma^2\omega_k, \qquad k = 1, 2, \cdots, n \tag{8}$$

where

$$\omega_k = \left(\frac{dP}{dY}\right)_k^2 \tag{9}$$

is the squared derivative of price with respect to yield for the k-th bond, taken at the current value of yield. The derivative $\mathrm{d}P/\mathrm{d}Y$ can easily be evaluated from time to maturity, the coupon rate, and the present yield. In addition, we will assume that the residuals for different bonds are uncorrelated,

$$E\varepsilon_k\varepsilon_j = 0, \qquad \text{for } k \neq j.$$

In specification of the effect of taxes, we will assume that the term Q_k is proportional to the current yield C_k/P_k on the bond,

$$Q_k = q\frac{C_k}{P_k}\left(\frac{dP}{dY}\right)_k, \qquad k = 1, 2, \cdots, n. \tag{10}$$

For the call effect, the simplest specification is to introduce a dummy variable I_k, equal to 1 for callable bonds and to 0 for noncallable bonds, and put

$$W_k = wI_k, \qquad k = 1, 2, \cdots, n. \tag{11}$$

Although more complicated specifications (such as those based on option pricing) are possible, the form (11) seems to work well with Treasury bonds, which invariably have the same structure of calls five years prior to maturity at par.

We will now turn to the specification of the discount function $D(t)$. Earlier approaches (cf. McCulloch [1971], [1975b]) fit the discount function by means of polynomial splines of the second or third order. While splines constitute a very flexible family of curves, there are several drawbacks to their use in fitting discount functions. The discount function is principally of an exponential shape,

$$D(t) \sim e^{-\gamma t}, \qquad 0 \leq t < \infty.$$

Splines, being piecewise polynomials, are inherently ill suited to fit an exponential type curve. Polynomials have a different curvature from exponentials, and although a polynomial spline can be forced to be arbitrarily close to an exponential curve by choosing a sufficiently large number of knot points, the local fit is not good. A practical manifestation of this phenomenon is that a polynomial spline tends to "weave" around the exponential, resulting in highly unstable forward rates (which are the derivatives of the logarithm of the discount function). Another problem with polynomial splines is their undesirable asymptotic properties. Polynomial splines cannot be forced to tail off in an exponential form with increasing maturities.

It would be convenient if we can work with the logarithm log $D(t)$ of the discount function, which is essentially a straight line and can be fitted very well with splines. Unfortunately, the model given by Eq. (7) would then be nonlinear in the transformed function, which necessitates the use of complicated nonlinear estimation techniques (cf. Langetieg and Smoot [1981]).

A way out of this dilemma is provided by the following approach, which is used in our model. Instead of using a transform of the function $D(t)$, we can apply a transform to the *argument* of the function. Let α be some constant and put

$$t = -\frac{1}{\alpha}\log(1-x), \qquad 0 \leq x < 1. \tag{12}$$

Then $G(x)$ defined by

$$D(t) = D\left(-\frac{1}{\alpha}\log(1-x)\right) = G(x) \tag{13}$$

is a new function with the following properties: (a) $G(x)$ is a decreasing function defined on the finite interval $0 \leq x \leq 1$ with $G(0) = 1$, $G(1) = 0$; (b) to the extent that $D(t)$ is approximately exponential,

$$D(t) \sim e^{-\gamma t}, \qquad 0 \leq t < \infty$$

the function $G(x)$ is approximately a power function,

$$G(x) \sim (1 - x)^{\gamma/\alpha} \qquad 0 \leq x \leq 1;$$

(c) the model specified by Eq. (7) is linear in G. Thus, we have replaced the function $D(t)$ to be estimated by the approximately power function $G(x)$ which can be very well fitted by polynomial splines, while preserving the linearity of the model. Moreover, desired asymptotic properties can easily be enforced.

If $G(x)$ is polynomial with $G'(1) \neq 0$, then the parameter α constitutes the *limiting value of the forward rates*,

$$\lim_{t \to \infty} F(t) = \alpha.$$

Indeed, in that case

$$G(x) = -G'(1)(1 - x) + o(1 - x)$$

and consequently

$$D(t) = -G'(1)e^{-\alpha t} + o(e^{-\alpha t})$$

as $t \to \infty$. Using polynomial splines to fit the function $G(x)$ will thus assure the desired convergence of the forward rates. The limiting value α can be fitted to the data together with the other estimation parameters.

Let $g_i(x)$, $0 \leq x \leq 1, i = 1, 2, \ldots, m$ be a base of a polynomial spline space. Any spline in this space can be expressed as a linear combination of the base. If $G(x)$ is fitted by a function from this space,

$$G(x) = \sum_{i=1}^{m} \beta_i g_i(x), \qquad 0 \leq x \leq 1, \tag{14}$$

the model of Eq. (7) can be written as

$$P_k + A_k = \sum_{i=1}^{m} \beta_i (g_i(X_{k1}) + \sum_{j=1}^{L_k} C_k g_i(X_{kj})) - q\frac{C_k}{P_k}\left(\frac{\mathrm{d}P}{\mathrm{d}Y}\right)_k - wI_k + \varepsilon_k, \tag{15}$$

$$E\varepsilon_k = 0, \qquad E\varepsilon_k^2 = \sigma^2 \omega_k, \qquad E\varepsilon_k \varepsilon_j = 0 \text{ for } k \neq j$$

where

$$X_{kj} = 1 - e^{-\alpha(T_k - j + 1)}, \qquad j = 1, 2, \cdots, L_k.$$

The model described by Eq. (15) is used in the estimation of the term structure. It is linear in the parameters $\beta_1, \beta_2, \ldots, \beta_m, q, w$, with residual covariance matrix proportional to

$$\Omega = \begin{vmatrix} \omega_1 & & & & & \\ & \omega_2 & & & & \\ & & \cdot & & & \\ & & & \cdot & & \\ & & & & \cdot & \\ & & & & & \cdot \\ & & & & & & \omega_n \end{vmatrix}.$$

If we write

$$U_k = P_k + A_k$$

$$Z_{ki} = g_i(X_{k1}) + \sum_{j=1}^{L_k} C_k g_i(X_{k_j}), \qquad i = 1, 2, \cdots, m$$

$$Z_{k,m+1} = -\frac{C_k}{P_k}\left(\frac{\mathrm{d}P}{\mathrm{d}Y}\right)_k$$

$$Z_{k,m+2} = -I_k$$

for $k = 1, 2, \ldots, n$, then the least-squares estimate of $\beta = (\beta_1, \beta_2, \ldots, \beta_m, q, w)'$ conditional on the value of α can be directly calculated by the generalized least-squares regression equation

$$\hat{\beta} = (Z'\Omega^{-1}Z)^{-1}Z'\Omega^{-1}U$$

where $U = (U_k), Z = (Z_{ki})$. The sum of squares

$$S(\alpha) = U'\Omega^{-1}U - \hat{\beta}'Z'\Omega^{-1}U$$

is then a function of α only. We can then find the value of α that minimizes $S(\alpha)$ by use of numerical procedures, such as the three-point Newton minimization method.

Once the least-squares values of the regression coefficients $\beta_1, \beta_2, \ldots, \beta_m, q, w$ and the parameter α are determined, the fitted discount function is given by

$$\hat{D}(t) = \sum_{i=1}^{m} \hat{\beta}_i g_i(1 - e^{-\hat{\alpha}t}), \qquad t \geq 0. \tag{16}$$

As for the spline space, we choose cubic splines as the lowest odd order with continuous derivatives. The boundary conditions are $G(0) = 1$, $G(1) = 0$. The base $\{g_i(x)\}$ should be chosen to be reasonably close to orthogonal, in order that the regression matrix

$$Z'\Omega^{-1}Z$$

can be inverted with sufficient precision.

Although the model is fitted in its transformed version given by Eq. (15), it may be illustrative to rewrite it in the original parameter t. In any interval between consecutive knot points, $G(x)$ is a cubic polynomial, and therefore $D(t)$ takes the form

$$D(t) = a_0 + a_1 e^{-\alpha t} + a_2 e^{-2\alpha t} + a_3 e^{-3\alpha t}$$

on each interval between knots. The function $D(t)$ and its first and second derivatives are continuous at the knot points. This family of curves, used to fit the discount function, can be described as the *third order exponential splines*.

Since least-squares methods are highly sensitive to wrong data, we use a screening procedure to identify and exclude outliers. Observations with residuals larger than four standard deviations are excluded and the model is fitted again. This procedure is repeated until no more outliers are present.

REFERENCES

Brennan, M.J., and E.S. Schwartz. (1979). "A Continuous Time Approach to the Pricing of Bonds." *Journal of Banking and Finance*, 3, 133–155.

Brennan, M.J., and E.S. Schwartz. (1977). "Saving Bonds, Retractable Bonds, and Callable Bonds." *Journal of Financial Economics*, 5, 67–88.

Carleton, W.R., and I. Cooper. (1976). "Estimation and Uses of the Term Structure of Interest Rates." *Journal of Finance*, September, 1067–1083.

Cox, J.C., J.E. Ingersoll, and S.A. Ross. (1981). "A Theory of the Term Structure of Interest Rates." Working Paper #19, Graduate School of Business, Stanford University.

Dobson, S.W., R.C. Sutch, and D.E. Vanderford. (1976). "An Evaluation of Alternative Empirical Models of the Term Structure of Interest Rates." *Journal of Finance*, 31, 1035–1065.

Fama, E.F. (1976). "Forward Rates as Predictors of Future Spot Rates." *Journal of Financial Economics*, 3, 361–377.

Fisher, L., and R. Weil. (1971). "Coping with Risk of Interest Rate Fluctuations: Returns to Bondholders from Naive and Optimal Strategies." *Journal of Business*, October, 408–432.

Houglet, M.X. (1980). "Estimating the Term Structure of Interest Rates for Non-Homogeneous Bonds," dissertation, Graduate School of Business. Berkeley: University of California, Berkeley.

Langetieg, T.C. (1980). "A Multivariate Model of the Term Structure." *Journal of Finance*, 35, 71–97.

Langetieg, T.C., and S.J. Smoot. (1981). "An Appraisal of Alternative Spline Methodologies for Estimating the Term Structure of Interest Rates." Working Paper, University of Southern California, December.

McCulloch, J.H. (1971). "Measuring the Term Structure of Interest Rates." *Journal of Business*, January, 19–31.

McCulloch, J.H. (1975a). "The Tax Adjusted Yield Curve." *Journal of Finance*, 30, 811–830.

McCulloch, J.H. (1975b). "An Estimate of the Liquidity Premium." *Journal of Political Economy*, 83, 95–118.

Schaefer, S.M. (1981). "Tax Induced Clientele Effects in the Market for British Government Securities." *Journal of Financial Economics*. 10, 121–159.

Vasicek, O.A. (1977). "An Equilibrium Characterization of the Term Structure." *Journal of Financial Economics*, 5, 177–188.

CHAPTER 9

The Heath, Jarrow, Morton Model

The price $P(\tau, T)$ at time τ of a discount bond maturing at T is subject to the dynamics

$$\frac{\mathrm{d}P(\tau,T)}{P(\tau,T)} = \mu_P(\tau,T)\mathrm{d}\tau + \sigma_P(\tau,T)\mathrm{d}W(\tau)$$

with

$$\mu_P(\tau,T) = r(\tau) + \lambda(\tau)\sigma_P(\tau,T)$$

where $\lambda(\tau)$ is the market price of risk (see Vasicek, 1977, Chapter 6 of this volume). This can be written as

$$\frac{\mathrm{d}P(\tau,T)}{P(\tau,T)} = r(\tau)\mathrm{d}\tau + \sigma_P(\tau,T)\mathrm{d}W^*(\tau) \tag{1}$$

where

$$W^*(\tau) = \int_0^\tau \lambda(u)\mathrm{d}u + W(\tau).$$

Integrate Eq. (1) with respect to τ from 0 to t,

$$\log P(t,T) - \log P(0,T) = \int_0^t r(\tau)\mathrm{d}\tau - \frac{1}{2}\int_0^t \sigma_P^2(\tau,T)\mathrm{d}\tau + \int_0^t \sigma_P(\tau,T)\mathrm{d}W^*(\tau),$$

and differentiate with respect to T. This produces

$$F(t,T) - F(0,T) = \int_0^t \sigma_F(\tau,T)\sigma_P(\tau,T)\mathrm{d}\tau - \int_0^t \sigma_F(\tau,T)\mathrm{d}W^*(\tau) \tag{2}$$

Written in 1994; printed in *Economic Notes*, 36 (3) (2008), 205–207.

where σ_F is the volatility of the forward rates and

$$\sigma_P(t,T) = \int_t^T \sigma_F(t,s)ds.$$

Eq. (2) is the Heath, Jarrow, Morton (1992) model.

If W, λ, σ_F are vectors, their products are interpreted as inner products.

REFERENCES

Heath, D., R. Jarrow, and A. Morton. (1992). "Bond Pricing and the Term Structure of Interest Rates: A New Methodology for Contingent Claims Valuation." *Econometrica* 60, pp. 77–105.

Vasicek, Oldrich A. (1977). "An Equilibrium Characterization of the Term Structure." *Journal of Financial Economics*, 5, 177–188.

PART

Three

General Equilibrium

Suppose each participant in an economy maximizes the expected isoelastic utility of end-of-period wealth. When the technology risk is independent of the production risk, the equilibrium value of the short rate is given by

$$r(t) = \mu(t) - \sigma^2(t)E_t \frac{1}{\Gamma(T)} \frac{A(T)Y(T)}{A(t)Y(t)}$$

where $A(t)$ is the production process, $Y(t)$ is the state price density process, and

$$\Gamma(T) = \frac{\sum_{k=1}^{n} \gamma_k W_k(T-)}{W(T-)}$$

is the average coefficient of risk tolerance as of the end of the period. If $\gamma_k = \gamma$, $k = 1, 2, \ldots, n$, then

$$r(t) = \mu(t) - \frac{1}{\gamma}\sigma^2(t)$$

(page 108)

CHAPTER 10

Introduction to Part III

General equilibrium models investigate the pricing of real and financial assets resulting from the balance of supply and demand in an economy. The participants in the economy (often called agents) make their investment and consumption decisions to optimize their individual objectives, typically the maximum expected utility of end-of-period wealth, or the maximum expected utility of lifetime consumption. This creates a demand and supply for transactions, whose pricing is then set by the equality of supply and demand.

Equilibrium is not a stationary state. It changes at every moment, depending on the stochastic nature of the flow of capital and goods, of investment results, and of technology changes.

One result obtained from the solution of a general equilibrium model is the relationship of interest rates to economic variables. Interest rates are determined by economic forces through the equilibrium of supply and demand. Term structure models describe the behavior of interest rates of different maturities as joint stochastic processes; these models do not relate interest rates to economic variables. General equilibrium models explain why interest rates behave the way they do, not just how they behave.

Most of the modern general equilibrium models fall into two broad categories: pure exchange models and production models. Pure exchange models assume that each participant receives some endowment (such as income from labor) during his lifetime, which he can trade with other participants to maximize his expected utility of consumption. Thus, a participant who assigns large utility to immediate consumption will borrow from those participants who assign higher utility to consumption at a later date. The mechanism of supply and demand will determine the pricing of such contracts, resulting in a description of the term structure of interest rates and the pricing of bonds. For this kind of a model, see, for instance, Karatzas and Shreve (1998).

Models of production economies often start with an initial endowment assigned to each participant. The economy contains production opportunities, which consist of production processes with stochastic rates of return on investment. The production processes can be viewed as exogenously given assets that are available for investment in any amount. The amount of investment in the production, however, is determined endogenously. The parameters of the production process can themselves be stochastic. This can be interpreted as representing uncertain changes in production technology.

It is assumed that investors can issue and buy any derivatives of any of the assets and securities in the economy. The investors can lend and borrow among themselves, either at a floating short rate or by issuing and buying term bonds. The resultant market is complete. It is further assumed that there are no transaction costs and no taxes or other forms of redistribution of social wealth. The investment wealth and asset values are measured in terms of a medium of exchange that cannot be stored unless invested in the production process. For instance, this wealth unit could be a perishable consumption good. A model of production economy with these characteristics is described in Cox, Ingersoll, and Ross (1985a). They assume that the investors have identical preferences.

For a meaningful economic analysis, it is essential that a general equilibrium model allows heterogeneous participants. If all participants have the same preferences, they will all hold the same portfolio. Since there is no borrowing and lending in the aggregate, there is no net holding of debt securities by any participant, and no investor is exposed to interest rate risk. Moreover, if the utility functions are the same, it does not allow for study of how asset pricing and interest rates depend on differences in investors' preferences.

The main difficulty in developing a general equilibrium model of production economies with heterogeneous participants had been the need to carry the individual wealth levels as state variables, because the equilibrium depends on the distribution of wealth across the participants. It is shown in the 2005 paper "The Economics of Interest Rates" (Chapter 11) that the individual wealth levels can be represented as functions of a single process, which is jointly Markov with the technology state variable. This allows construction of equilibrium models with just two state variables, regardless of the number of participants in the economy.

The papers in Part Three investigate an economy in continuous time with production subject to uncertain technological changes described by a state variable. Each investor maximizes the expected utility from lifetime consumption. The participants have different utility functions and different time preferences.

The economy contains a production process whose rate of return dA/A on investment is

$$\frac{dA}{A} = \mu dt + \sigma dy$$

where $y(t)$ is a Wiener process. The process $A(t)$ represents a constant return-to-scale production opportunity.

The parameters of the production process are stochastic, reflecting the fact that production technology evolves in an unpredictable manner. It is assumed that their behavior is driven by a Markov state variable $X(t)$, $\mu = \mu(X(t), t), \sigma = \sigma(X(t), t)$. The state variable can be interpreted as representing the state of the production technology. The process $X(t)$, which can be a vector, may be correlated with the production process $A(t)$.

In equilibrium, the total wealth must be invested in the production process (which justifies referring to the production process as the *market portfolio*). Any lending and borrowing (including lending and borrowing implicit in issuing and buying contingent claims) is among the participants in the economy, and its sum must be zero.

It may seem more realistic to have a model of the economy with multiple production processes: factories for different goods, farming of different commodities, and so on. It may be noted, however, that the equilibrium conditions would simply determine in which proportion these production processes are held by the aggregate of the economy participants. Now, this total is actually known and observed: It is the market portfolio. Rather than specifying the vectors of expected returns for each production and the covariance matrix of their risks (and perhaps arriving at a market portfolio different from the observed one due to misspecification of the inputs for the individual productions), it serves the purpose of investigating an economic equilibrium better to model the properties of the market portfolio directly.

An economy cannot be in equilibrium if arbitrage opportunities exist. A necessary and sufficient condition for absence of arbitrage is that there exists a process $Y(t)$, called the state price density process, such that the price P of any asset in the economy satisfies the equation

$$P(t) = \mathrm{E}_t P(s) \frac{Y(s)}{Y(t)}.$$

Equilibrium is fully described by specification of the process $Y(t)$, which determines the pricing of all assets in the economy, such as bonds and derivative contracts, by means of the previous equation. Bond prices in turn determine the term structure of interest rates. The state price density process also determines each participant's optimum investment strategy. Solving for the equilibrium means solving for the process $Y(t)$.

In "The Economics of Interest Rates" (Chapter 11), it is assumed that consumption takes place continuously at rates based on the investor's optimal investment and consumption strategy. The equilibrium conditions are used to derive a nonlinear partial differential equation whose solution determines the state price density process and consequently the term structure of interest rates. (The results are stated in terms of the so-called numeraire portfolio $Z(t) = 1/Y(t)$). While the solution to the equation can be approximated by numerical methods, the nonlinearity of the equation could present some difficulties.

The 2013 article "General Equilibrium with Heterogeneous Participants and Discrete Consumption Times" (Chapter 12) provides the exact solution for the case that consumption takes place at a finite number of discrete times. If the time points are chosen to be dense enough, the discrete case will approximate the continuous case with the desired precision. This solution does not require solving partial differential equations, and explicit computational procedure is provided. The algorithm requires no more complicated mathematical tools than finding the root of a monotone function.

In many applications, the technology risk is independent of the production risk. For instance, if the production is farming, the progress in development of new agricultural methods, hybrids, fertilizers, and so on is independent of weather. The unpublished 2013 memorandum "Independence of Production and Technology Risks" (Chapter 13) provides an intriguing formula for the equilibrium value of the short rate in the case that each participant maximizes the expected utility of end-of-period wealth.

The paper "Risk-Neutral Economy and Zero Price of Risk" (Chapter 14), written in 2014, investigates the equilibrium in an economy in which all participants are indifferent to risk. The mechanism of asset and derivative pricing in such an economy is identified. It is shown that no economy in equilibrium with stochastic interest rates can be simultaneously risk-neutral and have zero market price of risk. On the other hand, there exist equilibrium economies with risk-averse participants and zero prices of risk. The paper explains the paradox: In a risk-neutral economy in equilibrium, the expected returns are the same on all assets, regardless of their riskiness, over the one period that is relevant to the investors, namely to the point of consumption. Due to the nonlinearity of compounding, however, this precludes the expected instantaneous returns to be the same, unless they are deterministic. The market price of risk will not be zero.

CHAPTER 11

The Economics of Interest Rates

ABSTRACT

The paper looks at the behavior of investors in an economy consisting of a production process controlled by a state variable representing the state of technology. The participants in the economy maximize their individual utilities of consumption. Each participant has a constant relative risk aversion. The degrees of risk aversion, as well as the time preference functions, differ across participants. The participants may lend and borrow among themselves, either at a floating short rate or by issuing or buying term bonds. We derive conditions under which such an economy is in equilibrium, and obtain equations determining interest rates.

INTRODUCTION

What determines interest rates? Intuitively, it seems that interest rates should be set by supply and demand for borrowing and lending, given the production opportunities in the economy (both current and as they may change in the future depending on technological developments), the time preference for consumption and the attitude toward risk and return of the participants in the economy, and the distribution of wealth across the participants. This would necessitate a general equilibrium model of the economy under the optimal consumption and investment decisions of the players. So far, however, such a model does not seem to have been developed in sufficient generality.

Cox, Ingersoll, and Ross (1985a, 1985b) postulate an economy with endogenous production subject to technological changes described by state variables. After identifying the optimal investment and consumption strategies, they derive conditions under which the total riskless lending and the

Journal of Financial Economics, 76 (2)(2005), 293–307.

total holdings in debt securities and contingent claims are zero. They then obtain a specific interest rate model under the assumption that the means and variances of the production rates of return are proportional to a single state variable following a square-root process.

This analysis, however, is limited by their assumption that all participants in the economy are identical in their preferences (namely, all with a logarithmic utility function). All investors will thus hold the same portfolio. If there is no borrowing and lending in aggregate, there is no holding of debt securities by any participant. In such an economy, the bond market does not exist. Moreover, since the utility functions are fixed, it does not allow us to study how interest rates depend on the investors' preferences. Dumas (1989) investigates equilibrium conditions in an economy with no technology change and with two investors. Wang (1996) looks at a pure exchange economy with two heterogeneous participants. Chan and Kogan (2002) analyze an exchange economy with heterogeneous participants, where each individual's utility is a function of consumption measured in units of an average aggregate endowment.

What is attempted here is an investigation of the term structure of interest rates imposed by equilibrium in a production economy consisting of participants with heterogeneous preferences. When the participants in an economy have different objectives, some will borrow from others in optimizing their investment strategies. Bond prices will be set in such a way that the total demand for borrowing at any maturity equals the total supply. Bond repricing changes the excess returns expected on the production processes and on bonds and thus alters the relative attractiveness of the different investment opportunities. The bond market provides a means of reapportioning the investments in production among the participants in the economy to accommodate their diverse preferences.

We postulate a very simple economy, namely one consisting of a single production process whose behavior is affected by a single variable representing the state of technology. The members of the economy maximize their individual utilities of consumption. It will be assumed that each participant has a constant relative risk aversion. The degrees of risk aversion, as well as the time preference functions, differ across the participants. The participants may lend and borrow among themselves, either at a floating short rate or by issuing or buying term bonds. In this economy, the total social wealth is invested in the production process and the sum of the bond investments is zero. This provides equilibrium conditions from which we derive equations for the short rate and for the market prices of risk. These relations will allow us to investigate the nature of interest rates. The main difficulty in developing a general equilibrium model with heterogeneous participants, namely, that the aggregate preferences in the economy shift due to changes in the distribution of wealth across the participants, is resolved by showing that the individual wealth levels can be represented as functions of a single process.

We will assume that investment wealth and asset values are measured in terms of a medium of exchange that cannot be stored unless invested in the production process. For instance, this wealth unit may be a perishable consumption good. In this case, interest rates can become negative, because no participant will hold the exchange medium physically but will instead invest it in the production process or lend it to other participants who will put it into production.

OPTIMAL INVESTMENT STRATEGIES

Consider an economy consisting of a production process whose rate of return $\mathrm{d}A/A$ on an investment A is

$$\frac{\mathrm{d}A}{A} = \mu \mathrm{d}t + \sigma \mathrm{d}y, \tag{1}$$

where $y(t)$ is a Wiener process. The rate of return on an investment in the production process is independent of the investment amount. The development of the production process is affected by a state variable X, $\mu = \mu(X(t), t), \sigma = \sigma(X(t), t)$. The dynamics of the state variable, which can be interpreted as measuring technological change, is given by

$$\mathrm{d}X = \zeta \mathrm{d}t + \psi \mathrm{d}y + \varphi \mathrm{d}x, \tag{2}$$

where $x(t)$ is a Wiener process independent of $y(t)$. The parameters ζ, ψ, and φ are functions of $X(t)$ and t.

In addition to the production process, the economy allows unrestricted borrowing and lending at any maturity. Denote the interest rate on instantaneous borrowing (the *short rate*) by $r(t)$. An asset $M(t)$ consisting of reinvestment at the short rate,

$$M(s) = M(t)\exp\left(\int_t^s r(\tau)\,\mathrm{d}\tau\right), \tag{3}$$

will be called the money market account.

It will be assumed that it is possible to issue and buy any derivatives of any of the assets and securities in the economy. Specifically, it is possible to short the production process by writing futures against it. It will further be assumed that there are no transaction costs and no taxes or other forms of redistribution of social wealth. We do not explicitly consider firms, since an equity participation in a firm is equivalent to holding a contingent claim on the value of the firm's business.

We will take a shortcut in the development of the equilibrium model. If asset pricing is not free of arbitrage, the economy cannot be in equilibrium. Since there are only two sources of uncertainty, namely the processes y and x, there exist processes λ, η, called the *market prices of risk* for the risk sources y, x, respectively, such that the price P of any asset in the economy must satisfy the equation

$$\frac{\mathrm{d}P}{P} = (r + \beta\lambda + \delta\eta)\mathrm{d}t + \beta\mathrm{d}y + \delta\mathrm{d}x, \tag{4}$$

where β, δ are the exposures of the asset to the two risk sources. In particular, we have

$$r = \mu - \sigma\lambda. \tag{5}$$

Alternatively stated, there will exist a numeraire portfolio Z of Long (1990) with the dynamics

$$\frac{\mathrm{d}Z}{Z} = (r + \lambda^2 + \eta^2)\mathrm{d}t + \lambda\mathrm{d}y + \eta\mathrm{d}x \tag{6}$$

such that the price P of any asset satisfies

$$P(t) = Z(t)\mathrm{E}_t\frac{P(s)}{Z(s)}. \tag{7}$$

Here and throughout, the symbol E_t denotes expectation conditional on a filtration $\Im_t$ generated by $y(t), x(t)$. In integral form, the numeraire portfolio can be written as

$$Z(s) = Z(t)\exp\left(\int_t^s r\mathrm{d}\tau + \frac{1}{2}\int_t^s \left(\lambda^2 + \eta^2\right)\mathrm{d}\tau + \int_t^s \lambda\mathrm{d}y + \int_t^s \eta\mathrm{d}x\right). \tag{8}$$

The price $B(t, s)$ at time t of a default-free bond with unit face value maturing at time s is given by the equation

$$B(t,s) = \mathrm{E}_t\frac{Z(t)}{Z(s)} = \mathrm{E}_t\exp\left(-\int_t^s r\mathrm{d}\tau - \frac{1}{2}\int_t^s \left(\lambda^2 + \eta^2\right)\mathrm{d}\tau - \int_t^s \lambda\mathrm{d}y - \int_t^s \eta\mathrm{d}x\right). \tag{9}$$

Term rates will be defined by

$$R(t, \tau) = -\frac{1}{\tau}\log B(t, t + \tau), \tag{10}$$

with $r(t) = R(t, 0+)$. Bonds of all maturities, together with the money market account, will be referred to as the bond market. We see from Eqs. (5), (9), and (10) that interest rates are completely described by specifying the market prices of risk $\lambda(t)$ and $\eta(t)$, so our goal is to find out how the two processes are determined in an equilibrium economy.

Suppose that the economy has n participants and let $W_k(0)$ be the initial wealth of the k-th investor. Suppose each investor maximizes the expected utility of lifetime consumption,

$$\max E \int_0^T p_k(t) U_k(c_k(t)) \mathrm{d}t, \tag{11}$$

where $c_k(t)$ is the rate of consumption at time t, $U_k(c)$ is a utility function with $U'_k > 0$, $U''_k < 0$, and $p_k(t) \geq 0, 0 \leq t \leq T$ is a time preference function. We will consider specifically the class of isoelastic utility functions, which we will write in the form

$$\begin{aligned} U_k(c) &= \frac{c^{(\gamma_k - 1)/\gamma_k}}{\gamma_k - 1} && \gamma_k > 0, \gamma_k \neq 1 \\ &= \log c && \gamma_k = 1. \end{aligned} \tag{12}$$

Here γ_k is the reciprocal of the relative risk aversion coefficient, $1/\gamma_k = -cU''_k/U'_k$. We will call γ_k the *risk tolerance*.

An investment strategy is fully described by the exposures $\beta_k(t)$ and $\delta_k(t)$ to the sources of risk y and x. The wealth $W_k(t)$ at time t grows by the increment

$$\mathrm{d}W_k = W_k(r + \beta_k \lambda + \delta_k \eta)\mathrm{d}t + W_k \beta_k dy + W_k \delta_k \mathrm{d}x - c_k \mathrm{d}t. \tag{13}$$

Let $V_k(t)$ be the value at time t of the expected utility of consumption under an optimal investment and consumption strategy,

$$V_k(t) = \max E_t \int_t^T p_k(s) U_k(c_k(s)) \mathrm{d}s. \tag{14}$$

Under some mild regularity conditions (cf. Fleming and Rishel, 1975), a necessary and sufficient condition for optimality is given by the Bellman equation

$$\max(E \mathrm{d}V_k + p_k U_k(c_k) \mathrm{d}t) = 0. \tag{15}$$

Put

$$\begin{aligned} V_k &= \frac{1}{\gamma_k - 1} {Q_k}^{1/\gamma_k} {W_k}^{(\gamma_k - 1)/\gamma_k} && \gamma_k > 0, \gamma_k \neq 1 \\ &= Q_k \log W_k + G_k && \gamma_k = 1, \end{aligned} \tag{16}$$

with the dynamics of Q_k written as

$$\frac{dQ_k}{Q_k} = \vartheta_k dt + \theta_k dy + \omega_k dx. \tag{17}$$

Calculating EdV_k yields the equation

$$\max\left(\left(\frac{1}{\gamma_k(\gamma_k - 1)}\vartheta_k + \frac{1}{\gamma_k}\left(r + \beta_k\lambda + \delta_k\eta - \frac{c_k}{W_k}\right)\right.\right.$$

$$\left.\left.-\frac{1}{2}\frac{1}{\gamma_k^2}\left((\beta_k - \theta_k)^2 + (\delta_k - \omega_k)^2\right)\right)Q_k^{1/\gamma_k}W_k^{(\gamma_k-1)/\gamma_k} + p_k U_k(c_k)\right) = 0. \tag{18}$$

Maximization over the values of β_k, δ_k, and c_k yields a unique maximum attained at the point

$$\beta_k = \gamma_k\lambda + \theta_k \tag{19}$$

$$\delta_k = \gamma_k\eta + \omega_k \tag{20}$$

$$c_k = \frac{p_k^{\gamma_k} W_k}{Q_k}. \tag{21}$$

The investment position of each participant is independent of his current wealth level W_k and the rate of consumption is proportional to the current wealth.

Substituting these values back into (18), we get the equation

$$\vartheta_k + (\gamma_k - 1)(r + \lambda\theta_k + \eta\omega_k) + \frac{1}{2}\gamma_k(\gamma_k - 1)(\lambda^2 + \eta^2) + \frac{p_k^{\gamma_k}}{Q_k} = 0 \tag{22}$$

and consequently

$$\frac{dQ_k}{Q_k} = \left(-(\gamma_k - 1)(r + \lambda\theta_k + \eta\omega_k) - \frac{1}{2}\gamma_k(\gamma_k - 1)(\lambda^2 + \eta^2) - \frac{p_k^{\gamma_k}}{Q_k}\right)dt$$

$$+ \theta_k dy + \omega_k dx. \tag{23}$$

We note that

$$Ed(Q_k Z^{\gamma_k - 1}) = -p_k^{\gamma_k} Z^{\gamma_k - 1} dt \tag{24}$$

and integrating subject to the condition

$$Q_k(T) = 0, \tag{25}$$

we get

$$Q_k(t) = Z^{1-\gamma_k}(t)\mathrm{E}_t \int_t^T p_k{}^{\gamma_k}(\tau) Z^{\gamma_k - 1}(\tau)\mathrm{d}\tau. \tag{26}$$

The wealth increment can be determined as

$$\frac{\mathrm{d}W_k}{W_k} = (r + \lambda\theta_k + \eta\omega_k + \gamma_k(\lambda^2 + \eta^2))\mathrm{d}t + (\gamma_k\lambda + \theta_k)dy + (\gamma_k\eta + \omega_k)\mathrm{d}x - \frac{p_k^{\gamma_k}}{Q_k}\mathrm{d}t. \tag{27}$$

Comparing equations (6), (23) and (27), we find that

$$\mathrm{d}\left(\frac{W_k}{Q_k} Z^{-\gamma_k}\right) = 0. \tag{28}$$

On integration,

$$W_k(t) = v_k Z^{\gamma_k}(t) Q_k(t) \tag{29}$$

and therefore

$$W_k(t) = v_k Z(t)\mathrm{E}_t \int_t^T p_k{}^{\gamma_k}(\tau) Z^{\gamma_k - 1}(\tau)\mathrm{d}\tau, \tag{30}$$

where

$$v_k = \frac{W_k(0)}{Q_k(0)} Z^{-\gamma_k}(0) = \frac{W_k(0)}{Z(0)\mathrm{E} \int_0^T p_k{}^{\gamma_k}(\tau) Z^{\gamma_k - 1}(\tau)\mathrm{d}\tau} \tag{31}$$

is a constant. The behavior of the individual wealth levels W_k is fully determined by the process Z.

The optimal rate of consumption is, from Eqs. (21) and (29),

$$c_k = v_k p_k^{\gamma_k} Z^{\gamma_k}. \tag{32}$$

We see from equations (30), (32) that, when measured in units of the numeraire portfolio, the current wealth is equal to the expected future consumption.

THE EQUILIBRIUM ECONOMY

If we consider the economy as a whole, the total wealth must be invested in the production process. Any lending and borrowing is among the participants in the economy, and its sum must be zero. Thus, the total exposure to the process y is that of the total wealth invested in the production, and the total exposure to the process x is zero. The conditions for equilibrium are then

$$\sum_{k=1}^{n} \beta_k W_k = \sigma W \tag{33}$$

$$\sum_{k=1}^{n} \delta_k W_k = 0, \tag{34}$$

where

$$W = \sum_{k=1}^{n} W_k \tag{35}$$

is the total social wealth.

Using the relation (29) and substituting back from (19) and (20), write equation (27) as

$$dW_k = W_k(r + \beta_k \lambda + \delta_k \eta)dt + W_k \beta_k dy + W_k \delta_k dx - \nu_k p_k^{\gamma_k} Z^{\gamma_k} dt \tag{36}$$

and sum over all investors. This produces the equation

$$dW = \mu W dt + \sigma W dy - \sum_{k=1}^{n} \nu_k p_k^{\gamma_k} Z^{\gamma_k} dt \tag{37}$$

describing the dynamics of the total wealth. The first two terms on the right-hand side correspond to the investment of the total social wealth in the production, and the third term represents the total consumption. The terminal condition is $W(T) = 0$.

The unique solution of the stochastic differential equation (37) is given by

$$W(t) = Z(t) E_t \int_t^T \sum_{k=1}^{n} \nu_k p_k^{\gamma_k}(\tau) Z^{\gamma_k - 1}(\tau) d\tau. \tag{38}$$

Indeed, we can write (37) as

$$d\left(\frac{W}{A}\right) = -\frac{1}{A} \sum_{k=1}^{n} \nu_k p_k^{\gamma_k} Z^{\gamma_k} dt \tag{39}$$

and therefore

$$\mathrm{Ed}\left(\frac{W}{Z}\right) = \mathrm{Ed}\left(\frac{W}{A}\frac{A}{Z}\right) = \frac{A}{Z}\mathrm{d}\left(\frac{W}{A}\right) + \frac{W}{A}\mathrm{Ed}\left(\frac{A}{Z}\right) = -\sum_{k=1}^{n} v_k p_k^{\gamma_k} Z^{\gamma_k - 1}\mathrm{d}t, \tag{40}$$

due to the property (7) of the numeraire process. Eq. (38) follows by integration.

To determine the process Z, however, we need the solution of Eq. (37) in a more explicit form. We see from Eq. (37) that the only state variable for W besides X is the value of Z. Write $W(t) = W(X, Z, t)$ as a function of the state variables. Then

$$\begin{aligned} \mathrm{d}W = {} & W_t \mathrm{d}t + (\zeta \mathrm{d}t + \psi \mathrm{d}y + \varphi \mathrm{d}x) W_X \\ & + ((\mu - \sigma\lambda + \lambda^2 + \eta^2)\mathrm{d}t + \lambda \mathrm{d}y + \eta \mathrm{d}x) Z W_Z \\ & + \frac{1}{2}(\psi^2 + \varphi^2) W_{XX}\mathrm{d}t + (\psi\lambda + \varphi\eta) Z W_{XZ}\mathrm{d}t + \frac{1}{2}(\lambda^2 + \eta^2) Z^2 W_{ZZ}\mathrm{d}t, \end{aligned} \tag{41}$$

where the subscripts X, Z, and t denote partial derivatives with respect to these variables. Comparing Eqs. (37) and (41), we must have

$$\psi W_X + \lambda Z W_Z = \sigma W \tag{42}$$

$$\varphi W_X + \eta Z W_Z = 0. \tag{43}$$

Solving for λ, η and substituting produces the equation

$$W_t = -\mathfrak{R}[W, t] - \sum_{k=1}^{n} v_k p_k^{\gamma_k} Z^{\gamma_k}, \tag{44}$$

where

$$\begin{aligned} \mathfrak{R}[W, t] = {} & (\zeta + \sigma\psi) W_X + \mu Z W_Z + \frac{1}{2}(\psi^2 + \varphi^2) W_{XX} \\ & + (\sigma\psi W - (\psi^2 + \varphi^2) W_X) \frac{W_{XZ}}{W_Z} \\ & + ((\psi^2 + \varphi^2) {W_X}^2 - 2\sigma\psi W W_X + \sigma^2 W^2) \left(\frac{1}{Z W_Z} + \frac{1}{2}\frac{W_{ZZ}}{{W_Z}^2}\right) \\ & - (\mu + \sigma^2) W \end{aligned} \tag{45}$$

is an operator that involves only derivatives with respect to X and Z. Eq. (44) is subject to the condition

$$W(T) = 0. \tag{46}$$

The value of $\Re[W,T]$ is defined by its limit for $t \to T$. From (38), we have

$$W(t) \sim \sum_{k=1}^{n} \nu_k Z^{\gamma_k}(t) \int_t^T p_k^{\gamma_k}(\tau) d\tau, \quad t \to T. \tag{47}$$

If none of the time preference functions $p_k(t)$ has an atom at T, the limit is $\Re[W,T] = 0$. This assumes that the sum of the integrals in Eq. (47) is nonzero for all $t < T$, in other words, that at least one participant in the economy assigns positive utility to consumption up to the date T. If it is zero for $T_1 < t < T$ but positive for all $t < T_1$, the boundary conditions are applied to T_1.

Once the function $W(X, Z, t)$ has been determined, λ and η are calculated as

$$\lambda = \frac{\sigma W - \psi W_X}{Z W_Z} \tag{48}$$

$$\eta = -\frac{\varphi W_X}{Z W_Z}. \tag{49}$$

To demonstrate that the process W is indeed a function of X, Z, and t only, assume to the contrary that there are other state variables (for instance, the current and past values of the individual wealth levels W_k) of which W is a function. Suppose Y (possibly a vector) is such a variable, $W(t) = W(X, Y, Z, t)$. In that case, the market prices of risk $\lambda = \lambda(X, Y, Z, t), \eta = \eta(X, Y, Z, t)$ are functions of Y as well and the dynamics of Z depends on Y. Write the dynamics of Y as $dY = \chi_0 dt + \chi_1 dy + \chi_2 dx$, where $\chi_i = \chi_i(X, Y, Z, t), i = 0, 1, 2$. Expressing dW by Ito's lemma and comparing the coefficients of dt, dy, and dx with those of (37), we can again eliminate λ, η and obtain a partial differential equation in X, Y, Z, and t. But the only coefficients in that equation that depend on Y are the χ_i, all of which are multiplied by derivatives with respect to Y. Therefore, any solution of (44) is also a solution of that equation. Since W is unique, it must be independent of Y. Consequently, λ and η are functions of X, Z, and t only. The process $(X(t), Z(t))$ is Markov.

Eqs. (44), (48), and (49) define λ and η, and the process Z is given by its dynamics (6). Bond prices and rates are then determined by (5), (9), and (10). This constitutes a complete solution of the problem.

Eq. (44) is an evolution equation. Very little is known about nonlinear partial differential equations in general, and the equation needs to be investigated case by case. For some of the problems that may be encountered in the presence of nonlinearity see, for instance, Li and Chen (1992) or Logan (1994). We can expect, however, that the reasons for ill behavior of the solution will often be an economic misspecification rather than mathematical irregularity. For instance, if $\mu(X,t)$ is too steep a function of the state variable X, and X is allowed to drift to large values too freely (as in Example 7), the production process $A(t)$ may explode or have an infinite expectation. The process Z will not exist, and Eq. (44) will have no solution.

In well-posed situations, Eq. (44) is easy to solve computationally. The simplest method is to replace the derivative W_t by the difference quotient and recursively calculate $W(t-h)$ from $W(t)$. For some guidance on numerical methods see, for instance, Ganzha and Vorozhtsov (1996). The main computational difficulty is the necessity to iterate on the values of the constants $\nu_1, \nu_2, \ldots, \nu_n$, since they are determined (up to a scalar) by (31) only after Z has been found.

EXAMPLES

Example 1. Suppose $\gamma_k = \gamma, k = 1, 2, \ldots, n$ (although the investors may still differ by their time preference functions $p_k(t)$). Then the solution of Eq. (44) is

$$W = Z^{\gamma} F, \tag{50}$$

where $F = F(X, t)$ is the solution of

$$F_t + \left(\zeta + \frac{\gamma - 1}{\gamma}\sigma\psi\right) F_X + \frac{1}{2}(\psi^2 + \varphi^2) F_{XX} - \frac{\gamma - 1}{2\gamma}(\psi^2 + \varphi^2)\frac{{F_X}^2}{F}$$
$$+(\gamma - 1)\left(\mu - \frac{1}{2\gamma}\sigma^2\right) F + \sum_{k=1}^{n} \nu_k p_k^{\gamma} = 0 \tag{51}$$

subject to $F(X, T) = 0$. The process Z is given by

$$Z(t) = W^{1/\gamma}(0) A^{-1/\gamma}(0) A^{1/\gamma}(t) F^{-1/\gamma}(X(t), t) \exp\left(-\frac{1}{\gamma}\int_0^t \frac{\sum \nu_k p_k^{\gamma}(\tau)}{F(X(\tau), \tau)} d\tau\right).$$

The constants $\nu_1, \nu_2, \ldots, \nu_n$ are determined by the equations

$$W_k(0) = \nu_k W(0) A^{(1-\gamma)/\gamma}(0) F^{-1/\gamma}(X(0), 0)$$
$$\times \mathrm{E}\int_0^T p_k^{\gamma}(t) A^{(\gamma-1)/\gamma}(t) F^{(1-\gamma)/\gamma}(X(t), t) \exp\left(\frac{1-\gamma}{\gamma}\int_0^t \frac{\sum \nu_k p_k^{\gamma}(\tau)}{F(X(\tau), \tau)} d\tau\right) dt.$$

Then

$$\lambda = \frac{1}{\gamma}\left(\sigma - \psi\frac{F_X}{F}\right)$$

$$\eta = -\frac{\varphi F_X}{\gamma F}.$$

The dynamics of $\lambda = \lambda(X, t)$ and $\eta = \eta(X, t)$, as well as that of the short rate $r = \mu - \sigma\lambda$, follow from the dynamics of X.

Example 2. If, in particular, $\gamma_k = 1, k = 1, 2, \ldots, n$, then

$$F(X, t) = \sum_{k=1}^{n} v_k \int_t^T p_k(\tau)\mathrm{d}\tau$$

and

$$Z(t) = \frac{W(0)}{A(0)F(X(0), 0)}A(t).$$

Solving Eq. (31) for $v_1, v_2, \ldots, v_n$, we get

$$v_k = \frac{NW_k(0)}{\int_0^T p_k(\tau)\mathrm{d}\tau},$$

where N is an arbitrary multiplier. On substitution, we have

$$F(X, t) = N\sum_{k=1}^{n} W_k(0)\int_t^T p_k(\tau)\mathrm{d}\tau \Big/ \int_0^T p_k(\tau)\mathrm{d}\tau.$$

The prices of risk are

$$\lambda = \sigma$$

$$\eta = 0$$

and the short rate is

$$r = \mu - \sigma^2.$$

Example 3. Let $\gamma_k = \gamma, k = 1, 2, \ldots, n$ and suppose there are no unforeseen technological changes, so that μ and σ are functions of time only. Then F is a function of t only and we have $\lambda = \sigma/\gamma, \eta = 0$, and

$$r = \mu - \frac{1}{\gamma}\sigma^2.$$

Interest rates are deterministic, independent of the time preference functions $p_k(t)$.

Example 4. Suppose that the time preference functions of all participants are concentrated at the point T. In other words, each participant maximizes the expected utility of end-of-period wealth. Then

$$W(t) = \frac{W(0)}{A(0)}A(t) \quad t < T$$
$$= 0 \quad t = T.$$

At T, we have

$$W(T-) = \sum_{k=1}^{n} \nu_k Z^{\gamma_k}(T).$$

Put

$$K(Z) = \frac{A(0)}{W(0)} \sum_{k=1}^{n} \nu_k Z^{\gamma_k}$$

and denote by K^{-1} the inverse function of K. Since

$$\frac{A(t)}{Z(t)} = \mathrm{E}_t \frac{A(T)}{Z(T)},$$

we get

$$Z(t) = \frac{A(t)}{\mathrm{E}_t \dfrac{A(T)}{K^{-1}(A(T))}}$$

and bond prices are given by

$$B(t,s) = \frac{A(t)}{\mathrm{E}_t \dfrac{A(T)}{K^{-1}(A(T))}} \mathrm{E}_t \frac{A(T)}{A(s)K^{-1}(A(T))}.$$

Example 5. Suppose that the time preference functions of all participants are concentrated at the point T, and assume moreover that $\gamma_k = \gamma, k = 1, 2, \ldots, n$ (so that investors have homogeneous preferences). Then

$$K^{-1}(A) = NA^{1/\gamma},$$

where N is a constant multiplier, and

$$Z(t) = \frac{NA(t)}{\mathrm{E}_t A^{(\gamma-1)/\gamma}(T)}. \tag{52}$$

For instance, suppose that

$$\mu = X$$
$$\zeta = \alpha(\overline{X} - X)$$

and let σ, ψ, and φ be constant. Evaluating the expectation in Eq. (52) gives

$$Z(t) = A^{1/\gamma}(t)\exp\left(\frac{1-\gamma}{\gamma}D(t,T)\,X + g(t)\right),$$

where $g(t)$ is a function of t alone, and

$$D(t,T) = \frac{1}{\alpha}\left(1 - e^{-\alpha(T-t)}\right). \tag{53}$$

Alternatively, we can solve equation (51) and find F in the form

$$F(X,t) = \exp((\gamma - 1)D(t,T)X + h(t)). \tag{54}$$

Consequently, we have

$$\lambda = \frac{\sigma}{\gamma} + \frac{1-\gamma}{\gamma}\psi D \tag{55}$$

$$\eta = \frac{1-\gamma}{\gamma}\varphi D \tag{56}$$

$$r = X - \frac{\sigma^2}{\gamma} + \frac{\gamma - 1}{\gamma}\sigma\psi D. \tag{57}$$

The dynamics of r is given by

$$dr = \alpha(\overline{r} - r)dt + \psi dy + \varphi dx,$$

where $\overline{r}$ is a function of time. Interest rates of all maturities are Gaussian, and market prices of both sources of risk are functions of time only. All investors hold the same portfolio, $\beta_k = \sigma, \delta_k = 0$.

Example 6. Make the same assumptions as in Example 5, but let

$$\sigma^2 = \widehat{\sigma}^2 X$$
$$\psi^2 = \widehat{\psi}^2 X$$
$$\varphi^2 = \widehat{\varphi}^2 X,$$

where $\widehat{\sigma}$, $\widehat{\psi}$, and $\widehat{\varphi}$ depend on time only. The function F still has the form of Eq. (54), with D given by a different expression than in Eq. (53) but still independent of X. Equations (55), (56), and (57) hold, and we have

$$\lambda = \widehat{\lambda}\sqrt{X}$$

$$\eta = \widehat{\eta}\sqrt{X}$$

$$r = \zeta X$$

with $\widehat{\lambda}$, $\widehat{\eta}$, and ζ being functions of time only. The dynamics of r are described by

$$dr = \kappa(\bar{r} - r)dt + \sqrt{r}(\xi_1 dx + \xi_2 dy),$$

where $\kappa, \bar{r}, \xi_1, \xi_2$ are functions of time. This is a model of the Cox, Ingersoll, Ross type.

Example 7. Consider the same situation as in the previous two examples, but let

$$\sigma = \widehat{\sigma}X$$

$$\psi = \widehat{\psi}X$$

$$\varphi = \widehat{\varphi}X$$

with $\widehat{\sigma}$, $\widehat{\psi}$, and $\widehat{\varphi}$ constant. If $\gamma > 1$, the expectation in (52) is infinite. We have $Z(t) \equiv 0$ and the numeraire portfolio does not exist. Equilibrium cannot be attained in this economy.

TERM STRUCTURE MODELS

A number of specific models of the term structure of interest rates have been proposed, derived from the principle of no arbitrage. We wish to ask the following question: For a given term structure model, does an equilibrium economy of the kind investigated here exist in which interest rates are governed by that model?

If an equilibrium exists, the expectations in Eq. (30) must be finite. For that, it is necessary that

$$E_t Z^{\gamma_k - 1}(s) < \infty \tag{58}$$

for all $k = 1, 2, \ldots, n, 0 \le t \le s \le T$. On the other hand, if Eq. (58) holds, it is always possible to construct an economy in equilibrium (cf. Harrison and Kreps, 1979). We will therefore investigate whether condition (58) is satisfied by a given term structure model.

We will look specifically at one-factor interest rate models. We obtain such models in the economy proposed here if there is only one source of risk. This will happen if, for instance, $\sigma = 0, \psi = 0$. These models then have the form

$$B(t,s) = E_t\frac{Z(t)}{Z(s)} = E_t \exp\left(-\int_t^s r\mathrm{d}\tau - \frac{1}{2}\int_t^s \eta^2\mathrm{d}\tau - \int_t^s \eta\mathrm{d}x\right).$$

This question was investigated in some detail in Vasicek (2000), who gives a somewhat different rationale for the condition (58). It is shown that a Gaussian model always satisfies the finiteness condition. On the other hand, consider the Cox, Ingersoll, Ross model described by

$$\mathrm{d}r = \alpha(\overline{r} - r)\mathrm{d}t + \xi\sqrt{r}\mathrm{d}x$$

$$\eta = \hat{\eta}\sqrt{r}.$$

Note that $\xi\hat{\eta}$ is negative when the bond risk premia $\mathrm{E}\mathrm{d}B/B - r\mathrm{d}t = \eta\mathrm{E}\mathrm{d}x\mathrm{d}B/B$ are positive. Put

$$a = \gamma_{\max}\alpha^2 + \left(1 - \gamma_{\max}\right)\left(\left(\alpha + \xi\hat{\eta}\right)^2 + 2\xi^2\right)$$

$$b = \alpha + \left(1 - \gamma_{\max}\right)\xi\hat{\eta},$$

where $\gamma_{\max}$ is the largest of $\gamma_k, k = 1, 2, \ldots, n$. The expectation in (58) is finite if and only if $a \geq 0$, or $a < 0$ and

$$s < t + \frac{2}{\sqrt{-a}}\left(\pi - \arctan\left(\sqrt{-a}/b\right)\right).$$

When applying a term structure model (for instance, in derivatives pricing), one does not want to make assumptions about the preferences of the participants in the economy that generated that model. In other words, it is desirable to know under what conditions the model is consistent with an equilibrium economy with *any* participant preferences. For the Cox, Ingersoll, Ross model, in order that Eq. (58) holds for all γ_k and all $t \leq s$, it is necessary (and sufficient) that

$$(\alpha + \xi\hat{\eta})^2 + 2\xi^2 \leq \alpha^2. \tag{59}$$

The inequality in Eq. (59) (which can be written as $\gamma \leq \kappa$ in the notation of their 1985b paper) is a restriction on the parameters of the model in order that it may describe the behavior of interest rates in an economy with arbitrary preferences of the participants.

For the Black, Derman, Toy (1990) model, the expectation in (58) is infinite for all $\gamma_k > 1$ and $s > t$. No equilibrium economy exists in which the bond market follows this model. There would be an infinite demand for interest rate swaps (receiving floating and paying fixed rates) with no supply.

CONCLUSIONS

This chapter looks at the behavior of heterogeneous investors in an economy consisting of a production process and a bond market. If each participant in the economy pursues a strategy optimal with respect to his preferences, the market has to accommodate the resultant demand and supply of credit by pricing risk so that the economy stays in equilibrium. We derive conditions under which such equilibrium is possible, and obtain equations determining interest rates. These results can be used for quantitative analyses of various economic phenomena.

REFERENCES

Black, F., Derman, E., and W. Toy. (1990). "A One-Factor Model of Interest Rates and Its Application to Treasury Bond Options." *Financial Analysts Journal*, 33–39.

Chan, Y., and L. Kogan. (2002). "Catching up with the Joneses: Heterogeneous Preferences and the Dynamics of Asset Prices." *Journal of Political Economy*, 110, 1255–1285.

Cox, J., Ingersoll, J. Jr., and S. Ross. (1985a). "An Intertemporal General Equilibrium Model of Asset Prices." *Econometrica*, 53, 363–384.

Cox, J., Ingersoll, J. Jr., and S. Ross. (1985b). "A Theory of the Term Structure of Interest Rates." *Econometrica*, 53, 385–407.

Dumas, B. (1989). "Two-Person Dynamic Equilibrium in the Capital Market." *Review of Financial Studies*, 2, 157–188.

Fleming, W., and R. Rishel. (1975). *Deterministic and Stochastic Optimal Control*. New York: Springer-Verlag.

Ganzha, V., and E. Vorozhtsov. (1996). *Computer-Aided Analysis of Difference Schemes for Partial Differential Equations*. New York: John Wiley & Sons.

Harrison, J., and D. Kreps. (1979). "Martingales and Arbitrage in Multiperiod Securities Markets." *Journal of Economic Theory*, 20, 381–408.

Li, T.-T., and Y. Chen. (1992). *Global Classical Solutions for Nonlinear Evolution Equations*. Harlow, Great Britain: Longman Group.

Logan, J. (1994). *An Introduction to Nonlinear Partial Differential Equations*. New York: John Wiley & Sons.

Long, J. Jr. (1990). "The Numeraire Portfolio." *Journal of Financial Economics,* 26, 29–69.

Vasicek, O. (2000). "Bond Market Clearing." In Hughston, L. (Ed.), *The New Interest Rate Models*. London: Risk Books, 157–168.

Wang, J. (1996). "The Term Structure of Interest Rates in a Pure Exchange Economy with Heterogeneous Investors." *Journal of Financial Economics,* 41, 75–110.

CHAPTER 12

General Equilibrium with Heterogeneous Participants and Discrete Consumption Times

ABSTRACT

The paper investigates the term structure of interest rates imposed by equilibrium in a production economy consisting of participants with heterogeneous preferences. Consumption is restricted to an arbitrary number of discrete times. The paper contains an exact solution to market equilibrium and provides an explicit constructive algorithm for determining the state price density process. The convergence of the algorithm is proven. Interest rates and their behavior are given as a function of economic variables.

INTRODUCTION

Interest rates are determined by the equilibrium of supply and demand. Increased demand for credit brings interest rates higher, while an increase in demand for fixed-income investment causes rates to go down. To determine the mechanism by which economic forces and investors' preferences cause changes in supply and demand, it is necessary to develop a general equilibrium model of the economy. Such model provides a means of quantitative analysis of how economic conditions and scenarios affect interest rates.

Vasicek (2005) (Chapter 11 of this volume) investigates an economy in continuous time with production subject to uncertain technological changes described by a state variable. Consumption is assumed to be in continuous time, with each investor maximizing the expected utility from

Journal of Financial Economics, 108, (2013), pp. 608–614; short version published in *FAMe*, 2013.

lifetime consumption. The participants have constant relative risk aversion, with different degrees of risk aversion and different time preference functions. After identifying the optimal investment and consumption strategies, the paper derives conditions for equilibrium and provides a description of interest rates.

For a meaningful economic analysis, it is essential that a general equilibrium model allows heterogeneous participants. If all participants have identical preferences, then they will all hold the same portfolio. Since there is no borrowing and lending in the aggregate, there is no net holding of debt securities by any participant, and no investor is exposed to interest rate risk. Moreover, if the utility functions are the same, it does not allow for study of how interest rates depend on differences in investors' preferences.

The main difficulty in developing a general equilibrium model with heterogeneous participants had been the need to carry the individual wealth levels as state variables, because the equilibrium depends on the distribution of wealth across the participants. This can be avoided if the aggregate consumption can be expressed as a function of a Markov process, in which case only this Markov process becomes a state variable. This is often simple in models of pure exchange economies, where the aggregate consumption is exogenously specified.

The situation is different in models of production economies. In such economies, the aggregate consumption depends on the social welfare function weights. Because these weights are determined endogenously, it is necessary that the individual consumption levels themselves be functions of a Markov process. This has precluded an analysis of equilibrium in a production economy with any meaningful number of participants; most explicit results for production economies had previously been limited to models with one or two participants.

The above approach is exploited here. Vasicek (2005) shows that the individual wealth levels can be represented as functions of a single process, which is jointly Markov with the technology state variable. This allows construction of equilibrium models with just two state variables, regardless of the number of participants in the economy.

In Vasicek (2005), the equilibrium conditions are used to derive a nonlinear partial differential equation whose solution determines the term structure of interest rates. While the solution to the equation can be approximated by numerical methods, the nonlinearity of the equation could present some difficulties.

The present paper provides the exact solution for the case that consumption takes place at a finite number of discrete times. This solution does not require solving partial differential equations, and explicit computational procedure is provided. If the time points are chosen to be dense enough, the discrete case will approximate the continuous case with the desired precision. Some may in fact argue that, in reality, consumption is discrete rather than continuous, and therefore the discrete case addressed here is the more relevant.

The following section summarizes the relevant results from Vasicek (2005). The next section contains the solution for the equilibrium state price density process and the structure of interest rates in the discrete consumption case. The final section gives a proof that the proposed algorithm converges to the market equilibrium.

THE EQUILIBRIUM ECONOMY

Assume that a continuous time economy contains a production process whose rate of return $\mathrm{d}A/A$ on investment is

$$\frac{\mathrm{d}A}{A} = \mu \mathrm{d}t + \sigma \mathrm{d}y, \tag{1}$$

where $y(t)$ is a Wiener process. The process $A(t)$ represents a constant return-to-scale production opportunity. An investment of an amount W in the production at time t yields the amount $WA(s)/A(t)$ at time $s > t$. The production process can be viewed as an exogenously given asset that is available for investment in any amount. The amount of investment in production, however, is determined endogenously.

The parameters of the production process can themselves be stochastic. It will be assumed that their behavior is driven by a Markov state variable X, $\mu = \mu(X(t), t)$, $\sigma = \sigma(X(t), t)$. The dynamics of the state variable, which can be interpreted as representing the state of the production technology, is given by

$$\mathrm{d}X = \zeta \mathrm{d}t + \psi \mathrm{d}y + \varphi \mathrm{d}x, \tag{2}$$

where $x(t)$ is a Wiener process independent of $y(t)$. The parameters ζ, ψ, and φ are functions of $X(t)$ and t.

It is assumed that investors can issue and buy any derivatives of any of the assets and securities in the economy. The investors can lend and borrow among themselves, either at a floating short rate or by issuing and buying term bonds. The resultant market is complete. It is further assumed that there are no transaction costs and no taxes or other forms of redistribution of social wealth. The investment wealth and asset values are measured in terms of a medium of exchange that cannot be stored unless invested in the production process. For instance, this wealth unit could be a perishable consumption good.

Suppose that the economy has n participants and let $W_k(0) > 0$ be the initial wealth of the k–th investor. Each investor maximizes the expected utility from lifetime consumption,

$$\max E\int_0^T p_k(t)U_k(c_k(t))\mathrm{d}t, \tag{3}$$

where $c_k(t)$ is the rate of consumption at time t, $U_k(c)$ is a utility function with $U_k' > 0,\ U_k'' < 0$, and $p_k(t) \geq 0,\ 0 \leq t \leq T$ is a time preference function. Consider specifically the class of isoelastic utility functions, written in the form

$$\begin{aligned} U_k(c) &= \frac{c^{(\gamma_k-1)/\gamma_k}}{\gamma_k - 1} && \gamma_k > 0,\ \gamma_k \neq 1 \\ &= \log c && \gamma_k = 1. \end{aligned} \tag{4}$$

Here γ_k is the reciprocal of the relative risk aversion coefficient, $1/\gamma_k = -\,cU_k''/U_k'$, which will be called the risk tolerance.

An economy cannot be in equilibrium if arbitrage opportunities exist in the sense that the returns on an asset strictly dominate the returns on another asset. A necessary and sufficient condition for absence of arbitrage is that there exist processes $\lambda(t),\ \eta(t)$, called the market prices of risk for the risk sources $y(t),\ x(t)$, respectively, such that the price P of any asset in the economy satisfies the equation

$$\frac{\mathrm{d}P}{P} = (r + \beta\lambda + \delta\eta)\mathrm{d}t + \beta\mathrm{d}y + \delta\mathrm{d}x, \tag{5}$$

where β, δ are the exposures of the asset to the two risk sources. In particular,

$$\mu = r + \sigma\lambda. \tag{6}$$

It is assumed that Novikov's condition holds,

$$\mathrm{E}\exp\left(\frac{1}{2}\int_0^T \left(\lambda^2 + \eta^2\right)\mathrm{d}t\right) < \infty. \tag{7}$$

Let Z be the numeraire portfolio of Long (1990) with the dynamics

$$\frac{\mathrm{d}Z}{Z} = (r + \lambda^2 + \eta^2)\mathrm{d}t + \lambda\mathrm{d}y + \eta\mathrm{d}x, \tag{8}$$

such that the price P of any asset satisfies

$$\frac{P(t)}{Z(t)} = \mathrm{E}_t \frac{P(s)}{Z(s)}. \tag{9}$$

Specifically, the price $B(t,s)$ at time t of a default-free bond with unit face value maturing at time s is given by the equation

$$B(t,s) = E_t \frac{Z(t)}{Z(s)}. \tag{10}$$

Here and throughout, the symbol E_t denotes expectation conditional on a filtration $\mathfrak{I}_t$ generated by $y(t)$, $x(t)$. In integral form, the numeraire portfolio can be written as

$$Z(s) = Z(t)\exp\left(\int_t^s r\mathrm{d}\tau + \frac{1}{2}\int_t^s (\lambda^2+\eta^2)\mathrm{d}\tau + \int_t^s \lambda \mathrm{d}y + \int_t^s \eta \mathrm{d}x\right). \tag{11}$$

The process $Z(t)$ is the reciprocal of the state price density process.

Vasicek (2005) shows that the optimal consumption rate of the k-th investor is a function of the numeraire process only, given as

$$c_k(t) = v_k p_k^{\gamma_k}(t) Z^{\gamma_k}(t), \tag{12}$$

where

$$v_k = \frac{W_k(0)}{Z(0)\mathrm{E}\int_0^T p_k^{\gamma_k}(t) Z^{\gamma_k - 1}(t)\mathrm{d}t} \tag{13}$$

is a constant. The individual wealth level W_k under an optimal strategy is

$$W_k(t) = v_k Z(t) \mathrm{E}_t \int_t^T p_k^{\gamma_k}(\tau) Z^{\gamma_k - 1}(\tau)\mathrm{d}\tau. \tag{14}$$

The behavior of the wealth level $W_k(t)$ is fully determined by the process $Z(t)$. Moreover, the process $(X(t),\ Z(t))$ is Markov. That means that $W_k(t) = W_k(X(t), Z(t), t)$ is a function of two state variables X and Z only.

In equilibrium, the total wealth

$$W(t) = \sum_{k=1}^{n} W_k(t) \tag{15}$$

must be invested in the production process (which justifies referring to the production process as the *market portfolio*). Any lending and borrowing (including lending and borrowing implicit in issuing and buying contingent claims) is among the participants in the economy, and its sum must be zero. Thus, the total exposure to the process y is that of the total wealth invested in the production, and the total exposure to the process x is zero. This produces the equation

$$dW = \mu W dt + \sigma W dy - \sum_{k=1}^{n} v_k p_k^{\gamma_k} Z^{\gamma_k} dt \tag{16}$$

describing the dynamics of the total wealth. The terminal condition is

$$W(T) = 0. \tag{17}$$

The process Z is further subject to the requirement that

$$\frac{A(t)}{Z(t)} = \mathrm{E}_t \frac{A(s)}{Z(s)}. \tag{18}$$

The unique solution of the stochastic differential Eq. (16) subject to Eqs. (17) and (18) is given by

$$W(t) = Z(t)\mathrm{E}_t \int_t^T \sum_{k=1}^{n} v_k p_k^{\gamma_k}(\tau) Z^{\gamma_k - 1}(\tau) d\tau. \tag{19}$$

In Vasicek (2005), the process $Z(t)$ is determined in the following manner: Write $W(t) = W(X, Z, t)$ as a function of the state variables. Expanding dW in Eq. (16) by Ito's lemma and comparing the coefficients of dt, dy, and dx provides equations from which λ, η can be eliminated, resulting in a nonlinear partial differential equation with known coefficients. Once the function $W(X, Z, t)$ has been determined as the unique solution of this equation, λ and η are calculated from $W(X, Z, t)$ as functions of X, Z, and t. The process $Z(t)$ is obtained by integrating the stochastic differential equation (8). Bond prices are determined from Eq. (10).

In the case of discrete consumption dealt with in this paper, the partial differential equation and the subsequent integration of Eq. (8) is replaced by an explicit algorithm described in the next section.

Equilibrium is fully described by specification of the process $Z(t)$, which determines the pricing of all assets in the economy, such as bonds and derivative contracts, by means of Eq. (9). Solving for the equilibrium requires determining the values of the constants $v_1, v_2, \ldots, v_n$. The algorithm proposed in this paper utilizes the fact that any choice of the constants is consistent with a unique equilibrium described by the process $Z(t)$, except that the corresponding initial wealth levels calculated as

$$W_k'(0) = Z(0)\mathrm{E}\int_0^T v_k p_k^{\gamma_k}(t) Z^{\gamma_k - 1}(t)\mathrm{d}t \tag{20}$$

do not agree with the given initial values $W_k(0)$. Repeatedly replacing v_k by $v_k W_k(0)/W_k'(0)$ and recalculating Z converges to the required equilibrium, as proven in "Proof of Convergence" section later in this chapter. This is analogous to the method proposed by Negishi (1960) in a deterministic economy.

In economic literature, the usual approach to investigating the existence and uniqueness of equilibrium has been the concept of a representative agent (see Negishi, 1960, and Karatzas and Shreve, 1998). The representative agent maximizes an objective (the social welfare function)

$$\max E\int_0^T \max_{c_1+c_2+\ldots+c_n=c} \sum_{k=1}^{n} \Lambda_k p_k(t) U_k(c_k(t))\mathrm{d}t, \tag{21}$$

where $c(t)$ is the consumption rate of the agent (equal to the aggregate consumption of all participants) and $\Lambda_1, \Lambda_2, \ldots, \Lambda_n$ are weights assigned to the individual participants. The constants $v_1, v_2, \ldots, v_n$ in Eq. (12) are related to the representative agent weights. Eq. (4.5.7) in Theorem 4.5.2 of Karatzas and Shreve (1998) can be written as

$$c_k(t) = \gamma_k^{-\gamma_k} \Lambda_k^{\gamma_k} p_k^{\gamma_k}(t) Z^{\gamma_k}(t). \tag{22}$$

Comparing Eqs. (22) and (12) yields the relationship

$$\Lambda_k = \gamma_k v_k^{1/\gamma_k} \tag{23}$$

for $k = 1, 2, \ldots, n$.

DISCRETE CONSUMPTION TIMES

This chapter considers an economy in which consumption takes place only at specific discrete dates. The economy exists in continuous time, and between the consumption dates the participants are continuously trading and the production is continuous. The market is assumed to be complete.

Suppose each investor's time preference function is concentrated at positive points $t_1 < t_2 < \ldots < t_m = T$, so that the k-th investor maximizes the expected utility

$$\max E \sum_{i=1}^{m} p_{ik} U_k(C_{ik}), \tag{24}$$

where C_{ik} is the consumption at time t_i, and U_k is a utility function given by Eq. (4). It is assumed that

$$\sum_{k=1}^{n} p_{mk} > 0. \tag{25}$$

Let $Y(t) = 1/Z(t)$ be the state price density process. Put

$$\begin{aligned} A_i &= A(t_i), \\ X_i &= X(t_i), \\ Y_i &= Y(t_i) \end{aligned} \tag{26}$$

for $i = 0, 1, \ldots, m$, with $t_0 = 0$. The state variable $X(t)$ can be a vector. Furthermore, let

$$N_i = \frac{W(t_i+)}{A_i} \tag{27}$$

for $i = 0, 1, \ldots, m-1$, and $N_m = 0$.

The optimal individual consumption is given from Eq. (12) by

$$C_{ik} = v_k p_{ik}^{\gamma_k} Y_i^{-\gamma_k} \tag{28}$$

for $i = 1, 2, \ldots, m$, $k = 1, 2, \ldots, n$, where v_k are positive constants satisfying the equation

$$v_k = \frac{Y_0 W_k(0)}{E \sum_{i=1}^{m} p_{ik}^{\gamma_k} Y_i^{-\gamma_k+1}}. \tag{29}$$

Eq. (16) takes the form

$$W(t) = N_i A(t) \text{ for } t_i \le t < t_{i+1}, \quad i = 0, 1, \ldots, m-1 \tag{30}$$

and

$$N_{i-1} - N_i = \frac{K_i(Y_i)}{A_i} \quad i = 1, 2, \ldots, m, \tag{31}$$

where

$$K_i(Y) = \sum_{k=1}^{n} \nu_k p_{ik}^{\gamma_k} Y^{-\gamma_k} \quad i = 1, 2, \dots, m. \tag{32}$$

From Eq. (31),

$$N_0 = \sum_{i=1}^{m} \frac{K_i(Y_i)}{A_i}. \tag{33}$$

From Eq. (18),

$$Y_{i-1} = \mathrm{E}_{t_{i-1}} \frac{A_i}{A_{i-1}} Y_i, \quad i = 1, 2, \dots, m. \tag{34}$$

Note that Eqs. (33) and (34) imply

$$W(0) = \frac{1}{Y_0} \mathrm{E} \sum_{i=1}^{m} Y_i K_i(Y_i), \tag{35}$$

as is easily established by multiplying Eq. (33) by $A_m Y_m / Y_0$ and taking expectation.

The solution to Eqs. (31) and (34) subject to $N_m = 0$, $N_0 = W(0)/A(0)$ is obtained by successive elimination of $Y_m, Y_{m-1}, \dots, Y_1$ and N_{m-1}, $N_{m-2}, \dots, N_1$. Let K_m^{-1} be the inverse of the function K_m and define recursively two sets of functions G, H as follows:

$$G_m(N, A, X) = K_m^{-1}(NA) \tag{36}$$

and $G_i(N, A, X) = Y$ is the positive solution of the equation

$$Y = H_i \left(N - \frac{K_i(Y)}{A}, A, X \right) \tag{37}$$

for $i = 1, 2, \dots, m-1$; and

$$H_i(N, A, X) = \mathrm{E}_{t_i} \left[\frac{A_{i+1}}{A_i} G_{i+1} \left(N, A_{i+1}, X_{i+1} \right) \middle| A_i = A, X_i = X \right] \tag{38}$$

for $i = 0, 1, \dots, m-1$. Then

$$\begin{aligned} Y_i &= H_i(N_i, A_i, X_i) \quad i = 0, 1, \dots, m-1 \\ &= G_i(N_{i-1}, A_i, X_i) \quad i = 1, 2, \dots, m. \end{aligned} \tag{39}$$

It will be now shown that the functions $G_i(N,A,X)$, $H_i(N,A,X)$ are decreasing functions of the first argument. Suppose, for some $1 \le i \le m$, $G_i(N,A,X)$ is a decreasing function of N. It follows from Eq. (38) that $H_{i-1}(N,A,X)$ is also decreasing in N. Denote by $N = H_i^{-1}(Y,A,X)$ the inverse of the function $Y = H_i(N, A, X)$ with respect to the first argument while keeping the remaining arguments constant. Then from Eq. (37),

$$H_{i-1}^{-1}(G_{i-1}(N,A,X),A,X) + \frac{K_{i-1}(G_{i-1}(N,A,X))}{A} = N. \tag{40}$$

The expression on the left-hand side of this equation is a decreasing function of G_{i-1}, and therefore the function $G_{i-1}(N,A,X)$ is decreasing in N. Because $G_m(N,A,X)$ is decreasing in N, it follows by induction that $G_i(N,A,X)$, $i = 1, 2, \ldots, m$, and consequently $H_i(N,A,X)$, $i = 0, 1, \ldots, m-1$, are all decreasing functions of the first argument.

Then from Eq. (39),

$$Y_i = G_i\left(H_{i-1}^{-1}\left(Y_{i-1}, A_{i-1}, X_{i-1}\right), A_i, X_i\right) \tag{41}$$

for $i = 1, 2, \ldots, m$. Eq. (41) together with $Y_0 = H_0(N_0, A_0, X_0)$ determines $Y_1, Y_2, \ldots, Y_m$ recursively. The state price density process at time t is

$$Y(t) = \mathrm{E}_t \frac{A_i}{A(t)} Y_i \text{ for } t_{i-1} \le t \le t_i,\ i = 1, 2, \ldots, m. \tag{42}$$

Eqs. (41), (42) represent the exact solution to the equilibrium economy in the case that consumption is limited to a number of discrete times, provided Eq. (29) holds.

Calculation of the equilibrium solution proceeds as follows: Choose initial values of the constants $\nu_1, \nu_2, \ldots, \nu_n$. A reasonable initial guess is

$$\nu_k = \frac{W_k(0) A_0^{\gamma_k - 1}}{\mathrm{E}\sum_{i=1}^{m} p_{ik}^{\gamma_k} A_i^{\gamma_k - 1}} \tag{43}$$

for $k = 1, 2, \ldots, n$. Calculate recursively the functions G_i, $i = 1, 2, \ldots, m$ and H_i, $i = 0, 1, \ldots, m-1$ from Eqs. (36), (37), and (38). Calculate $Y_0 = H_0(N_0, A_0, X_0)$ and determine $Y_1, Y_2, \ldots, Y_m$ from Eq. (41). Calculate $W_k'(0)$ as

$$W_k'(0) = \frac{\nu_k}{Y_0} \mathrm{E} \sum_{i=1}^{m} p_{ik}^{\gamma_k} Y_i^{-\gamma_k + 1} \tag{44}$$

for $k = 1, 2, \ldots, n$. Set new values of constants $v_1, v_2, \ldots, v_n$ as

$$v'_k = v_k \frac{W_k(0)}{W'_k(0)}. \tag{45}$$

Repeat the above calculations with the new values of the constants until $W'_k(0)$ are sufficiently close to $W_k(0)$, $k = 1, 2, \ldots, n$. The state price density process is given by Eq. (42). Bond prices are given as

$$B(t,s) = \mathrm{E}_t \frac{Y(s)}{Y(t)}. \tag{46}$$

Interest rates are determined by bond prices.

In the special case that $\gamma_k = \gamma$, $k = 1, 2, \ldots, n$, the functions take the form $G_i(N,A,X) = (NA)^{-1/\gamma}(F_i(X) + q_i)^{1/\gamma}$, $i = 1, 2, \ldots, m$, $H_i(N,A,X) = (NA)^{-1/\gamma}F_i^{1/\gamma}(X)$, $i = 0, 1, \ldots, m-1$, where $F_m(X) = 0$,

$$F_i(X) = \left(\mathrm{E}_{t_i} \left[\left(\frac{A_{i+1}}{A_i} \right)^{(\gamma-1)/\gamma} (F_{i+1}(X_{i+1}) + q_{i+1})^{1/\gamma} \middle| X_i = X \right] \right)^{\gamma}$$

$$i = 0, 1, \ldots, m-1 \tag{47}$$

and

$$q_i = \sum_{k=1}^{n} v_k p_{ik}^{\gamma}. \tag{48}$$

Then

$$Y_0 = N_0^{-1/\gamma} A_0^{-1/\gamma} F_0^{1/\gamma}(X_0) \tag{49}$$

and

$$Y_i = N_0^{-1/\gamma} A_i^{-1/\gamma} (F_i(X_i) + q_i)^{1/\gamma} \prod_{j=1}^{i-1} \left(1 + \frac{q_j}{F_j(X_j)} \right)^{1/\gamma} \quad i = 1, 2, \ldots, m. \tag{50}$$

PROOF OF CONVERGENCE

Define the function Q_m as

$$\begin{aligned} &Q_m(N, A_1, A_2, \ldots, A_m, X_1, X_2, \ldots, X_m) \\ &= G_m(H_{m-1}^{-1}(G_{m-1}(\ldots H_1^{-1}(G_1(N, A_1, X_1), A_1, X_1) \ldots, \\ &\quad A_{m-1}, X_{m-1}), A_{m-1}, X_{m-1}), A_m, X_m). \end{aligned} \tag{51}$$

Since there is an odd number of decreasing functions in the nested expression (51), Q_m is a decreasing function of N. Then

$$Y_m = Q_m(N_0, A_1, A_2, \ldots, A_m, X_1, X_2, \ldots, X_m). \tag{52}$$

Note that Eq. (52) represents the solution to Eqs. (33) and (34), since the intermediate values of $N_1, N_2, \ldots, N_{m-1}$ have been eliminated.

Assume that $\gamma_k \geq 1$, $k = 1, 2, \ldots, n$ (corresponding to the sufficient condition (4.6.4) for uniqueness of the equilibrium solution in Theorem 4.6.1 in Karatzas and Shreve, 1998). Let $v_1, v_2, \ldots, v_n$ be arbitrary positive constants and determine $Y_0, Y_1, \ldots, Y_m$ from Eq. (39). Calculate $W'_k(0)$ from Eq. (44) and v'_k from Eq. (45), $k = 1, 2, \ldots, n$. Put

$$K'_i(Y) = \sum_{k=1}^{n} v'_k p_{ik}^{\gamma_k} Y^{-\gamma_k} \tag{53}$$

and denote by $Y'_0, Y'_1, \ldots, Y'_m$ the variables calculated using the constants $v'_1, v'_2, \ldots, v'_n$ in place of $v_1, v_2, \ldots, v_n$. Then

$$N_0 = \sum_{i=1}^{m} \frac{K'_i(Y'_i)}{A_i} \tag{54}$$

and

$$Y'_{i-1} = \mathrm{E}_{t_{i-1}} \frac{A_i}{A_{i-1}} Y'_i, \quad i = 1, 2, \ldots, m. \tag{55}$$

Put

$$W''_k(0) = \frac{v'_k}{Y'_0} \mathrm{E} \sum_{i=1}^{m} p_{ik}^{\gamma_k} Y'^{-\gamma_k+1}_i \tag{56}$$

and

$$v''_k = v'_k \frac{W_k(0)}{W''_k(0)}. \tag{57}$$

Define

$$a_k = \frac{v_k}{v'_k} = \frac{W'_k(0)}{W_k(0)},$$

$$a'_k = \frac{v'_k}{v''_k} = \frac{W''_k(0)}{W_k(0)}. \tag{58}$$

Then

$$a'_k = \frac{Y_0 E \sum_{i=1}^{m} p_{ik}^{\gamma_k} Y_i'^{-\gamma_k+1}}{Y'_0 E \sum_{i=1}^{m} p_{ik}^{\gamma_k} Y_i^{-\gamma_k+1}}. \tag{59}$$

Set

$$b_k = a_k^{1/\gamma_k},$$
$$b'_k = a_k'^{1/\gamma_k}, \tag{60}$$

$k = 1, 2, \ldots, n$. Let $b_{\min}$, $b_{\max}$ be the lowest and highest value, respectively, of $b_1, b_2, \ldots, b_n$, and $b'_{\min}$, $b'_{\max}$ be the lowest and highest value, respectively, of $b'_1, b'_2, \ldots, b'_n$. Put

$$\alpha_k = \frac{W_k(0)}{W(0)}, \tag{61}$$

$k = 1, 2, \ldots, n$. Note that

$$\sum_{k=1}^{n} \alpha_k a_k = \sum_{k=1}^{n} \alpha_k a'_k = \sum_{k=1}^{n} \alpha_k = 1 \tag{62}$$

and therefore

$$b_{\min} \leq 1 \leq b_{\max}. \tag{63}$$

Define

$$V_i = b_{\min} Y'_i \tag{64}$$

and put

$$M_0 = \sum_{i=1}^{m} \frac{K_i(V_i)}{A_i}. \tag{65}$$

The values $V_1, V_2, \ldots, V_m$ satisfy the relationship

$$V_{i-1} = E_{t_{i-1}} \frac{A_i}{A_{i-1}} V_i, \quad i = 1, 2, \ldots, m. \tag{66}$$

Eqs. (65) and (66) have the solution

$$V_m = Q_m(M_0, A_1, A_2, \ldots, A_m, X_1, X_2, \ldots, X_m). \tag{67}$$

Now

$$K_i'(Y) = \sum_{k=1}^{n} \frac{v_k}{a_k} p_{ik}^{\gamma_k} Y^{-\gamma_k} = \sum_{k=1}^{n} v_k p_{ik}^{\gamma_k} (b_k Y)^{-\gamma_k} \le \sum_{k=1}^{n} v_k p_{ik}^{\gamma_k} (b_{\min} Y)^{-\gamma_k}$$
$$= K_i(b_{\min} Y) \tag{68}$$

for $i = 1, 2, \ldots, m$, and consequently

$$N_0 = \sum_{i=1}^{m} \frac{K_i'(Y_i')}{A_i} \le \sum_{i=1}^{m} \frac{K_i(b_{\min} Y_i')}{A_i} = M_0. \tag{69}$$

Because Q_m is a decreasing function of its first argument, Eqs. (52) and (67) imply

$$Y_m \ge V_m = b_{\min} Y_m'. \tag{70}$$

It is proven similarly that

$$Y_m \le b_{\max} Y_m', \tag{71}$$

and from Eqs. (34) and (55) it then follows that

$$b_{\min} Y_i' \le Y_i \le b_{\max} Y_i' \tag{72}$$

for $i = 0, 1, \ldots, m$.

From Eq. (59),

$$b_{\min}^{\gamma_k - 1} \frac{Y_0}{Y_0'} \le a_k' \le b_{\max}^{\gamma_k - 1} \frac{Y_0}{Y_0'} \tag{73}$$

and consequently

$$b_{\min}^{1-1/\gamma_k} (Y_0/Y_0')^{1/\gamma_k} \le b_k' \le b_{\max}^{1-1/\gamma_k} (Y_0/Y_0')^{1/\gamma_k}. \tag{74}$$

If $Y_0/Y_0' \le 1$, then

$$b_{\min} \le b_k' \le b_{\max}^{1-1/\gamma_k} \le b_{\max}^{1-1/\gamma_{\max}} \tag{75}$$

and

$$\frac{b_{\max}'}{b_{\min}'} \le \frac{b_{\max}}{b_{\min}} b_{\max}^{-1/\gamma_{\max}}. \tag{76}$$

If $Y_0/Y_0' \geq 1$, then

$$b_{\min}^{1-1/\gamma_{\max}} \leq b_{\min}^{1-1/\gamma_k} \leq b_k' \leq b_{\max} \tag{77}$$

and

$$\frac{b'_{\max}}{b'_{\min}} \leq \frac{b_{\max}}{b_{\min}} b_{\min}^{1/\gamma_{\max}}. \tag{78}$$

Thus, either the inequality in Eq. (76) or (78) holds.

Put $b_{\max}/b_{\min} = s \geq 1$ and let l be such that $b_l = b_{\min}$. Then

$$\begin{aligned}1 &= \sum_{k=1}^{n} \alpha_k b_k^{\gamma_k} = \alpha_l b_{\min}^{\gamma_l} + \sum_{\substack{k=1\\k\neq l}}^{n} \alpha_k b_k^{\gamma_k} = \alpha_l s^{-\gamma_l} b_{\max}^{\gamma_l} + \sum_{\substack{k=1\\k\neq l}}^{n} \alpha_k b_k^{\gamma_k} \leq \alpha_l s^{-\gamma_l} b_{\max}^{\gamma_l}\\ &+ \sum_{\substack{k=1\\k\neq l}}^{n} \alpha_k b_{\max}^{\gamma_k} \leq \alpha_l s^{-\gamma_{\min}} b_{\max}^{\gamma_{\max}} + \sum_{\substack{k=1\\k\neq l}}^{n} \alpha_k b_{\max}^{\gamma_{\max}} = b_{\max}^{\gamma_{\max}}(\alpha_l s^{-\gamma_{\min}} + 1 - \alpha_l)\\ &\leq b_{\max}^{\gamma_{\max}}(\alpha_{\min} s^{-\gamma_{\min}} + 1 - \alpha_{\min})\end{aligned} \tag{79}$$

and therefore

$$b_{\max} \geq (\alpha_{\min} s^{-\gamma_{\min}} + 1 - \alpha_{\min})^{-1/\gamma_{\max}}. \tag{80}$$

Similarly, if l is such that $b_l = b_{\max}$, then

$$\begin{aligned}1 &= \sum_{k=1}^{n} \alpha_k b_k^{\gamma_k} = \alpha_l b_{\max}^{\gamma_l} + \sum_{\substack{k=1\\k\neq l}}^{n} \alpha_k b_k^{\gamma_k} = \alpha_l s^{\gamma_l} b_{\min}^{\gamma_l} + \sum_{\substack{k=1\\k\neq l}}^{n} \alpha_k b_k^{\gamma_k} \geq \alpha_l s^{\gamma_l} b_{\min}^{\gamma_l}\\ &+ \sum_{\substack{k=1\\k\neq l}}^{n} \alpha_k b_{\min}^{\gamma_k} \geq \alpha_l s^{\gamma_{\min}} b_{\min}^{\gamma_{\max}} + \sum_{\substack{k=1\\k\neq l}}^{n} \alpha_k b_{\min}^{\gamma_{\max}}\\ &= b_{\min}^{\gamma_{\max}}(\alpha_l s^{\gamma_{\min}} + 1 - \alpha_l) \geq b_{\min}^{\gamma_{\max}}(\alpha_{\min} s^{\gamma_{\min}} + 1 - \alpha_{\min})\end{aligned} \tag{81}$$

and therefore

$$b_{\min} \leq (\alpha_{\min} s^{\gamma_{\min}} + 1 - \alpha_{\min})^{-1/\gamma_{\max}}. \tag{82}$$

Here $\gamma_{\min}, \gamma_{\max}$ are the lowest and highest value, respectively, of $\gamma_1, \gamma_2, \ldots, \gamma_n$, and $\alpha_{\min}$ is the lowest value of $\alpha_1, \alpha_2, \ldots, \alpha_n$. Put

$$q(s) = \max((\alpha_{\min} s^{-\gamma_{\min}} + 1 - \alpha_{\min})^{1/\gamma^2_{\max}}, (\alpha_{\min} s^{\gamma_{\min}} + 1 - \alpha_{\min})^{-1/\gamma^2_{\max}}) \le 1. \tag{83}$$

Combining the inequalities in Eqs. (76), (78), (80), and (82) produces

$$\frac{b'_{\max}}{b'_{\min}} \le \frac{b_{\max}}{b_{\min}} q(s). \tag{84}$$

Now consider the sequence of iterations $b^{(0)}_{\min} = b_{\min}$, $b^{(1)}_{\min} = b'_{\min}, \ldots$ and $b^{(0)}_{\max} = b_{\max}$, $b^{(1)}_{\max} = b'_{\max}, \ldots$. The series $s^{(j)} = b^{(j)}_{\max}/b^{(j)}_{\min}$, $j = 0, 1, \ldots$ is nonincreasing due to the inequality (84) and bounded from below by unity, so it converges to a limit $s^* \ge 1$. Assume that $s^* > 1$. Because $q(s)$ is a decreasing function of s, $q(s^{(j)}) \le q(s^*) < 1$ and the series $s^{(j)}$ decrease at least as fast as a geometric series with quotient $q(s^*)$. In a finite number of terms, it falls below the level s^*. Therefore, the assumption that $s^* > 1$ is false, and $s^{(j)}$ converges to unity. Then $b^{(j)}_1, b^{(j)}_2, \ldots, b^{(j)}_n$ and therefore $a^{(j)}_1, a^{(j)}_2, \ldots, a^{(j)}_n$ converge to unity and from Eq. (58), the sequence of the iterated values $W^{(j)}_k(0)$ converges to $W_k(0)$, $k = 1, 2, \ldots, n$.

CONCLUDING REMARKS

This paper provides explicit procedure to obtain the exact solution of equilibrium pricing in a production economy with heterogeneous investors. Each investor maximizes the expected utility from lifetime consumption, taking place at discrete times. Interest rates are determined by economic variables such as the characteristics of the production process, the individual investors' preferences, and the wealth distribution across the participants. Such a model provides a tool for quantitative study of the effect of changes in economic conditions on interest rates.

The algorithm is constructive and converges to the equilibrium solution. The convergence is proven for the case of $\gamma_k \ge 1$, $k = 1, 2, \ldots, n$, for which the uniqueness of the equilibrium has been established (cf. Karatzas and Shreve, 1998). All other steps of the procedure, however, are valid in general for any positive values of the risk tolerance coefficients. If some of the $\gamma_1, \gamma_2, \ldots, \gamma_n$ are smaller than unity and the values $W^{(j)}_k(0)$ fail to converge to the input values $W_k(0)$, $k = 1, 2, \ldots, n$ after a reasonable number of iterations, a search over the space of positive values of $v_1, v_2, \ldots, v_n$ needs to be made.

While this paper concentrates on the case that the participants have isoelastic utility functions (4), it can be extended to more general class of utilities. Suppose the k-th investor maximizes the objective (24), where $U_k(C)$ has a positive, decreasing continuous derivative $U'_k(C)$ with $U'_k(0) = \infty$, $U'_k(\infty) = 0$, $k = 1, 2, \ldots, n$. Denote the inverse of the derivative by $I_k(x) = U'^{-1}_k(x)$. Then the optimal consumption is given by

$$C_{ik} = I_k\left(\frac{Y_i}{\Lambda_k p_{ik}}\right), \tag{85}$$

where Λ_k is a positive constant satisfying the condition

$$W_k(0) = \frac{1}{Y_0} \mathrm{E} \sum_{i=1}^{m} Y_i I_k\left(\frac{Y_i}{\Lambda_k p_{ik}}\right) \tag{86}$$

for $k = 1, 2, \ldots, n$ (cf. Karatzas and Shreve, 1998, Theorems 3.6.3 and 4.4.5). Put

$$K_i(Y) = \sum_{k=1}^{n} I_k\left(\frac{Y}{\Lambda_k p_{ik}}\right) \quad i = 1, 2, \ldots, m. \tag{87}$$

Then Eqs. (30), (31), and (33) through (42) still hold. The algorithm consisting of making an initial choice of the constants $\Lambda_1, \Lambda_2, \ldots, \Lambda_n$, determining $Y_0, Y_1, \ldots, Y_m$ from Eqs. (39) and (31), setting new values of the constants from Eq. (86), and repeating the calculations may still be applicable, although a proof of convergence is not provided here.

REFERENCES

Karatzas, I., and S. Shreve. (1998). *Methods of Mathematical Finance.* New York: Springer-Verlag.

Long, J. (1990). "The Numeraire Portfolio." *Journal of Financial Economics, 26,* 29–69.

Negishi, T. (1960). "Welfare Economics and Existence of an Equilibrium for a Competitive Economy." *Metroeconomica,* 12, 92–97.

Vasicek, O. (2005). "The Economics of Interest Rates." *Journal of Financial Economics,* 76, 293–307.

CHAPTER 13

Independence of Production and Technology Risks

The economies investigated in Vasicek (2005, 2013) (Chapters 11 and 12 of this volume) contain a production process whose rate of return $\mathrm{d}A/A$ on investment is

$$\frac{\mathrm{d}A}{A} = \mu \mathrm{d}t + \sigma \mathrm{d}y, \tag{1}$$

where $y(t)$ is a Wiener process. The process $A(t)$ represents a constant return-to-scale production opportunity. The amount of investment in production is determined endogenously.

The parameters of the production process can themselves be stochastic, reflecting the fact that production technology evolves in an unpredictable manner. It is assumed that their behavior is driven by a Markov state variable $X(t)$, $\mu = \mu(X(t), t)$, $\sigma = \sigma(X(t), t)$. The dynamics of the state variable, which can be interpreted as representing the state of the production technology, is given by

$$\mathrm{d}X = \zeta \mathrm{d}t + \psi \mathrm{d}y + \varphi \mathrm{d}x, \tag{2}$$

where $x(t)$ is a Wiener process independent of $y(t)$. The parameters ζ, ψ, and φ are functions of $X(t)$ and t. The stochastic part of $\mathrm{d}A/A$ will be called the production risk, and the stochastic part of $\mathrm{d}X$ will be called the technology risk.

In many applications, it is realistic to assume that the technology risk is independent of the production risk—that is, $\psi = 0$. For instance, if the production is farming, progress in development of new agricultural methods, hybrids, fertilizers, and so on is independent of weather. When the two risks are independent, some special cases attain.

Unpublished memorandum, 2013.

Case 1. Suppose all investors have the same degree of risk tolerance, $\gamma_k = \gamma, k = 1, 2, \ldots, n$. Then the short rate of interest in the economy in equilibrium is

$$r(t) = \mu(t) - \frac{1}{\gamma}\sigma^2(t). \tag{3}$$

This is a consequence of the equation for λ in Example 1 of Vasicek (2005) with $\psi = 0$. Eq. (3) holds for any specification of the processes $\mu(t), \sigma^2(t)$, and for any investors' consumption time preferences.

Case 2. Suppose that the time preference functions of all participants are concentrated at the point T. In other words, each participant maximizes the expected utility of end-of-period wealth. Let $Y(t)$ be the state price density process (in Vasicek (2005), results are stated in terms of the so-called numeraire portfolio $Z(t) = 1/Y(t)$). The equilibrium value of the short rate is given by

$$r(t) = \mu(t) - \sigma^2(t)\mathrm{E}_t \frac{1}{\Gamma(T)} \frac{A(T)Y(T)}{A(t)Y(t)} \tag{4}$$

where

$$\Gamma(T) = \frac{\sum_{k=1}^{n} \gamma_k W_k(T-)}{W(T-)} \tag{5}$$

is the average coefficient of risk tolerance, weighted by the end-of-period wealth levels.

To derive Eq. (4), note that

$$W(t) = N_0 A(t) \quad 0 \leq t < T$$
$$W(T-) = K(Y(T)) \tag{6}$$

where $N_0 = W(0)/A(0)$ and

$$K(Y) = \sum_{k=1}^{n} \nu_k Y^{-\gamma_k}. \tag{7}$$

The state price density process given by

$$Y(t) = \frac{1}{A(t)} \mathrm{E}_t A(T) K^{-1}(N_0 A(T)) \tag{8}$$

is a function of $X(t), A(t)$, and t. Put

$$L(t) = \log A(t) \tag{9}$$

and write $Y = Y(X, L, t)$. The process $R(t) = A(t)Y(t)$ is a martingale,

$$\mathrm{E}dR = 0. \tag{10}$$

Expand the left-hand side of (10) by Ito's lemma to obtain a partial differential equation for R in the variables X, L, t. Since the coefficients of that equation are all independent of L, differentiating both sides with respect to L produces the same equation for the derivative R_L. Consequently, $R_L = R + AY_L$ and therefore also AY_L are martingales and

$$A(t)Y_L(t) = \mathrm{E}_t A(T)Y_L(T)). \tag{11}$$

At T,

$$Y_L(T) = \frac{A(T)}{A_Y(T)} = -\frac{\sum_{k=1}^{n} \nu_k Y^{-\gamma_k}(T)}{\sum_{k=1}^{n} \gamma_k \nu_k Y^{-\gamma_k - 1}(T)}. \tag{12}$$

The individual end-of-period wealths are given by

$$W_k(T-) = \nu_k Y^{-\gamma_k}(T), \quad k = 1, 2, \ldots, n \tag{13}$$

and Eq. (12) can be written in the form

$$Y_L(T) = -\frac{Y(T)}{\Gamma(T)}. \tag{14}$$

From the coefficients of dy in the expansion of dY (or from Eq. (48) of Vasicek (2005) with $\psi = 0$), it follows that

$$\lambda(t) = -\sigma(t)\frac{Y_L(t)}{Y(t)} \tag{15}$$

and therefore

$$\lambda(t) = -\frac{\sigma(t)}{A(t)Y(t)} \mathrm{E}_t A(T)Y_L(T)). \tag{16}$$

Eq. (4) follows from the relationship $r = \mu - \sigma\lambda$ and from Eqs. (16), (14).

In terms of the underlying economic variables, Eq. (4) can be written as

$$r(t) = \mu(t) + \sigma^2(t)\frac{\mathrm{E}_t \dfrac{N_0 A^2(T)}{K'(K^{-1}(N_0 A(T)))}}{\mathrm{E}_t A(T) K^{-1}(N_0 A(T))}. \tag{17}$$

REFERENCES

Vasicek, O. A. (2005). "Economics of Interest Rates." *Journal of Financial Economics*, 76, 293–307.

Vasicek, O. A. (2013). "General Equilibrium with Heterogeneous Participants and Discrete Consumption Times." *Journal of Financial Economics*, 108, 608–614.

CHAPTER 14

Risk-Neutral Economy and Zero Price of Risk

ABSTRACT

The paper investigates the equilibrium in an economy in which all participants are indifferent to risk. The mechanism of asset and derivative pricing in such economy is identified. It is shown that no economy in equilibrium with stochastic interest rates can be simultaneously risk-neutral and have zero market price of risk. On the other hand, there exist equilibrium economies with risk-averse participants and zero prices of risk.

INTRODUCTION

The concept of the risk-neutral economy, that is, an economy in which all participants are indifferent to risk and only care about expected return, is often used in finance as a standard of reference. That is due to the supposition that in such an economy there is no compensation for risk and all assets have the same expected return, which is therefore equal to the risk-free rate.

In general, a complete economy (an economy that allows all derivative contracts) in which there are no opportunities for riskless arbitrage will contain a process, called the market price of risk, for each source of uncertainty it involves. If x is a Wiener process of the risk sources and λ is the vector of the corresponding market prices of risk, and if r is the short riskless rate, then the expected instantaneous rate of return μ on an asset whose exposure to the sources of risk is β satisfies the relationship

$$\mu = r + \beta' \lambda. \tag{1}$$

It is often assumed that in the risk-neutral economy the market prices of risk are all zero and therefore $\mu = r$ for all assets. Why should there be compensation for risk if all investors are risk-neutral?

Mathematics and Financial Economics, 8 (2014), 229–239.

This is used in a number of conceptual conjectures. For instance, the general bond pricing formula

$$B(t,s) = \mathrm{E}_t \exp\left(-\int_t^s r \mathrm{d}\tau - \frac{1}{2}\int_t^s \lambda'\lambda \mathrm{d}\tau - \int_t^s \lambda' \mathrm{d}x \right) \tag{2}$$

is claimed in the risk-neutral economy to take the simple form

$$B(t,s) = \mathrm{E}_t \exp\left(-\int_t^s r \mathrm{d}\tau \right), \tag{3}$$

called the expectation hypothesis. Note that when the short rate $r(t)$ is deterministic, the expectation hypothesis holds trivially.

It has been noted in Cox, Ingersoll, and Ross (1981) that the returns on different assets in a risk-neutral economy are in general not all the same, and the price of risk is not identically zero. They show that in a production economy of the Cox, Ingersoll, and Ross (1985) type, the expected instantaneous return on any bond (in fact, on any asset) can be written as

$$\mathrm{E}\frac{\mathrm{d}B}{B} = r\mathrm{d}t - \mathrm{E}\frac{\mathrm{d}B}{B}\frac{\mathrm{d}Q}{Q} \tag{4}$$

where

$$Q(t) = \mathrm{E}_t \exp\left(\int_t^{T^*} r(\tau) \mathrm{d}\tau \right) \tag{5}$$

and T^* is the time of consumption. The second term on the right-hand side of (4), which is the instantaneous covariance of the bond price with the expected return to the consumption date on the money market account, is in general nonzero.

This chapter investigates the relationship between risk neutrality of investors and zero prices of risk in an equilibrium economy. Two questions are posed: First, if all investors are indifferent to risk, are the prices of risk identically zero? Second, are there economies with risk-averse participants and zero price of risk?

The chapter gives an explicit characterization of the risk-neutral economy in equilibrium. It is shown that there is no consumption by the participants until a certain moment, given by the first entry of the state price density process into an absorbing boundary. At that time, the total social wealth is consumed. The pricing of assets in such an economy is explicitly given, and equations for interest rates are provided.

In answer to the two questions, it is shown that no economy in which all participants are indifferent to risk can have zero market price of risk, unless interest rates are deterministic. On the other hand, there exist economies with risk-averse participants and stochastic interest rates in which the price of risk is identically zero.

In the derivative asset pricing theory, the term *risk-neutral probabilities* is often used to refer to the martingale probability measure under which the expected returns on risky assets are equal to the riskless rate r. It is a misnomer, since the martingale measure does not correspond to the probability measure in a risk-neutral economy.

This chapter draws heavily on the results and methodology of Vasicek (2005, 2013) (Chapters 11 and 12 of this volume).

AN ECONOMY IN EQUILIBRIUM

Consider a continuous time economy with n participants endowed with initial wealth $W_k(0)$, $k = 1, 2, \ldots, n$. It is assumed that investors can issue and buy any derivatives of any of the assets and securities in the economy. The investors can lend and borrow among themselves, either at a floating short rate or by issuing and buying term bonds. The resultant market is complete. It is further assumed that there are no transaction costs and no taxes or other forms of redistribution of social wealth. The investment wealth and asset values are measured in terms of a medium of exchange that cannot be stored unless invested in production.

Production in the economy is described by a production process $A(t)$ whose rate of return on investment is

$$\frac{\mathrm{d}A}{A} = \mu \mathrm{d}t + \sigma \mathrm{d}y \tag{6}$$

where $y(t)$ is a Wiener process. The process $A(t)$ represents a constant return-to-scale production opportunity. The amount of investment in production is determined endogenously.

The parameters of the production process can themselves be stochastic, reflecting the fact that production technology evolves in an unpredictable manner. It will be assumed that their behavior is driven by a Markov state variable X, $\mu = \mu(X(t), t)$, $\sigma = \sigma(X(t), t)$. The dynamics of the state variable, which represents the state of the production technology, is given by

$$\mathrm{d}X = \zeta \mathrm{d}t + \psi \mathrm{d}y + \varphi \mathrm{d}x \tag{7}$$

where $x(t)$ is a Wiener process independent of $y(t)$. The parameters ζ, ψ, and φ are functions of $X(t)$ and t.

In equilibrium, the total wealth must be invested in the production process (which could thus be referred to as the market portfolio). Individual investors may hold financial securities and contracts, such as bonds, futures, and derivatives, in order to optimize their objectives. Because these securities and contracts were issued by other participants in the economy, however, the net borrowing and lending (including lending and borrowing implicit in issuing and buying contingent claims) is zero and the total available wealth is put into production.

An economy cannot be in equilibrium if arbitrage opportunities exist in the sense that the returns on an asset strictly dominate the returns on another asset. A necessary and sufficient condition for absence of arbitrage is that there exist processes $\lambda(t)$, $\eta(t)$, called the market prices of risk for the risk sources $y(t)$, $x(t)$, respectively, such that the price P of any asset in the economy satisfies the equation

$$\frac{\mathrm{d}P}{P} = (r + \beta\lambda + \delta\eta)\mathrm{d}t + \beta\mathrm{d}y + \delta\mathrm{d}x \tag{8}$$

where β, δ are the exposures of the asset to the two risk sources. It is assumed that Novikov's condition holds,

$$\mathrm{E}\exp\left(\frac{1}{2}\int_0^T (\lambda^2 + \eta^2)\mathrm{d}t\right) < \infty. \tag{9}$$

Let $Y(t)$ be the state price density process,

$$Y(s) = Y(t)\exp\left(-\int_t^s r\mathrm{d}\tau - \frac{1}{2}\int_t^s (\lambda^2 + \eta^2)\,\mathrm{d}\tau - \int_t^s \lambda\mathrm{d}y - \int_t^s \eta\mathrm{d}x\right). \tag{10}$$

The price P of any asset satisfies

$$P(t) = \mathrm{E}_t P(s)\frac{Y(s)}{Y(t)}. \tag{11}$$

Here and throughout, the symbol E_t denotes expectation conditional on a filtration $\mathfrak{F}_t$ generated by $y(t)$, $x(t)$.

Equilibrium is fully described by specification of the process $Y(t)$, which determines the pricing of all assets in the economy, such as bonds and derivative contracts, by means of Eq. (11). Specifically, the price $B(t, s)$ at time t of a default-free bond with unit face value maturing at time s is given by the equation

$$B(t,s) = E_t \frac{Y(s)}{Y(t)}. \tag{12}$$

The short rate is given by

$$r = \mu - \sigma\lambda. \tag{13}$$

An asset $M(t)$ consisting of reinvestment at the short rate,

$$M(t) = \exp\left(\int_0^t r(\tau)\,d\tau\right) \tag{14}$$

will be called the money market account.

THE RISK-NEUTRAL ECONOMY

In a risk-neutral economy, where each participant is indifferent to risk, each investor maximizes the expected present value of lifetime consumption,

$$\max E \int_0^T p_k(t) c_k(t) dt \tag{15}$$

where $c_k(t)$ is the rate of consumption at time t and $p_k(t) \geq 0,\ 0 \leq t \leq T$ is a time preference function. An investment strategy is fully described by the exposures $\beta_k(t)$, $\delta_k(t)$ to the sources of risk $y(t)$, $x(t)$. The wealth $W_k(t)$ at time t grows by the increment

$$dW_k = W_k(r + \beta_k\lambda + \delta_k\eta)dt + W_k\beta_k dy + W_k\delta_k dx - c_k dt. \tag{16}$$

Let $V_k(t)$ be the value at time t of the expected remaining consumption under an optimal investment and consumption strategy,

$$V_k(t) = \max E_t \int_t^T p_k(s) c_k(s) ds. \tag{17}$$

The process $V_k(t)$ satisfies the Bellman equation for optimality

$$\max(E\,dV_k + p_k c_k dt) = 0. \tag{18}$$

Put

$$V_k = Q_k W_k \tag{19}$$

with the dynamics of Q_k written as

$$\frac{\mathrm{d}Q_k}{Q_k} = \vartheta_k \mathrm{d}t + \theta_k dy + \omega_k \mathrm{d}x. \tag{20}$$

Calculating $\mathrm{E}dV_k$ yields the equation

$$\max((\vartheta_k + r + \beta_k(\theta_k + \lambda) + \delta_k(\omega_k + \eta))Q_k W_k + c_k(p_k - Q_k)) = 0. \tag{21}$$

The function to be maximized is linear in the decision variables β_k, δ_k, and c_k. Because β_k, δ_k are unrestricted, in order to get a final maximum it must be that

$$\theta_k = -\lambda$$

$$\omega_k = -\eta. \tag{22}$$

If $Q_k > p_k$, the rate of consumption will be zero and consequently from (21),

$$\vartheta_k = -r \quad \text{if } Q_k > p_k. \tag{23}$$

When $Q_k \leq p_k$, the rate of consumption will be infinite, with the total consumption equal to the available wealth. Thus, the investor refrains from consuming until the process $Q_k(t)$ hits the boundary $p_k(t)$, at which time the whole wealth $W_k(t)$ is consumed. Eq. (17) takes the form

$$V_k(t) = \max_{t \leq s \leq T} E_t p_k(s) W_k(s) \tag{24}$$

Because the investment strategy is immaterial in virtue of Eqs. (21) and (22), it can be assumed that each participant is fully invested in the market portfolio,

$$W_k(t) = W_k(0)\frac{A(t)}{A(0)} \quad \text{if } Q_k(t) > p_k(t). \tag{25}$$

From Eqs. (19), (24), and (25),

$$Q_k(t) = \frac{1}{A(t)} \max_{t \leq s \leq T} \mathrm{E}_t\, p_k(s) A(s) \quad \text{if } Q_k(t) > p_k(t). \tag{26}$$

From Eq. (10), the dynamics of the state price density process $Y(t)$ is

$$\frac{dY}{Y} = -r\mathrm{d}t - \lambda \mathrm{d}y - \eta \mathrm{d}x \tag{27}$$

Comparing Eqs. (20), (22), (23), and (27), it follows that

$$\frac{dQ_k}{Q_k} = \frac{dY}{Y} \quad \text{if } Q_k > p_k \tag{28}$$

and therefore

$$v_k Q_k(t) = Y(t) \quad \text{if } Q_k > p_k \tag{29}$$

where v_k is a constant. It follows that

$$Y(t) = \frac{1}{A(t)} \max_{t \le s \le T} \mathrm{E}_t\, v_k p_k(s) A(s). \tag{30}$$

For equilibrium pricing to exist, the right-hand side of Eq. (30) must be the same for all $k = 1, 2, \ldots, n$, which requires that the preference functions all be the same. Equilibrium cannot attain in a risk-neutral economy if the participants have differing time preferences. It will therefore be assumed that $p_k(t) = p(t)$ for $k = 1, 2, \ldots, n$. In that case,

$$Y(t) = \frac{1}{A(t)} \max_{t \le s \le T} \mathrm{E}_t\, p(s) A(s). \tag{31}$$

Note that $Y(t) \geq p(t)$ for all t. Total consumption takes place when $Y(t) = p(t)$ for the first time. If $S(t)$ is the time point at which the maximum in (31) occurs,

$$\max_{t \le s \le T} \mathrm{E}_t p(s) A(s) = E_t p(S(t)) A(S(t)),$$

then $Y(t) = p(t)$ is equivalent to $S(t) = t$.

The expectation

$$U(X, t, s) = \mathrm{E}_t \left[\frac{A(s)}{A(t)} \middle| X(t) = X \right] \tag{32}$$

is a function of X, t only, and therefore the state price density process given by Eq. (31) is likewise a function of the state variable and time, $Y = Y(X, t)$. The market prices of risk are given by

$$\lambda = -\psi \frac{1}{Y} \frac{\partial Y}{\partial X} \tag{33}$$

$$\eta = -\varphi \frac{1}{Y} \frac{\partial Y}{\partial X} \tag{34}$$

In order that $\lambda = \eta = 0$ in a risk-neutral economy, it follows from Eqs. (33) and (34) that either X is deterministic or Y does not depend on X.

In either case, $Y(t)$ is deterministic and so are interest rates. No economy with stochastic interest rates can be simultaneously risk-neutral (i.e., with all participants being indifferent to risk) and have zero market price of risk.

The expected instantaneous returns on different assets in a risk-neutral economy are not in general equal. The same is true for expected returns on the assets over a given finite period. If T^* is the point of absorption of the process $Y(t)$ into the boundary $p(t)$, however, then

$$\mathrm{E}_t \exp\left(\int_t^{T^*} r(\tau)\, \mathrm{d}\tau \right) = \mathrm{E}_t \frac{A(T^*)}{A(t)}. \tag{35}$$

The expected return over the term T^* on the money market account is the same as on the market portfolio, and in fact the same on any asset in the economy. Indeed, conditionally on the value of T^*, Eqs. (31) and (11) reduce to

$$Y(t) = p(T^*)\mathrm{E}_t \frac{A(T^*)}{A(t)} \tag{36}$$

and

$$P(t) = p(T^*)\mathrm{E}_t \frac{P(T^*)}{Y(t)} \tag{37}$$

respectively, and therefore

$$\mathrm{E}_t \frac{P(T^*)}{P(t)} = \mathrm{E}_t \frac{A(T^*)}{A(t)} \tag{38}$$

for any asset P. Because this is valid conditionally for any value of T^*, it is valid unconditionally.

This explains the paradox: In risk-neutral economy in equilibrium, the expected returns are the same on all assets, regardless of their riskiness, over the one period that is relevant to the investors, namely, to the point of consumption. Due to the nonlinearity of compounding, however, this precludes the expected instantaneous returns to be the same, unless they are deterministic. The market price of risk will not be zero.

Two examples of risk-neutral economies follow.

Example 1. Let the time preference function of all participants be

$$p(t) = e^{-\kappa t}$$

and suppose that

$$\mu = X$$
$$\mathrm{d}X = \alpha(\overline{X} - X)\mathrm{d}t + \psi \mathrm{d}y + \varphi \mathrm{d}x$$

with α, ψ, φ, and σ constant. Put

$$a = \frac{\psi^2 + \varphi^2}{\alpha^2}$$

$$b = \overline{X} + \frac{\sigma\psi}{\alpha} + \frac{1}{2}a$$

and assume for simplicity that $\kappa \geq b$. Evaluating the expectation in (32) gives

$$U(X, t, s) = \exp\left(D(t, s)\,(X - b) + b(s - t) - \frac{1}{4}a\alpha D^2(t, s) \right)$$

where

$$D(t, s) = \frac{1}{\alpha}\left(1 - e^{-\alpha(s-t)}\right)$$

Denote by $S(t) = S(X(t), t)$ the time point at which the maximum in Eq. (31) occurs. The state price density process is given by

$$Y(X, t) = \exp\left(D(t, S)\,(X - b) + b(S - t) - \frac{1}{4}a\alpha D^2(t, S) - \kappa S \right).$$

Total consumption takes place when $Y(X(t), t) = e^{-\kappa t}$ for the first time, which is equivalent to $S(t) = t$ for the first time. Here $S(X, t)$ is given as

$$\begin{aligned}
S(X, t) &= T && \text{if } X \geq (\kappa - b)e^{\alpha(T-t)} + b + \frac{1}{2}a - \frac{1}{2}ae^{-\alpha(T-t)} \\
&= t - \frac{1}{\alpha}\log\left(\frac{1}{a}\left(-X + b + \frac{1}{2}a + \sqrt{\left(X - b - \frac{1}{2}a\right)^2 + 2a(\kappa - b)}\right)\right) \\
& && \text{if } \kappa < X < (\kappa - b)e^{\alpha(T-t)} + b + \frac{1}{2}a - \frac{1}{2}ae^{-\alpha(T-t)} \\
&= t && \text{if } X \leq \kappa.
\end{aligned}$$

If $X(0) \leq \kappa$, consumption takes place immediately at time zero. If $X(0) > \kappa$, consumption occurs when $X(t) = \kappa$ for the first time, or at the end date T if $X(t)$ fails to reach κ.

The risk premia are

$$\lambda = -\psi D(t, S(t))$$

$$\eta = -\varphi D(t, S(t))$$

Example 2. Suppose that the time preference functions of all participants are concentrated at the point T. In other words, each participant maximizes the expected end-of-period wealth. Then

$$Y(t) = \frac{\mathrm{E}_t A(T)}{A(t)}.$$

Bond prices are given by

$$B(t,s) = \frac{A(t)}{\mathrm{E}_t A(T)} \mathrm{E}_t \frac{A(T)}{A(s)}.$$

Specifically,

$$B(t,T) = \frac{A(t)}{\mathrm{E}_t A(T)} = \frac{1}{Y(t)}.$$

A contingent claim that pays a random amount $C(T)$ at time T is priced as

$$P(t) = B(t,T)\mathrm{E}_t C(T).$$

In an economy with risk-averse participants, this pricing will hold only when the payout $C(T)$ is uncorrelated with $Y(T)$.

AN ECONOMY WITH ZERO PRICE OF RISK

There are equilibrium economies with risk-averse participants in which the price of risk is zero. There is no practical significance of such economies, and they are investigated here solely to demonstrate the disconnection between risk neutrality and zero price of risk.

Suppose each investor maximizes the expected utility of lifetime consumption,

$$\max \mathrm{E} \int_0^T p_k(t) U_k(c_k(t)) dt \tag{39}$$

where $U_k(c)$ is an isoelastic utility function

$$\begin{aligned} U_k(c) &= \frac{c^{(\gamma_k - 1)/\gamma_k}}{\gamma_k - 1} & \gamma_k > 0,\ \gamma_k \neq 1 \\ &= \log c & \gamma_k = 1 \end{aligned} \tag{40}$$

Here γ_k is the reciprocal of the relative risk aversion coefficient, called the risk tolerance.

It is shown in Vasicek (2005) that the optimal consumption rate of the k-th investor is a function of his own preference parameters and initial wealth and of the state price density process only, given as

$$c_k(t) = v_k p_k^{\gamma_k}(t) Y^{-\gamma_k}(t) \tag{41}$$

where

$$v_k = \frac{Y(0) W_k(0)}{\mathrm{E} \int_0^T p_k^{\gamma_k}(\tau) Y^{-\gamma_k+1}(\tau) \mathrm{d}\tau} \tag{42}$$

is a constant determined by the initial wealth. The investor's wealth $W_k(t)$ at time t is

$$W_k(t) = v_k \frac{1}{Y(t)} \mathrm{E}_t \int_t^T p_k^{\gamma_k}(\tau) Y^{-\gamma_k+1}(\tau) \mathrm{d}\tau. \tag{43}$$

(This and other results in Vasicek (2005) are expressed in terms of the so-called numeraire process $Z(t) = 1/Y(t)$.)

In equilibrium, the total wealth in the economy

$$W(t) = \sum_{k=1}^{n} W_k(t) \tag{44}$$

is invested in the production process. This produces the equation

$$\mathrm{d}W = \mu W \mathrm{d}t + \sigma W \mathrm{d}y - \sum_{k=1}^{n} v_k p_k^{\gamma_k} Y^{-\gamma_k} \mathrm{d}t \tag{45}$$

subject to the terminal condition $W(T) = 0$.

Eq. (45) has a unique solution

$$W(t) = \frac{1}{Y(t)} \mathrm{E}_t \int_t^T \sum_{k=1}^{n} v_k p_k^{\gamma_k}(\tau) Y^{-\gamma_k+1}(\tau) \mathrm{d}\tau. \tag{46}$$

The state price density $Y(t)$ is determined as the unique process satisfying Eqs. (45) and (11) (cf. Vasicek (2005)). In the special case that $\gamma_k = \gamma$, $k = 1, 2, \ldots, n$, it is given by

$$Y(t) = W^{-1/\gamma}(0) A^{1/\gamma}(0) A^{-1/\gamma}(t) F^{1/\gamma}(X(t), t) \exp\left(\frac{1}{\gamma} \int_0^t \frac{\sum v_k p_k^{\gamma}(\tau)}{F(X(\tau), \tau)} \mathrm{d}\tau \right) \tag{47}$$

where the function $F(t) = F(X(t), t)$ is

$$F(X,t) = Y^{\gamma-1}(t)\mathrm{E}_t\left[\int_t^T \sum_{k=1}^{n} \nu_k p_k^{\gamma}(\tau)\, Y^{-\gamma+1}(\tau)\mathrm{d}\tau \,\middle|\, X(t) = X\right]. \tag{48}$$

Now assume that the prices of risk in the economy are all identically zero. Then

$$r(t) = \mu(t) \tag{49}$$

and

$$Y(t) = \frac{1}{M(t)} = \exp\left(-\int_0^t \mu(\tau)\,\mathrm{d}\tau\right). \tag{50}$$

From Eq. (46), the total wealth is given by

$$W(t) = \sum_{k=1}^{n} M^{\gamma_k}(t)F_k(X(t),t) \tag{51}$$

where

$$F_k(X,t) = \mathrm{E}_t\left[\int_t^T \nu_k p_k^{\gamma_k}(\tau)\exp\left((\gamma_k - 1)\int_t^{\tau} \mu(s)\mathrm{d}s\right)\mathrm{d}\tau \,\middle|\, X(t) = X\right]. \tag{52}$$

The stochastic part of $\mathrm{d}W/W$, given by

$$\frac{\displaystyle\sum_{k=1}^{n} M^{\gamma_k}(t)\frac{\partial F_k(X,t)}{\partial X}}{\displaystyle\sum_{k=1}^{n} M^{\gamma_k}(t)F_k(X,t)}\mathrm{d}X \tag{53}$$

must by Eq. (45) be equal to $\sigma(X,t)\mathrm{d}y$ and therefore independent of $M(t)$. This is only possible if the values of $\gamma_1, \gamma_2, \ldots, \gamma_n$ are all equal. It will therefore be assumed that $\gamma_k = \gamma$, $k = 1, 2, \ldots, n$. The investors may still differ by their time preference functions $p_k(t)$. Eq. (48) becomes

$$F(X,t) = \mathrm{E}_t\left[\int_t^T \sum_{k=1}^{n} \nu_k p_k^{\gamma}(\tau)\exp\left((\gamma - 1)\int_t^{\tau} \mu(s)\mathrm{d}s\right)\mathrm{d}\tau \,\middle|\, X(t) = X\right]. \tag{54}$$

It follows from Eq. (47) that the economy will have zero price of risk if (and only if) the market portfolio satisfies

$$A(t) = \frac{A(0)}{F(0)} M^{\gamma}(t) F(X(t), t) \exp\left(\int_{0}^{t} \frac{\sum \nu_k p_k^{\gamma}(\tau)}{F(X(\tau), \tau)} \mathrm{d}\tau \right). \tag{55}$$

Equation (55) does not seem to have an economic interpretation. It is just a technical condition that needs to be satisfied in order that the prices of risk are zero.

There are two kinds, both rather singular, of economies in equilibrium with risk-averse participants and stochastic interest rates in which the price of risk is identically zero:

1. The market portfolio is instantaneously riskless, $A(t) = A(0)M(t)$, and the investors are myopic with logarithmic utility function of consumption. Each participant is fully invested in the market portfolio $A(t)$ (or any combination of derivative contracts equivalent to it).
2. The market portfolio is risky, investors have the same degree of risk tolerance, and the stochastic part of $\mathrm{d}F/F$ equals $\sigma \mathrm{d}y$. This last condition is sufficient, and necessary, for (55) to hold. This implies $\varphi = 0$. Bond prices, as well as prices of any derivatives, are perfectly instantaneously correlated with the market portfolio.

Example. All investors maximize the expected value of their investments at time T and $\gamma_k = \gamma$, $k = 1, 2, \ldots, n$. The condition (55) becomes

$$A(t) = \nu M(t) \mathrm{E}_t M^{\gamma-1}(T) \tag{56}$$

where $\nu = A(0)/\mathrm{E}M^{\gamma-1}(T)$ is a constant. For instance, if the dynamics of $\mu(t) = r(t)$ is as in the Cox, Ingersoll, Ross model of interest rates

$$\mathrm{d}\mu = \alpha(\overline{\mu}(t) - \mu)\mathrm{d}t + \widehat{\psi}\sqrt{\mu}\mathrm{d}y$$

where α, $\widehat{\psi}$ are constants and $\overline{\mu}(t)$ is a deterministic function of time, the expectation in (56) will be finite when $\gamma \leq 1 + \frac{1}{2}\alpha^2/\widehat{\psi}^2$. The price of risk will be zero if the volatility of the production process is

$$\sigma(t) = (\gamma - 1)D(t, T)\widehat{\psi}\sqrt{\mu(t)}$$

where

$$D(t,T) = \frac{1 - e^{-\kappa(T-t)}}{\kappa + \frac{1}{2}(\alpha - \kappa)(1 - e^{-\kappa(T-t)})}$$

$$\kappa = \sqrt{\alpha^2 + 2(1-\gamma)\widehat{\psi}^2}.$$

The production process has the form

$$A(t) = M^{\gamma}(t)\exp((\gamma - 1)D(t,T)\mu(t) + f(t,T))$$

with $f(t,T)$ deterministic.

REFERENCES

Cox, J.C., Ingersoll, J.E. Jr., and S.A. Ross. "A Re-examination of Traditional Hypotheses about the Term Structure of Interest Rates." *Journal of Finance,* 36 (4), 769–799.

Cox, J.C., Ingersoll, J.E. Jr., and S.A. Ross. (1985). "An Intertemporal General Equilibrium Model of Asset Prices." *Econometrica,* 53, 363–384.

Vasicek, O.A. (2005). "The Economics of Interest Rates." *Journal of Financial Economics,* 76, 293–307.

Vasicek, O.A. (2013). "General Equilibrium with Heterogeneous Participants and Discrete Consumption Times." *Journal of Financial Economics*, 108, 608–614.

PART Four

Credit

The probability of loss on a homogeneous portfolio of corporate loans converges with the number of loans $n \to \infty$ to the distribution function

$$\mathrm{P}[L \le x] = \mathrm{N}\left(\frac{\sqrt{1-\rho}\,\mathrm{N}^{-1}(x) - \mathrm{N}^{-1}(p)}{\sqrt{\rho}}\right)$$

where L is the portfolio gross loss, p is the probability of default on any one loan, and ρ is the correlation coefficient between the asset values of any two of the borrowing companies. (page 148)

CHAPTER 15

Introduction to Part IV

Contemporary credit analysis comprises the following three areas:

1. Credit valuation of individual borrowers, as expressed in probability of default, and in the risk-neutral probability of default needed for debt pricing;
2. Portfolio risk measurement, taking into account the correlation of defaults, resulting in determining the probability distribution of portfolio losses, and of changes in the portfolio value; and
3. Structuring and pricing of credit derivatives, such as credit default swaps or collateralized debt obligations.

The theory of derivative asset pricing (options pricing) of Black, Scholes, and Merton opened up means of quantitative assessment of creditworthiness and pricing of debt securities. By being able to derive values of corporate liabilities from the market price of equity and its volatility, it became possible to measure credit risk in terms of probabilities of default rather than ordinal ratings.

The paper "Philosophy of Credit Valuation"(Chapter 16), written in 1984, provides an extensive argument for such methodology, as opposed to the previously established approach. Traditional approaches to credit valuation, such as agency ratings, involve a detailed examination of company's operations, projection of cash flows, measures of leverage and coverage, an assessment of the firm's future earning power, and so on. An assessment of the company's future, however, has already been made by all market participants and is reflected in the firm's current market value. Both current and prospective investors constantly perform this analysis, and their actions set the price for the company's equity. If the value of the company's assets can be inferred from the market valuation of equity, it will take advantage of the information contained in market prices.

The firm's liabilities are all claims, in one form or another, on the firm's assets. The firm's asset value is the worth of the firm's ongoing business. If all liabilities were traded, the market value of assets could be obtained as the sum of the market value of liabilities. It is asking the question: How much would it cost, *in today's markets*, to become the sole owner of the firm's business? It would necessitate buying all the stock, all the preferreds, convertibles, and so on, and all the firm's outstanding bonds, to pay off the bank debt, current obligations, and other costs. The total cost is the current market value of the firm's assets.

Typically, only the equity has observable price. The asset value must be inferred from equity value alone. This can be done by the options pricing theory. Merton's equation can be solved for the firm's asset value, provided we are able to supply the following information: Equity market value, stock price volatility, a complete description of the firm's liability structure including the terms of the liabilities (such as convertibility and callability), and the cash flows (such as interest payments and dividends). The author's work in this area could not be included in this publication, because it is the property of KMV Corporation and its successor, Moody's Corporation.

The market value of assets changes as the firm's future prospects change. The volatility of the asset value reflects the firm's business risk. The asset volatility needs to be estimated simultaneously with asset value from stock price and stock volatility.

If the asset value falls below the default point, the firm does not have the resources to repay its debt obligations. The *default point* is the cumulative amount of obligations payable within the given time frame. The probability of default is then calculated as the probability that the asset value falls below the default point.

Such an approach based on a causal relationship between the state of the firm and the probability of the firm defaulting allows for utilizing market information. It provides frequent updates and early warning of deterioration (or improvement) of credit quality.

Besides the valuation of credit for individual borrowers, it is necessary to measure the risks of *portfolios* of debt securities. The portfolio risk cannot be inferred solely from knowledge of the probabilities of default for the individual loans in the portfolio; it necessitates taking into account the *correlation* of defaults, resulting from the dependences of the asset values among the firms. The values of the firms' businesses are correlated, because they depend on common factors such as the state of the economy, the industries they have in common, and their mutual business relationships.

There is a number of useful measures of portfolio risk characteristics—for example, the expected loss, standard deviation of loss (unexpected loss), value-at-risk, various measures of diversification and concentration, and tail risk contribution. All these characteristics are determined by the probability distribution of the portfolio value as of a given future date. This is the subject of the article "Loan Portfolio Value" (Chapter 19).

There are three types of such probability distributions:

1. The distribution of portfolio realized losses
2. The distribution of portfolio market value at horizon date due to credit migration
3. The risk-neutral portfolio distribution (needed for pricing portfolio derivatives, such as CDOs)

Typically, bank loan portfolios are large, containing hundreds or thousands of names. A question naturally arises: How does the loss behave for large portfolios? Is there an asymptotic distribution type?

This question can be answered in affirmative for homogeneous portfolios, that is portfolios that have the same amount outstanding in each loan, same default probability for each loan, same maturity of each loan, and the same asset correlations between any two borrowers. In the limit, the distribution function of the loss on a homogeneous loan portfolio has a particular form, given in the 1987 memoranda "Probability of Loss on Loan Portfolio" and 1989 "Limiting Loan Loss Probability Distribution" (Chapters 17 and 18). This formula, which was incorporated into Basel II, has been shown empirically to provide a good approximation to the loss distribution for large portfolios, provided that the parameters in the formula are estimated from the *actual* portfolio composition, default characteristics, and correlations.

The note "The Empirical Test of the Distribution of Loan Portfolio Losses" (Chapter 20) reports the results of a test of the portfolio loss distribution performed by Patrick McAllister of Federal Reserve Bank. The test is based on the realization that it is not possible to obtain a sufficiently long time series of loan losses on a single loan portfolio, and that the only meaningful way of testing the distribution of loan losses is by using a cross-sectional sample of data on many portfolios. The sample contained about 23,000 actual annual gross losses reported to the FRB by U.S. banks over a period of several years. The frequency of losses were plotted in a histogram and compared with that calculated from the formula for the asymptotic loan loss distribution. The agreement in the shape of the distribution is remarkable.

The asymptotic distribution was derived as the limit distribution for a homogeneous portfolio. The sample in the FRB study is certainly as nonhomogeneous as possible: Each of the bank portfolios in the sample is a mix of loans of different qualities, maturities, and amounts outstanding, with nonequal diversification or concentration in specific industries; in addition, they are portfolios of different banks. There is nevertheless a conformity with the theoretical distribution; as is the case with many limit theorems, the asymptotic laws often appear to apply beyond their strict assumptions.

CHAPTER 16

Credit Valuation

THE APPROACH

Credit valuation is a necessary prerequisite to lending. It ensures a desired quality of the asset portfolio, and results in loan pricing that corresponds to the risks assumed. It also provides means to reduce the likelihood of substantive losses through portfolio diversification.

Credit valuation is an objective and quantitative process. It should not depend on the judgment of a particular person or committee. Instead, it should be based on observable quantities, most particularly the market value of the borrower's assets. Credit risk should be measured in terms of probabilities and mathematical expectations, rather than assessed by qualitative ratings. When performed in this manner, we can refer to a credit valuation model.

A credit valuation model requires a theory that describes the causality between the attributes of the borrowing entity (a corporation) and its potential bankruptcy. This does not mean merely an empirical analysis that consists of examining a large number of different variables until a fit is found to the data. Statistical correlations among data do not necessarily signify causal relationships, and therefore provide no assurance of predictive power.

The credit model should be consistent with the modern financial theory, particularly with the theory of option pricing. The various liabilities of a firm are claims on the firm's value, which often take the form of options. The option pricing theory provides means to determine the value of each of the claims, and consequently allows one to price the firm's debt.

If the credit model provides a realistic description of the relationship between the state of the firm and the probability of default on its obligations,

---

Written in 1984; printed in *NetExposure*, Issue 1, 1997; reprinted on CD in *Derivatives: Theory and Practice of Financial Engineering*, P. Wilmott (ed.) (London: John Wiley & Sons, 1998).

it will also reflect the development in the borrower's credit standing through time. This means that the model can be used to monitor changes and give an early warning of potential deterioration of credit. Obviously, this is only possible if the model is based on current, rather than historical, measurements. It also implies that the relevant variables are the actual market values rather than accounting values.

Pursuing this kind of approach to credit valuation means parting ways with some of the traditional credit analysis. Conventional analysis involves detailed examination of the company's operations, projection of cash flows, and assessment of the future earning power of the firm. Such analysis is not necessary. This is not because future prospects of the firm are not of primary importance—they most definitely are. It is because an assessment, based on all currently available information of the company's future, has already been made by the aggregate of the market participants, and reflected in the firm's current market value. Both current and prospective investors perform this analysis, and their actions set the price at an equilibrium value through the means of supply and demand. We do not assume that this assessment is accurate in the sense that its implicit forecasts of future prospects will be realized. We only assume that any one person or institution is unlikely to arrive at a superior valuation. The most junior claim on the firm's assets is equity. If the future earnings of the corporation start looking better or worse than before, the stock price will be the first to reflect the changing prospects. Our challenge is to properly interpret the changing share prices.

It is also not essential to determine whether the firm will have enough cash flow for payment of interest and maturing debt. What is important is whether the market value of the company's assets (i.e., its business) will be adequate. If the assets of the firm have sufficient market value, the firm can easily raise cash it needs by selling off a portion of its assets. If the assets are not easily transferable, the firm can sell them indirectly, by issuing additional equity or additional debt. In any case, the firm's ability to pay its debt is dependent upon its future market value, rather than on its future cash position.

THE FIRM'S VALUE

The value of a firm is the value of its business as a going concern. This value depends on the future prospects and profitability of the firm's business, its risks, and its standing relative to other investment opportunities existing in the economy. The firm's business constitutes its assets, and the present assessment of the future returns from the firm's business constitutes the current value of the firm's assets.

The value of the firm's assets is different from the bottom line on the firm's balance sheet. The book asset value is a fairly arbitrary statement of the initial cost of the physical assets of the company and their depreciation. When the firm is bought or sold, the value traded is the ongoing business. The difference between the amount paid for that value and the amount of the book assets is usually accounted for as the *goodwill*.

The value of the firm's assets can be measured by the price at which the total of the firm's liabilities can be bought or sold. The various liabilities of the firm are claims on its assets. The sum of the market value of the liabilities is the amount for which sole possession of the total of the firm's assets can be obtained (or disposed of) and that is exactly what the firm is worth. The market value of the individual liabilities is directly observable if the liabilities are publicly traded. Thus, the value of equity can be usually obtained by multiplying the share price by the number of shares outstanding. The various bond issues can often be valued as the current price per unit of face value times the total face amount of the issue. If the debt is privately placed, an approximate valuation can be achieved by pricing the debt at current interest rates. Current liabilities can be typically valued at their nominal amount, since they are usually immediately payable.

Although the sum of the market values of liabilities is a convenient way to determine the value of the assets, the asset value does not depend on the structure and composition of the liabilities. If the firm decides to raise additional equity to retire part of its debt, or to borrow in order to buy back some of its outstanding stock, the value of the firm's assets does not change. What changes is merely the division of the ownership of these assets. The same is true even in bankruptcy proceeding. Bankruptcy is a transfer of ownership from the stockholders to the holders of debt. If the firm is worth more as a going concern than its liquidation value, the debt holders will keep it going. If the debt holders do not want to run the firm, they can sell it to somebody who does.

LOAN DEFAULT

We will start with a simple situation. Consider a corporation that at present has no debt, and wants to borrow. Assume the debt is in the form of a discount note issued by the company (such as commercial paper). How much risk does the buyer of the note (the lender) take, and how much should he pay for it? In other words, how does he value the credit?

In buying the note, the lender purchases a claim on the firm's assets, and thereby becomes a partial owner of the company. The value of the company's assets increases by the amount received on the note (the stock price itself does not change by the issuance of the debt). The new total value of the firm's assets is equal to the value of the stock and the value of the debt.

With time, the market value of the company's assets will change. (Perhaps not the book value, but we are not concerned with book values.) The value of assets will be changing as the market's perception of the future earning power of the company changes. These changes obviously involve considerable uncertainty. We can characterize these changes as a stochastic (random) process, subject to a probability law.

What concerns the lender is the market value of the firm's assets when the note matures. Two situations are possible. The asset value is at least that of the face value of the debt, or the asset value is less than the debt.

In the first situation, the stockholders will pay the debt. The total value of the company is sufficient for them to do so. If the firm does not have enough cash, the stockholders can raise it by selling a part of the assets at their market value. Moreover, it is in the interest of the stockholders to pay the loan, since otherwise the lenders would force the firm to bankruptcy and the stockholders would lose control of the firm (although not money, apart from bankruptcy costs). Since the borrower is both willing and able to repay the loan, the lender will realize no loss.

In the situation that the market value of the firm's assets falls below the amount due on the loan, the company cannot repay the lender. There is no way to raise the cash. No other lender would refinance the loan, because that would mean taking over the loss from the original lender. It is also not possible to raise additional equity, since the stock is worthless. The company has to declare bankruptcy. The stockholders get nothing, while the lenders take over the assets. The lenders will thus realize a loss equal to the difference between the face value of the debt and the market value of the assets.

The risk to the lender at the time he contemplates making the loan is that the second situation may arise. The probability of this situation is the probability that the asset value at the maturity of the loan will be less than the loan balance. If we can describe the process governing the changes in the asset value, this probability can be explicitly calculated. This calculation provides a measure of credit risk.

A reasonable specification of the behavior of the asset value is that the change in market value over an interval of time is independent of its past changes, and has an expected component and a random component. The magnitude of both the expected and random components is proportional to the asset value (that is, it is the same for each dollar of assets). This type of process is variously referred to as a logarithmic Wiener process, or a proportional Brownian motion, or a geometric random walk.

The probability of default calculated under this assumption depends on the following quantities: the initial value of assets; the expected rate of return on assets; the variability of the asset value; the face value of the debt; and the loan term.

The higher the initial asset value in relation to the loan amount, the lower is the probability of default on the loan. If the company borrows little relative to the market value of its equity, the loan is comparatively safe. If the company levers itself considerably (in market value terms), the riskiness of the loan is high.

The default probability also depends highly on the variability of the asset value. If the assets grow more or less along the firm's expected growth path, the loan carries little risk even with relatively high leverage. If, on the other hand, the asset value fluctuates wildly, the likelihood of default on the loan is considerable.

As to the length of the loan term, typically the default probability will increase with the term. In effect, more things can go wrong with the company over a long interval than over a short one. For very long loans, however, the probability of default may start decreasing again, as the long-term asset growth asserts itself over the fluctuations.

The probability of default does not in itself provide a measure of the magnitude of the possible loss. It only characterizes the occurrence of loss, rather than the dollar amount. This latter quantity can be measured by the expected loss. Naturally, we care about both the probability of default and the size of loss.

The expected value of a quantity is defined as the average of the possible values of that quantity, each value being weighted by the probability of its occurrence. The expected loss is therefore the probability weighted mean dollar amount of the difference between the face value of the loan and the actual receipts by the lender.

The same considerations that led to a formula for the probability of default also allow deriving an equation for the expected loss. In the example of a commercial borrower whose liabilities consist of equity and one class of debt, the formula for the expected loss turns out to depend on the same quantities as the probability of default: namely, the current market value of total assets, the expected asset return, the variability of the asset value, the face value of debt, among others. The expected loss is given as the difference of two terms; the first term is the loan face value multiplied by the probability of default. This would be the expected loss if default meant losing the entire loan. As it is, there is a recovery equal to the assets of the bankrupt firm, and the formula for the expected loss has a second term subtracted from the first, which represents the expected amount recovered.

DEBT STRUCTURE

The financial structure of most corporations is more complicated than the one with which we have dealt so far. The liabilities will include current liabilities (such as accounts payable, provisions for taxes, etc.), debt of various terms, and equity. The whole structure of liabilities needs to be considered in valuing the company's credit from the viewpoint of a particular lender.

The first question to address is determining the hierarchy of the claims on the firm's assets. In other words, the priority and subordination of the claims in the event of dissolution of the firm has to be considered. From the viewpoint of a particular lender, the relevant distinction is between the claims that take precedence over that lender's claim, claims that are at par, and claims that are subordinated to the lender's claim. This last category includes the firm's equity.

It is obvious that we need to talk about valuation of the borrower's credit for a given lender, not for the lenders in general. Depending on the standing of the lender's claim in the hierarchy of debt, a company may be a good credit risk, or a poor one, even though the probability of bankruptcy is the same for everybody. As a matter of fact, the same event can improve the firm's credit for one lender and make it worse for another lender. For instance, issuing additional debt reduces the expected loss for holders of claims with a higher priority, while it increases the expected loss for holders of claims subordinated to the new debt.

In general, the credit standing of a commercial borrower from the viewpoint of a particular lender improves whenever debt with lower priority is added, or debt with higher priority is retired. It deteriorates with decreasing the total amount of more junior debt and with increasing the total amount of more senior debt. Lower priority debt, like equity, is a protection for the lender; the corresponding assets provide a cushion between the value of total assets and the face value of his claim.

In addition to categorizing liabilities of a firm by their priority, it is necessary to distinguish among them on the basis of their term. The firm goes bankrupt if its assets are less than the face value of debt that is due at that time; if the value of the assets is less than the amount of debt, which is not yet due, the firm can, and will, continue operating. A lender must therefore determine which of the firm's liabilities mature within the term of his claim.

This can lead to a very complicated situation if the structure of debt by priority and by term takes the most general form. In a simple situation when all debt matures at the same time, the holder of a claim is not concerned about any subordinated claims. His loss may only come if the company's assets at the maturity of the debt are less than the total of his loan and all debt with a higher priority. Moreover, the lender only needs to consider the possible value of the company's assets as of the date his loan is due.

If, however, different claims mature on different dates, claims that mature early may trigger a bankruptcy even if they are junior to the lender's claim. His loan may still be paid in full, if the firm's assets at that time exceed the total of his and the more senior debt. It is no longer sufficient, however, to consider only the more senior claims; and it is no longer sufficient for the lender to be concerned about the value of the firm's assets on the maturity date of his claim only.

Fortunately, from the viewpoint of the provider of short-term credit to a commercial borrower, the situation is relatively simple. It is reasonable to assume that the more senior claims (such as employee wages and benefits, and provisions for taxes) are also short-term; and that debt at par with ours is either similarly short (bank revolving credit, etc.) or, as with notes and bonds, matures after the term of our debt.

In this case, default occurs if, on the maturity date of our loan, the market value of the borrower's assets is less than the maturing debt amount (the total short-term obligations). The probability of default is then given by a similar formula to the one obtained in the case of a single class of debt, except that the face value of debt in that formula is replaced by the value of the short-term debt only. In other words, the term debt is treated like equity.

The expected loss amount, however, needs now to be calculated by a different formula than in the simple case of one type of debt. If, on the maturity of our loan, the market value of the firm's assets exceeds the total maturing debt, there is no loss. If the assets are less than the total maturing debt but more than the higher priority debt, the loss is equal to the maturing debt amount less the value of assets. Finally, if the assets are less than the higher priority debt, the loss is complete and we recover nothing. This is a more complex loss function than in the case of one class of debt. Nevertheless, it is still possible to derive a formula for the expected loss—it is just a more complicated equation.

Here it may seem that if the value of the firm's assets is less than the total maturing debt, the amount received by the short-term lender would be further decreased by payments to the holders of the long-term debt. Indeed, if the firm were forced into bankruptcy, the long-term debt would become payable and the short-term lender would only receive a proportional part of the remaining assets. This, however, can be avoided. The short-term lender should in this situation renew a partial credit to the firm that is equal to the exact difference between the amount due and the value of the firm's assets. This will keep the firm from going bankrupt and prevent the long-term lenders from collecting on their claim. The loss to the short-term lender will thus be limited to the same amount as if the long-term debt was a subordinated claim. From our viewpoint, long-term debt is as good as capital.

CAPITAL FLOWS

An explicit consideration must be paid to flows of value from the firm to its owners (stockholders as well as holders of debt). Unlike other cash flows, payments to owners are not reflected in the current market value of the firm, since they do not change the total owners' wealth. For example, if the company decides to double its dividends, or to accelerate repayment of its outstanding debt, the total current value of the firm will not change. In contrast, if taxes double, the firm's value will decline. Now, although changes in policy concerning payments to owners do not affect the firm's total value, they do affect the distribution of value between the different classes of claims. Thus, an extra dividend will transfer some value from the lenders to the stockholders. Consequently, payments to owners, such as dividends and interest on debt, need to be included in the lender's credit valuation.

When considering short-term lending, it is a reasonable, indeed conservative, approximation to assume that the total dividends expected to be paid during the term of the loan are paid at the beginning date. This means that the market value of the firm's assets is reduced by the total expected dividend payout. Similarly, interest on existing debt expected to be paid during the term of our loan is taken to reduce the initial assets.

Since these payments decrease the initial asset value, the probability of default and the expected loss increase. These payments are withdrawals of capital from the firm and as such change the relative value of the different claims. It should be noted that if the stockholders vote themselves additional dividends that have not been anticipated, they transfer wealth from the debt holders to themselves. It is important for the creditor not to underestimate the dividend payments.

LOAN PRICING

The purpose of credit valuation is for loan pricing. Pricing a loan means determining the current value of the loan as a function of its risks. A loan is an asset that can be bought and sold like any other asset. A lender has no economic reason to refuse making the loan if the price is right. If the riskiness of the loan does not suit the lender's preferences, he can sell the loan to somebody whose preferences it does fit.

Of course, determining the interest rate to be charged on a given loan (which is what is usually meant by loan pricing) is the same thing as determining the present value of the loan payments. It is just more convenient in view of the general theory of asset pricing to obtain the value of the loan first and then derive the interest rate from it.

It would seem that a loan should be priced at the present value of the expected payoff (that is, the face amount less the expected loss), using the risk-free rate as the discount rate. Indeed, by subtracting the expected loss from the face amount, a provision is made for the possibility of default; and discounting this amount to present at the risk-free rate then simply accounts for the time value of money.

This, however, is not correct. If it were, then the expected rate of return on the loan would be the risk-free rate, while risky assets in general earn higher than the risk-free rate. In particular, the assets of the firm to which the loan is made may be earning a rate of return whose expected value is higher than the risk-free rate. Since the loan is a claim on these assets, sharing the risks associated with these assets, it should also share the higher expected return.

The exact answer to the pricing of the loan is provided by the option pricing theory. The option pricing theory is in turn a special case of the theory of pricing derivative assets, that is assets whose value depends solely on the value of another, underlying asset. This is the situation at hand: the value of the loan is a function of the value of the firm's assets on which the loan is a claim.

It turns out, on the basis of this theory, that the value of the loan cannot be determined from the knowledge of the expected loss alone. As a matter of fact, it cannot be determined even from knowing the whole probability distribution of the loss. What is needed is the joint probability distribution of the loss together with the value of the underlying assets of the firm.

The equation for the value of the loan provided by the derivative asset pricing theory has a curious form. The loan value is equal to the present value of the expected payoff, discounted by the risk-free rate, with the expected payoff calculated as if the firm's assets earned the risk-free rate rather than its actual expected rate. In other words, we can take the formula for the expected loan loss, but substitute in it the risk-free rate for the expected asset rate of return. This hypothetical expected loss is subtracted from the loan face value, and the difference is discounted to present at the risk-free rate. This provides the correct loan price.

If the expected rate of return on the assets of the firm is higher than the risk-free rate (which in general it will be), the premium to be charged on the loan over the risk-free rate will actually be higher than the expected loss. This extra increment above the expected loss is a compensation for the variance of loss, or more accurately, for a component of that variance that is related to the systematic factors in the economy. The possible deviation of the loss from its expected value is in part due to factors specific to the firm, and in part due to more general factors, such as the market in general. It is this second source of variance that carries compensation to the lender beyond the amount of the expected loss itself.

PORTFOLIO DIVERSIFICATION

Portfolio diversification is a means of reducing the probability of large losses. Even if the expected loss on an individual loan is small, the loan can still result in a large loss. If this loan is a part of a portfolio, such a loss is a smaller percentage of the total assets. The portfolio can only incur a large loss if a number of loans in the portfolio realize losses simultaneously. This is less likely than the default on a single loan.

Diversification does not reduce the expected loss. The expected loss on a portfolio is the average of the expected losses on the individual loans, weighted by their relative proportions in the portfolio. If each loan in the portfolio had an expected loss of 0.1 percent, the expected loss on the portfolio would still be 0.1 percent.

What changes is the certainty of that loss. With a single loan, there may be no loss, but there may also be a big or total loss. In other words, there is a large dispersion of the possible loss amount around its expected, or mean, value. With a diversified portfolio, the dispersion of the portfolio loss around its expected value is much smaller.

An ideally diversified portfolio would have no deviation of the actual loss from the expected amount. It would be like playing the statistical odds in an infinite population. Since the expected loss is a probability weighted average of the possibilities, and in such an ideal situation the frequencies of the occurrence of each possibility conform to their probabilities, the portfolio loss would be guaranteed to be no more, or less, than the expected value. Some loans in the portfolio would realize losses larger than those expected, and some would realize no losses or losses smaller than expected. These individual deviations would average out.

In reality, an ideally diversified portfolio is not possible. For one thing, it would take an infinite number of loans in the portfolio to achieve this. More importantly, however, it would necessitate that there is a sufficient degree of independence among the individual loans. It would be necessary that an occurrence of larger than expected losses on some loans does not substantially decrease the likelihood of smaller than expected losses on other loans. Now, the loss on a loan results from a decline of the assets of the borrowing firm below the face value of the loan. The changes in the value of assets among firms in the economy are correlated, that is, tend to move together. There are factors common to all firms, such as their dependence on economy in general. Such common factors affect the asset values of all companies, and consequently the loss experience on all loans in the portfolio. This common, or systematic, risk cannot be diversified away. Only the risks that are specific for the individual companies, unrelated from one to another, can be reduced by diversification.

What this means is that even a very large portfolio of loans will have a substantial likelihood of a loss which is larger, or smaller, than that expected. There is a limit to the extent to which the variation of the actual loss from the expected loss can be reduced. This limit is the systematic portfolio risk. A well-diversified loan portfolio will have only this systematic risk, with very little of the specific risk. The goal of diversification is to bring the riskiness of the portfolio close to this minimum.

This goal can be achieved by ensuring that the loans in the portfolio are not unduly concentrated in any one segment of the market, such as a particular industry or particular type of firms. The less the companies in the portfolio have in common, the lower is the probability of large portfolio losses. The degree of diversification can be measured quantitatively by the variance of loss (variance characterizes the degree to which a quantity can deviate from its expected value), and this measure should be minimized subject to the portfolio requirements and constraints.

SUMMARY

The approach to credit valuation presented here differs in many aspects from traditional credit analysis. It does not involve judgmental evaluation of the company's operations and prospects. Instead, it is based on an explicit economic theory of bankruptcy and default, applied within the context of the modern financial theory. It thus relies on a belief in market values and the efficiency of the market to reflect all available information in security prices.

The model considers the borrower's credit to be a function of the value of his assets. For a corporate borrower, the assets are the firm's ongoing business. The market value of the firm's assets can be determined from the market price of the company's stock.

A default on a loan occurs if the value of the firm at the maturity of the loan is less than the amount due. Given a description of the firm's value as a stochastic process, the probability of default on the loan can be calculated. This probability depends on the initial market value of the firm, the total amount of debt and the hierarchy of debt, dividends and interest expense, the expected rate of return on assets, the variability of the asset value, and the loan term. The expected loss on the loan can also be calculated from these quantities.

The loan is priced to compensate the lender for the expected loss and for the systematic component of the variance of loss. The pricing formulas are derived from the theory of option pricing.

Portfolio diversification, although it does not reduce the expected loss, decreases the variance of the possible loss around its expected value. The limit to diversification is given by the amount of systematic (nondiversifiable) risk. This risk arises from dependence of the individual companies on the total economy.

CHAPTER 17

Probability of Loss on Loan Portfolio

Consider a portfolio consisting of n loans in equal dollar amounts. Let the probability of default on any one loan be p, and assume that the values of the borrowing companies' assets are correlated with a coefficient ρ for any two companies. We wish to calculate the probability distribution of the percentage gross loss L on the portfolio, that is,

$$P_k = \mathrm{P}\left[L = \frac{k}{n}\right], \ k = 0, 1, \ldots, n.$$

Let A_{it} be the value of the i-th company's assets, described by a logarithmic Wiener process

$$\mathrm{d}A_i = \mu_i A_i \mathrm{d}t + \sigma_i A_i \mathrm{d}z_i$$

where $z_{it}, i = 1, 2, \ldots, n$ are Wiener processes with

$$\mathrm{E}(\mathrm{d}z_i)^2 = \mathrm{d}t$$
$$\mathrm{E}(\mathrm{d}z_i)(\mathrm{d}z_j) = \rho\,\mathrm{d}t, i \neq j.$$

The company defaults on its loan if the value of its assets drops below the contractual value of its obligations D_i payable at time T. We thus have

$$\begin{aligned} p &= \mathrm{P}[A_{iT} < D_i] \\ &= \mathrm{N}(-c_i) \end{aligned}$$

Written in 1987; printed in *Derivatives Pricing: The Classic Collection*, P. Carr (ed.), London: Risk Books, 2004.

where

$$c_i = \frac{1}{\sigma\sqrt{T}}\left(\log A_{i0} - \log D_i + \mu_i T - \frac{1}{2}\sigma^2 T\right)$$

and N is the cumulative normal distribution function.

Because of the joint normality and the equal correlations, the processes z_i can be represented as

$$z_i = bx + a\varepsilon_i,\ i = 1, 2, \ldots, n$$

where

$$b = \sqrt{\rho}, a = \sqrt{1-\rho}$$

and

$$\begin{aligned}
&\mathrm{E}(\mathrm{d}x)^2 = \mathrm{d}t \\
&\mathrm{E}(\mathrm{d}\varepsilon_i)^2 = \mathrm{d}t \\
&\mathrm{E}(\mathrm{d}x)(\mathrm{d}\varepsilon_i) = 0 \\
&\mathrm{E}(\mathrm{d}\varepsilon_i)(\mathrm{d}\varepsilon_j) = 0, \quad i \neq j.
\end{aligned}$$

The term bx can be interpreted as the i-th company exposure to a common factor x (such as the state of the economy), and the term $a\varepsilon_i$ represents the company's specific risks. Then

$$\begin{aligned}
P_k &= \mathrm{P}\left[L = \frac{k}{n}\right] \\
&= \binom{n}{k} \mathrm{P}\left[A_{1T} < D_1, \ldots, A_{kT} < D_k, A_{k+1T} \geq D_{k+1}, \ldots, A_{nT} \geq D_n\right] \\
&= \binom{n}{k} \int_{-\infty}^{\infty} \mathrm{P}\left[A_{1T} < D_1, \ldots, A_{kT} < D_k, A_{k+1T} \geq D_{k+1}, \ldots,\right. \\
&\qquad \left. A_{nT} \geq D_n | x_T = u\right] \mathrm{dP}\left[x_T < u\right] \\
&= \binom{n}{k} \int_{-\infty}^{\infty} \mathrm{P}\left[c_1\sqrt{T} + bx_T + a\varepsilon_{1T} < 0, \ldots, c_k\sqrt{T} + bx_T + a\varepsilon_{kT} < 0,\right. \\
&\qquad \left. c_{k+1}\sqrt{T} + bx_T + a\varepsilon_{k+1T} \geq 0, \ldots, c_n\sqrt{T} + bx_T + a\varepsilon_{nT} \geq 0 \,|\, x_T = u\,]\right] \\
&\qquad \times \mathrm{dP}\left[x_T < u\right] \\
&= \binom{n}{k} \int_{-\infty}^{\infty} \left(\mathrm{N}\left(-\frac{c+bu}{a}\right)\right)^k \left(1 - \mathrm{N}\left(-\frac{c+bu}{a}\right)\right)^{n-k} \mathrm{dN}(u).
\end{aligned}$$

In terms of the original parameters p and ρ, we have

$$P_k = \binom{n}{k} \int_{-\infty}^{\infty} \left(N\left(\frac{1}{\sqrt{1-\rho}} \left(N^{-1}(p) - \sqrt{\rho}u\right)\right)\right)^k \times \left(1 - N\left(\frac{1}{\sqrt{1-\rho}} \left(N^{-1}(p) - \sqrt{\rho}u\right)\right)\right)^{n-k} dN(u)$$

Note that the integrand is the conditional probability distribution of the portfolio loss given the state of the economy, as measured by the market increase or decline in terms of its standard deviations.

CHAPTER 18

Limiting Loan Loss Probability Distribution

The cumulative probability that the percentage loss on a portfolio of n loans does not exceed θ is

$$F_n(\theta) = \sum_{k=0}^{[n\theta]} P_k$$

where P_k are given by an integral expression in Oldrich Vasicek's memo, "Probability of Loss on Loan Portfolio," February 1987 (Chapter 17 of this volume). The substitution

$$s = N\left(\frac{1}{\sqrt{1-\rho}}\left(N^{-1}(p) - \sqrt{\rho}u\right)\right)$$

in the integral gives $F_n(\theta)$ as

$$F_n(\theta) = \sum_{k=0}^{[n\theta]} \binom{n}{k} \int_0^1 s^k (1-s)^{n-k} dW(s)$$

where

$$W(s) = N\left(\frac{1}{\sqrt{\rho}}\left(\sqrt{1-\rho}\,N^{-1}(s) - N^{-1}(p)\right)\right).$$

Written in 1989; printed in *Derivatives Pricing: The Classic Collection*, P. Carr (ed.). London: Risk Books, 2004.

By the law of large numbers,

$$\lim_{n\to\infty} \sum_{k=0}^{[n\theta]} \binom{n}{k} s^k (1-s)^{n-k} = 0 \quad \text{if} \quad \theta < s$$

$$= 1 \quad \text{if} \quad \theta > s$$

and therefore the cumulative distribution function of loan losses on a very large portfolio is

$$F_\infty(\theta) = W(\theta).$$

This is a highly skewed distribution. Its density is

$$f_\infty(\theta) = \sqrt{\frac{1-\rho}{\rho}} \exp\left(-\frac{1}{2\rho}\left(\sqrt{1-\rho}\, \mathrm{N}^{-1}(\theta) - \mathrm{N}^{-1}(p)\right)^2 + \frac{1}{2}\left(\mathrm{N}^{-1}(\theta)\right)^2\right).$$

Its mean, median, and mode are given by

$$\overline{\theta} = p$$

$$\theta_{med} = \mathrm{N}\left(\frac{1}{\sqrt{1-\rho}}\mathrm{N}^{-1}(p)\right)$$

$$\theta_{mode} = \mathrm{N}\left(\frac{\sqrt{1-\rho}}{1-2\rho}\mathrm{N}^{-1}(p)\right) \quad \text{for} \quad \rho < \frac{1}{2}.$$

The α-quantile, $\mathrm{P}[L < L_\alpha] = \alpha$, is given by

$$L_\alpha = \mathrm{N}\left(\frac{\sqrt{\rho}\,\mathrm{N}^{-1}(\alpha) + \mathrm{N}^{-1}(p)}{\sqrt{1-\rho}}\right)$$

CHAPTER 19

Loan Portfolio Value

The amount of capital necessary to support a portfolio of debt securities depends on the probability distribution of the portfolio loss. Consider a portfolio of loans, each of which is subject to default resulting in a loss to the lender. Suppose the portfolio is financed partly by equity capital and partly by borrowed funds. The credit quality of the lender's notes will depend on the probability that the loss on the portfolio exceeds the equity capital. To achieve a certain credit rating of its notes (say Aa on a rating agency scale), the lender needs to keep the probability of default on the notes at the level corresponding to that rating (about .001 for the Aa quality). It means that the equity capital allocated to the portfolio must be equal to the percentile of the distribution of the portfolio loss that corresponds to the desired probability.

In addition to determining the capital necessary to support a loan portfolio, the probability distribution of portfolio losses has a number of other applications. It can be used in regulatory reporting, measuring portfolio risk, calculation of value-at-risk (VaR), portfolio optimization and structuring, and pricing debt portfolio derivatives such as collateralized debt obligations (CDO).

In this chapter, we derive the distribution of the portfolio loss under certain assumptions. It is shown that this distribution converges with increasing portfolio size to a limiting type, whose analytical form is given here. The results of the first two sections of this paper are contained in the author's technical notes, Vasicek (1987) and (1991) (Chapters 17 and 18 of this

---

Risk, 15 (12) (2002), 160–162; reprinted in *Risk* 20 (7) (2007), 130–133; reprinted in A. Lipton (ed.), *Theory and Practice of Credit Risk Modelling*, London: Risk Books, 2008.

volume). For a review of recent literature on the subject, see, for instance, Pykhtin and Dev (2002).

THE LIMITING DISTRIBUTION OF PORTFOLIO LOSSES

Assume that a loan defaults if the value of the borrower's assets at the loan maturity T falls below the contractual value B of its obligations payable. Let A_i be the value of the i-th borrower's assets, described by the process

$$dA_i = \mu_i A_i dt + \sigma_i A_i dx_i.$$

The asset value at T can be represented as

$$\log A_i(T) = \log A_i + \mu_i T - \frac{1}{2}\sigma_i^2 T + \sigma_i \sqrt{T} X_i \quad (1)$$

where X_i is a standard normal variable. The probability of default of the i-th loan is then

$$p_i = P[A_i(T) < B_i] = P[X_i < c_i] = N(c_i)$$

where

$$c_i = \frac{\log B_i - \log A_i - \mu_i T + \frac{1}{2}\sigma_i^2 T}{\sigma_i \sqrt{T}}$$

and N is the cumulative normal distribution function.

Consider a portfolio consisting of n loans in equal dollar amounts. Let the probability of default on any one loan be p, and assume that the asset values of the borrowing companies are correlated with a coefficient ρ for any two companies. We will further assume that all loans have the same term T.

Let L_i be the gross loss (before recoveries) on the i-th loan, so that $L_i = 1$ if the i-th borrower defaults and $L_i = 0$ otherwise. Let L be the portfolio percentage gross loss,

$$L = \frac{1}{n}\sum_{i=1}^{n} L_i.$$

If the events of default on the loans in the portfolio were independent of each other, the portfolio loss distribution would converge, by the central limit theorem, to a normal distribution as the portfolio size increases. Because the defaults are not independent, however, the conditions of the central limit theorem are not satisfied and L is not asymptotically normal. It turns out, however, that the distribution of the portfolio loss does converge to a limiting form, which we will now proceed to derive.

The variables X_i in Eq. (1) are jointly standard normal with equal pairwise correlations ρ, and can therefore be represented as

$$X_i = Y\sqrt{\rho} + Z_i\sqrt{1-\rho} \tag{2}$$

where $Y, Z_1, Z_2, \ldots, Z_n$ are mutually independent standard normal variables. (This is not an assumption, but a property of the equicorrelated normal distribution.) The variable Y can be interpreted as a portfolio common factor, such as an economic index, over the interval $(0, T)$. Then the term $Y\sqrt{\rho}$ is the company's exposure to the common factor and the term $Z_i\sqrt{(1-\rho)}$ represents the company-specific risk.

We will evaluate the probability of the portfolio loss as the expectation over the common factor Y of the conditional probability given Y. This can be interpreted as assuming various scenarios for the economy, determining the probability of a given portfolio loss under each scenario, and then weighting each scenario by its likelihood.

When the common factor is fixed, the conditional probability of loss on any one loan is

$$p(Y) = P[L_i = 1 | Y] = \mathrm{N}\left(\frac{\mathrm{N}^{-1}(p) - Y\sqrt{\rho}}{\sqrt{1-\rho}}\right). \tag{3}$$

The quantity $p(Y)$ provides the loan default probability under the given scenario. The unconditional default probability p is the average of the conditional probabilities over the scenarios.

Conditional on the value of Y, the variables L_i are independent equally distributed variables with a finite variance. The portfolio loss conditional on Y converges, by the law of large numbers, to its expectation $p(Y)$ as $n \to \infty$. Then

$$\mathrm{P}[L \le x] = \mathrm{P}[p(Y) \le x] = \mathrm{P}[Y \ge p^{-1}(x)] = \mathrm{N}(-p^{-1}(x))$$

and on substitution, the cumulative distribution function of loan losses on a very large portfolio is in the limit

$$\mathrm{P}[L \le x] = \mathrm{N}\left(\frac{\sqrt{1-\rho}\,\mathrm{N}^{-1}(x) - \mathrm{N}^{-1}(p)}{\sqrt{\rho}}\right). \tag{4}$$

This result is given in Vasicek (1991).

The convergence of the portfolio loss distribution to the limiting form in Eq. (4) actually holds even for portfolios with unequal weights. Let the portfolio weights be $w_1, w_2, \ldots, w_n$ with $\Sigma w_i = 1$. The portfolio loss

$$L = \sum_{i=1}^{n} w_i L_i$$

conditional on Y converges to its expectation $p(Y)$ whenever (and this is a necessary and sufficient condition)

$$\sum_{i=1}^{n} w_i^2 \to 0.$$

In other words, if the portfolio contains a sufficiently large number of loans without it being dominated by a few loans much larger than the rest, the limiting distribution provides a good approximation for the portfolio loss.

PROPERTIES OF THE LOSS DISTRIBUTION

The portfolio loss distribution given by the cumulative distribution function

$$F(x; p, \rho) = \mathrm{N}\left(\frac{\sqrt{1-\rho}\,\mathrm{N}^{-1}(x) - \mathrm{N}^{-1}(p)}{\sqrt{\rho}}\right) \tag{5}$$

is a continuous distribution concentrated on the interval $0 \le x \le 1$. It forms a two-parameter family with the parameters $0 < p, \rho < 1$. When $\rho \to 0$, it converges to a one-point distribution concentrated at $L = p$. When $\rho \to 1$, it converges to a zero-one distribution with probabilities p and $1 - p$, respectively. When $p \to 0$ or $p \to 1$, the distribution becomes concentrated at $L = 0$ or $L = 1$, respectively. The distribution possesses a symmetry property

$$F(x; p, \rho) = 1 - F(1 - x; 1 - p, \rho).$$

The loss distribution has the density

$$f(x; p, \rho) = \sqrt{\frac{1-\rho}{\rho}} \exp\left(-\frac{1}{2\rho}\left(\sqrt{1-\rho}\,\mathrm{N}^{-1}(x) - \mathrm{N}^{-1}(p)\right)^2 + \frac{1}{2}(\mathrm{N}^{-1}(x))^2\right)$$

which is unimodal with the mode at

$$L_{mode} = \mathrm{N}\left(\frac{\sqrt{1-\rho}}{1-2\rho}\mathrm{N}^{-1}(p)\right)$$

TABLE 19.1 Values of $(L_\alpha - p)/s$ for the portfolio loss distribution

p	ρ	$\alpha = .9$	$\alpha = .99$	$\alpha = .999$	$\alpha = .9999$
.01	.1	1.19	3.8	7.0	10.7
.01	.4	.55	4.5	11.0	18.2
.001	.1	.98	4.1	8.8	15.4
.001	.4	.12	3.2	13.2	31.8
Normal		1.28	2.3	3.1	3.7

when $\rho < 1/2$, monotone when $\rho = 1/2$, and U-shaped when $\rho > 1/2$. The mean of the distribution is $EL = p$ and the variance is

$$s^2 = \mathrm{Var}\, L = \mathrm{N}_2(\mathrm{N}^{-1}(p), \mathrm{N}^{-1}(p), \rho) - p^2$$

where N_2 is the bivariate cumulative normal distribution function. The inverse of this distribution, that is, the α-percentile value of L, is given by

$$L_\alpha = F(\alpha; 1 - p, 1 - \rho).$$

The portfolio loss distribution is highly skewed and leptokurtic. Table 19.1 lists the values of the α-percentile L_α expressed as the number of standard deviations from the mean for several values of the parameters. The α-percentiles of the standard normal distribution are shown for comparison.

These values manifest the extreme non-normality of the loss distribution. Suppose a lender holds a large portfolio of loans to firms whose pairwise asset correlation is $\rho = .4$ and whose probability of default is $p = .01$. The portfolio expected loss is $EL = .01$, and the standard deviation is $s = .0277$. If the lender wishes to hold the probability of default on his notes at $1 - \alpha = .001$, he will need enough capital to cover 11.0 times the portfolio standard deviation. If the loss distribution were normal, 3.1 times the standard deviation would suffice.

THE RISK-NEUTRAL DISTRIBUTION

The portfolio loss distribution given by Eq. (4) is the actual probability distribution. This is the distribution from which to calculate the probability of a loss of a certain magnitude for the purposes of determining the necessary capital or of calculating VaR. This is also the distribution to be used in structuring collateralized debt obligations—that is, in calculating the probability of loss and the expected loss for a given tranche. For the purposes of pricing the tranches, however, it is necessary to use the risk-neutral probability distribution. The risk-neutral distribution is calculated in the same way, except that the default probabilities are evaluated under the risk-neutral measure P*,

$$p^* = \mathrm{P}^*[A(T) < B] = \mathrm{N}\left(\frac{\log B - \log A - rT + \frac{1}{2}\sigma^2 T}{\sigma\sqrt{T}} \right)$$

where r is the risk-free rate. The risk-neutral probability is related to the actual probability of default by the equation

$$p^* = \mathrm{N}\left(\mathrm{N}^{-1}(p) + \lambda \rho_M \sqrt{T}\right) \tag{6}$$

where ρ_M is the correlation of the firm asset value with the market, and $\lambda = (\mu_M - r)/\sigma_M$ is the market price of risk. The risk-neutral portfolio loss distribution is then given by

$$\mathrm{P}^*[L \leq x] = \mathrm{N}\left(\frac{\sqrt{1-\rho}\,\mathrm{N}^{-1}(x) - \mathrm{N}^{-1}(p^*)}{\sqrt{\rho}} \right). \tag{7}$$

Thus, a derivative security (such as a CDO tranche written against the portfolio) that pays at time T an amount $C(L)$ contingent on the portfolio loss is valued at

$$V = e^{-rT}\mathrm{E}^* C(L)$$

where the expectation is taken with respect to the distribution (7). For instance, a default protection for losses in excess of L_0 is priced at

$$V = e^{-rT}\mathrm{E}^*(L - L_0)_+ = e^{-rT}\left(p^* - \mathrm{N}_2\left(\mathrm{N}^{-1}(p^*), \mathrm{N}^{-1}(L_0), \sqrt{1-\rho}\right)\right).$$

THE PORTFOLIO MARKET VALUE

So far, we have discussed the loss due to loan defaults. Now suppose that the maturity date T of the loan is past the date H for which the portfolio value is considered (the horizon date). If the credit quality of a borrower deteriorates, the value of the loan will decline, resulting in a loss (this is often referred to as the loss due to *credit migration*). We will investigate the distribution of the loss resulting from changes in the marked-to-market portfolio value.

The value of the debt at time 0 is the expected present value of the loan payments under the risk-neutral measure,

$$D = e^{-rT}(1 - Gp^*)$$

where G is the loss given default and p^* is the risk-neutral probability of default. At time H, the value of the loan is

$$D(H) = e^{-r(T-H)}\left(1 - G\,\mathrm{N}\left(\frac{\log B - \log A(H) - r(T-H) + \frac{1}{2}\sigma^2(T-H)}{\sigma\sqrt{T-H}}\right)\right).$$

Define the loan loss L_i at time H as the difference between the riskless value and the market value of the loan at H,

$$L_i = e^{-r(T-H)} - D(H).$$

This definition of loss is chosen purely for convenience. If the loss is defined in a different way (for instance, as the difference between the accrued value and the market value), it will only result in a shift of the portfolio loss distribution by a location parameter.

The loss on the i-th loan can be written as

$$L_i = a\,\mathrm{N}\left(b\sqrt{\frac{T}{T-H}} - X_i\sqrt{\frac{H}{T-H}}\right)$$

where

$$a = Ge^{-r(T-H)}, b = \mathrm{N}^{-1}(p) + \lambda\rho_M\frac{T-H}{\sqrt{T}}$$

and the standard normal variables X_i defined over the horizon H by

$$\log A_i(H) = \log A_i + \mu_i H - \frac{1}{2}\sigma_i^2 H + \sigma_i\sqrt{H}X_i$$

are subject to Eq. (2).

Let L be the market value loss at time H of a loan portfolio with weights w_i. The conditional mean of L_i given Y can be calculated as

$$\mu(Y) = \mathrm{E}(L_i|Y) = a\,\mathrm{N}\left(b\sqrt{\frac{T}{T-\rho H}} - Y\sqrt{\frac{\rho H}{T-\rho H}}\right).$$

The losses conditional on the factor Y are independent, and therefore the portfolio loss L conditional on Y converges to its mean value $E(L \mid Y) = \mu(Y)$ as $\Sigma w_i^2 \to \infty$. The limiting distribution of L is then

$$P[L \le x] = P[\mu(Y) \le x] = F\left(\frac{x}{a}; N(b), \frac{\rho H}{T}\right). \quad (8)$$

We see that the limiting distribution of the portfolio loss is of the same type (5) whether the loss is defined as the decline in the market value or the realized loss at maturity. In fact, the results of the section on the distribution of loss due to default are just a special case of this section for $T = H$.

The risk-neutral distribution for the loss due to market value change is given by

$$P^*[L \le x] = F\left(\frac{x}{a}; p^*, \frac{\rho H}{T}\right). \quad (9)$$

When applying the limiting distribution to an actual portfolio, the parameters p, ρ should be chosen in such a way that the limiting distribution has the same mean and variance as the actual portfolio. The latter calculation is facilitated by the formula for covariance of the loan values at the horizon,

$$\begin{aligned} \mathrm{Cov}(D_i(H), D_j(H)) &= e^{-r(T_i+T_j-2H)} G_i G_j \\ &\quad \times N_2\left(N^{-1}(p_i), N^{-1}(p_j), \rho_{ij}\frac{\min(T_i, T_j, H)}{\sqrt{T_i T_j}}\right). \end{aligned}$$

ADJUSTMENT FOR GRANULARITY

Eq. (8) relies on the convergence of the portfolio loss L given Y to its mean value $\mu(Y)$, which means that the conditional variance $\mathrm{Var}(L|Y) \to 0$. When the portfolio is not sufficiently large for the law of large numbers to take hold, we need to take into account the non-zero value of $\mathrm{Var}(L|Y)$. Consider a portfolio of uniform credits with weights $w_1, w_2, \ldots, w_n$ and put

$$\delta = \sum_{i=1}^{n} w_i^2.$$

The conditional variance of the portfolio loss L given Y is

$$\mathrm{Var}(L|Y) = \delta a^2 \left(N_2\left(U, U, \frac{(1-\rho)H}{T-\rho H}\right) - N^2(U)\right)$$

where

$$U = b\sqrt{\frac{T}{T - \rho H}} - Y\sqrt{\frac{\rho H}{T - \rho H}}.$$

The unconditional mean and variance of the portfolio loss are $EL = a\mathrm{N}(b)$ and

$$\begin{aligned} \mathrm{Var}\,L &= \mathrm{EVar}\,(L|Y) + \mathrm{Var}\,\mathrm{E}(L|Y) \\ &= \delta a^2 \mathrm{N}_2\left(b, b, \frac{H}{T}\right) + (1 - \delta) a^2 \mathrm{N}_2\left(b, b, \frac{\rho H}{T}\right) - a^2 \mathrm{N}^2(b). \end{aligned} \tag{10}$$

Taking the first two terms in the tetrachoric expansion of the bivariate normal distribution function $\mathrm{N}_2(x, x, \rho) = \mathrm{N}^2(x) + \rho \mathrm{n}^2(x)$, where n is the normal density function, we have approximately

$$\begin{aligned} \mathrm{Var}\,L &= \delta a^2 n^2(b)\frac{H}{T} + (1 - \delta) a^2 n^2(b)\frac{\rho H}{T} \\ &= a^2 \mathrm{N}_2\left(b, b, (\rho + \delta\,(1 - \rho))\,\frac{H}{T}\right) - a^2 \mathrm{N}^2(b) \end{aligned}$$

Approximating the loan loss distribution by the distribution (5) with the same mean and variance, we get

$$\mathrm{P}[L \le x] = F\left(\frac{x}{a}; \mathrm{N}\left(b\right), (\rho + \delta(1 - \rho))\frac{H}{T}\right). \tag{11}$$

This expression is in fact exact for both extremes $n \to \infty, \delta = 0$ and $n = 1, \delta = 1$.

Equation (11) provides an adjustment for the "granularity" of the portfolio. In particular, the finite portfolio adjustment to the distribution of the gross loss at the maturity date is obtained by putting $H = T, a = 1$ to yield

$$\mathrm{P}[L \le x] = F(x; p, \rho + \delta(1 - \rho)). \tag{12}$$

SUMMARY

We have shown that the distribution of the loan portfolio loss converges, with increasing portfolio size, to the limiting type given by Eq. (5) (see Figure 19.1). It means that this distribution can be used to represent the loan loss behavior of large portfolios. The loan loss can be a realized loss on loans maturing prior to the horizon date, or a market value deficiency on loans whose term is longer than the horizon period.

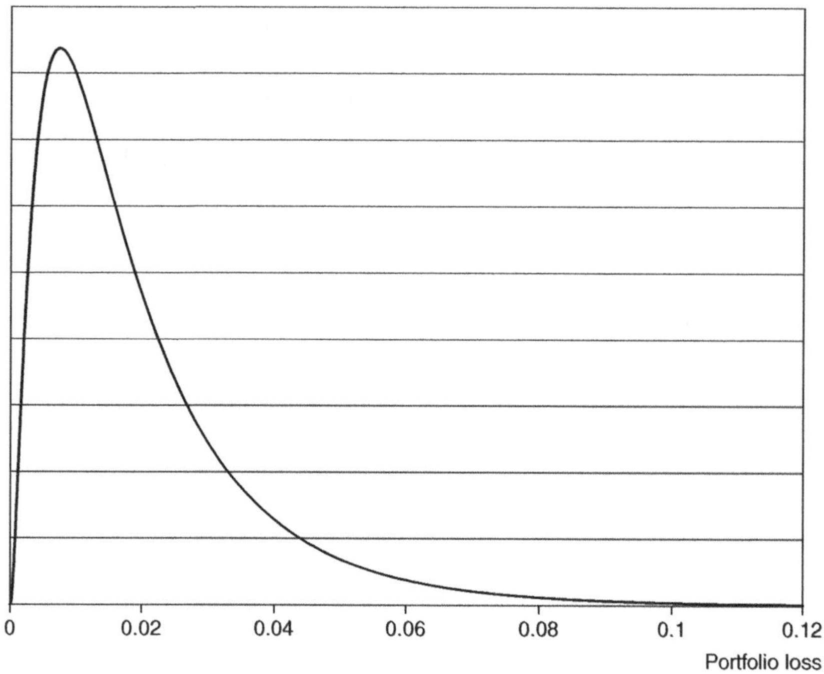

FIGURE 19.1 Portfolio Loss Distribution (p = .02, $\rho = .1$)

The limiting probability distribution of portfolio losses has been derived under the assumption that all loans in the portfolio have the same maturity, the same probability of default, and the same pairwise correlation of the borrower assets. Curiously, however, computer simulations show that the family (5) appears to provide a reasonably good fit to the tail of the loss distribution for more general portfolios. To illustrate this point, Figure 19.2 gives the results of Monte Carlo simulations of an actual bank portfolio. The portfolio consisted of 479 loans in amounts ranging from 0.0002 percent to 8.7 percent, with $\delta = .039$. The maturities ranged from 6 months to 6 years and the default probabilities from .0002 to .064. The loss given default averaged 0.54. The asset returns were generated with 14 common factors. Plotted is the simulated cumulative distribution function of the loss in one year (dots) and the fitted limiting distribution function (solid line).

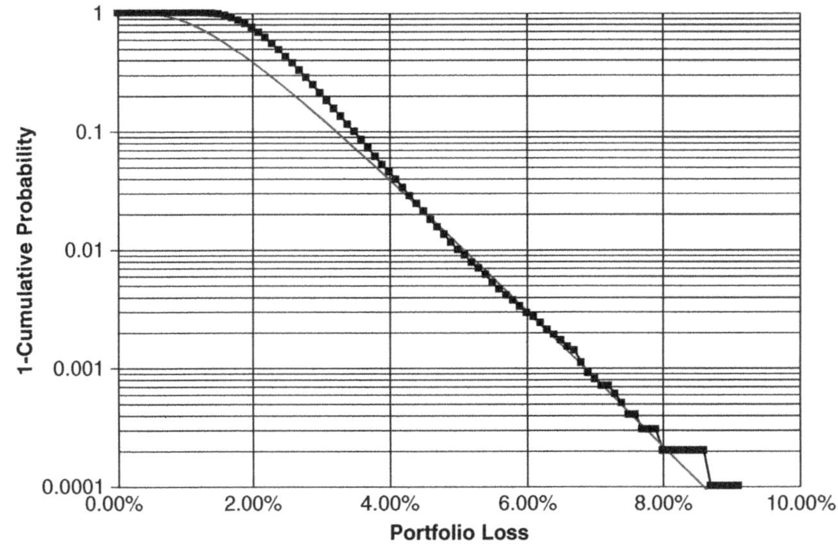

FIGURE 19.2 Simulated Loss Distribution for an Actual Portfolio

REFERENCES

Pykhtin, M., and A. Dev. (2002). "Credit Risk in Asset Securitisations: An Analytical Model." *Risk*, May, S16–S20.

Vasicek, O. (1987). *Probability of Loss on Loan Portfolio*, KMV Corporation.

Vasicek, O. (1991). *Limiting Loan Loss Probability Distribution*, KMV Corporation.

CHAPTER 20

The Empirical Test of the Distribution of Loan Portfolio Losses

This note reports the results of a test of the portfolio loss distribution performed in 1993 by Patrick McAllister of Federal Reserve Bank. The test is based on the realization that it is not possible to obtain a sufficiently long time series of loan losses on a single loan portfolio, and that the only meaningful way of testing the distribution of loan losses is by using a cross-sectional sample of data on many portfolios.

By law, every U.S. bank must report to the Federal Reserve Bank its actual losses for the previous year. The data used in the study consisted of the reported gross losses on commercial and industrial loans for small and medium-sized banks over the period 1984–1991 on some 4,000 banks. Altogether, the sample contained about 23,000 data points, each data point being the actual gross loss of a given bank in a given year.

The data points were plotted in the graph, using the kernel method of sample density estimation (see Figure 20.1). On the horizontal axis is the gross loss as a fraction of the bank portfolio: .05 is a loss of 5 percent of the portfolio value, .10 is a 10 percent loss, and so on. The vertical distance gives the number of observations of that size of loss. The graph is thus a histogram, plotting the frequency of gross loss of the given magnitude. This is the full line.

The dotted line is calculated from the formula for the density of the asymptotic loan loss distribution in Chapter 19 "The Loan Portfolio Value," using the values for the parameters p and ρ to have the same first two moments. The agreement in the shape of the distribution is striking.

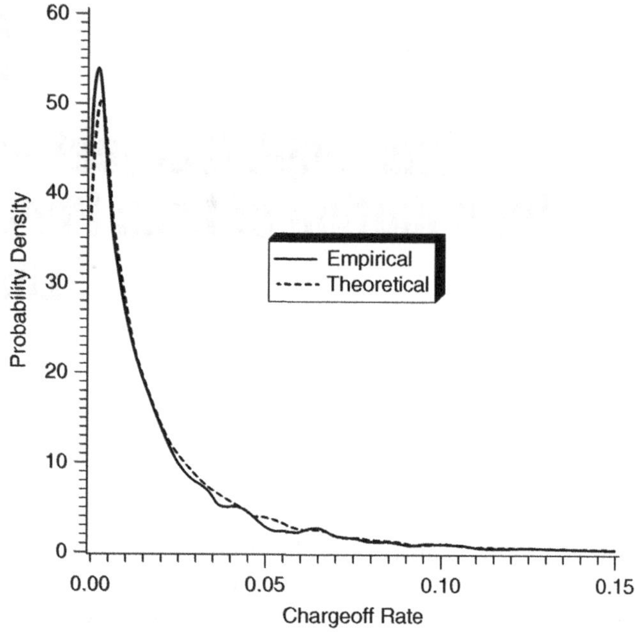

FIGURE 20.1 Loan losses as a fraction of total loan portfolio.

PART Five

Markets, Portfolios, and Securities

Let

$$I_0 = \sum_{j=1}^{m} C_j P_0(s_j)$$

be the value at time zero of a bond portfolio with payments C_j due at times $s_j, j = 1, 2, \ldots, m$ and let

$$D = \sum_{j=1}^{m} s_j C_j P_0(s_j)/I_0$$

be the Macaulay duration of the portfolio. Here

$$P_0(s) = \exp\left(-\int_0^s i(t)\,\mathrm{d}t\right)$$

and $i(t)$ are the forward rates. Let I_H be the future value of the portfolio at time $H = D$,

$$I_H = I_0/P_0(H).$$

Put

$$M^2 = \sum_{j=1}^{m} (s_j - H)^2 C_j P_0(s_j)/I_0$$

Suppose the forward rates change instantaneously to new values $i'(t) = i(t) + \Delta i(t), t \geq 0$. If K is an upper bound for the change in the slope of the forward rate curve,

$$\frac{d\Delta i(t)}{dt} \leq K, t \geq 0,$$

then the change ΔI_H in the portfolio value is bound from below by

$$\frac{\Delta I_H}{I_H} \geq -\frac{1}{2} K M^2.$$

(page 198)

CHAPTER 21

Introduction to Part V

The Capital Asset Pricing Model (CAPM) represented a significant step in the development of modern finance theory. It rested on Markowitz's concept of risk as the volatility of price, and on the ideas of mean-variance portfolio optimization, but it went a step further: It made a statement about the *market*, under the assumption that investors optimize their individual holdings. By postulating that the part of stock volatilities that are not correlated with the market portfolio (the *specific risks*) are mutually sufficiently independent to be diversified away, the model derives its powerful tenet: The risk of a security consists of two parts: the systematic risk and the specific risk. *Systematic risk*, measured by the covariance of the security price with the market portfolio price, carries a compensation in terms of expected return premium. The specific risk is not compensated for, since it can be reduced by diversification. Quantitatively, this is expressed by the equation for the *capital market line*,

$$\mu_i = r + \beta_i(\mu_M - r)$$

where μ_i is the expected rate of return on the i–th security, μ_M is the expected rate of return on the market portfolio, β_i is the regression coefficient of the security price on the market portfolio price, and r is the risk-free rate of return. A review of the model is provided in the paper "The Efficient Market Model" (Chapter 22) originally written in 1972 with John A. McQuown.

An interest in liability funding, such as fixed liabilities in pension plans, generated research in portfolio immunization strategies. Portfolio immunization is a technique of balancing long and short bonds in such a way that the portfolio value at a given horizon date (the date a liability is due) is guaranteed. Typically, this involves maintaining the Macaulay duration of the portfolio to be equal to the remaining horizon length. Such strategies are based on the assumption that interest rates of all maturities move up and down by the same amount (parallel shifts).

The paper "A Risk Minimizing Strategy for Portfolio Immunization" (Chapter 23), co-authored in 1984 with H. Gifford Fong, gives a lower bound on the portfolio value at the horizon date, should the assumption of parallel shifts be violated. The shortfall is bound by a quantity that is the product of two elements: the magnitude of a twist in the yield curve, as measured by the maximum value of the derivative with respect to term of the forward rate change; and a characteristic of the portfolio composition called M^2, which is a measure of dispersion of the portfolio cashflows around its duration. While the former quantity is outside the control of the bond investor, the latter can be minimized to assure a minimum risk of not meeting the fixed obligation on the horizon date.

This result is exploited in the 1983 paper "The Tradeoff Between Return and Risk in Immunized Portfolios" (Chapter 24), also written with H. G. Fong. It is argued that among portfolios with a fixed duration, some may offer higher return than others. An efficient frontier can be constructed that identifies the portfolio with the maximum expected return for a given level of risk, as measured by M^2. Investors can choose a portfolio on the efficient frontier that represents the desired tradeoff between return and risk.

The paper "Bond Performance: Analyzing Sources of Return" (Chapter 25), written in 1983 with H. G. Fong and C. J. Pearson, identifies the principal sources of the gains or losses in performance measurement. It is argued that the total return on a bond portfolio can be meaningfully attributed to two primary components: the effect of external interest rate development, and the contribution of the management process. The interest rate effect can be further decomposed into that due to the initial yield curve level and shape, and that due to the changes in the forward rates over the performance measurement period. The contribution of the portfolio management consists of the following components: return from management of the portfolio maturity composition; return from the management of the industry and quality sectors; and return due to the selection of the specific issues.

The method proposed in the paper for measurement of these components of performance consists of repricing of the securities in the portfolio. By pricing each bond as if it were a Treasury issue and calculating the return on such portfolio (including the actual changes in the portfolio composition over the period due to purchases, sales, swaps, etc.), the maturity management component is equal to the difference between this return and the external interest rate component. The next step is repricing each bond as if it were exactly in line with its own sector and quality group—that is, with the same average yield spread over Treasuries. The difference between the return on the portfolio with such pricing, and the sum of the external component and the maturity management, is the part of the total return due to the management of sectors and qualities. Finally, the difference between the actual total return and the sum of the previous components is due to the choice and management of the individual bonds.

A desirable property of this methodology is that the *timing* of any changes in the portfolio composition over the performance measurement period is properly allocated to each component of the management process.

Portfolio insurance is a technique that guarantees a minimum return over a specified horizon period even if the target asset, usually the market portfolio, is down by more than the minimum. This is achieved by a strategy that simulates the performance of a call on the target asset. Buying a call, together with an investment in a fixed-return bond, has the required property of having a guaranteed minimum return (in case the call is not exercised) together with sharing the performance of the target asset (in case the call is worth exercising). Creating a *synthetic* call, by maintaining the proportion of funds invested in the target asset equal to the hedge ratio of the call, achieves the same result. The cost of the strategy, equal to the cost of buying the call, is realized by a fixed and known return difference between the target asset return and the return on the portfolio.

A generalization of portfolio insurance is the *best return strategy*. Portfolio insurance can be viewed as a strategy that promises the better of two returns, each less a fixed return differential. The two assets are the target portfolio and a bond maturing on the horizon date. In the best return strategy, the objective is to get the best of several returns on different assets, each less a fixed return differential. The return on the strategy is thus

$$R_I = \max(R_1 - c_1, R_2 - c_2, \dots, R_n - c_n).$$

The costs $c_1, c_2, \dots, c_n$ are subject to a single condition, which corresponds to the pricing of the multiple asset call that the strategy creates synthetically. A detailed description of the strategy and examples of the strategy costs are given in the 1987 paper "The Best-Return Strategy" (Chapter 26).

Changes in interest rates are not the only source of risk in fixed-income investment. A bond portfolio value also depends on changes in interest rate volatility. Nearly all fixed-income instruments contain embedded options—callable bonds, pass-throughs, futures, and so on. Just as fixed-income investors need to know how changes in interest rates affect portfolio value, they need to be also concerned about changes in interest rate volatility.

The 1992 paper "Volatility: Omission Impossible" (Chapter 27) with H. Gifford Fong and D. Yoo presents a term structure model with two stochastic factors: the short rate and the short rate volatility. This model allows for measurement of the exposure to the risk of volatility changes.

The article "A Multidimensional Framework for Risk Analysis" (Chapter 28) was co-authored in 1997 with H. Gifford Fong. It provides a methodology for quantitative analysis of portfolio exposures to different types of risks, and the calculation of VaR measures. These risks can run from market risks (such as changes in stock market index or changes in interest rate levels) to credit or operations risks. As long as a given source of risk can be described by a risk factor, such as the level of interest rates or the quality spread of corporate yields over Treasuries, the sensitivity of the portfolio to changes in the risk source can be measured. By determining the covariance matrix of the different risk sources, value-at-risk can be calculated.

A characteristic of some commodities, foremost of which is electricity, is that they cannot be easily stored. For a storable commodity, the forward price is equal to the current spot price divided by the price of a zero coupon bond with the same maturity as the forward contract. This is because the forward contract to buy a commodity at a future date can be duplicated by issuing a bond maturing on the contract date and buying the commodity now. For electricity, this relationship between the spot and forward prices breaks down.

"Plugging into Electricity" (Chapter 29) was written in 2001 with Helyette Geman. (The article was originally called "Forward and Futures Contracts on Non-Storable Commodities: The Case of Electricity," but *Risk* likes to assign cute titles to its feature articles.) The paper investigates the relationship between spot and forward prices, and proposes a methodology for modeling electricity spot and futures prices.

The unpublished 2002 memorandum "Pricing of Energy Derivatives" (Chapter 30) goes further: It provides a general equation that represents a complete specification of the forward/spot process. The spot price behavior is fully described by the current forward curve and by forward contract volatilities, and it only includes processes whose stochastic properties under the martingale measure are known. Therefore, the prices of energy derivatives and contingent claims can be calculated without recourse to the market prices of risk, which are not directly observable.

CHAPTER 22

The Efficient Market Model

By Oldrich A. Vasicek and John A. McQuown

INTRODUCTION AND SUMMARY

The purpose of this chapter is to discuss what is known as the "efficient market model of capital market theory," the most significant part of which is the Capital Asset Pricing Model. The paper does not extend the model. It is a nontechnical summary of the papers by Treynor (1961),[1] Sharpe (1970), Lintner (1965), Black (1972), and others. Their writings require considerable familiarity with mathematical and econometric concepts, hence a more verbal exposition of the basic ideas may be helpful to some readers.

There are two appropriate caveats concerning the context of this chapter. They both follow from the fact that it is an exposition, and not an extension, of the thinking of the authors of capital market theory. The first is that this paper does not expose *all* of the work by all of these authors. It is not, therefore, a fully comprehensive exposition. In particular, completeness has been sacrificed in the treatment of some of the more advanced extensions and refinements of capital market theory, especially where considerable mathematical sophistication is involved. This incompleteness seems palatable on the grounds that the basic essentials should be exposed first. The second warning is that the authors are attempting to expose the basics of capital market theory and not to validate it per se. All theories are abstract simplifications of reality. No one theory encompasses

---

Financial Analysts Journal, 28 (5) (1972), 71–84 (received Graham and Dodd Award); reprinted in *Analyze Financière* 15, 21–35, 1973 (in French); reprinted in *Supplementary Readings in Financial Analysis*, Institute of Chartered Financial Analysts, University of Virginia, 1973.

[1]References appear at end of article.

all aspects of anything, nor is the most elaborate theory expected to go unchanged with the subsequent evolution of thought. Accordingly, all existing features of capital market theory do not inherently correspond to reality equally well. What the authors do assume, however, is that there is sufficient correspondence between reality and the extent of capital market theory exposed herein to warrant the attention of the financial community.

The chapter begins with a definition of the risk of investing in the capital markets and with a method of measuring return and risk. It is shown that risk can be decomposed into two parts: the *systematic* risk due to the response of any stock to changes in the market as a whole, and the *specific* risk attributable to a particular stock. It is shown how the market place compensates the investor for taking systematic risk with an appropriate expected return. It is also shown that specific risk is not compensated, since it can be essentially eliminated through diversification. It is shown that under the assumptions of borrowing and lending at a risk-free rate, the expected return is proportional to the systematic risk borne. The security market line, which represents the relationship between systematic risk and expected return, is derived. The concept of efficient portfolios is introduced. The capital market line is defined as the set of such combinations of risky and riskless assets that are superior to all other portfolios in terms of return and risk. It is shown that an investor's choice of a portfolio on the capital market line (or a well-diversified portfolio close to the capital market line) depends only on his attitude toward expected return and risk. A generalized form of the model is outlined for the case when borrowing at the risk-free rate is not possible.

As the name suggests, the efficient market model describes the equilibrium state of efficient capital markets. A perfectly efficient market is one in which new information is immediately and costlessly available to all investors and potential investors, and the cost of action (transaction costs, taxes, etc.) is zero. While actual capital markets do not conform exactly to "perfect" assumptions, empirical studies suggest that the main conclusions of the efficient market model hold very well in real markets. The theory of efficient markets represents the best description of capital markets available at present, and probably the only one that considers explicitly uncertainty and risk. Since it also offers important implications for investment decisions and portfolio construction, the efficient market model should command the attention of every practicing investor.

RISK, RISK AVERSION, AND COMPENSATION

Since the future prices of common stocks are uncertain, the outcome of an investment in common stocks cannot be determined in advance, and inevitably carries some risk. Risk is a chance of loss, which can be thought of either as an actual capital loss or a failure in achieving the return that was expected. There can be no risk if the outcome is certain; the investor, by definition, achieves the return he has expected. The more uncertain an investment opportunity is, the larger is the chance of loss, or the risk. Risk is therefore intrinsic to the existence of uncertainty about the outcome of an investment, and a formal quantitative definition of risk can be based on the concept of uncertainty.

Some financial instruments exhibit fixed return characteristics. Government bonds, for instance, when held to maturity, leave virtually no uncertainty about the total amount of money that will be returned. In accordance with the concept of risk as uncertainty, we will call these instruments, when held to maturity, *risk-free*. Common stocks, on the other hand, are *risky* issues. They may result in high gains, but may lead to large losses as well. A wide distribution of possible outcomes exists over all future horizons, since they do not mature.

Within the class of common stocks, not all issues exhibit the same risk. Some firms—for example, electronics or airlines—are generally engaged in endeavors whose outcome is less certain than those of other firms. For an investor, it means that there is less certainty that the future price of such stock is not going to decline considerably in value. On the other hand, the relatively stable and predictable nature of a utility company's business implies less uncertainty about the future price of its stock.

This leads to the following definition of risk in a capital asset market: The risk of an issue is the degree to which future price of that issue can differ from its expected value. Stated in different terms, risk is the dispersion of future price changes. The next section will deal with the question of how the dispersion can be measured *ex post* and estimated *ex ante*. Before addressing this issue, however, it is useful to discuss some aspects of this definition of risk.

There are several implications of the risky character of common stocks that generally make investors prefer (other things being equal) less risky investments to more risky ones. These include the so-called gambler's ruin, the consumption effects, and the liquidity requirement effects.

The phenomenon known as *gambler's ruin* refers to a particular outcome of an investment under uncertainty. It consists of losing effectively all funds in an extremely unlucky turn of events, thus being excluded from further participation in the investment. Thereby, the possibility of recovering from such loss is eliminated. Although this is an extreme case and it is generally very improbable (particularly in the short run), the effect—if it occurs—is fatal.

Another reason for investors' reluctance to bear risk relates to their consumption requirements. Most investors expect to consume some part of their income through time, and preservation of their wealth thus demands achieving a certain level of gain. Although a highly risky investment opportunity may have the prospect of high gains (as well as large losses), it may not, therefore, be as attractive to a particular investor as an opportunity to obtain more stable returns.

An even more important factor concerns liquidity requirements: the need to be able to convert stock holdings into another form of asset, namely cash, at any moment. An investment in highly risky stocks has a considerable disadvantage in this respect relative to an investment in more stable stocks, not because it is difficult to convert to cash, but because high-risk assets may happen to be at low values when cash is required, quite apart from the longer-term prospects.

For these reasons, it can be expected that investors are generally risk-averse. That is, they prefer more stable holdings to less stable ones, other things being equal. If this is true, how can one explain the behavior of market participants who place their investments in very risky positions? What would induce investors to hold these securities? The efficient market model suggests that the market pays higher rates of return for more risky holdings; otherwise, investors could not be induced to hold these issues. That is, the expected value of return on investment is higher for more risky issues than it is for less risky ones. The principle of risk compensation has been well established empirically (cf. Black, Jensen, and Scholes (1972)). It will be discussed again in quantitative terms in the Capital Asset Pricing Model section.

Different investors have different investment objectives, different consumption and liquidity requirements, and different planning horizons; thus, the degree of risk aversion differs from one investor to another. This means that some investors will be more comfortable at low risk levels with attendant comparatively small expectation of return, while others would prefer positions at higher risk levels with the attendant higher expected compensation. The actions of market participants, trading off their individual requirements with each other, then result in the appropriate pricing of risky assets.

Every investor can find a position in the market that corresponds to the degree of risk he considers adequate, given the compensation for risk the market offers. To avoid unnecessary risk (risk that can be diversified away) and to choose a proper tradeoff between the risk and expected return, are some of the practical applications of the efficient market model.

MEASUREMENT OF RISK AND RETURN

Risk has been introduced in the previous section as the dispersion of future price changes. This *ex ante* uncertainty manifests itself *ex post* as *volatility* in price series. The price of a company engaged in a business of highly unpredictable nature is likely to vary considerably as the prospects and outcomes of business ventures evolve. The price of a stock subject to less uncertainty is bound to change less swiftly.

These observations suggest that the risk is measured *ex post* by the variability of price changes. Since it has been established empirically that the degree of volatility of price changes of any stock is a reasonably stable quantity (cf. Blume (1971)), it can also be taken as an estimate of the *ex ante uncertainty*, or risk. This is a concept of great importance: It allows quantitative measurement and anticipation of risk.

Risk is one of the essential concepts of capital market theory, and the theory would lose much of its impact if techniques to measure risk were not provided. When risk is measured by price fluctuation, it is necessary to know to what extent *ex post* volatility of price can be taken as an estimate of *ex ante* uncertainty (i.e., risk). This depends on two factors: instability of the parameters of price change distributions, and sampling errors in estimating the parameters from data. The latter source of error can be minimized by using enough data for sampling and by choosing appropriate statistical techniques. The former source of misestimation depends on the speed with which the parameters change. In most cases, the rate of change is moderate, and past dispersion is as good an estimate of future dispersion as an estimate obtained by other means. Therefore, *ex post* measurements of price volatility provide a *usably accurate* proxy of *ex ante* risks.

To measure risk directly as the variability of price changes is not quite convenient, since it would mean that risk depends on the *level* of the price—the higher the price in dollars per share, the higher the dispersion. To avoid this scaling problem, variability of the rates of return is used. Another reason for choosing rates of return rather than price changes is that rates of return include dividends.

The rate of return R_t over a time period $(t-1)$ to t is defined as

$$R_t = \frac{P_t - P_{t-1} + D_t}{P_{t-1}}$$

where P_t is the price per share at time t, and D_t is the (cash) dividends per share paid during the period $(t-1)$ to t. The rate of return is thus expressed as total return on a dollar invested at the beginning of the period. Rate of return on a portfolio is defined in analogy, with return on an individual issue, as the increase in total wealth during the period divided by the original wealth.

Under uncertainty, future rates of return behave as random variables and can, accordingly, be described by the characteristics of their probability distribution. The *expected rate of return* is the mean value of the distribution of future returns. The expected rate of return is thus the value around which future rates are expected to center. The expected rate is the most likely estimate of what the future rates will be.

The expected rate of return may be different from the average performance of the company in previous periods. *If* a company is believed to maintain the same a priori distribution of rates of return, however, the expected value can be estimated by the average rate of return in the previous period,

$$\overline{R} = \frac{1}{n}\sum_{t=1}^{n} R_t.$$

Any investor certainly prefers investment opportunities with higher expectations to those with lower expectations, if other things are equal. The expected return alone, however, does not fully characterize an investment opportunity. It is necessary to consider the deviation of possible future returns from the expected value, which brings us back to the concept of uncertainty, or risk.

Risk has been defined as the dispersion of the rates of return from their expected value. The larger the dispersion, the less sure the investor is that the expected performance will be attained. The dispersion can be measured by the *variance*, which is the mean squared deviation of the distribution of returns from the expected value.

The variance in rates of return measures the expected degree of fluctuation of future returns about their expectation—that is, the probable variability of future payments. It is therefore a convenient measure of the riskiness of an investment. Investors, being risk-averse, will generally prefer smaller variance to larger variance on their investments.

The variance (which is, like the expected return, an unobservable *ex ante parameter* of the distribution of future returns) can be estimated by the *ex post* sample variance of rates of return attained:

$$V = \frac{1}{n}\sum_{t=1}^{n} (R_t - \overline{R})^2.$$

If the sample variance of past rates of return is used to estimate future dispersion, it must be assumed that the degree of fluctuation in the series of returns remains relatively stable over time. Stated differently: The variation in returns must be "usably" constant—a question that can be empirically tested.

The variance V is a quadratic measure of volatility. It is sometimes useful to consider its square root,

$$S = \sqrt{V}$$

which is called *standard deviation*. Since these two measures of risk are so closely related, we will occasionally use one and occasionally the other in referring to risk. The difference between them is a matter of mathematical convenience, not economic significance.

The prices, and consequently the rates of return, of two common stocks or of a stock and the stock market as a whole do not move independently. When the market advances, a stock listed on that market is also likely to advance, and similarly for declines. This is due to the dependence among industries and among companies of the same industry. It is estimated that about 50 percent of the price fluctuation of a particular company can be explained by overall market movements, and some 10 percent by the fluctuation of that industry. Then, the remaining 40 percent fluctuation is that due to the characteristics of the individual company (cf. King (1966)).

Since the comovement of stocks plays an eminent role in constructing a portfolio (e.g., in diversification), it is necessary to introduce a measure of dependence between rates of return, in addition to measures of expected return and dispersion. A convenient measure of comovement is what statisticians call the *covariance*.

Covariance between two rates of return is defined as the mean value of the product of the deviations of the two rates from their respective expected values. A positive covariance means that the two issues are likely to move in the same direction (which is typically the case in the stock market). Negative covariance means that the two stocks tend to move in different directions.

On past rates of return, the covariance can be estimated by the sample covariance, which is defined as

$$C_{ij} = \frac{1}{n}\sum_{t=1}^{n}(R_{it} - \overline{R}_i)(R_{jt} - \overline{R}_j)$$

where R_{it}, R_{jt} are the rates of return on two stocks, and $\overline{R}_i$, $\overline{R}_j$ are their respective averages.

It will be shown in a later section on the role of the portfolio that nearly all fluctuations of returns on a well-diversified portfolio are due to the average covariance of the issues with the market as a whole. The total dispersions of individual companies do not, therefore, add directly to form the dispersion of the portfolio. Rather, there are dispersion components of individual companies that cancel each other out. The result is that total portfolio dispersion is less than for any individual company. This is, of course, the desirable impact of diversification.

EFFICIENT MARKET HYPOTHESIS

Capital markets can be characterized by two important factors: divisibility, and liquidity. *Divisibility* means that real assets are divided into a large number of shares, which can be purchased by investors in arbitrary amounts. Therefore, an asset can be held in various proportions by a number of investors, and conversely, an investor can distribute his wealth among "shares" of many assets. Thus, divisibility in a marketplace permits diversification.

Liquidity means that each investor can easily and at relatively small expense trade his share in any real asset for shares of other assets, or convert his shares into cash, and vice versa. This implies that each investor can hold a portfolio of assets perceived to correspond best to his requirements. He may shift his holdings at any time when either his requirements or his perceptions of the characteristics of the assets change.

It is in the interest of each investor to collect information about the shares of real assets traded in capital markets. Such information allows the investor to evaluate the prospects of each investment opportunity, and therefore to invest in the portfolio with the most promising performance. The demand for this information generates the existence of various information channels expected to provide the investor with pertinent knowledge, such as periodic income statements and balance sheets of companies, stock prices, and volumes; there are also newspapers specializing in bringing and evaluating news relevant to investments, and reports from financial intermediaries who engage in estimating the prospects of corporations.

These channels are efficient in that information spreads rapidly, and each new piece of information quickly becomes public property. Because shares are both divisible and liquid, investors are able to react very quickly to perceived changes in the value of any company. This information-induced buying and selling affects the market price to the point where the price quickly corresponds to value again. Thus, information is rapidly discounted into the market price.

It thereby becomes very difficult for any individual investor to find a stock that is not priced correctly. In fact, it is hypothesized that the capital markets are very close to what is called an *efficient market*. In an efficient market, each common stock is, at any moment, priced fairly with respect to its value. This premise will be referred to as the *efficient market hypothesis*.

While it is very difficult to decide once and for all through empirical tests whether the capital markets are efficient, most empirical studies suggest that the principle of efficiency holds very closely. Only rarely does the performance record of an investor show results that can confidently be attributed to stock selection skill. More often than not, superior performances can be attributed to investors having systematically taken high risk (since the expected return on a high-risk portfolio exceeds the expected return of a market index).

In an efficient market, all currently available information about future prices is discounted in today's price. If the price were confidently expected to advance tomorrow by 10 percent, investors would buy the stock until that 10 percent expectation is arbitraged out of today's price. Hence tomorrow's expected price change is thereby reduced to zero. In this process of discounting information, today's price becomes an unbiased estimate of tomorrow's price. Strictly speaking, of course, this statement needs refinement, since the market exhibits a positive long-term trend. The principle of efficiency therefore asserts that today's price is an unbiased estimate of tomorrow's price, discounted by the expected long-term growth.

The process described in the preceding paragraph is called a *martingale*. Such a process implies that all information about future prices is already impounded in the current price. A special case of a martingale, with an additional assumption of independent distribution of price changes, is the well-known and frequently misunderstood random walk process.

The term *random walk* is often misinterpreted as implying that price changes "randomly," that is, by chance alone and without any causal reasons. This is not what the efficient market hypothesis states. Prices change because the characteristics and prospects of the company or the general economy change, and because investors' perception and evaluation of these characteristics and prospects change. In other words, an investor's knowledge evolves with the continuous supply of new information and with the revision of old information. What the efficient market hypothesis does state, however, is that at any given moment in time, the next period price change is random with respect to the state of knowledge at this moment. Moreover, the hypothesis of efficiency asserts that the current price fully reflects the present state of knowledge in the sense that it is equal to the (discounted) mean value of the distribution of the next period price as given by the present state of knowledge.

To summarize, under the efficient market hypothesis all the information available at any given moment is discounted into the current market price. The market price at any moment is an unbiased estimate of the next period price. In an efficient market, no investor can expect consistently to obtain information not already discounted into the market price by actions of other investors. Consequently, no investor can consistently achieve abnormal returns (i.e., returns in excess of that paid for risk taking, as discussed later in this chapter). In an efficient market, benefits from security analysis cannot be expected to exceed the costs of trading.

Since most of the discussion thus far has dealt with price changes, a word about the role of dividends is in order. Capital market theory deals with total rates of return, generally without distinction between the capital appreciation component and the component due to dividend income. Empirical studies by Black and Scholes (1970) have established that, while for a taxpaying investor it may be important whether the return on his investment comes in the form of dividend or capital gains, it makes no difference for the equilibrium of the market as a whole.

The next two sections will deal with the Capital Asset Pricing Model. In these sections, it will be assumed that the (total) rates of return over nonoverlapping periods are independently distributed random variables, and that each investor tries to maximize his expected rate of return subject to consideration of risk, without regard to whether the rate of return is composed of dividends or of capital gains. The assumption here that investors are indifferent between capital gains and dividends is not a realistic assumption when the component returns are taxed differently. The usefulness of this assumption is only to simplify the analysis, and the conclusions reached are, in fact, affected unimportantly.

THE ROLE OF THE PORTFOLIO IN RISK REDUCTION

It is intuitively obvious that "risk" of the volatility of future returns can be reduced by diversifying into several stocks rather than investing one's total wealth in a single stock. Let us, however, characterize this diversification phenomenon quantitatively.

Consider two different common stocks. Assume for simplicity that they both have the same expected rate of return, E. If a part of the wealth available for investment, call it x_1, is allocated to one stock and the remaining part $x_2 = 1 - x_1$ is invested in another, the expected rate of return, E_P, on this two-issue portfolio is a weighted average of the two expected returns, or

$$E_P = x_1 E + x_2 E = E.$$

The expected return on the portfolio is thus equal to that of either stock, since we, of course, assumed them to be the same. The volatility of the two-issue portfolio, however, is less (as will be seen) than the volatility of either stock, if only we assume them to move together through time imperfectly.

According to a theorem in statistics, the variance V_P of the portfolio is computed as:

$$V_P = x_1^2 V_1 + x_2^2 V_2 + 2x_1 x_2 C_{12}.$$

In this equation, V_1 and V_2 are variances of the two stocks, respectively; C_{12} is the covariance of their returns; and x_1, x_2 are their weights in the portfolio. The covariance term is crucial to the effect of diversification. If the two issues fluctuate in price independently of each other, then the covariance term is zero, and it is always possible to choose the relative proportions x_1, x_2 in such a way that the risk of the portfolio is smaller than that of either stock taken separately. This is due to the effect of squaring numbers less than one. For instance, when the volatility of both stocks is the same, $V_1 = V_2$, and the covariance is zero, the risk of a portfolio of equal investment in each stock is

$$V_P = (.5)^2 V_1 + (.5)^2 V_2 = .5 V_1.$$

Thus, the portfolio has a variance equal to only one half of the variance of either stock. Since the expected return on the portfolio is not reduced (i.e., as shown earlier, $E_P = E$), such a portfolio is clearly preferable to a single-issue portfolio for any investor who is averse to risk.

Typically, two stocks exhibit some positive co-movement; therefore, the covariance term cannot be realistically assumed to be zero. The reduction of risk in that case is not as large as if the two stocks were independent, but it always can be made smaller than the simple average risk of the two stocks. Hence, the amount of risk per unit of expected return can be decreased through diversification.

The foregoing illustration of a two-issue portfolio can be generalized to the case of any number of stocks in a portfolio. Assume for simplicity that the proportion of each of the *n* stocks in a portfolio is kept equal. Empirical studies conducted by Lorie and Fisher (1970) show the following relative risk reduction: If the average risk level of a single typical common stock is taken as the basis, the percentage reduction of risk for randomly selected portfolios with approximately the same expected return depends upon the number of issues as follows:

Number of Issues	Relative Risk with Respect to Average Stock
1	100%
2	81
8	64
16	60
32	59
128	57
510	57

Thus, diversification can provide a substantial reduction of risk. By diversifying funds among a large number of issues, the chances of heavy losses are lowered, since a price decline in some stocks is likely to be offset by price appreciation of others.

Common stocks are usually positively correlated with each other, and it is thereby not possible to eliminate variance completely. A down movement of a set of stocks in a portfolio will be only partly compensated by an up movement of some other stocks in the portfolio. There is, therefore, a part of the total variance of the portfolio that is due to the positive covariance between stocks and can never be eliminated by diversification. This part is called the *systematic risk* and will be dealt with in more detail in the next section.

Let us now investigate more thoroughly the impact of diversification on the expected return of the portfolio. Suppose an investor wants to maximize his expected rate of return but does not want to accept more than a particular risk level, call it V_0. His unwillingness to take more risk might, for instance, be attributable to the fact that the investor wants to keep the chances of failing to meet certain expected financial obligations below a particular level. Of all possible combinations of all stocks in various proportions that have the risk level of V_0, there will be one particular combination that has the highest expected return. This combination represents the optimal portfolio for that investor, since it is superior to all other portfolios of the same risk.

This portfolio can be constructed by means of so-called quadratic programming, provided all the prerequisite estimates of expected returns, variables, and covariances can be obtained. While it is difficult (and expensive) in practice to obtain the exact solution to this problem, due to the large number of stocks involved, there are methods that lead to a portfolio reasonably close to the optimal portfolio.

There will be a portfolio with maximal expected return for each different risk level. These portfolios are called efficient portfolios. The set of efficient portfolios, or the *efficient frontier*, as it is sometimes called, is a set of portfolios superior to all other portfolios. They are superior since, for each level of risk, there is no other portfolio with higher expected return. It is also possible, and often useful, to refer to efficient portfolios as those portfolios possessing minimum risk for a given level of expected return.

An investor's choice of a portfolio from the efficient frontier is a matter of finding a suitable tradeoff between expected return and risk. This choice depends on the investor's consumption, fixed obligations, time horizon, and other factors (which can be, at least for theoretical purposes, summarized in a so-called "utility function"). Whatever these factors might be, a rational risk-averse investor will select an investment portfolio that is at, or close to, the efficient frontier.

From what has been discussed, it should be apparent that the expected rate of return on portfolios on the efficient frontier increases with increasing risk. This is in agreement with the principle of risk compensation, as mentioned before. In the next section, this principle will be formulated quantitatively in the context of the efficient market model.

THE CAPITAL ASSET PRICING MODEL

The Capital Asset Pricing Model, or efficient market model, is usually derived under the assumption that there exists a riskless asset available for investment. The future return on this asset is not subject to uncertain fluctuations. It yields, therefore, a constant rate, R_F, called the risk-free rate. It is assumed, further, that any investor can borrow or lend as much as he desires at the risk-free rate. The assumption of unlimited borrowing at the risk-free rate has been properly viewed as unrealistic. In the next section, a generalized form of the efficient market model will be discussed, with this assumption relaxed. For the purposes of the present discussion, however, it will be retained.

In addition, two more assumptions will be made: First, that each investor is risk-averse; given his requirements in terms of expected wealth at the end of a period, each investor attempts to minimize the variance of his wealth at the end of the period. Second, that this period is the same for all investors, and all investors agree about the *distribution* of the end-of-period asset values. While the realism of the last assumption can again be disputed, it is important to note that it is not basically necessary to the model (cf. Lintner (1969)).

When an investor allocates part of his funds to the riskless asset and the remaining part to a portfolio of common stocks, the expected return on such holdings will be an average of the expected return on the (risky) common stock portfolio ER_P, and the risk-free rate R_F, weighted proportionally to the relative allocation. This can be expressed as

$$ER = xR_F + (1 - x)ER_P$$

where x is the proportion of money invested at the risk-free rate, and ER is the expected rate of return on the total holdings. Since the variance of the risk-free asset is (by definition) zero, the variance V of the total holding is

$$V = (1 - x)^2 V_P$$

where V_P is the variance of the risky assets. Expressed in terms of standard deviations, this same relation is linear:

$$S = (1 - x)S_P.$$

If an investor borrows some money at the risk-free rate R_F, the equations for ER and S will both still apply, with x now being a negative quantity expressing the proportion of borrowings to the investor's equity. Both the cases of lending and borrowing at the risk-free rate can be described as follows:

1. The expected rate of return in excess of the risk-free rate R_F (the *excess return*) is proportional to the expected excess return on the common stock portfolio,

$$ER - R_F = (1 - x)(ER_P - R_F).$$

2. The risk (in terms of standard deviation) is proportional to the risk of the common stock portfolio,

$$S = (1 - x)S_P.$$

These equations show that both expected return and risk are linear functions of the proportion x invested at the risk-free rate: If plotted in a coordinate system with expected return on the vertical axis and standard deviation on the horizontal axis (return-risk coordinates), the set of combinations of riskless asset and a common stock portfolio will be represented by a straight line with intercept equal to the risk-free rate.

Figure 22.1 gives a graphical representation of this relationship. The darkened area represents all possible portfolios of common stocks plotted in terms of their risk and return. The upper boundary of this set consists of portfolios with maximum expected return for a given level of risk, and is therefore the efficient frontier. The riskless asset, which has no risk, is represented by the point R_F on the vertical axis. Any combination of a common stock portfolio (point P) and the riskless asset is situated on a straight line determined by these two points (line R_FP). On this line, the points that fall

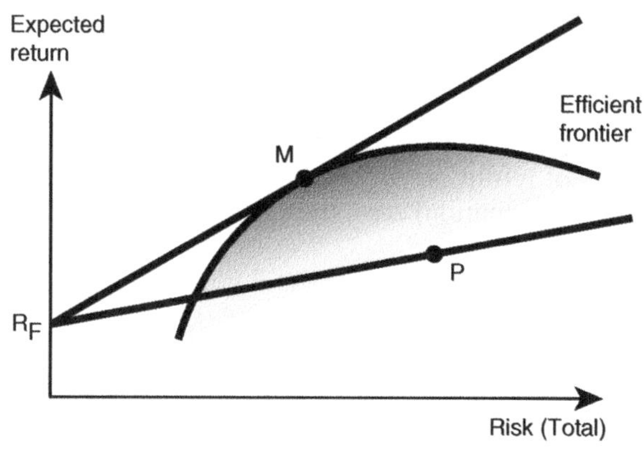

FIGURE 22.1

between R_F and P are alternative portfolios, each of which consists of some lending at the risk-free rate; portfolios which consist of some borrowing (at risk-free rate and investing in portfolio P) are depicted on this line to the right of point P.

Any straight line going through the risk-free rate and a point at or below the efficient frontier represents an available set of investment opportunities. Since these lines differ only in slope, it is clear that there is one of them, namely the line tangential to the efficient frontier (line R_FM in Figure 22.1), with investment opportunities that dominate all the efficient frontier portfolios. That is, every point on the line segment R_FM lies above the efficient frontier and therefore represents investment opportunities with superior expected returns for each level of risk.

Thus, when the riskless asset is available for borrowing and lending, optimal investment opportunities are described as combinations of the risk-free asset and one particular portfolio of common stocks (point M in Figure 22.1). An investor who wants to take a relatively low-risk position would allocate his assets between the riskless asset and the risky portfolio M. An investor wishing to take more risk (with increased expectation of return, of course) will borrow at the risk-free rate and invest all available funds in the risky portfolio M.

This analysis therefore leads to the conclusion that the equity holdings of all investors should consist of a share of the *same* portfolio of common stocks, namely the one lying at point M on the efficient frontier. Thus, the selection of the risk level can be separated from the problem of an optimal combination of risky securities. This important result is known as the separation theorem, first attributed to Tobin (1958). The crucial conclusion thereby suggested is that every investor must resolve what risk level he is willing to assume, but need not select particular stocks nor be concerned with combining them into a portfolio.

If every investor's equity holdings are made up of a part of the same portfolio, it follows that this portfolio comprises all the shares outstanding of all the common stocks in the market. This portfolio is called the *market portfolio*. The separation theorem can therefore be stated as: Every investor should hold a combination of the riskless asset and the market portfolio.

Thus, point M in Figure 22.1 is the market portfolio. The line R_FM, which represents the dominant investment opportunities, is called the *capital market line*. Since the line goes through the point of the market portfolio's expected return ER_M and its risk S_M, the equation of the capital market line is

$$ER - R_F = \frac{ER_M - R_F}{S_M} \cdot S \qquad (1)$$

where ER and S are the expected rate of return and standard deviation, respectively, of any particular portfolio on the capital market line.

This equation expresses quantitatively the principle of risk compensation. In words, it can be stated: For a portfolio on the capital market line, the expected rate of return in excess of the risk-free rate is proportional to the risk of that portfolio.

The constant of proportionality

$$\frac{ER_M - R_F}{S_M},$$

which represents the slope of the capital market line, is called the *market price of risk*. The price that one pays for his expected return is measured in risk, and hence the name "market price of risk." Thus expected return in excess of R_F is given by the amount of risk taken, multiplied by the market price of risk.

Individual stocks and imperfectly diversified portfolios will all fall below the capital market line, thus demonstrating that the market does not compensate for unnecessary risk—that is, for risk that can be diversified away. To give exact meaning to this statement, it is necessary to define what is meant by unnecessary risk. For this purpose, it is useful to return to the earlier discussion about the efficient frontier.

It has been seen that the market portfolio is the tangent point of the efficient frontier with the line of highest slope in Figure 22.1. Now, it can be shown (with the help of some complicated mathematical techniques) that this tangent-point portfolio must be such that the covariance of return on every security with this portfolio is proportional to the expected return on that security (in excess of the risk-free rate).[2] The expected rate of return ER_i for security i must fulfill the equation

$$ER_i - R_F = K.C_{iM}. \tag{2}$$

Here C_{iM} is the covariance of security i with the market portfolio, and K is a constant of proportionality. When combining securities into a portfolio, the expected return on the portfolio is equal to a weighted average of expected returns of individual securities, and similarly, the covariance of the portfolio with the market is a weighted average of the covariances of individual securities with the market portfolio. Consequently, the equation above holds for any portfolio as well as every individual stock. In particular, it holds also for the market portfolio, of which we must have

$$ER_M - R_F = K.S^2{}_M,$$

[2]To provide a proof of this statement is beyond the scope of this paper. It can be found, for instance, in the Sharpe book (1970), Chapter 5.

since the covariance of the market portfolio with itself is just the variance of the market.

The last equation allows us to identify this constant of proportionality:

$$K = \frac{ER_{\mathrm{M}} - R_{\mathrm{F}}}{S_{\mathrm{M}}^2}.$$

Then, upon substituting for K into Eq. (2), the following relation emerges:

$$ER - R_F = \frac{ER_{\mathrm{M}} - R_{\mathrm{F}}}{S_{\mathrm{M}}} \cdot C_{\mathrm{iM}}. \tag{3}$$

We can now compare Eq. (3), which holds for *any* security or portfolio, with Eq. (1), which holds only for the portfolios on the capital market line. It is seen that for portfolios *below* the capital market line, the market price of risk rewards only part of the total risk. The only part of the total risk-taking that has expected rate of return (reward) associated with it is the part:

$$\frac{C_{\mathrm{iM}}}{S_{\mathrm{M}}}.$$

This is the part of the total risk that is due to the covariance of that portfolio with the market portfolio. This part of the total risk is called the *systematic risk*.

The systematic risk $C_{\mathrm{iM}}/S_{\mathrm{M}}$ never exceeds the total risk S_{i}. In fact, it is smaller than the total risk for all portfolios that are not on the capital market line. But for the efficient portfolios on the capital market line, the systematic risk is equal to the total risk and, consequently, *all* the risk of these portfolios is rewarded.

The portfolios whose risk consists of the systematic risk only (portfolios on the capital market line) are called *perfectly diversified* portfolios. Those portfolios whose total risk is composed of systematic risk and some additional specific risk are imperfectly diversified. These are, of course, the portfolios that lie below the capital market line.

To summarize, the total risk of a security or of a portfolio is composed of two parts: the systematic risk, which is due to the covariance of that security or portfolio to the market, and the specific risk, which is due to any volatility of the security or portfolio that is independent of market fluctuations. The market price of risk rewards investors only for the systematic risk they assume; no compensation is paid for bearing specific risk. The expected rate of return on a portfolio or single security is, then, solely a function of the systematic risk; the higher the systematic risk, the higher the expected return.

Some portfolios, namely those on the capital market line, are perfectly correlated with the market portfolio and have no specific risk. Consequently, risk compensation applies to the total risk of such portfolios, and they represent investment opportunities superior to all other combinations of assets. These are the perfectly diversified portfolios.

The reason why only the systematic risk is compensated by appropriately higher expected return is that the systematic risk cannot be reduced by diversification, while the specific risk generally can. Specific risk can generally be reduced by diversification because it arises from fluctuations in the security price peculiar to that individual company, rather than from fluctuations in response to general market fluctuations.

Eq. (3) can be rewritten in a perhaps more familiar form:

$$ER_i - R_F = \frac{C_{iM}}{S^2{}_M}(ER_M - R_F).$$

Those familiar with least squares regression analysis will note at once that the term C_{iM} / S_M^2 is the slope coefficient in the regression of the security's rate of return on the market rate of return. This coefficient is customarily denoted by β_i and referred to as *beta* of that security. Since

$$\beta_i = \frac{C_{iM}}{S^2{}_M} = \left(\frac{C_{iM}}{S_M}\right) / S_M,$$

it is seen that beta of a security is merely its systematic risk expressed in units of market risk. For portfolios, beta is defined similarly as the covariance of that portfolio with the market, divided by the variance of the market portfolio itself. Since beta of the market portfolio is 1.0, beta is a suitable measure of *relative* riskiness. Portfolios whose betas are less than one have less systematic risk than the market as a whole; while those with betas greater than one have higher systematic risk.

Introducing β_i into Eq. (3), the following relation is obtained:

$$ER_i - R_F = \beta_i(ER_M - R_F). \tag{4}$$

When this equation is plotted in expected return/beta coordinates, it will yield a straight line (line R_FM in Figure 22.2). This line is called the *security market line*. It is determined by the risk-free rate (where $\beta = 0$) and the market expected rate of return ER_M for $\beta = 1$. Since beta is a measure of systematic risk only, *all* securities and *all* portfolios will be plotted along this line. This distinguishes the security market line from the capital market line, which depicts perfectly diversified portfolios only.

Eq. (4) represents one of the most important results of the Capital Asset Pricing Model. It states that expected rate of return of any security or

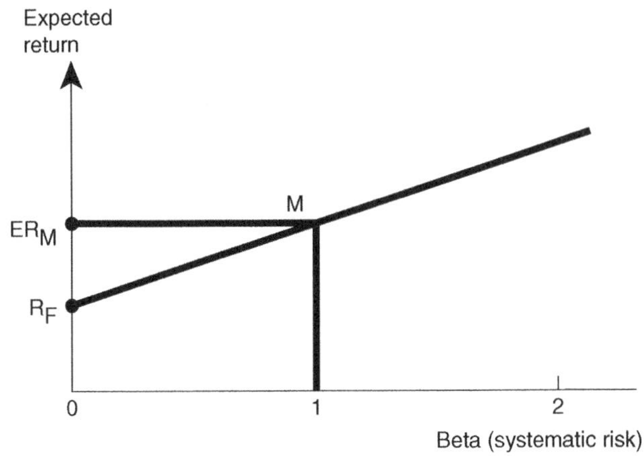

FIGURE 22.2

portfolio is determined solely by the beta of that security or portfolio, thus promoting beta to the most important single characteristic of any security or portfolio. In addition, betas are easy to estimate through regression analysis, and consequently play a central role in portfolio construction and analysis.

Beta was defined as the *systematic risk*; the return whose expectation is defined by Eq. (4) can appropriately be named *systematic return*. If the market advances 10 percent during a period, a stock with beta of 2 will, on average, appreciate by 20 percent. Similarly, a market decline of 10 percent will cause the stock to drop 20 percent on average. On the other hand, stocks with beta of 0.5 will reflect market movements with a magnitude of only one half as large. For this reason, betas are sometimes called *market sensitivities*.

The difference between the total price movement of a stock and the component explained by the market movement multiplied by beta, is what we call the "specific risk."

No applications of the Capital Asset Pricing Model to portfolio selection and management will be discussed in this paper. The reader interested in practical implications of the theory is referred to Wagner (1971).

GENERALIZATION OF THE MODEL

The principal conclusions of the capital asset pricing model previously developed are as follows:

1. In an efficient market, every investor should be expected to hold a combination of the riskless asset and the market portfolio. Such combinations

of assets dominate any other alternatives in the sense that they are subject to less risk for the same level of expected return. The proportions to be invested in the riskless asset and in the market portfolio depend solely on each investor's tradeoff of risk and expected return.

2. In an efficient market, the expected return on each stock in excess of the risk-free rate is related only to its beta. A stock with a beta twice as high as another stock exhibits twice as high an expected excess return. The relationship of the expected excess return on all stocks with their betas is called the security market line. Mathematically, the relationship for any stock is described by:

$$ER - R_F = \beta(ER_M - R_F). \tag{5}$$

The first of these two conclusions represents a *normative* rule; that is, it describes how a rational investor *should* behave in an efficient market. As such, it is not subject to direct empirical validation. The second conclusion, however, is of a *descriptive* nature; it predicts how an efficient market *would* appear if the assumptions of the model are fulfilled. The latter can therefore be tested empirically.

Of the studies that deal with empirical validation of the efficient market model, the work by Black, Jensen, and Scholes (1970) warrants attention for its rigorous character.[3] The principal conclusion of this study is that while the relationship between expected excess return of a stock or portfolio and its systematic risk is linear, it is not directly proportional. Rather, the empirical security market line exhibits a positive intercept, and a slope that is flatter than that is predicted by Eq. (5). The empirically observed market line appears to conform to a model of the form

$$ER - R_F = \gamma + \beta(ER_M - R_F - \gamma) \tag{6}$$

where γ is a positive quantity.

In intuitive terms, the observed relation (6) can be stated as follows: If the *expost* excess rates of return on a stock are regressed against the market excess rates of return in a simple regression model

$$R - R_F = \alpha + \beta(ER_M - R_F) + e, \tag{7}$$

estimates of the regression coefficients α, β can be obtained. The estimate of β is an estimate of the systematic risk (beta) as introduced in the previous

[3]There still can be some reservations with respect to accepting the empirical results of this study; the most important objection is that an equal weighted market index is employed there, rather than the theoretically justified value weighted index.

section. The regression coefficient α can be called the *abnormal return*, or simply *alpha*. It is the additional rate of return left after the stock's rate of return is adjusted for its systematic risk by subtracting the factor $\beta(R_M - R_F)$ from the total excess return.

Now, the simpler model (Eq. (5)) asserts that there should be no expected abnormal returns, or, more specifically, that

$$\alpha = 0.$$

This implication can be seen by comparing Eqs. (5) and (7), bearing in mind that the expected value of the error term in the regression (e in Eq. (7)) is zero by design. However, in reality, we observe that

$$\alpha = \gamma(1 - \beta), \tag{8}$$

which can be seen when Eqs. (6) and (7) are compared.

Thus, empirical measurements imply that stocks (and portfolios) with systematic risk (beta) lower than that of the market portfolio exhibit a positive abnormal return, whereas stocks and portfolios with betas higher than that of the market show negative abnormal returns. That is, high-risk stocks are observed to return less than what is predicted by the simple theory, and the converse for low-risk stocks. Moreover, the lower the beta, the higher the alpha, and conversely. This empirical result is sometimes called the *alpha effect*.

Thus, the actual behavior of capital markets differs in an important aspect from that predicted by the simple efficient market model described in the section "The Capital Asset Pricing Model." This, of course, casts some doubt on the validity of the assumptions on which this model is based. One questionable assumption is that each investor is able to borrow without limitation at a rate equal to the rate on the riskless asset. This, we know, does not correspond to actual behavior. Generally, borrowers pay more than the risk-free rate R_F. The question then naturally arises as to whether removing the unrealistic assumption of unlimited borrowing at the risk-free rate would produce a model that is in better agreement with empirical data than the Capital Asset Pricing Model.

Black (1972) investigated the market equilibrium under the assumption that there is no riskless asset, thereby preventing both borrowing at a risk-free rate and investing at a risk-free rate. Black has shown that ideally every investor holds a linear combination of the market portfolio and another portfolio that, though risky, possesses no market risk. This latter portfolio, which is called the *zero-beta portfolio,* is composed of long and short holdings in risky assets in such proportions that the systematic risk, or beta, of this portfolio is zero. The zero-beta portfolio (which, taken alone is not even an efficient portfolio in the sense developed previously in this chapter), takes on the general role previously played by the riskless asset in the Capital Asset Pricing Model. The expected rate of return on a security is still a linear function of the security's beta. The intercept of this relationship is the expected rate of return on the zero-beta portfolio. The security market line can thus be described by the equation

$$ER = ER_Z + \beta(ER_M - R_Z) \tag{9}$$

where ER_Z is the expected rate of return on the zero-beta portfolio. It is seen that this equilibrium equation is of the form of Eq. (6), and therefore consistent with the empirical results.

Vasicek (1971) dealt with the case when the riskless asset is available for investment, but investors cannot borrow at the risk-free rate. These assumptions correspond better to actual capital markets. This model is again based on each investor's minimizing the risk he assumes, while meeting his requirements in terms of expected return. Vasicek has shown that there exists a portfolio, called the *tangent portfolio,* which has the following properties: Every investor whose expected return requirements do not exceed the tangent portfolio's expected return, invests part of his assets into the riskless asset and the remaining part into the tangent portfolio. An investor with higher return requirements (which of course means taking more risk) will hold a combination of the tangent portfolio and the market portfolio.

The set of efficient portfolios is therefore composed of two parts: The first part consists of all combinations of the riskless asset and the tangent portfolio. The second part comprises all combinations of the tangent portfolio and a long position in the market portfolio. To select a portfolio satisfying his requirements, an investor can therefore separate the task of identifying suitable combinations of risky assets from the selection of risk level. The result can again be called the separation theorem.

The tangent portfolio itself is an efficient portfolio. It is a linear combination of the zero-beta portfolio and the market portfolio. Vasicek has shown that the tangent portfolio is that combination of assets with the highest expected excess return to standard deviation ratio of all combinations of risky assets.

In this model, the security market line is given by Eq. (9). Moreover, it is shown that the expected rate of return on the zero-beta portfolio is not smaller than the risk-free rate R_F,

$$ER_Z \geq R_F.$$

Since the constant γ in Eq. (8) is equal to $ER_Z - R_F$ (as is readily seen by comparing Eqs. (6), (7), and (9)), it follows that

$$\gamma \geq 0$$

and therefore, the possible existence of the alpha effect is admissible in the generalized efficient market model, providing substantially better correspondence between the theoretical model and empirical tests.

This generalized capital asset pricing model then permits replacement of the two propositions at the beginning of this section by the following two:

1. In an efficient market, each investor holds either a combination of the riskless asset and the tangent portfolio, or a combination of the tangent portfolio and long holdings in the market portfolio. The choice between the two alternatives, and within each alternative, depends solely on the investor's attitude towards risk and expected return.
2. In an efficient market, the expected excess rate of return on each security or portfolio is linearly related to the systematic risk, or beta, of that security. The intercept of the security market line is equal to the expected excess return on the zero-beta portfolio, and is non-negative. The generalized model thus takes the form

$$ER_i - R_F = ER_Z - R_F + \beta_i \ (ER_M - R_F).$$

The abnormal return α is related to beta by the relationship

$$\alpha_i = (ER_Z - R_F) \ (1 - \beta_i).$$

Thus, stocks or portfolios with low betas may have positive alphas, and stocks or portfolios with high betas may have negative alphas. But since alphas also may be zero, as well as positive, the efficient market model discussed in this chapter is a special case of the more generalized efficient market model.

The descriptive aspect of this generalized efficient market model, as summarized in the second point, is consistent with empirical results. While the normative aspect of the first point is not necessarily met by all investors, it may be noted that it still corresponds reasonably well to the actual behavior of large institutional investors. Those investors who exhibit strong risk aversion often hold a combination of riskless assets and a low to medium risk portfolio of common stocks. The equity portion of their holdings can be interpreted as an attempt to obtain the tangent portfolio. With increased total risk, the riskless portion decreases and the risky part increases, probably without a considerable shift in the composition of the equity portion.

Holdings of investors with even higher risk are often characterized by no riskless asset, while a portfolio of more risky common stocks is held in various proportions to the low-risk part.

In conclusion, it has been argued in this section that the capital asset pricing model can be generalized to correspond better to empirical observations by making the assumptions of the model more realistic. In particular, the possible existence of the alpha effect can be derived from the generalized model. While the more generalized models in this section certainly are not the final word in the theory of capital markets, the ability of the efficient market model to be generalized in various directions demonstrates the viability of the simplest form of the model.

CONCLUSION

The concluding remarks can appropriately contain some "so-what?" overtones, provided the reader is forewarned that we present these speculations without much support. We have, in fact, decided to exclude specific references to supporting materials since concluding remarks are hardly the appropriate point to introduce new evidence—especially since we have attempted, in this paper, to deal only with the concepts of the efficient market models and not with their empirical support. Having offered this warning, we now proceed to what we think are some plausible assertions.

If the efficient market model is to be applicable to *real* capital markets, and not idealized ones, it must be able to explain actual observed price changes. The beta coefficient in the model has been estimated by numerous investigators and found to be usefully stable and to be related in the predicted way to rate of return: the higher the beta, the higher the observed rate of return. This fact alone is sufficient to place the efficient market model in that rare class of theories that can be usefully employed. Given this fact, one may also expect that the efficient market model will be put to work in numerous ways (as, indeed, it has been) by practicing investors.

The efficient market model was developed under some simplifying assumptions concerning zero transactions costs and rapid information dissemination. However, the empirical findings to date tend to conform to the implications of the model, suggesting that these assumptions may be relaxed. Actually, it has been shown that the basic conclusions of the model hold under much more general assumptions—adding further confirmation to the empirical evidence. Thus, the reader should be cautious about rejecting the efficient market model for what he may correctively perceive to be unrealistic assumptions in the simplified model presented here.

The efficient market model is seen to be elegantly simple by many who have thoughtfully studied it. Less careful appraisals may tend to precipitate the view that a model containing considerably more variables is still waiting to be "discovered." The present model, it may be argued, does not take certain obvious effects into consideration—such as market ability, industry, management, foreign competition, and government policies. Still, the model works remarkably well—suggesting that these effects do get imbedded in prices, the behavior of which empirical studies find to be so efficient. The model is, we assert, much richer than its simplicity may suggest.

The thoughtful investor may find it profitable to ask himself: "Unless I know the beta of my portfolio, what evidence do I have that the returns are not systematic, rather than specific, returns? And if they are indeed specific returns, what assurance do I have that the portfolio has earned them consistently enough to justify the extra risk incurred in departing from perfect diversification?"

REFERENCES

Black, F. (1972). "Capital Market Equilibrium with Restricted Borrowing." *Journal of Business*, 45 (3) (July), 444–455.

Black, F., M.C. Jensen, and M. Scholes. (1972). "The Capital Asset Pricing Model: Some Empirical Tests." In Michael C. Jensen, ed., *Studies in the Theory of Capital Markets*. New York: Praeger Publishing Co.

Black, F., and M. Scholes. (1970). "Dividend Yields and Common Stock Returns: A New Methodology." *Proceedings of the Seminar on the Analysis of Security Prices*, U. of Chicago (November).

Blume, M. (1971). "On the Assessment of Risk." *Journal of Finance*, 26 (1) (March), 1–10.

Brealey, R.A. (1969). *An Introduction to Risk and Return from Common Stocks*. Cambridge, MA: M.I.T. Press.

Fama, E. (1971). "Risk, Return, and Equilibrium." *Journal of Political Economy*, 79 (1) (January/February), 30–55.

Jensen, M.C. (1971). "The Foundations and Current State of Capital Market Theory." *Studies in the Theory of Capital Markets*. New York: Praeger Publishers.

King, B.F. (1966). "Market and Industry Factors in Stock Price Behavior." *Journal of Business*, 39 (January), 139–190.

Lintner, J. (1965). "The Valuation of Risk Assets and the Selection of Risky Investments in Stock Portfolios and Capital Budgets." *Review of Economics and Statistics*, 47 (1) (February), 13–37.

Lintner, J. (1969). "The Aggregation of Investors' Diverse Judgment and Preferences in Perfectly Competitive Security Markets." *Journal of Finance and Quantitative Analysis* (December), 347–400.

Lorie, J.H., and L. Fisher. (1970). "Some Studies of Variability of Returns on Investment in Common Stocks." *Journal of Business*, 43 (2) (April), 99–134.

Miller, M.H., and M. Scholes. (1970). "Rates of Return in Relation to Risk: A Reexamination of Some Recent Findings." *Unpublished memorandum* (July).

Mossin, J. (1966). "Equilibrium in a Capital Asset Market." *Econometrica* (October), 768–83.

Sharpe, W.F. "Capital Asset Prices: A Theory of Market Equilibrium Under Conditions of Risk." *Journal of Finance* (September), 425–442.

Sharpe, W.F. (1970). *Portfolio Theory and Capital Markets*. New York: McGraw-Hill.

Tobin, J. (1958). "Liquidity Preference as Behavior Toward Risk." *Review of Economic Studies*, 25 (1) (February), 65–86.

Treynor, J. (1961). "Toward a Theory of Market Value of Risky Assets." Unpublished memorandum.

Vasicek, O.A. (1971). "Capital Asset Pricing Model with No Riskless Borrowing." Unpublished memorandum, Wells Fargo Bank (March).

Wagner, W.H. (1971). "Modern Portfolio Management Systems." Unpublished memorandum (February).

CHAPTER 23

A Risk Minimizing Strategy for Portfolio Immunization

By H. Gifford Fong and Oldrich A. Vasicek

ABSTRACT

Consider a fixed-income portfolio whose duration is equal to the length of a given investment horizon. It is shown that there is a lower limit on the change in the end-of-horizon value of the portfolio resulting from any given change in the structure of interest rates. This lower limit is the product of two terms, of which one is a function of the interest rate change only and the other depends only on the structure of the portfolio. Consequently, this second term provides a measure of immunization risk. If this measure is minimized, the exposure of the portfolio to any interest rate change is the lowest.

INTRODUCTION

The traditional theory of immunization as formalized by Fisher and Weil (1971) defines the conditions under which the value of an investment in a bond portfolio is protected against changes in the level of interest rates. The specific assumptions of this theory are that the portfolio is valued at a fixed horizon date, that there are no cash inflows or outflows within the horizon, and that interest rates change only by a parallel shift in the forward rates. Under these assumptions, a portfolio is said to be immunized if its value at the end of the horizon does not fall below the target value, where the

Journal of Finance 39, No. 5, 1541–1546, 1984.

target value is defined as the portfolio value at the horizon date under the scenario of no change in the forward rates. The main result of this theory is that immunization is achieved if the duration of the portfolio is equal to the length of the horizon.

The assumption that interest rates can only change by a parallel shift (that is, by the same amount for all maturities) has been the subject of considerable concern. Bierwag (1977; 1978), Bierwag and Kaufman (1977), Khang (1979), and others have postulated alternative models of interest rate behaviors. Each of these specifications implies a different measure of duration, with immunization attained if this duration measure is equal to the horizon length. A limitation of this approach is that the portfolio is protected only against the particular type of interest rate change assumed.

In a more recent development, Cox et al. (1979), Brennan and Schwartz (1981), and others have investigated immunization conditions when interest rates are governed by a continuous process consistent with a market equilibrium. Depending on the specification of the interest rate process, there is a duration-like measure (possibly multidimensional, as in Brennan and Schwartz) such that the portfolio is immunized if a proper value of this measure is maintained. This assumes a continuous rebalancing of the portfolio. Again, immunization is achieved only if interest rate changes conform to the specific process assumed.

In this chapter, we wish to pursue a different approach. If it turned out that the portfolio exposure to an *arbitrary* type of interest rate change were determined by some characteristic of the portfolio, then this characteristic could be considered a measure of immunization risk. By minimizing this risk measure, the portfolio could be structured to have as little vulnerability as possible to any interest rate movement.

It is shown in this chapter that there is a lower limit on the change in the end-of-horizon value of an immunized portfolio for an arbitrary interest rate change. This lower limit is a product of two terms. One of these terms depends only on the type and magnitude of the rate change, while the other term depends solely on the structure of the portfolio. This second term provides the desired measure of immunization risk, since, when it is small, the exposure of the portfolio to any interest rate change is small.

As in Fisher and Weil, we will consider interest rate shocks of finite magnitude, rather than infinitesimal rate changes with continuous portfolio rebalancing. This appears to be a more relevant approach for applications, since in practice rates will always move by a noninfinitesimal amount before the portfolio can be restructured.

The main result is stated in the form of a theorem in the next section, followed by a discussion of the concept. The mathematical proof of the theorem is given in the Appendix.

IMMUNIZATION RISK

Consider a portfolio at time $s_0 = 0$ to be immunized with respect to a given horizon H. Let $C_1, C_2, \ldots, C_m$ be the payments on the portfolio, due at times $s_1, s_2, \ldots, s_m$, and denote by I_0 the initial portfolio value,

$$I_0 = \sum_{j=1}^{m} C_j P_0(s_j). \tag{1}$$

Here $P_0(t)$ is the current discount function of term t. If $i(t)$ is the current forward rate of term $t, t \geq 0$, the discount function can be written as

$$P_0(t) = \exp\left(-\int_0^t i(\tau)\,\mathrm{d}\tau\right).$$

Let D be the Macaulay duration of the portfolio, defined as

$$D = \sum_{j=1}^{m} s_j C_j P_0(s_j)/I_0. \tag{2}$$

Define the target value I_H of the investment at the horizon date as the end-of-horizon value of the portfolio if the forward rates do not change,

$$I_H = I_0/P_0 H. \tag{3}$$

As shown by Fisher and Weil (1971), if the portfolio duration D is equal to the length of the horizon, the target value I_H is a lower bound of the terminal value of the portfolio regardless of any parallel shift in interest rates. If rates of different maturities change by different amounts, the I_H is not necessarily a lower bound on the end-of-horizon investment value. In order to establish a measure of immunization risk, we shall analyze the change in the terminal value of a given portfolio for a given (nonparallel) rate change.

The amount by which the terminal value of the portfolio may be short of the target, as a result of an interest rate change, will depend on the character and magnitude of the change as well as on the structure of the portfolio. The immunity of a portfolio to parallel rate changes is attained as a consequence of balancing the effect of changes in reinvestment rates on payments received during the horizon against the change in capital value of the portion of the portfolio still outstanding at the end of the horizon. For a nonparallel change in interest rates, such balancing may not take place. Consider the case when the change in short rates is algebraically less than the change in long rates (for example, short rates decline while long rates go up). Such a scenario, characterized by an increase in the slope of the interest rate structure, will result in a decline of the terminal portfolio value below the target. The larger the magnitude of such a twist of the yield curve, the bigger the resulting shortfall will be for a given portfolio.

Not all portfolios, however, will be affected by a given change equally. Consider a "barbell" portfolio composed of very short and very long bonds, and a "bullet" portfolio consisting of low-coupon securities with maturities close to the horizon date. Assume that both portfolios have durations equal to the horizon length. Should short rates go down and long rates go up, both portfolios will realize a decline in the end-of-horizon value, since they experience a capital loss in addition to lower reinvestment rates. The decline, however, would be substantially higher for the barbell portfolio for two reasons. First, the lower reinvestment rates are experienced on the barbell portfolio for longer time intervals than on the bullet portfolio, so that the opportunity loss is much greater. Second, the portion of the barbell portfolio still outstanding at the horizon date is much longer than that of the bullet portfolio, which means that the rate increase would result in a much steeper capital loss.

To characterize these arguments quantitatively, suppose that the forward rates change instantaneously from $i(t)$ to $i'(t) = i(t) + \Delta i(t)$, where $\Delta i(t)$ is an arbitrary function of the term t. Consider a portfolio whose duration is equal to the horizon length, and denote by ΔI_H the corresponding change in the portfolio value as of the horizon date. We will state the following theorem, a proof of which is given in the Appendix:

Theorem 1. Let K be an arbitrary constant. If $\mathrm{d}\Delta i(t)/\mathrm{d}t \le K$ for all $t \ge 0$, then

$$\Delta I_H / I_H \ge -{}^1\!/_2\, K \cdot M^2, \tag{4}$$

where

$$M^2 = \sum_{j=1}^{m} (s_j - H)^2 C_j P_0(s_j)/I_0. \tag{5}$$

The inequality in (4) provides a lower bound on the change in the terminal value of the portfolio. The theorem states that this lower bound is the product of two terms. The first term, $-{}^1\!/_2\, K$, is a function of the interest rate change only, while the second term, M^2, depends solely on the structure of the investment portfolio.

The quantity K can be interpreted as an upper bound, over maturity, on the *change in the slope of the term structure*. Note that the derivative $\mathrm{d}\Delta i(t)/\mathrm{d}t$ is with respect to the term, not time. In effect, this quantity characterizes the twist of the yield curve. Since the rate change can be arbitrary, the maximum slope change is an uncertain variable, outside the control of the investor.

The investor, however, can determine the portfolio composition and therefore the quantity M^2. This term, which is a multiplier of the unknown rate change, is a *measure of risk for an immunized portfolio*, since it determines the exposure of the portfolio to rate changes. The lower bound for the change in the end-of-horizon value of the investment as a result of an arbitrary rate change is proportional to M^2. Note that to justify M^2 as a measure of risk, no assumptions are necessary about the nature or dimensionality of the stochastic process that governs the behavior of the term structure of interest rates.

To gain insight into the meaning of the risk measure M^2, note the similarity in form of M^2 in Eq. (5) to the definition of duration in Eq. (2). While duration is a weighted *average* of time to payments on the portfolio, the weights being the present value of the payments, M^2 is a similarly weighted *variance* of time to payments around the horizon date. If the portfolio payments occur close to the end of the horizon, as with a portfolio of deep-discount bonds maturing close to the horizon date, M^2 is low. If the payments are widely dispersed in time, as with a portfolio consisting of very short bonds and very long bonds, M^2 is high. The theorem states that a low M^2 portfolio has less exposure to whatever the change in the interest rate structure may be than a high M^2 portfolio. An optimally immunized portfolio that has the minimum exposure to interest rate changes is obtained by minimizing the risk measure M^2, subject to the duration condition $D = H$ and any portfolio constraints. It may be noted that M^2 is linear in the portfolio weights, so that minimizing M^2 can be written as a linear program.

The risk measure M^2 is always nonnegative. It attains its lowest possible value of zero if and only if the portfolio consists of a single discount bond with maturity equal to the length of the horizon. This is indeed the perfectly immunized portfolio, since no interest rate change affects its end-of-horizon value. Any other portfolio is to some extent vulnerable to an adverse interest rate movement. The immunization risk M^2 in effect measures how much a given portfolio differs from this ideally immunized portfolio consisting of the single discount bond.

It may be pointed out that the previous theorem contains, as a special case, the main result of classical immunization theory. Indeed, for parallel shifts, we have

$$\frac{\mathrm{d}}{\mathrm{d}t}\Delta i(t) = 0$$

for all $t \geq 0$, which then implies $\Delta I_H \geq 0$ for any portfolio whose duration is equal to the horizon length.

APPENDIX: PROOF OF THE THEOREM

Suppose that forward rates change from $i(t)$ to $i'(t) = i(t) + \Delta i(t)$. The discount function then becomes

$$P_0'(t) = \exp\left(-\int_0^t i'(\tau)\,\mathrm{d}\tau\right)$$
$$= P_0(t)\exp\left(-\int_0^t \Delta i(\tau)\,\mathrm{d}\tau\right).$$

The change ΔI_H in the end-of-horizon value of the portfolio due to the change $\Delta i(t)$ in the forward rates is

$$\Delta I_H = \sum_{j=1}^{m} C_j P_0'(s_j)/P_0'(H) - \sum_{j=1}^{m} C_j P_0(s_j)/P_0(H)$$
$$= \sum_{j=1}^{m} C_j \exp\left(\int_{s_j}^{H} \Delta i(\tau)\,\mathrm{d}\tau\right) P_0(s_j)/P_0(H) - \sum_{j=1}^{m} C_j P_0(s_j)/P_0(H),$$

or

$$\Delta I_H = \sum_{j=1}^{m} f(s_j) C_j P_0(s_j)/P_0(H) - I_0/P_0(H), \tag{A1}$$

where

$$f(t) = \exp\left(\int_t^H \Delta i(\tau)\,\mathrm{d}\tau\right).$$

Let

$$g(t) = \frac{\mathrm{d}}{\mathrm{d}t}\Delta i(t).$$

Then

$$\Delta i(H) - \Delta i(\tau) = \int_\tau^H g(u)\mathrm{d}u$$

and

$$\int_t^H \Delta i(\tau)\mathrm{d}\tau = \Delta i(H)\cdot(H-t) - \int_t^H \mathrm{d}\tau \int_\tau^H g(u)\mathrm{d}u$$
$$= \Delta i(H)\cdot(H-t) - \int_t^H (u-t)g(u)\mathrm{d}u.$$

Assume that $g(t) \leq K$ for all $t \geq 0$. If $t \leq H$, then

$$\int_t^H (u-t)g(u)\mathrm{d}u \leq K \int_t^H (u-t)\mathrm{d}u = {}^1\!/\!_2 K(h-t)^2.$$

If $t > H$, then

$$\int_t^H (u-t)g(u)\mathrm{d}u = \int_H^t (t-u)g(u)\mathrm{d}u \leq K \int_H^t (t-u)\mathrm{d}u = {}^1\!/\!_2\, K(h-t)^2.$$

Therefore,

$$\int_t^H (u-t)g(u)\mathrm{d}u \leq {}^1\!/\!_2 K(H-t)^2$$

for all $t \geq 0$, and, consequently,

$$\int_t^H \Delta i(\tau)\mathrm{d}\tau \geq \Delta i(H)\cdot(H-t) - {}^1\!/\!_2\, K(H-t)^2.$$

Since $e^x \geq 1 + x$, we have

$$\begin{aligned} f(t) &= \exp\left(\int_t^H \Delta i(\tau)\,\mathrm{d}\tau\right) \\ &\geq 1 + \int_t^H \Delta i(\tau)\mathrm{d}\tau \\ &\geq 1 + \Delta i(H)\cdot(H-t) - {}^1\!/\!_2\, K(H-t)^2. \end{aligned}$$

From Eq. (A1), we then have

$$\begin{aligned} \Delta I_H &\geq \sum_{j=1}^{m} [1 + \Delta i(H)\cdot(H-s_j) - {}^1\!/\!_2 K(H-s_j)^2] C_j P_0(s_j)/P_0(H) - I_0/P_0(H) \\ &= -{}^1\!/\!_2\, K \sum_{j=1}^{m} (H-s_j)^2 C_j P_0(s_j)/P_0(H) \\ &= -{}^1\!/\!_2\, K M^2 I_H, \end{aligned}$$

which completes the proof.

REFERENCES

Bierwag, G.O. (1977). "Immunization, Duration, and the Term Structure of Interest Rates." *Journal of Financial and Quantitative Analysis,* 12, 725–742.

———. (1978). "Measures of Duration." *Economic Inquiry*, 497–507.

Bierwag, G.O., and G.G. Kaufman. (1977). "Coping with the Risk of Interest Rate Fluctuations: A Note." *Journal of Business*, 50, 364–370.

Brennan, M.J., and E.S. Schwartz. (1981). "Duration, Bond Pricing, and Portfolio Diversification." Working paper no. 793, University of British Columbia, June.

Cox, J.C., J.E. Ingersoll, Jr., and S.A. Ross. (1979). "Duration and the Measurement of Basis Risk." *Journal of Business*, 52, 51–61.

Fisher, L., and R. Weil. (1971). "Coping with Risk of Interest Rate Fluctuations: Returns to Bondholders from Naive and Optimal Strategies." *Journal of Business*, 44, 410–431.

Khang, C. (1979). "Bond Immunization When Short Rates Fluctuate More Than Long Rates." *Journal of Financial and Quantitative Analysis*, 14, 1085–1090.

CHAPTER 24

The Tradeoff between Return and Risk in Immunized Portfolios

By H. Gifford Fong and Oldrich Vasicek

ABSTRACT

The target value of an immunized portfolio at the horizon date defines the portfolio's target rate of return. If interest rates change by parallel shifts for all maturities, the portfolio's realized rate of return will not be below the target value. To the extent that nonparallel rate changes occur, however, the realized return may be less than the target value.

The relative change in the end-of-horizon value of an immunized portfolio resulting from such an arbitrary rate change will be proportional to the value of its immunization risk. Immunization risk equals the weighted variance of times to payment around the horizon date, hence depends on portfolio composition. For example, immunization risk will be low if portfolio payments cluster around the end of the horizon and high if payments are widely dispersed in time. One may minimize the extent to which a portfolio's realized return differs from its target return by minimizing the portfolio's immunization risk (while keeping the portfolio's duration equal to the remaining horizon length).

Although risk minimization is the traditional objective of immunization, the immunization risk measure may also be used to optimize the risk-return tradeoff. The standard deviation of an immunized portfolio's rate of return over the investment horizon will be proportional to the value

Financial Analysts Journal, 39 (5) (1983), 73–78.

of its immunization risk. Thus an investor may choose from immunized portfolios of equal duration a portfolio with a high level of immunization risk in order to maximize his expected return.

INTRODUCTION

The traditional theory of immunization, as formalized by Fisher and Weil in 1971, assumed that a portfolio is valued at a fixed horizon date, that there are no cash inflows or outflows within the horizon, and that interest rates can change only by a parallel shift (that is, by the same amount for rates of all maturities). Under these assumptions, a portfolio is said to be immunized if its value at the end of the horizon does not fall below the target value, the target being defined as the value at the horizon date under the scenario of no change in the forward rates. The main result of this theory is that immunization is achieved if the duration of the portfolio is equal to the length of the horizon.

Immunization theory and practice have developed in a number of directions since the work by Fisher and Weil. The most significant development has been in overcoming the limitations of a fixed horizon with no contributions or withdrawals. Marshall and Yawitz (1974), for instance, demonstrated that, even if the value of an immunized portfolio declines because of interest rate changes over the investment horizon, a lower bound on the value of the portfolio exists at any point during the investment period. Fong and Vasicek (1980) and Bierwag, Kaufman, and Toevs (1983) subsequently addressed the multiple liabilities situation. Multiple liability immunization involves an investment strategy that guarantees that a specified schedule of future liabilities will be met, regardless of any parallel interest rate shifts. The amount of initial investment necessary for multiple liability immunization is equal to the present value of the liability stream under the initial interest rate structure (cf., for instance, Fong and Vasicek (1980)).

Immunization theory has also been extended to allow relaxation of the assumption of parallel changes in interest rates. Most of the work in this area—such as Bierwag (1978), Cox, Ingersoll, and Ross (1979), and Brennan and Schwartz (1983)—postulates alternative models of interest rate behavior and derives modified definitions of duration corresponding to the assumed interest rate process. A limitation of this approach is that immunity is achieved only against the assumed type of rate changes. A different approach to nonparallel rate changes described in Fong and Vasicek (1980) is to establish a measure of immunization risk for an arbitrary interest rate change; this risk can then be minimized, subject to the duration condition and other constraints, to obtain an optimally immunized portfolio. Whereas duration measures the mean time to payment on a portfolio, the proposed risk measure represents the time-to-payment variance around the liability dates, hence the exposure of the portfolio to relative changes of rates of different maturities.

Finally, immunization techniques have recently been used in conjunction with elements of active bond investment strategies. The classical objective of immunization has been risk protection, with little consideration of possible returns. Leibowitz and Weinberger (1981) proposed a scheme called *contingent immunization,* which provides a degree of flexibility in pursuing active strategies while ensuring a certain minimum return in the case of parallel rate shifts. With this approach, immunization serves as a fall-back strategy if the actively managed portfolio does not grow at a certain rate.

This article explores the risk-return tradeoff for immunized portfolios using a very different approach. The strategy proposed here maintains the duration of the portfolio at all times equal to the horizon length (or, in the multiple-liability case, keeps the generalized immunization conditions satisfied). Thus, the portfolio always remains fully immunized in the classical sense. However, instead of attempting to minimize the portfolio's immunization risk—that is, its vulnerability to arbitrary rate changes—this strategy aims for an optimal tradeoff between risk and return. The immunization risk measure can be relaxed if the compensation in terms of expected return warrants it.

Specifically, the strategy maximizes a lower bound on the portfolio's return. The lower bound is defined as a confidence interval on the realized return for a given probability level. The optimal portfolio therefore has the following characteristics:

1. It is completely immunized against parallel rate shifts, so the target rate of return is guaranteed as long as rates of various maturities change by the same amount.
2. Its level of immunization risk for arbitrary nonparallel rate changes is measured and minimized in the tradeoff with expected return.
3. Maximization of the expected portfolio return is included in the objective function together with risk consideration by maximizing a lower bound on return.

PORTFOLIO VALUE AND INTEREST RATE CHANGES

The duration of a bond portfolio is defined as the weighted average time to all the portfolio payments, the weights being the present values of the payment amounts. Mathematically, duration can be written as:

$$D = \sum_{i=1}^{m} t_i C_i P_0(t_i)/I_0, \tag{1}$$

where:

m = the number of portfolio payments (interest and principal),
C_i = the amount of the payment due at time t_i, i = 1, 2, …, m,
$P_0(t)$ = the current discount function—that is, the present value of a unit payment expected at time t, and
I_0 = the initial portfolio value, equal (by definition of the discount function) to the sum of the present values of the payments.

Assume that a portfolio has been constructed to have its duration equal to the investment horizon H. If interest rates do not change (in the sense that the forward rates stay the same), the portfolio, including reinvestment of portfolio cash flows received over the horizon, will have a certain value at the horizon date. This value, denoted by I_H, is called the *target value*.

Now suppose that, after the portfolio has been constructed, interest rates do change, but in such a way that rates of all maturities move, up or down, by the same amount. This is called a parallel shift of interest rates. The resulting change in the portfolio value at the horizon date, ΔI_H, will never be negative. In other words, the portfolio's terminal value will not fall below the target value because of a parallel shift of the yield curve. This is the principal result of the traditional immunization theory.

This immunization against changes in the level of rates is achieved by balancing the changes in reinvestment rates against capital gains or losses. Suppose that rates of all maturities increase by a given amount. Because the average time to payments (the portfolio's duration) is equal to the length of the horizon, there are some portfolio payments before the horizon date and some after the horizon date. The portion of the portfolio still outstanding at the horizon date will experience a capital loss. This loss, however, will be compensated for by the reinvestment of the portfolio payments received over the horizon at rates higher than those originally expected. Conversely, if rates of all maturities decrease by a like amount, the lower value of reinvestment is balanced by capital gains on the longer portion of the portfolio. The condition that the portfolio duration be equal to the horizon length assures that the magnitudes of the opposing changes in the reinvestment amounts and the principal values are such as to keep the end-of-horizon portfolio value from falling below the target value.

This balancing act obviously works only if rates of various maturities move in the same direction and by the same amount. If, instead of a parallel shift of the initial yield curve, there is a more complicated rate change, immunization may not take place. If the yield curve twists in such a way that short rates decline while long rates increase, the portfolio will suffer both a decrease in reinvestment rates and a capital loss on the longer portion, and its value at the horizon date will be below the target. We refer to such a possibility as *immunization risk*.

If immunization risk could be measured, immunized portfolios could be constructed to minimize this risk. For instance, there may be a number of portfolios having the same investment horizon and duration, each having a different degree of exposure to nonparallel rate changes. A quantitative measure of this exposure, independent of assumptions about the character of the possible changes in the interest rate structure, would be desirable.

IMMUNIZATION RISK

Fong and Vasicek (1984) (Chapter 23 of this volume) have shown that the change ΔI_H in the end-of-horizon value of an immunized portfolio resulting from an *arbitrary* change in interest rates is approximated by the following equation:

$$\frac{\Delta I_H}{I_H} = -M^2 \Delta_s. \tag{2}$$

Here Δ_s is the change in the slope of the term structure of interest rates; this quantity characterizes the degree of twist of the yield curve. The term M^2 is given by the formula:

$$M^2 = \sum_{i=1}^{m} (t_i - H)^2 C_i P_0(t_i)/I_0. \tag{3}$$

Eq. (2) has an interesting structure. It expresses the relative change in the end-of-horizon portfolio value as a product of two terms. The first term, M^2, depends solely on the structure of the portfolio, whereas the second term, Δ_s, is a function of the interest rate change only. The investor has no control over the quantity Δ_s; it is an uncertain variable that can take any value. The investor can, however, determine the portfolio composition, hence the quantity M^2. As a multiplier of the unknown rate change, this term measures the extent to which the portfolio can be affected by such a change. The change in the end-of-horizon value of the investment resulting from an arbitrary rate change is thus proportional to M^2, and M^2 is a *measure of immunization risk*.

To gain an insight into the meaning of the risk measure M^2, note the similarity in form between M^2 in Eq. (3) and the definition of duration in Eq. (1).

Whereas duration is a weighted *average* of time to portfolio payments, the weights being the present values of the payments, M^2 is a similarly weighted *variance* of times to payment around the horizon date. If the portfolio payments occur close to the end of the horizon (as would be the case with a portfolio of deep-discount bonds maturing close to the horizon date), M^2 is low. If the payments are widely dispersed in time (as would be the case with a portfolio consisting of very short bonds and very long bonds), M^2 is high.

It is not difficult to see why a *barbell* portfolio composed of very short and very long bonds should be more risky than a *bullet* portfolio consisting of low-coupon issues with maturities close to the horizon date. Assume that both portfolios have durations equal to the horizon length, so that both portfolios are immune to parallel rate changes. When interest rates change in an arbitrary nonparallel way, however, the effect on the two portfolios is very different.

Suppose, for instance, that short rates decline and long rates increase. The end-of-horizon values of both portfolios would fall below the target, since both portfolios would experience a capital loss in addition to lower reinvestment rates. The decline, however, would be substantially higher for the barbell portfolio than for the bullet portfolio, for two reasons. First, the barbell portfolio experiences lower reinvestment rates for a longer time interval than the bullet portfolio, so its opportunity loss is much greater. Second, the portion of the barbell portfolio still outstanding at the horizon date is much longer than that of the bullet portfolio, which means that the same rate increase will result in a much steeper capital loss for the former. The low M^2 bullet portfolio has less exposure to whatever the change in the interest rate structure may be than the high M^2 barbell portfolio.

Note that the risk measure M^2 is always nonnegative. It attains its lowest possible value of zero if and only if the portfolio consists of a single discount bond with maturity equal to the length of the horizon. This is indeed the perfectly immunized portfolio; no interest rate change can affect its end-of-horizon value. Any other portfolio is to some extent vulnerable to an adverse interest rate movement. The immunization risk M^2 in effect measures how much a given portfolio differs from this ideally immunized portfolio consisting of the single discount bond.

CONFIDENCE INTERVALS

The target value of an immunized portfolio at the horizon date I_H defines the *target rate of return* R^* over the horizon. If immunization works as assumed, the realized rate of return R will not be below the target value. This will be the case if interest rates change only by parallel shifts for all maturities.

To the extent that nonparallel rate changes occur, the realized return may be less than the target return.

Minimizing immunization risk M^2 during the horizon (while keeping the portfolio duration equal to the remaining horizon length) will minimize the extent to which the realized return differs from the target return. Unless a portfolio can be constructed with zero M^2, however, the immunized portfolio is subject to some risk. A common way of characterizing the effect of this risk on the investment is by the variance of return (or its square root, the standard deviation).

Eq. (2) can be used in deriving an expression for the standard deviation of the rate of return over the horizon, but not without further work. This equation only characterizes the portfolio's response to a single, instantaneous change in interest rates (an interest rate shock). Over an entire investment horizon, changes in the level and shape of the yield curve can be thought of as a series of interest rate shocks, each of which affects the portfolio's terminal value. The resulting change in value over the whole horizon is then an aggregate of these individual impacts. By Eq. (2), each such impact is proportional to what the portfolio M^2 was at the time. To measure the total impact, it is necessary to establish the statistical properties of the variable Δ_s, the change in the slope of the term structure.

Assuming that the subsequent values of change in the slope of the yield curve are independent random variables with a common variance σ_s^2, the effects of the individual rate shocks can be integrated over the total horizon, subject to a function describing how M^2 changes with the remaining time to horizon. This results in a formula for the standard deviation of return:

$$\sigma_R = a_H M^2 \sigma_s, \tag{4}$$

where:

σ_R = the standard deviation of the rate of return over the horizon,
σ_s = the standard deviation of the change in slope of the term structure (which can be estimated from historical data),
M^2 = the risk measure for the initial immunized portfolio, and
a_H = a constant that depends only on the horizon length.

Note that the standard deviation of return in Eq. (4) is again proportional to M^2. A portfolio whose M^2 is half the value of another portfolio's can be expected to produce half the dispersion of realized returns around the target value, when submitted to a variety of interest rate scenarios, than the other portfolio.

The standard deviation of return as given by Eq. (4) can be used in the construction of *confidence intervals*. A confidence interval represents an uncertainty band around the target return within which the realized return can be expected with a given probability. It can be provided in the form:

$$R = R^* \pm k\sigma_R, \tag{5}$$

where k is the critical value corresponding to the given confidence level. The value of k can be obtained from tables of normal distribution. For instance, to construct an interval within which the realized return can be expected with 95 percent probability, the value of k is 1.96.[1]

RISK AND RETURN

In a narrow sense, the objective of immunization is risk minimization. Given M^2 as a measure of a portfolio's exposure to general interest rate changes, construction of an immunized portfolio then becomes an optimization problem of the following structure:

Minimize the immunization risk M^2 subject to

1. immunization condition $D = H$ and
2. investment policy requirements.

The investment policy requirements can include restrictions such as minimum or maximum holdings of individual securities or groups of securities (for instance, issuing sector or quality requirements). It is also possible to include transaction constraints or turnover limits in the optimization.

In some situations, strict risk minimization may be deemed too restrictive. Because not all bonds are priced exactly on the current term structure of interest rates, there are yield differentials within the available universe that may be exploited to enhance the target return. If a substantial increase in the target return can be accomplished with little effect on immunization risk, then the higher yielding portfolio may be preferred in spite of its higher risk.

Consider an optimally immunized portfolio that has a target return of 13 percent over the horizon, with a 95 percent confidence interval of ±0.20 percent. This means that the minimum risk portfolio would have a 1 in 40 chance of realizing a return less than 12.8 percent. Suppose that another portfolio, less well immunized, can produce a target return of 13.3 percent with a 95 percent confidence interval of±0.30 percent. In all but one case

[1]The use of normal tables is justified by the fact that the return differential can be thought of as the result of a large number of independent interest rate changes, so that the central limit theorem is in effect.

out of 40, this portfolio would realize a return above 13 percent, compared with 12.8 percent on the minimum-risk portfolio. For many investors, this may be a preferred tradeoff.

It is possible to set up the optimization problem in such a way that, instead of risk minimization, the risk-return tradeoff is optimized. This can be accomplished by maximizing a *lower bound* on the realized return corresponding to a given confidence level. Since the confidence interval width in Eq. (5) is proportional to M^2, the objective function is a linear combination of the target return R^* and the risk measure M^2. It could be written in an equivalent form as:

$$\text{Minimize}\, M^2 - \lambda R^*$$

where the value of the coefficient λ depends on the desired confidence level.

This objective function represents a tradeoff between immunization risk and target return. If the parameter λ is small (corresponding to a high confidence level for the lower bound), the emphasis in the construction of the optimal portfolio is on risk. In the extreme case of λ being equal to zero, the objective would be strict risk minimization. On the other hand, if λ is high (such as for low confidence levels), the primary concern of the optimization is maximum return. The other extreme case of λ being equal to infinity would correspond to maximization of return subject only to the requirement that the portfolio be immunized against parallel rate shifts. This would mean selecting the highest return portfolio among all portfolios with durations equal to the horizon length.

By varying the coefficient λ over its range, it is in fact possible to obtain *efficient frontiers* for immunized portfolios, analogous to those in the mean-variance framework.

REFERENCES

Bierwag, G.O. (1978). "Measures of Duration." *Economic Inquiry*, October 16, 497–507.

Bierwag, G.O., G.G. Kaufman, and A. Toevs. (1983). "Immunizing Strategies for Funding Multiple Liabilities." *Journal of Financial and Quantitative Analysis*, (March) 18, 113–123.

Brennan, M., and E. Schwartz. (1983). "Duration, Bond Pricing and Portfolio Management." In G.O. Bierwag, G.G. Kaufman, and A. Toevs, eds., *Innovations in Bond Portfolio Management: Duration Analysis and Immunization*. Greenwich, CT: JAI Press.

Cox, J., J.E. Ingersoll, and S.A. Ross. (1979). "Duration and Measurement of Basis Risk." *Journal of Business*, January, 52, 51–61.

Fisher, L., and R. Weil. (1971). "Coping with the Risk of Interest Rate Fluctuations: Returns to Bondholders from Naive and Optimal Strategies." *Journal of Business*, October, 44 (4), 408–431.

Fong, H.G., and O. Vasicek. (1980)."A Risk Minimizing Strategy for Multiple Liability Immunization." *Institute for Quantitative Research in Finance*.

Fong, H.G., and O. Vasicek. (1984)."A Risk Minimizing Strategy for Portfolio Immunization". *Journal of Finance*, December 39 (5), 1541–1546.

Leibowitz, M.L., and A. Weinberger. (1981). *Contingent Immunization*. New York: Salomon Brothers Inc., January.

Marshall, W., and J.B. Yawitz. (1974). *Lower Bounds on Portfolio Performance: A Generalized Immunization Strategy*. St. Louis: Graduate School of Business, Washington University.

CHAPTER 25

Bond Performance: Analyzing Sources of Return

By Gifford Fong, Charles Pearson, and Oldrich Vasicek

Measuring the performance of bond portfolios has been an evolutionary effort. Early work focused on measuring the total return of the portfolio (Bank Administration Institute 1968). This involved establishing alternative measures of performance suitable for comparing the total return of one portfolio with another. The performance of a given portfolio can then be contrasted with that of an index, other portfolios, and the investment objectives of the fund sponsor. While this allows an assessment of the total portfolio results relative to the market conditions, it provides an insufficient insight into the underlying causes of the experienced performance. Explaining *how* the actual portfolio return was achieved is also an important objective of performance analysis.

Understanding the sources of the return of a portfolio can help in monitoring the effectiveness of the management process and in identifying its strengths and weaknesses. The manager can more effectively evaluate the consequences of the decision-making process. A framework providing sources of return may also serve as a communication aid for clients or for marketing purposes. For the portfolio sponsor, this analysis promotes insight into where and how much contribution to return has been made from the various sources of return. This is useful again as an aid to communication and also in the selection of managers by desired skill or style.

Journal of Portfolio Management, 9 (3) (1983), 46–50.

An explanation of the observed performance takes the form of decomposing the total return into components corresponding to the various sources of return. For equity portfolios, a framework for such analysis was presented in Fama (1972). A component analysis of bond portfolio performance was given in Dietz, Fogler, and Hardy (1980). These break the total bond return into yield to maturity, interest rate effect, sector/quality effect, and a residual. While this approach represents a significant development in bond performance measurement, it has several limitations. Yield to maturity is taken to represent the holding-period return under the assumption of no change in interest rates, which is not quite correct. The sector/quality component may be misleading, since the way it is calculated does not account for the differences in the maturity composition of the sectors. Most important, the return components are identified only for the portfolio as it existed at the beginning of the evaluation period. Thus, any actual management of the portfolio other than the initial portfolio selection is not included in the appropriate return components.

The goal of this paper is to extend the capabilities of bond performance analysis to provide a precise and comprehensive structure both for the measurement of the total realized return and for attribution of the return to its sources. The approach presented here is based on recent investment technology developments, including term structure modeling, which permit a more refined and precise methodology. The emphasis will be first on identifying the macro sources of return: external market conditions and the management contribution. In further analysis, we will define the micro components of return, including maturity management, spread/quality management, and individual security selection.

An important aspect of the performance analysis system outlined next is that it includes the portfolio *activity* over the evaluation period. Rather than just reviewing the performance of a static portfolio as it existed at the beginning of the period, we include as an integral part of the analysis all transactions, cash flows, contributions and withdrawals, cash account activity, and any other changes in the portfolio structure. The components of the performance also reflect the timing of the managerial decisions.

ANALYSIS OF RETURN

In the evaluation of bond portfolio performance, the first step is the measurement of return on the portfolio over the evaluation period. The next step is an analysis of return. We can think of analysis of return as the identification of the factors that contributed to the realized performance and a quantitative assessment of the contribution of each factor to the total return.

The total portfolio return is partitioned into components, each component representing the effect of the given factor.

The first level of this decomposition aims at distinguishing between the effect of the external interest rate environment and the management contribution. If we separate the effect of circumstances that are outside the control of the portfolio manager from the effect of the portfolio management process, we can gain valuable insight into the nature of the portfolio performance. Denoting the total realized portfolio return by R, such a partition can be written as:

$$R = I + C, \tag{1}$$

where:

I = the effect of the external interest rate environment beyond the portfolio manager's control, and
C = the contribution of the management process.

If the portfolio had no element of management, then the return would be I, or the return due to the environment. This portfolio can be considered to be randomly selected from an available universe of fixed-income securities. As a proxy for this management-free randomly selected portfolio, we can use the total of all default-free securities, best approximated by all outstanding U.S. Treasury issues. These are the only available securities that are truly fixed-income securities in the sense that the promised payments can be expected with virtual certainty. Including corporate, municipal, or agency issues constitutes an element of the management process: It involves a decision to accept a degree of default risk in exchange for higher yields typically expected on lower quality securities. The standard for identification of the effect of the internal interest rate environment is thus a value-weighted Treasury index.

One might argue that the relevant portfolio bogey should vary according to investor preference. In the determination of the investor's investment objectives, individual preferences are certainly appropriate. The intent here, however, is to measure the interest rate effect on a universe that involves no other aspect, such as credit risk or spread relationships. That does not mean that a comparison of the portfolio return to a broader bond market index is inappropriate. Such comparison is in fact an integral part of the performance analysis as discussed in this article. It is done by performing the return analysis for the chosen bogey as well, thus allowing a direct comparison of the resulting components of return between the actual portfolio and the specialized bogey.

We can achieve a more refined analysis of the external factor component by partitioning the actual holding-period return on the Treasury index into two sources: interest rate *level* and interest rate *change*. Higher interest rate levels mean higher holding-period returns, on which the effect of interest rate changes is then superimposed. The effect of the interest rate environment thus consists of two components: return that would be realized if interest rates did not change, and the return due to the actual interest rate change.

To assign a precise meaning to the assumption of no change in interest rates, we use the basic concepts of the term structure of interest rates. The discount rates that determine the present value of a unit payment at a given time in the future are called spot rates. Spot rates are essentially yields on pure discount bonds. The market value of a coupon bond can be considered the sum of the present values of its payments, each payment being discounted by the spot rate corresponding to the maturity of that payment. The yield to maturity, or the internal rate of return on the bond payments, is a mixture of spot rates of various maturities.

The future one-period rates implied by the current spot rates are called forward rates. Forward rates are defined by the property that we can obtain the spot rates by compounding the forward rates over the term of the spot rate. If the forward rates do not change, future spot rates will be formed by compounding the current forward rates over the appropriate future interval. This implies that an investment in a long security would realize the same return as rolling over a short-term security. As a consequence, forward rates exhibit the following property: *Under the scenario of no change in the forward rates, the holding period returns over a given period are the same for securities of all maturities and coupons*. No other scenario of interest rate development would make the holding period returns independent of the maturity of the security or portfolio. In this sense, no change in the forward rates is the most "neutral" forecast, since under this assumption no maturities or payment schedules would be *ex ante* preferred to others. This scenario is often referred to as the *market implicit forecast*.

One can therefore define the effect of the current level of interest rates as the return on Treasury bonds under the assumption of no change in the current forward rates. The effect of the interest rate change is then defined as the difference between the actual realized return on the Treasury index and the return under the market-implicit forecast. We can then decompose the effect of I, the external interest rate environment, in the following way:

$$I = E + U, \tag{2}$$

where:

E = return on the default-free securities under the market-implicit scenario of no change in the forward rates, and

U = return attributable to the actual change in forward rates.

We can interpret the component E as the expected return on a portfolio of default-free Treasury securities. The component U is then the unexpected part of the actual return on the Treasury index, due to the forward rate change. The sum I of these components is then the actual return on the Treasury index. We can attribute the difference between the actual portfolio return and the actual Treasury index return, termed C in Eq. (1), to the management process.

In evaluating the management contribution C, consider the means by which the management process can affect the portfolio. Three principal management skills that have an effect on performance include maturity management, sector/quality management, and selection of the individual securities. A partitioning of the management contribution is as follows:

$$C = M + S + B, \tag{3}$$

where:

M = return from maturity management,
S = return from spread/quality management, and
B = return attributable to the selection of specific securities.

Maturity management (which might more correctly be called duration management) is an important tool of a bond portfolio manager and one that typically has the largest impact on performance. The successful application of this skill is related to the ability of the manager to anticipate interest rate changes. Holding long duration portfolios during periods of decreasing interest rates and short duration portfolios during periods of rate increases will typically result in superior performance. Being short when rates decline or long when rates go up will have a negative impact on performance.

Sector and quality management allocates the portfolio among the alternative issuing sectors and quality groups of the bond market. There may be spread relationships among the individual sector/quality groups that the manager may be able to exploit. Having a portfolio concentrated in high-quality industrial issues, for instance, during a period when high-quality industrials generally perform better than other sectors, would increase the portfolio return. The ability to select the right issuing sector and quality group at the right time constitutes the sector/quality management skill.

Selectivity, or individual bond picking, is the skill of selecting specific securities within a given sector/quality group to enhance the portfolio return. Individual securities show specific returns over and above the average performance of their sector/quality group. While sector/quality management means selecting the right market segment, selectivity means concentrating on the bonds, within that segment, whose specific returns are the most advantageous. As with the other two management skills, selectivity is involved in the initial portfolio construction as well as in subsequent activities such as purchases, sales, or swaps within a sector/quality group.

There is a fourth important skill of bond portfolio management, namely, timing. Timing is not a separate skill, but rather, an aspect of each of the skills identified earlier. Timing the shift of the portfolio from short to long duration or vice versa is really an element of maturity management, rather than an independently exercised ability. Without timing, there would be no maturity management. Similarly, timing is an essential part of sector/quality management and a part of choosing the proper bonds within a given sector/quality group. To provide a meaningful analysis of the portfolio return, the timing aspect must be included in the calculation of the return components.

MEASUREMENT OF RETURN COMPONENTS

We can measure the return components by security repricing. Consider maturity management first. If all securities held during the evaluation period were Treasury issues and if each issue were consistently priced exactly on the term structure of default-free rates (so that there would be no specific returns on any security), the maturity management component M of the total return would be equal to the difference between the realized total return R and the effect I of the external environment. In other words, if the sector/quality effect and the selectivity effect were eliminated, the total management contribution can be attributed to maturity management. This means that we can reprice each security as if it were a Treasury issue priced from the term structure, measure the total return under such pricing, and subtract the external effect component I to obtain the effect of maturity management.

Practically, this is accomplished by estimating the term structure of default-free rates from the universe of Treasury issues as of each valuation date throughout the evaluation period. The default-free price of each security held on that date is then calculated as the present value of its payments discounted by the spot rates corresponding to the maturity of that payment. The total return over the evaluation period is then calculated using the default-free prices, but otherwise maintaining all actual activity in the portfolio, including all transactions, contributions and withdrawals, cash account changes, and the like. Finally, the actual Treasury index return over the evaluation period is subtracted to arrive at the maturity management component M.

To determine the spread/quality management component S of the total return, we price each security as if it were exactly in line with its own sector/quality group (that is, with no specific returns), calculate the total return under such prices, and subtract the total of the external component I and the maturity management component M.

Here we have to be careful to determine the sector/quality prices correctly. It is not correct to base the sector/quality pricing on sector/quality indexes, since the differences in actual performance among various sector/quality indexes is primarily due to the different maturity composition of the market segments. For instance, the telephone issues would generally perform poorly during periods of increasing interest rates, not because they are telephones but because they are longer than the bond market as a whole.

We therefore adopt the following approach: First, we define a meaningful classification of the bond market by sector/quality groups. We then estimate the term structure of default-free rates from U.S. Treasury issues. Next, for each valuation date, we calculate the default-free prices for all securities existing in the market at that date. We then calculate the spreads, or yield premia, for each security as the difference between the actual yield and yield determined from the default-free price. These yield premia are then averaged over all securities in the given sector/quality group to determine the average yield premium for the sector/quality group as of the given date. After all this is done, we can calculate the sector/quality prices of the securities in the given portfolio by determining their default-free prices from the term structure, calculating the yield, adding the appropriate average yield premium depending on the sector/quality of that security, and converting this yield back to price. When all securities in the portfolio have been priced according to their sector/quality group at each of the valuation dates, we calculate the total portfolio return with the sector/quality prices. Again, the portfolio return with these prices is calculated including all actual purchases, sales, swaps, contributions, and withdrawals. We then obtain the sector/quality component S of the portfolio management by subtracting the external effect component and the maturity management component from the return calculated on the sector/quality prices.

Finally, to determine the selectivity component of the management contribution, we use the actual prices, which reflect the specific returns on each security. The selectivity component B is thus calculated by subtracting the total of all previously determined components from the actual total portfolio return.

In this way, we partition the total portfolio return into five components as follows:

$$R = \underbrace{E + U}_{I} + \underbrace{M + S + B}_{C} \tag{4}$$

These components are the effect of interest rate level (E), the effect of interest rate change (U), the maturity management (M), sector/quality management (S), and selectivity (B). The first component can also be interpreted as the expected return on default-free securities, and the second as the unexpected component of the actual return on the default-free Treasury market index. The first two components are the effect of external factors beyond the control of the portfolio manager, namely, the interest rate environment. Their sum is the actual return on the Treasury index. The last three components reflect factors within the control of the manager, that is, management skill. Together, they add up to the total management contribution. The sum of all five components is the actual return on the portfolio.

An alternative way of looking at the composition of the total return given by Eq. (4), which will reflect the way these components are actually calculated, is to consider the cumulative totals. The first total, E, is the expected return on a randomly selected portfolio of Treasury issues, calculated assuming no change in interest rates. The second total, $E + U$, is the actual return on a randomly selected portfolio of Treasury issues. The third total, $E + U + M$, is the return on the actual portfolio (including all activity) as if all securities were Treasury issues priced on the term structure (i.e., no sector/quality effects and no specific returns). The fourth total, $E + U + M + S$, is the return on the actual portfolio as if all securities were priced according to their issuing sector and quality (i.e., no specific returns). Finally, the fifth total, $E + U + M + S + B$, is the actual portfolio return. The decomposition of the total return into its components as specified in Eq. (4) provides a meaningful and informative analysis of the portfolio performance.

The effect of transaction costs is also included by this analysis. As a transaction is made, the cost is reflected in the price paid for a purchase and the price received for a sale. This, in turn, is captured in the return due to the selectivity component. Hence, excessive turnover of the portfolio would be reflected in the selectivity component of the portfolio.

After we have calculated components of return for the portfolio being analyzed, we can repeat the same return decomposition for a total bond market index such as the Lehman Government/Corporate Bond Index. The return components of the bond index provide benchmarks against which we can compare the return components of the portfolio.

We will conclude our exposition of the performance measurement by a discussion of risk adjustments. For equity portfolios, it is customary to calculate a risk-adjusted return, defined as the actual portfolio beta. Crude attempts at a similar adjustment for bond portfolios have been made by substituting the bond portfolio duration relative to an index for the beta of a stock portfolio. This is incorrect, since duration would measure the portfolio response only if interest rates always changed by parallel shifts of the forward rates.

It turns out that the correct adjustment for interest rate risk would actually be the maturity management component *M* as defined previously. Similarly, the sector/quality component *S* would be an adjustment for the second source of risk in the bond market, namely, the default risk. If the investment policy of a fund constrains the manager as to the maturity composition and/or sector and quality composition of the portfolio, it may be appropriate to consider the maturity and/or the sector/quality return components risk adjustments. For instance, if both maturity and sector composition of the portfolio are specifically prescribed by policy, the risk-adjusted return is equal to the selectivity component *B*. In general, however, interpretation of the maturity and sector/quality components as risk adjustments would mean removing the principal sources of return from the observed performance.

SUMMARY

This paper has described a framework for comprehensively measuring and understanding the performance of a fixed-income portfolio. Macro components include the external interest rate environment and the managerial contribution to total returns. A more refined perspective is achieved by partitioning the external interest rate environment into expected and unexpected components. The managerial contribution is further partitioned into the return components of maturity, sector/quality, and individual security selection. These components are then contrasted with those of a total bond market index. An example of the analysis is contained in Table 25.1.

TABLE 25.1 Bond performance analysis

Portfolio: Sample portfolio		Beginning date: 1-1-82 Ending date: 3-31-82 Evaluation period returns (%) Portfolio	LBKL Govt/Corp Index
I.	Interest Rate Effect		
	1. Expected	2.89	2.89
	2. Unexpected	0.34	0.34
	Subtotal	3.23	3.23
II.	Management Effect		
	3. Maturity	0.48	0.10
	4. Sector/Quality	1.54	0.23
	5. Individual Bonds	−0.72	0.00
	Subtotal	1.30	0.33
III.	Total Return	4.53	3.56

REFERENCES

Bank Administration Institute. (1968). *Measuring the Investment Performance of Pension Funds*. Park Ridge, Illinois: B.A.I.

Dietz, P.O., H.R. Fogler, and D.J. Hardy. (1980). "The Challenge of Analyzing Bond Portfolio Returns." *Journal of Portfolio Management*, 6, Spring, 53–58.

Fama, E.F. (1972). "Components of Investment Performance." *Journal of Finance*, 27, 551–567.

Vasicek, O.A., and H.G. Fong. (1982). "Term Structure Modeling Using Exponential Splines." *Journal of Finance*, 37 (May), 339–348.

CHAPTER 26

The Best-Return Strategy

INTRODUCTION

Portfolio insurance is a technique that allows the investor to participate in the upside potential of a risky portfolio (called the target asset), while reducing or eliminating the downside risk. Typically, this means guaranteeing a specified minimum return over a given investment horizon. The cost of the insurance is paid in terms of a return differential by which the investment return lags behind the performance of the target asset.

The target asset itself can be a portfolio containing a number of investment assets. For instance, the target portfolio can be a balanced fund consisting of equities, bonds, and mortgages. The allocation of funds within this portfolio can be fixed, or can vary according to a passive or active strategy. The insurance then applies to the total fund, and depends only on its total performance rather than on the performance of the individual components. Although the insured portfolio consists of multiple assets, from the viewpoint of the insurance strategy it is a single target asset.

In this chapter, we address a different type of multiple asset strategy, called the best return strategy. Instead of ensuring the performance of a combination of assets, this strategy assures that the return on the total investment will be that of the best performance of the individual assets, less the known cost of the strategy. Thus, if the individual assets are stocks, bonds, and mortgages, and if stocks happen to perform the best of the three, the return on the strategy will be that of the stock portion, less the known cost. If bonds perform better over the investment horizon than stocks and mortgages, the investment return will equal the return on bonds, less cost. If mortgages do better than stocks or bonds, the investor will realize the return, after costs, of the mortgage portfolio on his total investment.

Moreover, if one of the assets has a fixed return over the investment horizon, this strategy guarantees a specified minimum return in addition to assuring the best of the remaining asset returns. This minimum guaranteed return is the return on such safety asset less the known costs. Thus, if the assets include a pure discount bond maturing at the end of the investment horizon in addition to stocks, bonds, and mortgages, the strategy will yield a specified minimum return even if stocks, bonds, and mortgages all perform poorly.

There is no restriction on the number of assets used in the best return strategy. It can be applied to individual securities (such as getting the best of several individual stock returns), to portfolios (for example, assuring that the return achieved by the best—or luckiest—of several portfolio managers is realized on the total plan), or to whole markets (for instance, obtaining the best performing of several international equity markets). The cost of the strategy, of course, increases with the number of assets involved. In addition to the number of assets, the costs depend on the riskiness of the assets (the riskier the assets, the higher the costs), on the correlations among the assets (the higher correlated they are, the lower the costs), and on the length of the investment horizon (the costs per year decrease with increasing horizon length).

The strategy is implemented by a dynamic allocation of the investment funds among the several assets. The proportions of the total investment allocated to the individual assets are continuously monitored and adjusted, depending on their performance to date, and on the time remaining to the horizon date.

THE OBJECTIVE

The best-return strategy is a generalization of portfolio insurance to multiple assets. To understand the connection, consider the objective of portfolio insurance. The objective function can be written in the following form:

$$R_I = \max(R_T - c, R_{\min})$$

where R_I is the total investment return, R_T is the target asset return, $R_{\min}$ is the assured minimum return, and c is the insurance cost. (Throughout this chapter, all returns are assumed to be expressed in terms of annual, continuously compounded rates.)

Portfolio insurance is nothing other than getting the better of two asset returns. Indeed, when the insurance plan is implemented by means of dynamic asset allocation, it is necessary to utilize a second asset that has a fixed return over the insurance horizon, such as a pure discount bond with no default risk. The difference between the second asset return and the assured minimum return can be viewed as a second insurance cost, assigned to this second asset. The objective function can then be written as

$$R_I = \max(R_1 - c_1, R_2 - c_2)$$

where R_1, R_2 are returns on the two assets and c_1, c_2 are the corresponding insurance costs. A minimum return guarantee is just a special case when one of the two assets has a fixed terminal value. (In a world of changing interest rates, however, that asset is also risky, since its value fluctuates during the horizon.)

The two insurance costs, c_1, c_2 (both of which must be positive) are subject to a pricing equation that determines one of them if a value for the other is selected. This equation reduces to a version of the Black-Scholes (1973) option pricing formula if one of the assets is a bond and interest rates are deterministic and constant, and to Merton's (1973) extension of that formula if one asset is a pure discount bond and the variability of interest rates is independent of their level. Margrabe (1978) has provided a formula for two risky assets. In general, the insurance costs will depend on the risk structure of the two assets throughout the horizon (i.e., their instantaneous covariance matrix as a function of time and state variables) and the length of the horizon.

It is a natural generalization of the two-asset case to postulate an objective function of the form

$$R_I = \max(R_1 - c_1, R_2 - c_2, \ldots, R_n - c_n)$$

where $n \geq 2$ is the number of assets, $R_1, R_2, \ldots, R_n$ are their returns, and $c_1, c_2, \ldots, c_n$ are the corresponding insurance costs. This objective is to get the best of multiple risky asset returns, less the cost of insurance. This constitutes the goal of the best-return strategy.

THE COSTS

The valuation formula from which the costs of the best-return strategy are calculated is a single equation for the n costs, so that $n - 1$ of the costs can be independently chosen (subject to feasibility constraints) and the remaining one is then determined. Alternatively, $n - 1$ relationships can be imposed on the costs (such as that they be all equal) to determine their values.

The formula depends on the number of assets, the risk structure of the n-dimensional stochastic process that describes their behavior over the horizon, and the horizon length. For diffusion processes, the valuation formula involves $(n - 1)$-dimensional cumulative normal distribution functions with covariance matrices that are transformations of the n-dimensional instantaneous covariance matrix of the assets, integrated over the horizon. In addition to the two-asset formulas of Black and Scholes, Merton, and Margrabe mentioned earlier, the other result previously available is Stulz's (1982) formula for two risky and one riskless asset.

The values of the costs are determined by the investor's preferences, much like in the case of portfolio insurance. In that special case of two assets, the investor chooses a tradeoff between the minimum guaranteed return (which is the fixed return of the safety asset less the cost attributed to the safety asset), and the return differential between the target asset return and the total investment return (which is the cost attributed to the target asset). Thus, portfolio insurance strategies can guarantee a relatively high minimum return at a high cost of the insurance, or a lower minimum return at a more modest insurance cost.

In the best return strategy, one alternative is to choose the costs to be all equal,

$$c_1 = c_2 = \ldots = c_n.$$

In that case, the objective function of the strategy has a particularly simple form

$$R_I = \max(R_1, R_2, \ldots, R_n) - c,$$

where the common value c of the n costs is determined from the valuation formula. This case, which will be called *uniform cost allocation*, assigns the costs equally to all of the assets included in the objective.

As an example, consider n assets whose stochastic behavior is described by a logarithmic Wiener process. Let the instantaneous covariance matrix be specified by standard deviations all equal to 15 percent annual, with correlations among the assets all equal to 0.4, and assume a five-year horizon. Table 26.1 lists the value c of the uniform costs, in annual percent, as a function of the number of assets.

TABLE 26.1 Uniform costs in annual percent

Number of Assets							
$n =$	2	3	4	5	6	8	10
$c =$	2.7	4.1	5.0	5.7	6.2	7.0	7.6

These costs are the price to pay for getting the best out of a number of asset returns. Suppose that the values of the parameters chosen for the example are descriptive of the international equity markets. It is possible to implement a strategy whose realized return is equal to the highest of six separate national stock markets, over a five-year period, less 6.2 percent annual. It goes without saying that no prediction is needed as to which of these markets will have the highest return, or, for that matter, what are the expected returns of each.

Table 26.1 is an extract from Table 26.2, which lists the values of the uniform costs as a function of the number of assets and of the correlation

TABLE 26.2 Best-return strategy

Uniform Costs (in Annual %)
Horizon Length (yrs): 5.0
Standard Deviation (%): 15.0

Number of Assets

Corr.	2	3	4	5	6	7	8	9	10	11	12
.0	3.4	5.2	6.3	7.2	7.9	8.4	8.9	9.2	9.6	9.9	10.2
.1	3.3	4.9	6.0	6.9	7.5	8.0	8.4	8.8	9.1	9.4	9.7
.2	3.1	4.7	5.7	6.5	7.1	7.6	8.0	8.3	8.7	8.9	9.2
.3	2.9	4.4	5.4	6.1	6.7	7.1	7.5	7.8	8.1	8.4	8.6
.4	2.7	4.1	5.0	5.7	6.2	6.6	7.0	7.3	7.6	7.8	8.0
.5	2.5	3.8	4.6	5.2	5.7	6.1	6.4	6.7	6.9	7.2	7.4
.6	2.3	3.4	4.1	4.7	5.1	5.5	5.8	6.0	6.2	6.4	6.6
.7	2.0	3.0	3.6	4.1	4.5	4.8	5.0	5.2	5.4	5.6	5.8
.8	1.6	2.4	3.0	3.4	3.7	3.9	4.1	4.3	4.5	4.6	4.7
.9	1.2	1.7	2.1	2.4	2.6	2.8	2.9	3.1	3.2	3.3	3.4

among them, assumed to be the same between any pair. The investment horizon is taken to be five years, and the standard deviations of the individual asset returns are assumed to be all equal to 15 percent per year. It can be seen that the costs decrease drastically with an increase in the correlation among the assets. The uniform costs under the same assumptions but for a one-year horizon are given in Table 26.3.

NONUNIFORM COSTS

The costs of the strategy do not have to be made equal. It is possible to choose them in such a way that a disproportionate part of the burden is borne by those assets in which the investor has a secondary interest. For instance, consider the case of four assets with standard deviations of 15.7 percent, 11.7 percent, 15.2 percent, and 1.3 percent, and a correlation matrix as shown in Table 26.4. These values correspond to historical estimates of volatilities and correlations (over the period January 1979 to December 1980) for S&P 500 stock index, Lehman government/corporate bond index, GNMA index, and Treasury bill index. For a five-year horizon, the uniform costs are 3.8 percent annually. This means that the best return strategy applied to these four assets assures the investor a return equal to the highest of the realized annual returns over the five-year period of stocks, bonds, mortgages, and cash, less 3.8 percent. For instance, if stocks turned out to do the best of these four

TABLE 26.3 Best-return strategy, one-year horizon

Uniform Costs (in Annual %)
Horizon Length (yrs): 1.0
Standard Deviation (%): 15.0

	Number of Assets										
Corr.	2	3	4	5	6	7	8	9	10	11	12
0	8.1	12.2	14.9	16.8	18.4	19.6	20.7	21.6	22.3	23.1	23.7
0.1	7.7	11.6	14.1	16	17.4	18.6	19.6	20.5	21.2	21.9	22.5
0.2	7.3	11	13.4	15.1	16.5	17.6	18.5	19.3	20.1	20.7	21.3
0.3	6.8	10.3	12.5	14.2	15.4	16.5	17.4	18.1	18.8	19.4	19.9
0.4	6.3	9.5	11.6	13.1	14.3	15.3	16.1	16.8	17.4	18	18.5
0.5	5.8	8.7	10.6	12	13.1	14	14.7	15.4	16	16.5	16.9
0.6	5.2	7.8	9.5	10.8	11.8	12.6	13.2	13.8	14.3	14.8	15.2
0.7	4.5	6.8	8.3	9.4	10.2	10.9	11.5	12	12.4	12.8	13.2
0.8	3.7	5.6	6.8	7.7	8.4	8.9	9.4	9.8	10.2	10.5	10.8
0.9	2.6	4	4.8	5.5	5.9	6.3	6.7	7	7.2	7.5	7.7

assets with an annual return of 20 percent, the investor would realize 16.2 percent annually over the horizon. If stocks, bonds, and the GNMA portfolio all lost money, the strategy would still provide a return equal to that realized on Treasury bills, less 3.8 percent.

Now suppose that it is essential to the investor to maintain a five-year return of no less than that of Treasury bills less 2 percent, while retaining as much of the upside potential of stocks, bonds, and GNMAs as possible. The costs of a best-return strategy can be chosen as

$$c_1 = 4.9\%, c_2 = 4.9\%, c_3 = 4.9\%, c_4 = 2.0\%.$$

(See Case #4 in Table 26.4.) This choice of costs would assure a minimum performance of Treasury bill return less 2 percent, while keeping the possibility open to participate in the performance of the three riskier assets if any one of them turns out to do well.

If mortgages were less important to the investor than stocks and bonds, perhaps the following cost assignment may be a preferred choice:

$$c_1 = 4.2\%, c_2 = 4.2\%, c_3 = 7.3\%, c_4 = 2.0\%.$$

(See Case #5 in Table 26.4.) This cost allocation would attribute lower costs to stocks and bonds than the previous case, and higher costs to the less important mortgage portfolio.

TABLE 26.4 Best-return strategy costs

Number of assets:	4			
Horizon length (years):	5.0			
Standard deviations (%):	15.7	11.7	15.2	1.3
Correlation matrix:	1.00	.25	.24	−.08
		1.00	.97	.74
			1.00	.75
				1.00
Costs (in annual %):				
Case	Stocks	Bonds	Mortgage	Bills
Uniform	3.8	3.8	3.8	3.8
1	4.1	4.1	4.1	3.0
2	3.0	5.8	5.8	3.0
3	2.2	9.0	9.0	3.0
4	4.9	4.9	4.9	2.0
5	4.2	4.2	7.3	2.0
6	3.4	7.0	8.0	2.0
7	6.4	6.4	6.4	1.0
8	2.0	5.0	5.0	6.0

Table 26.4 lists a number of possible alternatives for the cost allocation. Note that these are just a few possibilities out of an infinite range of feasible cost allocations, with no particular meaning to the order in which the cases are listed.

STRATEGY IMPLEMENTATION

The strategy is executed by a dynamic allocation of investment funds among the several assets. The amounts allocated to the individual assets are maintained to be proportional to the partial derivatives, with respect to the asset values, of the valuation function (the same function that is also used initially to determine the costs of the strategy). The required allocation changes continuously as a function of the asset performance to date, and the remaining time to the horizon.

An example of the strategy is provided in Table 26.5. The strategy is simulated over a one-year investment horizon from January 1, 1981, to December 31, 1981, using the four assets described. The risk parameters are those listed in Table 26.4, as measured over a prior period from January 1979 to December 1980. The costs, allocated uniformly, are 8.8 percent for each asset. The simulations assume monthly rebalancing, with transaction costs of 0.25 percent round-trip (since the rebalancing can be executed by trading futures).

TABLE 26.5 Best-return strategy simulation

Plan #5: Best of Four Assets

Best	Name	Costs (%)	Description		
1	Stocks	8.76	Standard & Poor's 500 Stock Index	Inception date	1-01-81
2	Bonds	8.76	Shearson Lehman Government Corporate Bond Index	Horizon date	12-31-81
3	Morg	8.76	Shearson Lehman GNMA Pass Through Index	Horizon length	1.00 yrs
4	Bills	8.76	U.S. Treasury Bill Index		
				Init'l. investment	$10,000,000
				Rnd. trip trans. costs	.25%

Date	Yrs to Horiz	Stocks	Bonds	Mortg	Bills	Plan Sched.	Plan Actual Before T/costs	Plan Actual After T/costs		
1-01-81	1.00									
Required allocation		36.07%	8.71%	28.79%	26.42%				Investment value	$10,000,000
2-01-81	.91									
Return in last period		−4.20%	−0.03%	0.68%	1.21%	−1.03%	−1.00%	−1.00%	Investment value	$9,899,676
Return since inception		−4.20%	−0.03%	0.68%	1.21%	−1.03%	−1.00%	−1.00%	Turnover	13.65%
Current allocation		34.90%	8.80%	29.28%	27.01%				Transaction costs	$3,391
Required allocation		23.28%	6.78%	34.46%	35.49%					
3-01-81	.84									
Return in last period		1.71%	−1.63%	−3.68%	1.18%	−.55%	−.56%	−.60%	Investment value	$9,840,655

Return since inception	−2.57%	−1.66%	−3.03%	2.41%	−1.57%	−1.56%	−1.59%	Turnover	14.23%
Current allocation	23.81%	6.70%	33.38%	36.11%				Transaction costs	$3,517
Required allocation 4-01-81 .75	28.06%	8.00%	19.13%	44.81%					
Return in last period	4.03%	2.39%	2.05%	1.62%	2.09%	2.44%	2.40%	Investment value	$10,077,098
Return since inception	1.36%	0.68%	−1.04%	4.06%	.49%	.84%	.77%	Turnover	6.55%
Current allocation	28.50%	7.99%	19.06%	44.45%				Transaction costs	$1,662
Required allocation 5-01-81 .67	33.79%	9.25%	17.03%	39.93%					
Return in last period	−1.97%	−3.22%	−6.28%	0.64%	−1.62%	−1.77%	−1.79%	Investment value	$9,896,627
Return since inception	−0.63%	−2.56%	−7.26%	4.73%	−1.14%	−.95%	−1.03%	Turnover	16.41%
Current allocation	33.72%	9.12%	16.25%	40.91%				Transaction costs	$4,074
Required allocation 6-01-81 .59	29.60%	9.01%	4.06%	57.33%					
Return in last period	0.21%	3.19%	6.97%	1.25%	1.24%	1.35%	1.31%	Investment value	$10,026,188
Return since inception	−0.42%	0.55%	−0.79%	6.05%	.09%	.39%	.26%	Turnover	11.79%
Current allocation	29.27%	9.18%	4.28%	57.28%				Transaction costs	$2,965
Required allocation 7-01-81 .50	23.49%	5.60%	16.06%	54.85%					
Return in last period	−0.63%	0.15%	−3.04%	1.46%	.12%	.18%	.15%	Investment value	$10,040,793

(continued)

TABLE 26.5 *(Continued)*

Plan #5: Best of Four Assets

Best Name	Costs (%)	Description							
Return since inception	−1.05%	0.70%	−3.81%	7.60%	.21%	.57%	.41%	Turnover	16.97%
Current allocation	23.30%	5.60%	15.54%	55.56%				Transaction costs	$4,275
Required allocation	18.08%	10.15%	3.78%	67.98%					
8-01-81 .42									
Return in last period	0.23%	−1.79%	−3.28%	1.07%	.31%	.46%	.42%	Investment value	$10,082,992
Return since inception	−0.82%	−1.10%	−6.96%	8.75%	.52%	1.03%	.83%	Turnover	11.24%
Current allocation	18.04%	9.93%	3.64%	68.39%				Transaction costs	$2,848
Required allocation	15.04%	4.63%	0.69%	79.64%					
9-01-81 .33									
Return in last period	−5.81%	−1.68%	−4.58%	1.16%	.36%	−.06%	−.09%	Investment value	$10,074,200
Return since inception	−6.58%	−2.77%	−11.22%	10.01%	.88%	.97%	.74%	Turnover	15.80%
Current allocation	14.17%	4.56%	0.66%	80.61%				Transaction costs	$3,997
Required allocation	2.25%	1.30%	0.01%	96.43%					
10-01-81	.25								
Return in last period	−4.94%	0.02%	−0.67%	1.57%	1.47%	1.40%	1.36%	Investment value	$10,211,184
Return since inception	−11.19%	−2.75%	−11.82%	11.73%	2.36%	2.39%	2.11%	Turnover	3.12%

Current allocation	2.11%	1.29%	0.01%	96.59%				Transaction costs	$810
Required allocation 11-01-81 .17	0.06%	0.22%	0.00%	99.72%					
Return in last period	5.43%	5.45%	9.27%	1.56%	1.57%	1.57%	1.57%	Investment value	$10,371,085
Return since inception	−6.37%	2.55%	−3.65%	13.48%	3.96%	4.00%	3.71%	Turnover	.31%
Current allocation	0.07%	0.23%	0.00%	99.71%				Transaction costs	$94
Required allocation 12-01-81 .08	0.05%	0.53%	0.01%	99.41%					
Return in last period	4.11%	8.04%	12.22%	1.51%	1.62%	1.55%	1.54%	Investment value	$10,531,296
Return since inception	−2.52%	10.79%	8.13%	15.19%	5.65%	5.60%	5.31%	Turnover	8.07%
Current allocation	0.05%	0.56%	0.01%	99.38%				Transaction costs	$2,135
Required allocation 12-31-81 .00		0.00%	7.10%	1.54%	91.37%				
Return in last period	−2.55%	−3.19%	−7.37%	0.79%	.69%	.38%	.36%		
Return since inception	−5.01%	7.25%	0.16%	16.10%	6.37%	6.01%	5.69%	Investment value	$10,569,185

The initial allocation was 36.1 percent, 8.7 percent, 28.8 percent, and 26.4 percent among stocks, bonds, mortgages, and cash, respectively. One month later, based on the market moves over the month, the allocation was changed to 23.3 percent, 6.8 percent, 34.5 percent, and 35.5 percent, respectively, for a turnover of 13.6 percent. The rebalancing is continued each month until the horizon date.

Table 26.5 lists, for each rebalancing period, the last month performance and the performance since inception of the four assets, as well as the scheduled performance of the plan (the performance, calculated from the valuation formula, that is expected from the strategy given the performance of the individual assets), and the actual performance of the plan before and after transaction costs.

The summary of the strategy performance is provided in Table 26.6. Over the one-year horizon, the annual continuously compounded returns for the four assets were −5.1 percent for stocks, 7.0 percent for bonds,

TABLE 26.6 Simulation summary

Plan #5: Best of Four Assets					
Plan Inception Date		1/1/1981	Horizon Length		1.00 Yrs
Plan Horizon Date		12/31/1981	Initial Investment		$10,000,000
	Stocks	Bonds	Mortgage	Bills	
Return Since Inception:					
Total	−5.01%	7.25%	0.16%	16.10%	
Per/yr (Annl. Comp)	−5.01%	7.25%	0.16%	16.10%	
Per/yr (Cont. Comp)	−5.14%	7.00%	0.16%	14.93%	
	Plan Scheduled	Plan Actual			
		Before T/Costs	After T/Costs	Investment Value	$10,569,185
Return Since Inception:				Total Turnover	118.14%
Total	6.37%	6.01%	5.69%	Total Trans. Costs	$29,768
Per/yr (Annl. Comp)	6.37%	6.01%	5.69%		
Per/yr (Cont. Comp)	6.18%	5.83%	5.54%		

0.2 percent for mortgages, and 14.9 percent for cash. The scheduled return was 6.2 percent, equal to the best of the four asset returns (Treasury bills in this case) less 8.8 percent. The actual performance of the plan was 5.8 percent before and 5.5 percent after transaction costs, very close to the schedule. The difference between the actual and promised performance is due to monthly (rather than continuous) rebalancing and to the actual risk parameters over the investment horizon differing from the assumed values (which were estimated over a previous period).

CHAPTER 27

Volatility: Omission Impossible

By Gifford Fong, Oldrich Vasicek, and Daihyun Yoo

INTRODUCTION

Investors have long understood the need to measure how changes in interest rates will affect the value of fixed-income portfolios. Duration and convexity, used to measure these effects, belong in every portfolio manager's tool kit. But these alone do not give a complete picture of the risk in a portfolio. Changes in interest rates are not the only source of risk in fixed-income investment. What about changes in interest rate volatility?

Nearly all fixed-income instruments contain embedded options. The price of a callable bond, for example, depends on the value of the call option; this, in turn, depends on the volatility of interest rates. Measuring an instrument's sensitivity to interest rate volatility is thus central to valuing the instrument as a whole.

The Black-Scholes formula shows that options' sensitivity to volatility, and the value of callable bonds, pass-throughs, futures, and other instruments with option-like features also depends on market volatility. Even noncallable bonds are volatility-dependent. The published results from Vasicek (1977) (Chapter 6 of this volume), Cox, Ingersoll, and Ross (1985), and others on the behavior of the term structure of interest rates show the presence of the volatility parameter in the bond pricing formula.

Just as the fixed-income investor needs to know how changing interest rates affect portfolio value, he or she should be concerned about the effects of random (stochastic) changes in volatility. This article outlines a

Risk, 5 (2) (1992), 62–65.

new two-factor term structure model that explicitly incorporates volatility as a stochastic factor and produces a new risk measure—volatility exposure.

STOCHASTIC VOLATILITY TERM STRUCTURE

Term structure theory attempts to define the behavior of interest rates. Its starting point is to identify the stochastic factors that explain the movement of interest rates. The stochastic processes that govern the behavior of the factors are then specified.

The next step is to derive an equilibrium condition that precludes riskless arbitrage, and to define the risk premia associated with the factors. This results in a partial differential equation for the bond price. For the theory to be practicable, a closed-form solution should be achievable. The exposure of the bond price to the stochastic factors can then be evaluated, and the risk measures quantified. Finally, the pricing can be extended to more complex instruments such as interest rate–contingent claims.

The stochastic volatility term structure (SVTS) describes the behavior of the short rate r by a diffusion process:

$$dr = \alpha(\bar{r} - r)dt + \sqrt{v}dx \tag{1}$$

where

dr = change in the short rate,
α = speed of reversion to the mean $\bar{r}$,
$\bar{r}$ = long-term mean of the short rate,
dt = change in time,
v = instantaneous variance (volatility), and
dx = random element.

Eq. (1) describes the short rate as a continuous process with a tendency to revert to a long-term mean value. The strength of this tendency is proportional to its current deviation from the mean. Thus, high rates have a tendency to come down, while low rates tend to go up. In all cases, however, there is a random component associated with the change in interest rates, which can make high rates go higher or low rates go lower. The magnitude of this random component is described by its variance $v = \sigma^2$.

If the variance v is a constant, as previous models have assumed, a one-factor description of the term structure can be derived. In the SVTS specification, the variance (volatility) v is a second stochastic factor, described by the following equation:

$$dv = \gamma(\bar{v} - v)dt + \xi\sqrt{v}dx \tag{2}$$

where

$$\begin{aligned} dv &= \text{change in volatility,} \\ \gamma &= \text{speed of reversion to the mean } \overline{v}, \\ \overline{v} &= \text{long-term average volatility,} \\ dt &= \text{change in time,} \\ \xi^2 v &= \text{instantaneous variance, and} \\ dy &= \text{random element.} \end{aligned}$$

Similar in form to the short-rate equation, the volatility equation (2) also has a mean reverting tendency with strength proportional to the current deviation from the mean level. Unlike the equation for the short rate, however, the random component has a variance proportional to the current level of volatility. This means that volatility changes less abruptly in very quiet markets than in very unstable markets.

In addition, the random element dx of the short rate and the random element dy of the volatility can be correlated with a correlation coefficient ρ. Thus, increasing levels of rates are typically accompanied by an increase in their volatility and vice versa, as indeed happens in reality.

Under this description of the term structure, the price $P = P(t, r, v)$ of a zero coupon bond with term t depends on the values of the two stochastic factors, r and v. From Ito's lemma, the price change is then governed by the factor changes dr, dv according to the equation

$$\frac{dP}{P} = \frac{1}{P}\left(-\frac{\partial P}{\partial t} + \tfrac{1}{2}v\frac{\partial^2 P}{\partial r^2} + \xi\rho v\frac{\partial^2 P}{\partial r \partial v} + \tfrac{1}{2}\xi^2 v\frac{\partial^2 P}{\partial v^2}\right)dt + \frac{1}{P}\frac{\partial P}{\partial r}dr + \frac{1}{P}\frac{\partial P}{\partial v}dv. \tag{3}$$

Given the nature of the price changes specified by Eq. (3), it is possible to form a portfolio of three bonds of different maturities in such proportions that the dependence on the risk factors dr, dv is eliminated. Since this portfolio is riskless, its rate of return must be equal to the riskless rate r.

This is the arbitrage argument first invoked by Black and Scholes in their 1973 article. Indeed, the impossibility of a riskless arbitrage is a necessary condition in an efficient market. If excess profits are to be achieved, then risk must be assumed.

Formalizing the argument results in the partial differential equation

$$\begin{aligned} &-\frac{\partial P}{\partial t} + (\alpha\overline{r} - \alpha r + \lambda v)\frac{\partial P}{\partial r} + (\gamma\overline{v} - \gamma v - \xi\eta v)\frac{\partial P}{\partial v} \\ &+ \tfrac{1}{2}v\frac{\partial^2 P}{\partial r^2} + \xi\rho v\frac{\partial^2 P}{\partial r \partial v} + \tfrac{1}{2}\xi^2 v\frac{\partial^2 P}{\partial v^2} - rP = 0 \end{aligned} \tag{4}$$

that must be satisfied by the bond prices $P(t, r, v)$ in order for the market to be efficient.

Eq. (4) contains terms that capture the pricing of risk in a risk-averse market. We have assumed that the market price of risk corresponding to each of the stochastic factors is proportional to the level of risk in the market, with the proportionality constants λ and η.

The solution of Eq. (4) subject to the boundary condition $P(0, r, v) = 1$ is given by the expression

$$P(t, r, v) = \exp(-rD(t) + vF(t) + G(t)). \tag{5}$$

The quantities $D(t), F(t), G(t)$ in Eq. (5) are functions of the term t alone. They are obtained as the solutions of ordinary differential equations to which the partial differential equation reduces. In particular, the function $D(t)$ is given by

$$D(t) = (1 - e^{-\alpha t})/\alpha. \tag{6}$$

The functions $F(t)$ and $G(t)$ are given by more complicated (but closed-form) expressions, involving the confluent hypergeometric function. For the exact formulas, refer to Fong and Vasicek (1991).

We may point out that the form of the bond pricing equation (5) and the specifications of the functions D, F, and G are deduced from the condition of market efficiency, rather than simply declared. This provides a rigorous framework that goes beyond the intuitive description that is commonly the first and only step in many term structure formulations.

The term structure of interest rates is determined from the pricing Eq. (5). If we define $R(t, r, v)$ as the spot rate of term t, then

$$R(t, r, v) = rD(t)/t - vF(t)/t - G(t)/t. \tag{7}$$

Eq. (7) describes the behavior of interest rates as a function of the term and the development in time of the two stochastic factors r and v. The resulting spot rate curves can be monotone or have one or two humps. Figures 27.1 to 27.3 show the shapes of the spot rate curves for several values of the parameters. Note in particular in Figure 27.3 that the SVTS allows for the possibility of different yield curves when both the short and the long end of the curves are fixed, which cannot happen in a single-factor model. From the form of the solution for the bond price in Eq. (5), we note that

$$D(t) = -\frac{1}{P}\frac{\partial P}{\partial r} \tag{8}$$

$$F(t) = \frac{1}{P}\frac{\partial P}{\partial v}. \tag{9}$$

The quantities D and F are thus, respectively, the rate exposure (i.e., duration) and the exposure to volatility. Together, duration and volatility exposure constitute the risk parameters of a bond. Moreover, the expected rate of return is also fully determined by the two measures. Two securities or portfolios will have the same returns over a given period if their durations and their volatility exposures are kept matched during that period.

TERM STRUCTURES OF INTEREST RATES

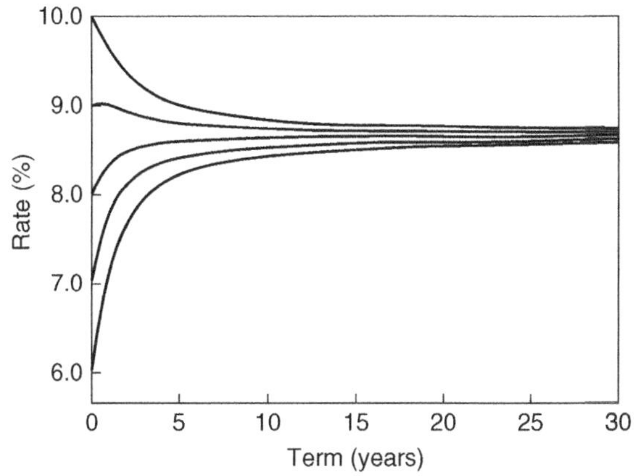

FIGURE 27.1 For Different Values of the Short Rate

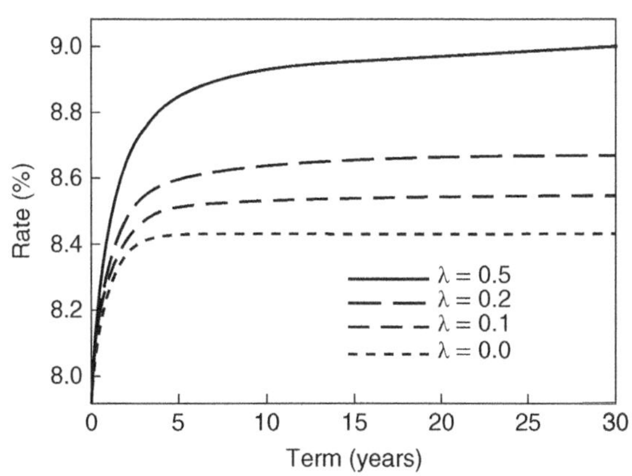

FIGURE 27.2 For Different Values of Risk Premium

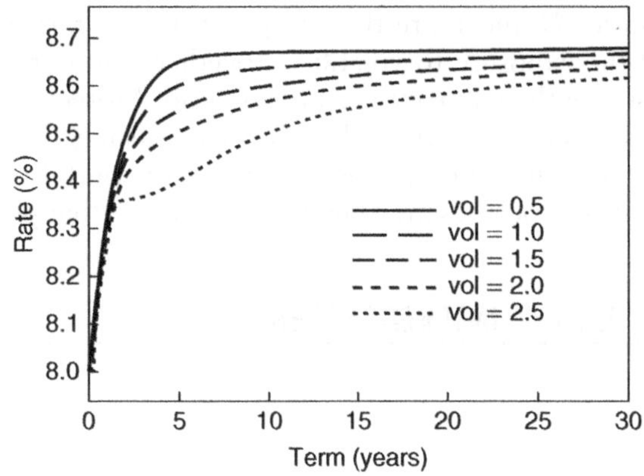

FIGURE 27.3 For Different Values of Current Volatility

VOLATILITY EXPOSURE

Figure 27.4 depicts the shape of the function $F(t)$ that constitutes the measure of volatility exposure for a zero coupon bond. We note that in most of its range, it is a concave function, unlike, for instance, Macauley duration (linear) or convexity (convex quadratic).

Simple calculation shows that duration or volatility exposure for a coupon bond is each weighted averages of the duration or volatility exposures of its individual cash flows. The same principle applies to portfolios of fixed-income instruments: Both risk measures combine linearly as a function of the market value of the portfolio components.

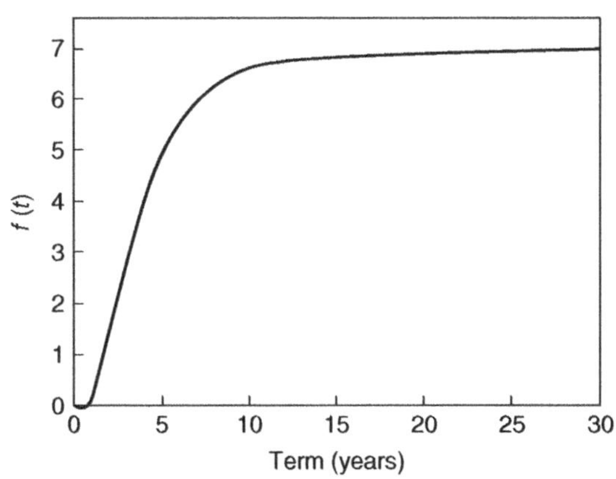

FIGURE 27.4 Volatility Exposure

INDEX TRACKING

One possible application of volatility management is in index tracking. The approach is to apply volatility analysis and control using a strategic optimization system called Stratos. The effectiveness of this system can be measured by comparing the tracking error produced by a Stratos portfolio with that of a more traditional approach to bond tracking, Bondtrac, as shown in Table 27.1. (Both systems come from Gifford Fong Associates.)

We chose the period October 1990 to March 1991 for the simulations, since we wished to select a six-month time period in which the implied volatilities changed significantly. We used the spot rate on one-month T-bill for the risk-free short rate. The target index was the widely used Shearson Lehman Treasury Index. Since the SVTS theory asserts that even the prices of noncallable bonds are affected by volatility, we restricted ourselves to such securities.

To compare the effectiveness of Bondtrac versus Stratos, both systems optimized a portfolio containing the same assets and indexed against the same target index. To replicate the index using the traditional approach (Bondtrac), we separated the bonds into 10 cells; these cells were defined by coupon and maturity break points.

The index was first partitioned into two groups by coupon (0–10% and 10–30%), then both coupon groups were partitioned into five maturity groups (1 to 2 years, 2 to 5 years, 5 to 10 years, 10 to 20 years, and 20 to 30 years). These 10 cells gave a fair representation of the characteristics of the target index, which was made up of high-coupon and low-coupon bonds with short to long maturities.

After randomly selecting one bond from each cell to be included in the portfolio, we ran Bondtrac to calculate the optimal composition of the 10 bonds. In this optimization procedure, Bondtrac tries to match the duration, convexity, and cell representation of the portfolio with those of the index.

We then ran Stratos with the same bonds used by Bondtrac to get the optimal composition for the Stratos portfolio. Unlike Bondtrac, Stratos tries to match duration, convexity, and volatility exposure without aiming to match the index cell representation.

Once we had the optimal portfolio compositions, we calculated the actual returns from each portfolio strategy. The tracking error was defined as the deviation of the portfolio return from the index return ($R_B - R_I$ and $R_S - R_I$, where R_B is the return on the Bondtrac portfolio, R_S is the return on the Stratos portfolio, and R_I denotes the return on the index). The tracking errors found are reported in Table 27.1.

TABLE 27.1 Tracking error: stratos versus bondtrac

		Monthly returns (%)			Tracking error (%)	
Period	Volatility (%)	Bondtrac	Stratos	Index	Bondtrac	Stratos
October 1990	3.791	1.652	1.667	1.609	0.043	0.058
November 1990	3.710	2.267	2.150	2.107	0.160	0.043
December 1990	3.263	1.580	1.582	1.576	0.004	0.006
January 1991	4.037	1.071	1.042	1.042	0.029	0.000
February 1991	3.429	0.519	0.532	0.548	0.029	0.016
March 1991	3.158	0.439	0.503	0.477	0.038	0.026
Average	3.565				0.028	0.019
Standard deviation	0.338				0.065	0.025

With the randomly selected bond, Stratos generated lower tracking error in terms of absolute value in four out of six months. The average tracking error was 2.8 basis points (bp) for the Bondtrac portfolio and 1.9 bp for Stratos; theoretically, it should be zero for both. We tested the null hypothesis H_0: $\mu_B = \mu_S = 0$. The values of the t statistic were 0.43 and 0.76, too low to reject the null hypothesis.

The monthly standard deviations of the tracking errors were 6.5 bp and 2.5 bp, respectively. On an annualized basis, the corresponding figures are 23 bp and 9 bp—a substantial difference.

To test whether this difference in standard deviations in tracking error was statistically significant, we constructed another null hypothesis $H_0: \sigma_B^2 = \sigma_S^2$ against the alternative $H_1: \sigma_B^2 > \sigma_S^2$. To test these hypotheses, we computed the ratio of sample variances, which has F distribution if H_0 is true. The computed F value was $6.62 > 5.05 = F$ (5 percent). We therefore rejected the null hypothesis in favor of the alternative at the 5 percent significance level. The evidence proves that the variance of the tracking error of the Stratos portfolio was smaller than that of the Bondtrac portfolio.

Stratos generally tracked the index better than Bondtrac during the period covered in this study. In particular, it tended to work better when the volatility of the short rate changed significantly, as happened from November 1990 to January 1991.

Applying the concept of volatility exposure to an indexed Treasury portfolio can significantly reduce risk.

REFERENCES

Cox, J.C., J.E. Ingersoll Jr., and S.A. Ross. (1985). "A Theory of the Term Structure of Interest Rates." *Econometrica*, 53, 385–407.

Fong, H.G., and O.A. Vasicek. (1991). *Interest Rate Volatility as a Stochastic Factor*, unpublished, Gifford Fong Associates.

Fong, H.G., and O.A. Vasicek. (1991). "Fixed Income Volatility Management." *Journal of Portfolio Management* (Summer), 41–46.

Vasicek, O.A. (1977). "An Equilibrium Characterization of the Term Structure." *Journal of Financial Economics*, 5, 177–188.

CHAPTER 28

A Multidimensional Framework for Risk Analysis

By Gifford Fong and Oldrich A. Vasicek

ABSTRACT

The variety and complexity of portfolio holdings have given rise to the need for additional analyses for purposes of risk management. A framework for risk analysis includes three dimensions: sensitivity analysis, value at risk (VaR), and stress testing. This article describes each dimension and suggests a procedure for achieving a VaR measure. Once individual holdings are analyzed, attention can be directed to portfolio-level analyses and the types of output suitable for monitoring purposes. In combination, this framework can capture the important features of portfolio risk.

INTRODUCTION

Risk control in asset management is the ability to manage the uncertainty associated with the investment process. Fundamental to risk control is risk measurement, which can be thought of as quantification of the characteristics of risk.

Early attempts at risk quantification dealt with investments in relatively simple security types. This approach included both fixed and known cash flows, as is the case for Treasury securities and equities described

Financial Analysts Journal, 53 (4) (1997), 51–57.

by lognormal return distributions. Risk was characterized by volatility of returns, measured by quantities such as variance, standard deviation, or mean absolute deviation (Markowitz 1952, 1959).

As the concept of risk measurement and risk control evolved over time, additional approaches were introduced. In the case of fixed-income securities, the concept of duration, modified duration, and effective duration became widespread tools for risk management (see, e.g., Fabozzi 1988, Appendix A). For equities, beta coefficients and fundamental betas were introduced to provide additional capability in managing the risk of equity portfolios (Sharpe 1964; Rosenberg and Guy 1976a, 1976b). These analytical paths are indicative of specialization by asset type since the earlier attempts at risk management. Portfolio-oriented measures such as the concept of shortfall risk also have been introduced (Leibowitz and Henriksson 1989).

As the structure of marketable assets has become more complex and as market conditions have exposed the limitations of the traditional measures of risk, a number of recommendations have emerged to address the perceived need for additional risk analysis insight. The Group of Thirty (1993) reviewed the derivative product industry practice and suggested capital at risk as an appropriate risk measure. The Group of Thirty's Derivative Policy Group further described specific parameters for a capital-at-risk analysis.

The complexities of the many risk factors and their interaction call for a multidimensional approach to risk measurement. The nature of complex marketable assets has increased the requirements for the necessary analytical methods. In general, these methods represent a revisit to the early macro perspective in viewing risk from an overall portfolio standpoint.

These methods must deal with the multiplicity of risk sources and their correlations. They must also recognize the asymmetry of the return distribution. Derivative securities, such as options or swap transactions with embedded options, exhibit a skewed price distribution that cannot be adequately analyzed using the traditional risk measures suitable for simpler investments.

The objective of this study is to describe the methods appropriate for quantifying the risk of complex investments that are subject to a variety of risk sources. The overall methodology consists of three functional elements: sensitivity analysis, value at risk (VaR), and stress testing. Each element has its unique contribution to comprehensive risk measurement. Sensitivity analysis provides a basic building block to risk analysis and is a necessary input for hedging activities. VaR provides a useful summary, under prespecified conditions, of the amount at risk, given the risk characteristics of the portfolio. Stress testing complements VaR by providing the results of extreme scenarios of joint risk-factor change.

This chapter discusses ways of measuring and analyzing quantifiable risks, with emphasis on assessment of total portfolio risk and on the tools for risk management. The discussion, for illustrative purposes, focuses on fixed-income portfolios, because they typically contain the largest percentage of derivative securities and transactions. The principles of the analysis, however, apply to portfolios of all asset types.

RISK SOURCES

An investment portfolio of securities, derivatives, or contracts is exposed to many types of risk, including the following:

- *Market risks.* The value of a portfolio may change because of changes in market conditions, such as changes in a stock market index or in the level of interest rates.
- *Foreign exchange risks.* The value of foreign investments may change because of exchange rate movements.
- *Option risks.* The counterparty may exercise its options at a time that is disadvantageous to the security holder.
- *Prepayment risks.* Principal payments and other cash flows may be accelerated at a time when prepayments are undesirable.
- *Credit risks.* The counterparty or issuer of the security may be unable to fulfill its obligations.
- *Specific risks.* Individual securities may be subject to price changes not explained by changes in the level of the market.
- *Liquidity risks.* A security may be difficult or impossible to sell or liquidate at its proper value.
- *Management and operations risks.* The portfolio may be poorly managed or maintained, such as by engaging in disadvantageous transactions or executing trades improperly.
- *Administrative risks.* A loss in value may result from excessive fees or fraud.
- *Regulatory risks.* The governing laws and regulations may change, requiring adjustments to a portfolio that can affect its value.
- *Event risks.* The portfolio may be vulnerable to specific events such as political instability in a country in which the portfolio has an exposure.

The total risk of a portfolio is the potential decline in its market value. Measuring this risk requires quantification of possible market value changes, under probable as well as extreme circumstances, resulting from the individual risk sources and their interplay.

A quantitative measure of the contribution of the various types of risk to the market value change is possible for only some of them, including market, option, prepayment, foreign exchange, credit, and specific risks. Additional risk components, notably liquidity, management, administrative, regulatory, and specific event risks, must be determined by other means, including judgmental procedures, and incorporated into the total risk assessment.

An investor may be able to hedge or otherwise compensate for some of these risks; for example, the portfolio's interest rate risk can be easily counterbalanced by short positions in interest rate futures contracts, and foreign exchange risk can be eliminated by forward currency hedges. The specific risk of the portfolio may be diversified away by the investor's other holdings. Proper risk management, therefore, requires measuring the exposures to the sources of risk in such a way that they can be reduced or eliminated.

RISK EXPOSURES

An essential basis to risk measurement and management is determining the security and portfolio exposures to risk factors. Risk factors are market characteristics whose change affects the value of a given security or contract. For fixed-income derivatives, the principal risk factors are as follows (for each of the currencies involved):

- *Interest rate level*, the overall level of the term structure whose shifts will affect the portfolio value
- *Rates of benchmark maturities*, the specific maturity points along the term structure by which changes in interest rates can be measured
- *Spreads over government rates* (such as various corporate bond quality sectors, swap spreads, or mortgage-backed security spreads), the yield premiums attributable to specific nongovernment securities
- *Volatility of rates*, measures of interest rate variability for various maturities and forward horizons
- *Exchange rates*, measures of currency exchange rates

Denote the values of these risk factors by $F_1, F_2, \ldots, F_n$. If P is the value of a security, then the change in the security value resulting from the change in the risk factors can, in the first approximation, be given as

$$\frac{\Delta P}{P} = -\sum_{i=1}^{n} D_i \Delta F_i. \tag{1}$$

The quantities $D_1, \ldots, D_n$ in this equation are the exposures, or sensitivities, of the security to each of the risk factors. They measure the percentage change in the value of the security resulting from a unit change in the value of the factors.

A well-known example is the exposure to changes in the level of interest rates, which is the security duration. Another example is the exposure to changes in volatility (relevant especially for options), sometimes referred to as vega. In equities, the exposure of a stock to a stock market index move is proportional to its beta.

If we postulate a linear relationship between changes in the value of the factors and the percentage price change represented by Eq. (1), then the exposures to the factors are defined by the partial derivatives as

$$D_i = -\frac{1}{P}\frac{\partial P}{\partial F_i}. \tag{2}$$

If F_i *is* the interest rate level, Eq. (2) is the familiar definition of duration. It generalizes in the same form (apart from the choice of sign in Eqs. (1) and (2), which is strictly a matter of convention) to other risk factors as well. Care needs to be taken that the duration and all other exposures are correctly measured on an options-adjusted basis. If so, the price sensitivities will have already taken into account any embedded options affecting price changes.

For several reasons, except as a first-order approximation, Eqs. (1) and (2) are not a satisfactory representation for the price change of a security. First, the price change is not a linear function of the factor change, particularly for derivatives. Second, the changes in the factors are not instantaneous, so a change resulting from the passage of time needs to be incorporated. Third, the market move may not explain fully the change in the value of a security. Fourth, it is more appropriate to characterize the dollar change rather than the percentage value change because derivatives such as swaps and other contracts often start with a low or even zero value.

Assume that the change ΔP in the market value of a security over an interval Δt is governed by the equation

$$\Delta P = A - \sum_{i=1}^{n} D_i X_i + \tfrac{1}{2}\sum_{i=1}^{n} C_i X_i^2 + Y, \tag{3}$$

where $X_i = \Delta F_i$ are changes in the value of each risk factor, and Y is the risk specific to each security. The quantities D_i, C_i are then the linear and quadratic exposures of the security value to the factors. They are analogous to the dollar duration and dollar convexity measures of interest rate exposure. So that the nonlinear price response is properly approximated, however, D_i, C_i should be measured for a finite factor change rather than the infinitesimal one given by Eq. (2). The exposures are estimated as

$$D_i = -\frac{P_i' - P_i''}{2\Delta F_i} \tag{4}$$

and

$$C_i = \frac{P_i' + P_i'' - 2P}{(\Delta F_i)^2}, \tag{5}$$

where P_i' and P_i'' are the prices of the security calculated under the assumption that the risk factor F_i changed by the amount of ΔF_i and $-\Delta F_i$, respectively. Some considerations (related to the theory of Hermite integration) suggest that ΔF_i should be taken specifically to equal

$$\begin{aligned} \Delta F_i &= \sigma_i \sqrt{3} \\ &= 1.73\sigma_i, \end{aligned} \tag{6}$$

where σ_i is the volatility of F_i over the interval Δt. In Eqs. (4), (5), and (6), the exposures characterize the *global* response curve of the security price rather than the local behavior captured by durations and convexities.

The quantity A in Eq. (3) is equal to

$$A = \mu - \tfrac{1}{2}\sum_{i=1}^{n} C_i \sigma_i^2, \tag{7}$$

where μ is the expected return, $\mu = E\Delta P$.

This representation of price behavior facilitates risk analysis and measurement. The linear risk exposures D_i and the quadratic risk exposures C_i combine in the portfolio as simple sums of those exposures for the individual securities. Thus, if D_{ik} is the linear exposure of the k-th security to the i-th risk factor (and similarly for C_{ik}), then

$$D_{iP} = \sum_{k=1}^{m} D_{ik}$$

and

$$C_{iP} = \sum_{k=1}^{m} C_{ik}$$

would be the risk exposures for the portfolio.

A risk-management process may then consist of a conscientious program of keeping all the portfolio risk exposures close to zero,

$$D_{iP} = 0, i = 1, \ldots, n$$

$$C_{iP} = 0, i = 1, \ldots, n$$

to eliminate an undesirable dependence on market factors. This approach is equivalent to hedging against all sources of market risk. The specific risks, $s_k^2 = \mathrm{Var}(Y_k)$, which combine by the formula

$$s_P^2 = \sum_{k=1}^{m} s_k^2,$$

can only be reduced by diversification.

The overall variability of the portfolio or security value can be calculated from its risk exposures, using the formula

$$\begin{aligned}\sigma^2 &= \mathrm{Var}(\Delta P) \\ &= \sum_{i=1}^{n}\sum_{j=1}^{n} D_i D_j \sigma_{ij} + \tfrac{1}{2}\sum_{i=1}^{n}\sum_{j=1}^{n} C_i C_j \sigma_{ij}^2 + s^2, \end{aligned} \tag{8}$$

which is a consequence of the value change Eq. (3). Here, the σ_{ij} are the covariances in the changes of the i-th and j-th risk factors; that is,

$$\sigma_{ij} = \mathrm{Cov}(X_i, X_j).$$

To the extent possible, the variances and covariances should be obtained from current pricing of derivatives whose values depend on these variances (the implicit volatilities). For instance, quotes are available in the swap market for interest rate volatilities, calculated from market prices of swaptions. These volatilities reflect the market's estimate of the prospective, rather than past, interest rate variability. Only when such implicit volatilities are not available for a given risk factor should a historical variability be used. In that case, care should be taken that the historical period is long enough to cover most market conditions and cycles.

The calculations of the price variability of a portfolio, its sectors, and the individual securities can be an accurate picture of the structure of the risks.

In addition to the total price variabilities, risk may also be broken down by source. One possible presentation is

Source	Volatility (%)
Interest rate risk	10
Other market risk	2
Derivative risks	3
Specific risks	1
Foreign exchange risks	6
Total	22

These risks are defined as follows:

Interest rate risk = portfolio value vulnerability to changes in interest rates

Other market risks = additional components of the total market risk (spread changes, basis risk, etc.)

Derivative risks = nonmarket risks, including options and prepayment risks, generated by the portfolio's holding in derivative securities

Specific portfolio risk = component of total risk unexplained by the market factors (akin to a tracking error for index funds)

Foreign exchange risk = exchange rate fluctuations (to the extent they are not hedged)

Although the risks are measured by standard deviation, and standard deviations do not add, the component risks do add up to the total risk. This summation is accomplished by calculating the risk increment each component adds to the previous subtotal. This method makes the decomposition dependent on the order in which the components are listed, but it also makes the components meaningful: The 3 percent derivative risk, for example, means that the fund's derivative holdings add 3 percentage points to the 12 percent price variability attributable to market factors.

VALUE AT RISK

The capital at risk, also called the value at risk (VaR, not to be confused with variance, Var, of the previous section), is a single, highly useful number for the purposes of risk assessment. It is defined as the decline in the portfolio market value that can be expected within a given time interval (such as two weeks) with a probability not exceeding a given number (such as 1 percent). Mathematically, if

$$\text{Prob}(\Delta P \leq -\text{VaR}) = \alpha, \tag{9}$$

then VaR is equal to the value at risk at the probability level α.

To calculate the VaR, it is necessary to determine the probability distribution of the portfolio value change. This distribution can be derived from Eq. (3).

Assume that the factor changes X_i have a jointly normal distribution with zero mean and a covariance matrix $(\sigma_{ij}), i, j = 1, \ldots, n$. Then the first three moments of ΔP are given by Eqs. (7), (8), and (10), where

$$\begin{aligned} \mu_3 &= E(\Delta P - \mu)^3 \\ &= 3\sum_{i=1}^{n}\sum_{j=1}^{n}\sum_{k=1}^{n} D_i D_j C_k \sigma_{ik}\sigma_{jk} + \sum_{i=1}^{n}\sum_{j=1}^{n}\sum_{k=1}^{n} C_i C_j C_k \sigma_{ij}\sigma_{jk}\sigma_{ki}. \end{aligned} \tag{10}$$

Knowing the three moments, the probability distribution of ΔP can be approximated and the VaR calculated. There are theoretical reasons to use the gamma distribution as a proxy for that distribution. The resulting formula for the value at risk is then very simple:

$$\text{VaR} = k(\gamma)\sigma, \tag{11}$$

where σ is the standard deviation of the value of the portfolio or security, obtained as the square root of the variance given in Eq. (8), and γ is the skewness of the distribution,

$$\gamma = \frac{\mu_3}{\sigma^3}, \tag{12}$$

calculated using Eqs. (7) and (9). The ordinate $k(\gamma)$ is obtained from Table 28.1 (corresponding to the gamma distribution). Table 28.1 extends only to the values $\gamma = \pm 2.83$ because that is the highest magnitude attainable for the skewness of the quadratic form in Eq. (3).

Note that the value 2.33 in Table 28.1 corresponding to $\gamma = 0$ is the 1 percent point of the normal distribution. In other words, if the portfolio value change can be represented by the symmetric normal distribution, the VaR at the 1 percent probability will be

$$\text{VaR} = 2.33\sigma.$$

TABLE 28.1 0.01 ordinates as a function of skewness

γ	$k(\gamma)$
−2.83	3.99
−2.00	3.61
−1.00	3.03
−0.67	2.80
−0.50	2.69
0.0	2.33
0.50	1.96
0.67	1.83
1.00	1.59
2.00	0.99
2.83	0.71

For most derivative securities and portfolios, however, the probability distribution is highly skewed one way or the other, and the normal ordinates do not apply. The numbers in Table 28.1 represent the proper ordinate values.

In fact, the ratio of the ordinate in Table 28.1 corresponding to the skewness of the portfolio to the normal ordinate provides the increase (or reduction) of the VaR attributable to the portfolio composition. Thus, if the portfolio has a negative skewness of $\gamma = -0.50$ (such as a portfolio of callable bonds), the VaR is $2.69/2.33 = 115$ percent higher than it would be if the portfolio returns were symmetric. A portfolio with positive skewness of $\gamma = 0.50$ (for instance, holding bonds with puts) will require only $1.96/2.33 = 84$ percent as much capital to cover the VaR as a portfolio with normally distributed returns.

Eq. (11) does not include the expected return μ, because the mean is of a lower order of magnitude (namely Δt) than the standard deviation σ (which is of the order $\sqrt{\Delta t}$) and can be neglected.

The VaR can be calculated for individual securities, portfolio sectors, and the total portfolio, as well as by sources of risk. This approach can lead to a useful breakdown, such as that presented in Table 28.2. The numbers in Table 28.2 do not necessarily add up, either down or across. The reason is that the VaR resulting from, say, interest rate risk may come from rising interest rates for one security (as for most bonds) and declining interest rates for another (such as an income-only security or a short position in futures). The reason the numbers do not add up across the sources of risk is that events of a given probability (say, 1 percent) do not add up: An interest rate change that can happen with 1 percent likelihood when considered alone

TABLE 28.2 Example of value at risk calculation

Example Portfolio	Interest Rate Risk	Other Market Risks	Derivatives Risks	Specific Risks	Foreign Exchange Risks	Total Risk
Sector A						
Security 1	$103,400	$19,500	$52,100	$5,700	$0	$133,100
Security 2	85,600	0	0	2,300	0	86,700
Sector A total	$189,000	$19,500	$52,100	$6,100	$0	$217,500
Sector B						
Security 3	—	—	—	—	—	—
Security 4	—	—	—	—	—	—
Sector B total	—	—	—	—	—	—
Sector C (etc.)						
Portfolio Total	$2,358,100	$311,700	$827,700	$63,300	$556,900	$3,581,900

Note: The portfolio is assumed to be composed of several sectors (industries, etc.). Sector A amounts are given for illustrative purposes only; the dash represents amounts for the other sectors, which are not made explicit.

is not the same as if it would happen together with, say, an exchange rate movement.

An alternative to Table 28.2 would be to measure the component values at risk incrementally. This method would mean that the VaR attributable to derivative risks, for example, would be calculated as the difference between the VaR obtained when considering jointly interest rate risk, other market risks, and derivative risks and the VaR obtained when considering interest rate and other market risks alone. Such measurement depends on the order in which the sources of risk are taken, which seems somewhat arbitrary. Moreover, when applied down the table for securities and sectors, this method also presumes that the risks of, say, Security 2 are measured on top of those of Security 1, which may make sense in some situations (such as a futures position as a hedge on top of bond holdings), but makes less sense in others.

STRESS TESTING

Although VaR provides a useful assessment of potential losses from various sources of risk and their interplay, it should be complemented by a series of stress tests. A stress test consists of specifying a scenario of extreme and unfavorable market conditions occurring over a specific time interval and then evaluating the portfolio gains or losses under such scenarios. This approach is useful for a number of reasons: It allows for consideration of

TABLE 28.3 Stress tests

Scenario	Gain/Loss
1. USD interest rate up 100 basis points (bps)	–$10,123,900
2. USD interest rate down 100 bps	10,234,400
3. USD interest rate: 2 year up 50 bps, 10 year down 50 bps	410,500
4. USD interest rate: 2 year down 50 bps, 10 year up 50 bps	–410,200
5. JPY/USD up 10%	–1,200,700
6. JPY/USD down 10%	1,200,700
7. JPY interest rate up 30 bps	–210,800
8. JPY interest rate down 30 bps	210,400
9. JPY/USD up 10% and JPY interest rate up 30 bps	–1,035,300

path-dependent events such as cash flows on collateralized mortgage obligations; it does not rely on a specific form of the value-response curve, such as the quadratic form in Eq. (3); it appeals to intuition by showing the situations under which a loss can occur, which is lost in VaR alone; and last but not least, it is required or recommended by the various oversight agencies and auditors.

Table 28.3 shows a possible stress test output table. Scenarios 3 and 4 represent the US dollar interest rate term structure steepening or flattening, which may affect long/short rate basis swaps. Scenario 9 is a combination of an exchange rate change and foreign interest rate change, which may affect currency swaps and the like.

Stress tests are less systematic and somewhat ad hoc compared with VaR. Their usefulness is in an analysis of the portfolio response to market-condition changes that are more extreme or persistent than those likely to occur in a short time interval. Over large and protracted market movements, the value of a security or portfolio may show a response curve that is not well represented by a quadratic form such as Eq. (3). An example is provided in Figure 28.1, which shows the price response to interest rate movements for a callable bond.

The VaR calculations for this security would be based on an interest rate move possible with 1 percent probability over a time interval, such as two weeks, which may be some 50 basis points. Within that range, the price-response curve is adequately described by the assumptions of the VaR calculation. The VaR is therefore a proper measure of *instantaneous*, or current, portfolio riskiness, which is all that would be necessary if all securities in the portfolio were perfectly liquid and if the portfolio risk were managed on a continuous-time basis. Because this assumption is often unrealistic, it is advisable to measure portfolio value in response to extreme stress tests.

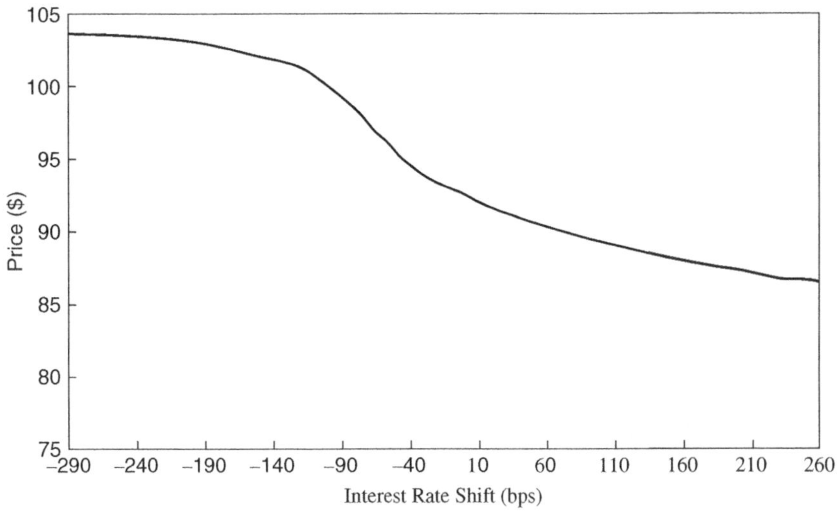

FIGURE 28.1 Price Response Curve

CONCLUSIONS

The risk in complex portfolios can be quantified. The market characteristics that affect the value of a security or portfolio are called risk factors. Risk factors that affect fixed-income derivatives include interest rate level, benchmark maturity rates, spread over government rates, volatility of rates, and exchange rates. A quadratic approximation may be used to quantify the risk exposure to those risk factors, and then a standard deviation may be calculated. The risk-summary number, value at risk (or capital at risk), is defined as the dollar amount that the total loss might exceed within a certain time period with a certain probability. The VaR may be calculated by a gamma distribution approximation. Although VaR gives a summary risk number, it does not tell the source or direction of the risk. To see the possible loss under extreme or least favorable market conditions, a series of stress tests must be performed. The VaR and the result of a comprehensive stress test give a better risk picture than either of them alone.

Risk measurement of fixed-income investments is an involved process. The result of using three methods—sensitivity analysis, value at risk, and stress testing—is an ability to evaluate complex return outcomes. Each of these techniques has an important role; in combination, they represent the comprehensive risk measurement necessary for portfolios with complex structures and interrelationships.

REFERENCES

Fabozzi, F.J. (1988). *Fixed Income Mathematics*. Chicago: Probus Publishing.

Group of Thirty. (1993). *Derivatives: Practices and Principles*. Washington, DC: Group of Thirty (July).

Leibowitz, M., and R.D. Henriksson. (1989). "Portfolio Optimization with Shortfall Constraints: A Confidence-Limit Approach to Managing Downside Risk." *Financial Analysts Journal*, 45 (2) (March/April), 34–41.

Markowitz, H.M. (1952). "Portfolio Selection." *Journal of Finance*, 7 (1) (March), 77–91.

—. (1959). *Portfolio Selection*. New Haven, CT: Yale University Press.

Rosenberg, B., and J. Guy. (1976a). "Beta and Investment Fundamentals." *Financial Analysts Journal*, 32 (3) (May/June), 60–72.

—. (1976b). "Beta and Investment Fundamentals—II." *Financial Analysts Journal*, 32 (4) (July/August), 62–71.

Sharpe, W.F. (1964). "Capital Asset Prices: A Theory of Market Equilibrium under Conditions of Risk." *Journal of Finance*, 19 (3) (September), 425–442.

CHAPTER 29

Plugging into Electricity

By Hélyette Geman and Oldrich Vasicek

FORWARD AND FUTURES CONTRACTS ON NONSTORABLE COMMODITIES: THE CASE OF ELECTRICITY

Most of the literature about modeling commodity spot and futures prices has dealt with storable commodities, such as wheat, gold, and oil. However, the deregulation of energy markets worldwide over the past few years has paved the way to free electricity markets, both for spot and derivatives trading, and made it necessary to focus on electricity's unique features as a commodity.

The most important feature is the nonstorability of power (except for hydroelectricity). It accounts for the spikes observed during periods of extreme weather conditions and/or lack of capacity: for example, in the U.S. Midwest in June 1998; on the U.S. East Coast in July 1999; and in California in much of 2000, followed by severe blackouts in early 2001.

From a financial economics standpoint, the nonstorability makes irrelevant (as argued by Eydeland & Geman, 1998) the notion of convenience yield, which represents the benefits accrued from "holding" the commodity. It also implies the collapse of the spot-forward relationship, as its proof involves cost-of-carry arguments between the current date and the maturity of the forward contract. Besides the nonstorability, electricity has unusual physical attributes that makes the design of well-functioning

Risk 14(8) (2001), 93–97; reprinted in A. Lipton (ed.), *Exotic Options: The Cutting Edge Collection* (London: Risk Books, 2003).

markets difficult: Rather than following regulatory rules or the rules of supply and demand balancing in each region, electricity obeys physical laws such as Kirchoff laws at each node. When there is congestion at a node, capacity becomes a good in its own right, distinct from electricity. The same fundamental observations would prevail in the case of cable-based telecommunications, wireless telecommunications, and bandwidth.

This chapter has three aims:

1. To examine the specific properties of forward contracts, since they play a central role in the electricity industry, not only in the trading agreements that have existed for decades but also for risk management purposes made necessary by today's highly volatile markets.
2. To analyze separately the behavior of futures contracts. In the general situation of stochastic interest rates that we consider (and without any assumption of independence between the shocks in the economy affecting electricity prices and interest rates), their prices are different from those of the forward contracts. This property was discussed in Cox, Ingersoll, & Ross (1981) and has to be taken into account when the length of the time period of analysis is too long to assume constant interest rates (which is the case, for instance, when investing in a power plant, a pipeline, or another physical asset).
3. To propose a process for the electricity spot price accounting for the spikes (upward jumps followed at some point by downward moves) observed in the power markets.

The first two points are discussed in the framework of diffusion processes, since our goal is to emphasize the specificities of forward and futures contracts in the case of nonstorability, namely the fact that they may not deserve the terminology of derivatives since they are *nonredundant* with the underlying asset (see Hakansson, 1979). The technical issues reside in the discussion of the martingale property satisfied under different probability measures by futures and forward prices.

FORWARD, FUTURES, AND OPTION PRICING IN A DIFFUSION SETTING

Let $B(t,T)$ be the price at time t of a bond with unit face value maturing at time T. Assume for simplicity that bond prices are governed by a one-factor model of the term structure of interest rates,

$$\frac{\mathrm{d}B(t,T)}{B(t,T)} = (r(t) + \lambda(t)\sigma_B(t,T))\mathrm{d}t + \sigma_B(t,T)\mathrm{d}X(t) \tag{1}$$

where $r(t)$ is the short rate, $\lambda(t)$ is the market price of bond risk, and $X(t)$ is a Wiener process. An asset $M(t)$ consisting of reinvestment at the short rate $r(t)$ will be called the money market account.

Assume that the spot price $S(t)$ of a unit of energy follows a diffusion process with mean μ_S, variance σ_S, and a correlation with bond prices ρ. The parameters μ_S , σ_S, and ρ may exhibit mean reversion, seasonality, and other aspects of the empirical spot price behavior. We can write the dynamics of S (under the actual probability measure) as

$$\frac{dS}{S} = \mu_S dt + \varphi_S dX + \psi_S dY \tag{2}$$

where $Y(t)$ is a Wiener process independent of $X(t)$ and $\varphi_S = \sigma_S \rho$, $\psi_S = \sigma_S \sqrt{1-\rho^2}$.

We wish to investigate the pricing of forward and futures contracts and options. Since energy cannot be stored, it is not possible to set up an arbitrage position between the spot price and the derivative. We can, however, apply the standard arbitrage argument to a position consisting of two derivatives, such as two futures contracts of different maturities, or a futures and a forward contracts. We will start with the pricing of the futures contract.

Let $F(t, T)$ be the price at time t of a futures contract with maturity T on the energy unit. In Appendix A, we show that there exists a process $v(t)$, which we can interpret as the market price of risk corresponding to the risk source $Y(t)$, such that

$$\frac{dF}{F} = (\lambda \varphi_F + v \psi_F) dt + \varphi_F dX + \psi_F dY. \tag{3}$$

There then exists an equivalent probability measure P* under which $F(t, T)$ is a martingale and

$$F(t, T) = E_t^* S(T). \tag{4}$$

This equation gives the pricing of the futures contracts.

The martingale property of the futures contracts and Eq. (4) are valid for storable commodities as well. The difference is that for storable commodities, the expected rate of return $E^* dS/S$ on the spot commodity under the risk-neutral measure is the risk-free rate, and consequently $S(t)/M(t)$ is a martingale under P*. (If there is a benefit/cost of storage accruing to the holder of the commodity at a rate y, called the convenience yield, then the martingale property is satisfied by the process $e^{yt} S(t)/M(t)$.) This is not true if the commodity is not storable. Both the long and the short position in the underlying commodity have, in effect, infinite carrying costs.

Denote by α the expected relative spot price change $E^*\mathrm{d}S/S$ under P*. We have

$$\alpha = \mu_S - \lambda\varphi_S - \nu\psi_S. \tag{5}$$

Since the spot process could not be involved in the arbitrage argument, we have in general $\alpha \neq r$. In other words, the price of risk $\nu(t)$ is in no relationship to the process describing the spot price. It means that the expectation in the formula for pricing of futures contracts will lead to a different value for a nonstorable commodity than it would have if the commodity could be stored. Due to the fact that $\alpha(t)$ is not observable, the futures contract pricing can be only applied relative to each other (i.e., giving the price of one contract in terms of the prices of other contracts).

Let us now turn to the pricing of forward contracts. Denote by $G(t,T)$ the price at time t of a forward contract on the energy unit with maturity at T. As shown in Appendix A, an arbitrage argument between the forward contract $G(t,T)$, a futures contract $F(t,T)$, the bond $B(t,T)$, and the money market account implies that $B(t,T)G(t,T)/M(t)$ is a martingale under P*. It follows that

$$G(t,T) = \frac{1}{B(t,T)} E_t^* S(T) \frac{M(t)}{M(T)}. \tag{6}$$

Again, this formula holds for pricing of forward contracts in general. If the commodity is storable, however, the expectation can be evaluated to yield

$$G(t,T) = \frac{S(t)}{B(t,T)}.$$

This could be established directly by the following well-known argument: The forward contract can be exactly duplicated by issuing a bond with the maturity value $G(t,T)$, buying the commodity with the proceeds today, and storing it until time T. When the commodity is not storable, this argument, and the aforementioned relationship, is not valid. For a discussion of the martingale property satisfied by the storable commodity forward price, see Geman (1989).

Consider now a European option on an energy unit with an expiration date T, and denote its price by $P(t,T)$. Let the terms of the option specify that

$$P(T,T) = f(S(T))$$

An arbitrage argument applied to the option, a futures contract $F(t,T)$, a bond $B(t,T)$, and the money market account implies that $P(t,T)/M(t)$ is a martingale under P*, and

$$P(t,T) = E_t^* f(S(T)) \frac{M(t)}{M(T)}. \tag{7}$$

EXAMPLES

Example 1. Suppose α is constant. Then

$$F(t, T) = S(t)\exp(\alpha(T - t)).$$

Since α is not directly observable, this equation provides only a relative pricing of futures contracts,

$$F(t, T_2) = F(t, T_1)^{(T_2-t)/(T_1-t)} S(t)^{(T_1-T_2)/(T_1-t)}.$$

In this case, the prices of futures contracts of all maturities can be calculated from the spot price and the price of one contract only.

Example 2. Suppose $\rho = 0$ and α, σ_S are functions of t and $S(t)$ only. Then $G(t, T) = F(t, T)$, and $F(t, T)$ is the solution of the partial differential equation

$$\frac{\partial F}{\partial t} + \alpha S\frac{\partial F}{\partial S} + \frac{1}{2}\sigma_S^2 S^2 \frac{\partial^2 F}{\partial S^2} = 0$$

subject to $F(t, T) = S(T)$. For instance, if $\log S$ follows a Gaussian mean-reverting process with the drift $\kappa(\theta - \log S)$ and $\kappa, \theta, \sigma_S, \nu$ are constant, then

$$F(t, T) = \exp\left(e^{-\kappa(T-t)}\log S(t) + \left(\theta - \frac{\nu\sigma_S}{\kappa} - \frac{\sigma_S^2}{2\kappa}\right)(1 - e^{-\kappa(T-t)}) + \frac{\sigma_S^2}{4\kappa}(1 - e^{-2\kappa(T-t)})\right).$$

Example 3. Suppose $\sigma_B(t, T)$ is deterministic (so that interest rates are Gaussian under the risk-neutral measure) and assume that $\alpha(t), \sigma_S(t), \rho(t)$ are also deterministic functions of t. Then

$$G(t, T) = S(t)\exp\left(\int_t^T \alpha(\tau)\,d\tau + \int_t^T \rho(\tau)\sigma_B(\tau, T)\sigma_S(\tau)d\tau\right)$$

$$F(t, T) = G(t, T)\exp\left(-\int_t^T \rho(\tau)\,\sigma_B(\tau, T)\sigma_S(\tau)d\tau\right).$$

Example 4. Let $\sigma_B(t,T), \sigma_S(t), \rho(t)$ be deterministic as in Example 3, but suppose that $\alpha = r + \eta$ with $\eta(t)$ deterministic. Then

$$G(t,T) = \frac{S(t)}{B(t,T)} \exp\left(\int_t^T \eta(\tau)\, d\tau \right)$$

and

$$F(t,T) = G(t,T) \exp\left(\int_t^T \left(\sigma_B^2(\tau,T) - \rho(\tau)\sigma_B(\tau,T)\sigma_S(\tau) \right) d\tau \right).$$

The relationship of the forward and future prices, which involves observable quantities only, is quite different in Examples 3 and 4.

Under the assumptions of Example 4, an option to buy an energy unit at time T for a fixed price X is valued as

$$\begin{aligned} P(t,T) = {} & G(t,T)B(t,T)N\left(\frac{\log G(t,T) - \log X + \frac{1}{2}\Sigma^2(t,T)}{\Sigma(t,T)} \right) \\ & - XB(t,T)N\left(\frac{\log G(t,T) - \log X - \frac{1}{2}\Sigma^2(t,T)}{\Sigma(t,T)} \right) \end{aligned} \tag{8}$$

where N is the cumulative normal distribution function and

$$\Sigma^2(t,T) = \int_t^T (\sigma_B^2(\tau) + \sigma_S^2(\tau,T) - 2\rho(\tau)\sigma_B(\tau,T)\sigma_S(\tau)) d\tau.$$

Note that the Black-Scholes (1973) formula for the valuation of calls, resulting from replacing $G(t,T)$ by $S(t)/B(t,T)$, does not apply to a nonstorable commodity such as electricity. For the pricing of options on nonstorable commodities, it is not sufficient to know the current spot price; such options can only be priced relative to the forward curve.

EXPECTATIONS AND RISK PREMIA

Leaving aside the issue of stochastic interest rates, in this section we discuss the relationship between forward (or futures) prices and the realized values of spot prices for the corresponding maturity.

The rational expectations hypothesis, first expressed in the framework of interest rates by economists such as Keynes and Lucas, states that forward prices are unbiased predictors of futures prices, namely that $F(t, T) = E_t S(T)$, where E_t denotes the expectation with respect to the true probability measure conditional on the information available at time t.

Other economic theories view these quantities as related but not identical, the differences accounting for risk premia (whose full specification, whether they are assumed to be constant or functions of time t and maturity T, is not straightforward to establish). On the other hand, the arbitrage theory developed in a thorough manner for the past twenty years in the framework of traded financial assets, establishes that futures prices are martingales under the risk-neutral probability measure P*, or in other words,

$$F(t, T) = E_t^* S(T).$$

Obviously, in the absence of risk premia, P = P* and the previous relationship reduces to the rational expectations hypothesis. Given the relatively short period of observations of electricity prices available in the framework of deregulated markets worldwide, we maximize the number of pairs (forward, spot prices) in our analysis by comparing day-ahead prices with realized prices of the following day. In order to avoid the specific problems of California, which would deserve a study by itself, we consider a database of 740 observations at the western hub of PJM (Pennsylvania–New Jersey–Maryland), another vibrant part of the U.S. economy. Figure 29.1 plots the differences between spot prices and day-ahead values and allows us to sketch the following conclusions:

1. The mean is negative.
2. The distribution is skewed to the left.
3. These features become more accentuated when one reduces the analysis to summer periods, times when the consumption of air-conditioning in businesses and households entails a sharp rise in demand, and explains why industrial corporations and wholesale marketers are prepared to pay a risk premium for hedging away the risk of power disruption.
4. Conversely, during the so-called shoulder months of April or October, this property is much less true and the distribution of the spreads becomes symmetric.

These elements tend to support the existence of risk aversion and risk premia in power markets (one expression of these being the development of weather derivatives), hence the probability measures earlier denoted as P and P* are distinct. When pricing options on futures, the use of a valuation formula written in terms of the forward prices only (as in Eq. (8)) is admissible from an economic standpoint, since all instruments satisfy the martingale

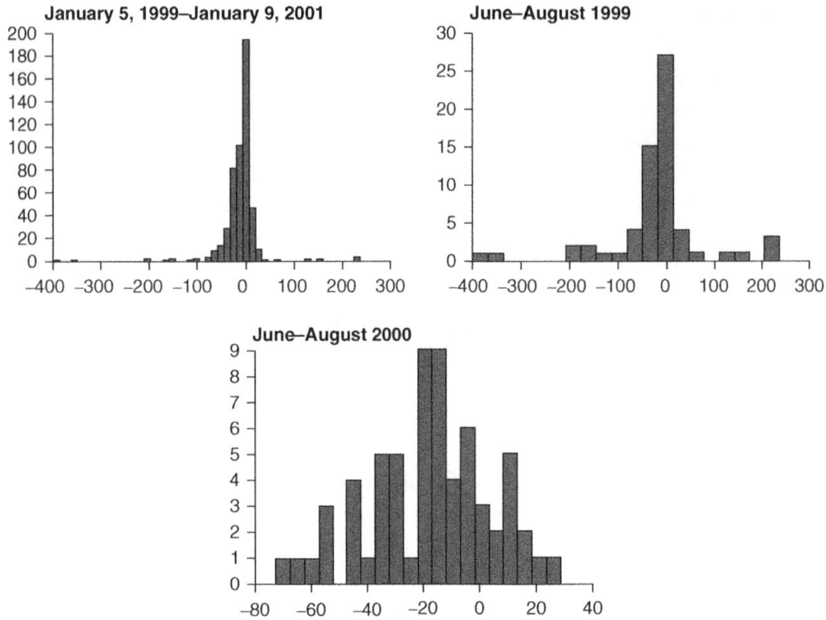

FIGURE 29.1 Differences (spot prices minus one-day forward prices) on the PJM Western Hub

property under P^*; hence the representation and calibration of the forward prices process should take place under P^*. The hedging portfolio held by the option seller only involves forward contracts; the underlying and the option are redundant instruments, as in the Black-Scholes world. Not surprisingly, these options represent a liquid market in all deregulated countries.

The remaining issues are of a mathematical nature and related to the consequences for forward prices of the spikes in the electricity price processes as discussed next. (One may arguably view the shocks as toned down when translated into forward prices.)

In the case of daily power options, however, the situation may be described as "bad news on all fronts": Not only does the option seller need to account for the spikes, fat tails, and stochastic volatility of the spot price process, but also the seller should bear in mind that these spot prices are observed under the true probability measure P while option prices should be computed under P^*. Or equivalently, the risk premium to be received for the risk bought should be incorporated in the option price. The daily power option market became very illiquid after the first major spike in the power markets, which took place in June 1998 in the East Central Area Reliability (ECAR) Coordination Agreement region of the United States, and has remained so since then.

ENERGY PRICE SPIKES

Energy prices exhibit sudden increases (often due to a heat wave and the corresponding sharp increase in energy consumption) that can be considered discontinuities in the spot price. If these discontinuities were modeled by a jump process, however, it would not take into account the fact that there is typically a discontinuity of a similar magnitude in the other direction (as when the heat wave ends). To address this issue, we propose the following simple model to describe the spot price spikes: A spike of a fixed magnitude occurs at the change from the normal situation to the heat-wave situation, corresponding to the transition from state 0 to state 1 of a Markov process. Such change is followed by a spike of the same magnitude in the opposite direction, occurring as a transition of the Markov process from state 1 to state 0.

Let $Z(t)$ be a Markov process in continuous time with state space $\{0, 1\}$, and denote the transition intensity from state 0 to state 1 by $\gamma_0(t)$ and the transition intensity from state 1 to state 0 by $\gamma_1(t)$,

$$P[Z(t+\mathrm{d}t) = 1 | Z(t) = 0] = \gamma_0(t)\mathrm{d}t$$
$$P[Z(t+\mathrm{d}t) = 0 | Z(t) = 1] = \gamma_1(t)\mathrm{d}t. \tag{9}$$

For simplicity, assume that Z is independent of X, Y.

Let the spot price of an energy unit be given by

$$S(t) = s_0(t)(1 - Z(t)) + s_1(t)Z(t) \tag{10}$$

where $s_0(t) < s_1(t)$ are deterministic functions. Obviously, this description of the spot price process is meaningful only if the commodity cannot be stored, because otherwise selling energy when $Z(t) = 1$ and buying the money market account guarantees a positive gain on no investment.

Let $F(t, T)$ be the price at time t of a futures contract with maturity T on the energy unit. It is shown in Appendix B that there exist values $\delta_0(t), \delta_1(t)$ such that $Z(t)$ is a Markov process with transition intensities $\delta_0(t), \delta_1(t)$ under an equivalent probability measure P*. The futures price is a martingale under P*, and consequently

$$F(t, T) = E_t^* S(T).$$

If δ_0, δ_1 are deterministic, the expectation can be evaluated to yield

$$F(t, T) = f_0(t, T)(1 - Z(t)) + f_1(t, T)Z(t) \tag{11}$$

where

$$f_0(t,T) = s_0(T) + (s_1(T) - s_0(T)) \int_t^T \delta_0(\tau) \exp(-\int_\tau^T (\delta_0(u) + \delta_1(u))du)d\tau$$

$$f_1(t,T) = s_1(T) - (s_1(T) - s_0(T)) \int_t^T \delta_1(\tau) \exp(-\int_\tau^T (\delta_0(u) + \delta_1(u))du)d\tau. \tag{12}$$

The pricing of the futures contracts can thus be described as follows: The futures price is equal to the expectation of its maturity value, calculated *as if* the transition intensities of the spot price process were not the actual values γ_0, γ_1, but rather some other values δ_0, δ_1. The intensities δ_0, δ_1 cannot be derived from the character of the spot price process, so the pricing is again only relative to the values of other contracts.

The same principle applies to pricing of options. As to the forward contracts, their price is the same as the price of the corresponding futures contracts, due to our assumption that Z is independent of X.

As an example, suppose δ_0, δ_1 are constant. Then

$$F(t,T) = G(t,T) = s_0(1 - Z(t)) + s_1 Z(t) + (s_1 - s_0)\frac{\delta_0(1 - Z(t)) - \delta_1 Z(t)}{\delta_0 + \delta_1}$$
$$\times (1 - e^{-(\delta_0+\delta_1)(T-t)}).$$

We note that here the value of long forward and futures contracts tends to a finite limit

$$F(t,\infty) = G(t,\infty) = \frac{s_1\delta_0 + s_0\delta_1}{\delta_0 + \delta_1}.$$

This cannot happen with contracts on storable commodities, where the contract prices increase without limits as the time to maturity increases.

THE SPOT PRICE

We can now propose the following description of the energy spot price process (see Figure 29.2): The spot price has a continuous component and a spike component,

$$S(t) = C(t) + D(t). \tag{13}$$

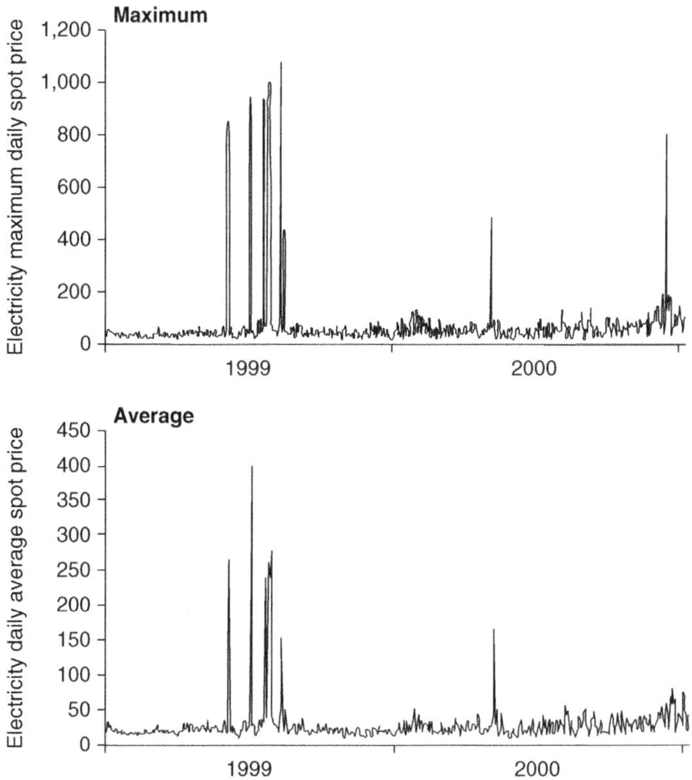

FIGURE 29.2 Electricity Daily Spot Prices at the PJM Western Hub: January 1, 1999–January 9, 2001

The continuous component is subject to the dynamics

$$dC = \mu_C C dt + \varphi_C C dX + \psi_C C dY \tag{14}$$

and the spike component is given by

$$D(t) = A(t)Z(t). \tag{15}$$

The quantity $A(t)$, which is the magnitude of the spike, is defined as follows: Let $A_1, A_2, \ldots$ be a series of identically distributed positive random variables independent of each other and of X, Y, Z. Let $t_1, t_2, \ldots$ be the consecutive transition times of the process $Z(t)$ from state 0 to state 1,

$$Z(t_i) - Z(t_i-) = 1.$$

Then

$$A(t) = A_i \quad \text{for} \quad t_i \le t < t_{i+1}.$$

Typically, the parameters of the continuous component $\mu_C(t), \varphi_C(t), \psi_C(t)$ and the transition intensities $\gamma_0(t), \gamma_1(t)$ of the spike component will show an annual periodicity, and $\gamma_0(t) << \gamma_1(t)$.

Futures contracts are priced as

$$F(t,T) = E_t^* S(T)$$

which can be evaluated as

$$F(t,T) = E^*(C(T)|J_t) + f_0(t,T)(1 - Z(t)) + f_1(t,T)Z(t) \tag{16}$$

where

$$f_0(t,T) = a\int_t^T \delta_0(\tau)\exp\left(-\int_\tau^T (\delta_0(u) + \delta_1(u))\,du\right)d\tau$$

$$f_1(t,T) = (A(t) - a)\exp\left(-\int_t^T \delta_1(\tau)\,d\tau\right) + a\left(1 - \int_t^T \delta_1(\tau)\right.$$

$$\left.\times \exp\left(-\int_\tau^T (\delta_0(u) + \delta_1(u))\,du\right)d\tau\right).$$

Here a is a quantity not necessarily equal to EA_i. For forward contracts, we have similarly

$$G(t,T) = \frac{1}{B(t,T)}E_t^* C(T)\frac{M(t)}{M(T)} + f_0(t,T)(1 - Z(t)) + f_1(t,T)Z(t). \tag{17}$$

CONCLUSION

The paper provides a general framework for the pricing of derivatives on nonstorable commodities. It is demonstrated that options and other derivatives can only be valued from the futures or forward curve, rather than from the spot price. A specific process is proposed to describe the observed spot price spikes and time-varying volatility.

APPENDIX A: PRICING OF FUTURES, FORWARDS, AND OPTIONS

Futures

We use the setting described by Eqs. (1), (2), and (3). Building a portfolio comprising futures F_1 with maturity T_1, futures F_2 with maturity T_2, and bonds with maturity T_1, one obtains through classical argument

$$\frac{\mu_{F1} - \lambda\varphi_{F1}}{\psi_{F1}} = \frac{\mu_{F2} - \lambda\varphi_{F2}}{\psi_{F2}}.$$

Hence

$$\frac{dF}{F} = (\lambda\varphi_F + v\psi_F)dt + \varphi_F dX + \psi_F dY.$$

Put

$$V(t) = \exp\left(-\int_0^t \lambda(\tau)\,dX(\tau) - \int_0^t v(\tau)dY(\tau) - \frac{1}{2}\int_0^t \lambda^2(\tau)d\tau - \frac{1}{2}\int_0^t v^2(\tau)d\tau\right)$$

and let P* be a probability measure whose Radon-Nikodym derivative with respect to P is defined by

$$\frac{dP^*}{dP} = V(t).$$

The processes

$$X^*(t) = X(t) + \int_0^t \lambda(\tau)d\tau,\; Y^*(t) = Y(t) + \int_0^t v(\tau)d\tau$$

are Wiener processes under P*. Then

$$\frac{dF}{F} = \varphi_F dX^* + \psi_F dY^*$$

and $F(t, T)$ is a martingale under P*. Since at the contract maturity $F(T, T) = S(T)$, we obtain

$$F(t, T) = E^*(S(T)|J_t).$$

This gives the pricing of the futures contracts.

If energy were storable, then $S(t)/M(t)$ (or $S(t)$ times a factor accounting for the convenience yield) would also be a martingale under P*, but this will not be the case for nonstorable commodities.

Forwards

Let $G(t, T)$ be the price at time t of a forward contract on the energy unit at maturity T, with

$$\frac{\mathrm{d}G}{G} = \mu_G \mathrm{d}t + \varphi_G \mathrm{d}X + \psi_G dY.$$

The wealth gain over an interval $\mathrm{d}t$ resulting from holding the forward contract is

$$(G(t + \mathrm{d}t, T) - G(t, T))B(t + \mathrm{d}t, T) = B(t, T)\mathrm{d}G(t, T) + \mathrm{d}B(t, T)\mathrm{d}G(t, T).$$

The presence on the left-hand side of $B(t + \mathrm{d}t, T)$ reflects the fact that gains or losses on G are *locked in the forward position* up to its maturity, hence need to be discounted when analyzed at time $t + \mathrm{d}t$. Such discounting does not apply to the future contract change in value, since futures are marked to market over time.

Again, standard arguments provide

$$\mu_G = \lambda\varphi_G - \sigma_B\varphi_G + \nu\psi_G.$$

Hence

$$\begin{aligned}\frac{M}{BG}\mathrm{d}\left(\frac{BG}{M}\right) &= \frac{\mathrm{d}B}{B} + \frac{\mathrm{d}G}{G} + \sigma_B\varphi_G \mathrm{d}t - r\mathrm{d}t \\ &= (\sigma_B + \varphi_G)\mathrm{d}X^* + \psi_G \mathrm{d}Y^*\end{aligned}$$

so that $B(t, T)G(t, T)/M(t)$ is a martingale under P^* and

$$G(t, T) = \frac{1}{B(t, T)} E^* \left(S(T) \frac{M(t)}{M(T)} |J_t \right).$$

Options

Finally, consider a European option on an energy unit with an expiration date T, and denote its price by $P(t, T)$. Let the terms of the option specify that

$$P(T, T) = f(S(T)).$$

An arbitrage argument applied to the option, a futures contract $F(t, T)$, a bond $B(t, T)$, and the money market account implies that

$$\begin{aligned}\frac{\mathrm{d}P}{P} &= r\mathrm{d}t + \lambda\varphi_P \mathrm{d}t + \nu\psi_P \mathrm{d}t + \varphi_P \mathrm{d}X + \psi_P \mathrm{d}Y \\ &= r\mathrm{d}t + \varphi_P \mathrm{d}X^* + \psi_P \mathrm{d}Y^*\end{aligned}$$

and therefore $P(t,T)/M(t)$ is a martingale under P*. The option price is then

$$P(t,T) = E^* \left(f(S(T)) \frac{M(t)}{M(T)} | J_t \right).$$

APPENDIX B: SPOT PRICE SPIKES

We work in the setting described by Eqs. (9), (10), and (11). Assume that Z is independent of X, Y, and that $\gamma_0(t), \gamma_1(t)$ are adapted to a filtration K_t generated by $Z(t)$ on an augmented probability space (Ω, L, P). Write

$$\mathrm{d}f_0 = \mu_0 \mathrm{d}t + \varphi_0 \mathrm{d}X$$

$$\mathrm{d}f_1 = \mu_1 \mathrm{d}t + \varphi_1 \mathrm{d}X.$$

Then

$$\mathrm{d}F = (\mu_0(1-Z) + \mu_1 Z)\mathrm{d}t + (\varphi_0(1-Z) + \varphi_1 Z)\mathrm{d}X + (f_1 - f_0)\mathrm{d}Z.$$

Consideration of an arbitrage position for $Z(t) = 0$ yields

$$\frac{\mu_{01} - \lambda\varphi_{01}}{f_{11} - f_{01}} = \frac{\mu_{02} - \lambda\varphi_{02}}{f_{12} - f_{02}} = -\delta_0.$$

The quantity δ_0 must be positive, because otherwise shorting φ_0/σ_B bonds for each future contract would generate a sure positive gain with no investment.

By the same argument for $Z(t) = 1$,

$$\frac{\mu_1 - \lambda\varphi_1}{f_1 - f_0} = \delta_1$$

with δ_1 positive. On substitution,

$$\mathrm{d}F = (\varphi_0(1-Z) + \varphi_1 Z)(\lambda \mathrm{d}t + \mathrm{d}X) + (f_1 - f_0)((-\delta_0(1-Z) + \delta_1 Z)\mathrm{d}t + \mathrm{d}Z).$$

The values of $\delta_0(t), \delta_1(t)$ are K_t adapted. Let P* be a probability measure that is the same as before on J, but under which $Z(t)$ is a Markov process with transition intensities $\delta_0(t), \delta_1(t)$. The measure P* is equivalent to P, with Radon-Nikodym derivative

$$\frac{\mathrm{d}P^*}{\mathrm{d}P} = V(T)\exp(\int_0^T ((\delta_0 - \gamma_0)(1-Z) - (\delta_1 - \gamma_1)Z)\mathrm{d}\tau$$

$$+\int_0^T ((\log \delta_0 - \log \gamma_0)(1 - Z) - (\log \delta_1 - \log \gamma_1)Z)dZ(\tau)).$$

Then

$$E^*[(-\delta_0(t)(1 - Z(t)) + \delta_1(t)Z(t))dt + dZ(t)|Z(t) = 0] = 0$$
$$E^*[(-\delta_0(t)(1 - Z(t)) + \delta_1(t)Z(t))dt + dZ(t)|Z(t) = 1] = 0$$

Therefore, $F(t, T)$ is a martingale under P^*, and

$$F(t, T) = E^*(S(T)|K_t).$$

NOTE

The authors wish to thank Alexander Eydeland of Mirant for providing the data on electricity prices and Vu-Nhat Nguyen, a doctoral student at Paris Dauphine, for processing them.

REFERENCES

Amin, K., and R. Jarrow. (1992). "Pricing Options on Risky Assets in a Stochastic Interest Rate Economy." *Mathematical Finance* 22, 217–237, reprinted as Chapter 15 in *Vasicek and Beyond*, L. Hughston (ed.), London: Risk Publications.

Black, F., and M. Scholes. (1973). "On the Pricing of Options and Corporate Liabilities." *Journal of Political Economics,* 81, 637–659.

Cox, J., J. Ingersoll, and S. Ross. (1981). "The Relation Between Forward Prices and Futures Prices." *Journal of Financial Economics*, 9, 321–346.

Eydeland, A., and H. Geman. (1998). "Pricing Power Derivatives." *Risk*, October, 71–73.

Geman, H. (1989). "The Importance of the Forward Neutral Probability Measure in a Stochastic Approach to Interest Rates." ESSEC working paper.

Geman, H., and A. Roncoroni. (2001). "A Class of Marked Point Processes for Modeling Electricity Prices." ESSEC working paper.

Hakansson, N. (1979). "The Fantastic World of Finance: Progress and the Free Lunch." *Journal of Quantitative and Financial Analysis* 14 (4), 717–734.

CHAPTER 30

Pricing of Energy Derivatives

It was shown in Geman and Vasicek (2001) (Chapter 29 of this volume) that the price $G(t, T)$ of a forward contract maturing at T is subject to

$$\frac{dG(t,T)}{G(t,T)} = -\sigma_B(t,T)\varphi_G(t,T)dt + \varphi_G(t,T)dX^*(t) + \psi_G(t,T)dY^*(t) \quad (1)$$

where $X^*(t)$, $Y^*(t)$ are Wiener processes under a risk-neutral probability measure P^* equivalent to P.

Integrating Eq. (1) from 0 to T and taking into account that $G(T, T) = S(T)$ yields

$$S(T) = G(0,T)\exp(\int_0^T \varphi_G(\tau,T)dX^*(\tau) + \int_0^T \psi_G(\tau,T)dY^*(\tau)$$
$$-\int_0^T \sigma_B(\tau,T)\varphi_G(\tau,T)d\tau - \frac{1}{2}\int_0^T \varphi_G^2(\tau,T)d\tau - \frac{1}{2}\int_0^T \psi_G^2(\tau,T)d\tau) \quad (2)$$

Eq. (2) represents a complete specification of the forward/spot process. It is fully described by the forward contract volatilities, and it only includes processes whose stochastic properties under the measure P^* are known. Therefore, the prices of energy derivatives and contingent claims can be calculated without recourse to the market prices of risk, which are not directly observable. In this sense, it is akin to the Heath/Jarrow/Morton (1992) model of interest rates (their Eq. (26)).

Unpublished memorandum, 2002.

The price of any derivative contract (e.g., a futures or a swap) is a martingale under the measure P*. The price of any derivative security (such as options, whether simple or compound, European, American, or Asian, etc.) expressed in units of the money market fund is also a martingale under P*. That is, if $P(t)$ is the price of a derivative security, then the quantity $P(t)/M(t)$ is a martingale.

Specifically, the forward contract is priced as

$$F(t, T) = E_t^* S(T). \tag{3}$$

A European option with a value $f(S(T))$ at the expiration date T is priced as

$$P(t, T) = E_t^* f(S(T)) \frac{M(t)}{M(T)}. \tag{4}$$

A compound option paying the amount $f(S(T_1), \ldots, S(T_n))$ at time T, which is dependent on the spot prices at times $T_1, \ldots, T_n$, is valued as

$$P(t) = E_t^* f(S(T_1), \ldots, S(T_1)) \frac{M(t)}{M(T)}. \tag{5}$$

These valuation relationships, applied to Eq. (2), give an exact meaning to the phrase that energy derivatives are priced off the forward price curve.

Write the dynamics of the spot price $S(t)$ under the risk-neutral probability measure as

$$\frac{dS}{S} = \alpha dt + \varphi_S dX^* + \psi_S dY^*. \tag{6}$$

Then

$$\varphi_S(t) = \varphi_G(t, t)$$

$$\psi_S(t) = \psi_G(t, t)$$

$$\alpha(t) = \frac{G'(t, t)}{S(t)}$$

where

$$G'(t, t) = \left. \frac{\partial G(t, s)}{\partial s} \right|_{s=t}$$

is the slope of the forward price curve at the present date. If the commodity can be stored, the expected rate of return on the commodity under the risk-neutral measure is the risk-free rate, $\alpha = r$. This imposes the condition

$$G(t, T) = \frac{S(t)}{B(t, T)}$$

for all $t \leq T$ that must be satisfied by the forward price curves. This is not so for nonstorable commodities, and the forward prices can be specified without restrictions.

EXAMPLES

Example A. Suppose $\sigma_B(t,\ T)$ is deterministic (so that interest rates are Gaussian under the risk-neutral measure) and assume that $\varphi_G(t,\ T)$ is also a deterministic function of t. Then the relationship of forward and future prices is given by

$$F(t,T) = G(t,T)\exp\left(-\int_t^T \sigma_B(\tau,T)\,\varphi_G(\tau,T)\mathrm{d}\tau\right). \tag{7}$$

Example B. If the commodity is storable, then

$$\varphi_G(t,T) = \varphi_S(t) - \sigma_B(t,T) \tag{8}$$

and the futures contract price is given by

$$F(t,T) = S(t)\mathrm{E}_t^* \exp\left(\int_t^T r(\tau)\,\mathrm{d}\tau\right).$$

For a nonstorable commodity, we have

$$F(t,T) = G(t,T)B(t,T)\mathrm{E}_t^* \exp\left(\int_t^T r(\tau)\,\mathrm{d}\tau\right)$$

whenever Eq. (8) holds.

Example C. Assume that

$$\varphi_G(t,T) = \varphi_S(t) - \sigma_B(t,T)$$
$$\psi_G(t,T) = \psi_S(t).$$

Then

$$G(t,T) = \frac{S(t)}{B(t,T)}\frac{G(0,T)B(0,T)}{G(0,t)B(0,t)}.$$

This is the Example 4 in Geman and Vasicek (2001).

Example D. Suppose $\sigma_B(t, T)$, $\varphi_G(t, T)$ are deterministic, and the forward price volatilities are independent of the contract maturity date T,

$$\varphi_G(t, T) = \varphi_S(t)$$
$$\psi_G(t, T) = \psi_S(t).$$

Then

$$G(t, T) = S(t)\frac{G(0, T)}{G(0, t)} \exp\left(\int_0^t \left(\sigma_B(\tau, t) - \sigma_B(\tau, T)\right) \varphi_S(\tau)\mathrm{d}\tau\right).$$

This corresponds to the Example 3 in Geman and Vasicek (2001).

REFERENCE

Geman, H., and O. Vasicek. (2001). "Plugging into Electricity." *Risk*, 14 (8), 93–106.

Heath, D., R. Jarrow, and A. Morton. (1992). "Bond Pricing and the Term Structure of Interest Rates: A New Methodology for Contingent Claims Valuation." *Econometrica*, 60, pp. 77–105.

PART Six

Probability Theory and Statistics

A Bayesian estimate of security beta β is obtained from its posterior distribution, which is approximately normal with mean

$$b'' = \frac{b'/s_b'^2 + b/s_b^2}{1/s_b'^2 + 1/s_b^2}$$

and variance

$$s_b''^2 = \frac{1}{1/s_b'^2 + 1/s_b^2}$$

where b is the least-squares estimate of β in a linear regression, s_b is the standard error of the estimate, and b' and s_b' are the mean and standard deviation, respectively, of prior information about the company's beta. In the absence of more specific knowledge about the company, the parameters of the prior distribution can be set to the mean ($b' = 1$) and standard deviation of the cross-sectional distribution of betas in the universe. (page 291)

CHAPTER 31

Introduction to Part VI

Estimation of security betas—that is, coefficients that measure the security's systematic risk—is crucial for application of the Capital Asset Pricing Model. The standard estimation procedure is to use the least-squares regression applied to historical data. This technique consists of fitting a linear relationship between the rates of return on the security and those on the market portfolio.

The regression coefficient estimate, however, does not capture all available information. Suppose the estimated beta of a stock is $b = .2$. In the absence of any additional information, this estimate is taken by the sampling theory as being the best estimate, because the true beta is equally likely to be overestimated as underestimated by the sample b. This, however, does not imply that given the sample estimate, the true parameter is equally likely to be below or above the value of .2. It is known from previous measurements that betas of all stocks are concentrated around unity, most of them ranging in value between .5 and 1.5. An observed beta of .2 is more likely to be a result of an underestimation than overestimation.

Bayesian decision theory provides a framework for incorporating prior information in estimation of unknown parameters. The paper "A Note on Using Cross-Sectional Information in Bayesian Estimation of Security Betas" (Chapter 32) from 1973 presents a method for Bayesian estimation of the regression coefficients that is optimal with respect to the minimization of the expected squared estimation error.

The bivariate normal distribution function appears often in mathematical finance. It is required in pricing of options whose payout depends on two assets, such as rainbow options, of calls on the maximum of three assets, of extendible options, cross-country swaps, and so on. It is also required for calculation of covariances of derivatives and corporate liabilities.

In some cases, the bivariate normal distribution involves correlations that are close to unity. Suppose an investor wants to calculate the variance of the portfolio value change over a horizon of length H, and suppose the portfolio contains options and derivatives. The variance over an interval of length H of the price of a call option with time to expiration $T > H$ is given by the bivariate normal function with correlation H/T. If the option expires shortly after the end of the horizon period, the correlation can be very high. The same correlation figures in the formula for variance in the change over the horizon H in the market value of a loan maturing at time T.

The standard method of evaluating the bivariate normal distribution function is the tetrachoric series. This series converges only slightly faster than a geometric series with quotient equal to the correlation coefficient. If the correlation is close to unity, the tetrachoric series is not practical. The paper "A Series Expansion for the Bivariate Normal Integral" (Chapter 33) from 1998 gives an alternative series that converges approximately as a geometric series with quotient equal to one minus the correlation squared, which makes it a convenient means of calculation when the correlation is close to one in absolute value.

The article "A Conditional Law of Large Numbers" (Chapter 34), originally written in 1980, is a purely mathematical work. The law of large numbers in probability theory justifies interpreting limiting frequencies as probabilities; the conditional law of large numbers provides a similar foundation for the principle of maximum entropy, an extremely useful proposition in many areas of physics, which had never been formally proven. Informally stated, the theorem asserts that in the equiprobable case, the frequencies conditional on given constraints converge in probability to the distribution that has the maximum entropy subject to these constraints.

A generalization of that result is also given, which relaxes the assumption of all states being equally likely. In the general case, the frequencies conditional on a set of constraints converge in probability to the distribution that maximizes the entropy relative to the underlying distribution.

The paper "A Test for Normality Based on Sample Entropy" (Chapter 35) written in 1976 also deals with the subject of entropy, although in a completely different setting and for a completely different purpose. This paper proposes a statistical goodness-of-fit test to determine whether a given sample came from the normal (Gaussian) distribution. It is based on the fact that the normal distribution has the maximum entropy among all distributions with the same variance. The test statistic is the exponential of a sample estimate of the population entropy, based on higher-order spacings, divided by the sample standard deviation. The test is shown to be a consistent test of the composite hypothesis of normality. The power of the test is estimated against a number of different alternative distributions. It is observed that the power of the test compares favorably to that of several standard tests of goodness-of-fit.

Another paper in probability theory is the joint 1998 work with Julian Keilson, "Monotone Measures of Ergodicity for Markov Chains" (Chapter 36). Finite irreducible Markov chains in continuous time approach ergodicity—that is, they possess a limiting state probability distribution. The speed of approaching the asymptotic distribution is provided by measures of ergodicity. The paper provides a systematic discussion of a certain set of norms, each a measure of ergodicity. Monotonicity of these norms is proven, *whether or not the chain is time-reversible*. That is a novel and useful result, because up to then monotonicity of these measures had been proven only for time-reversible chains, a small subset of Markov chains. Similar results are noted for Markov chains in discrete time.

The paper "An Inequality for the Variance of Waiting Time under a General Queueing Discipline" (Chapter 37), originally written in 1977, belongs to the field of operations research and, specifically, to the area of queueing systems. Queueing systems are mathematical models of structures into which "customers" arrive at random times to receive some kind of service that takes an uncertain amount of time. Typical examples are telephone exchanges connecting phone calls, or airports accommodating arriving planes. When all servers are busy, arriving customers must wait in line ("queue") until a server is available. The waiting customers are selected for service by some rule, called the *queueing discipline*. Of interest are various characteristics of the operation, such as the average waiting time, the number of customers in the queue, the idle periods of the servers, etc.

The chapter proves an interesting inequality about the variance of the waiting time. The queueing discipline can take a variety of forms, such as serving next the customer who came the earliest ("First-come-first-served"), or the most recent arrival ("Last-come-first-served") as is often the case in warehousing, or selecting a customer from the queue at random, or various priority rules. The expected, or average, waiting time is the same under any queuing discipline, as long as the selection rule does not depend on the serving time of the customers in the queue. The variance, however, is the lowest under the first-come-first-served discipline and the largest under the last-come-first-served discipline. For any other rule of selecting the next customer, the variance is in between these two extremes. It means that the waiting times are the most and the least equitably distributed, respectively, under the two extreme rules.

CHAPTER 32

A Note on Using Cross-sectional Information in Bayesian Estimation of Security Betas

ABSTRACT

Bayesian decision theory provides formal procedures that utilize information available prior to sampling, together with the sample information, to construct estimates that are optimal with respect to the minimization of the expected loss. This paper presents a method for generating Bayesian estimates of the regression coefficient of rates of return of a security against those of a market index. The distribution of the regression coefficients across securities is used as the prior distribution in the analysis. Explicit formulas are given for the estimates. The Bayesian approach is discussed in comparison with the current practice of sampling-theory procedures.

INTRODUCTION

The Capital Asset Pricing Model of Treynor (1961), Sharpe (1964), and Lintner (1965) states that the expected rate of return on a security in excess of the risk-free rate is proportional to the slope coefficient of the regression of that security's rates of return on a market index. The slope coefficient, or beta, is for this reason one of the basic concepts of modern capital market theory, and considerable attention has been devoted to its measurement.

Journal of Finance 28, (5) (1973), 1233–1239.
This paper is a minor revision of the author's unpublished memorandum "Bayesian Estimates of Beta," Wells Fargo Bank, August 1971.

Customarily, beta is estimated from past data by least-squares regression procedures. The least-squares technique consists of fitting a linear relationship between the rates of return on a security and the rates of return on a market index so that the sum of squared differences between the security's actual returns and those implied by the relationship is minimized.

If $y_t, t = 1, 2, \ldots, T$ and $x_t, t = 1, 2, \ldots, T$ are the series of rates of return on a security and on a market index, respectively, the least-squares estimates of the parameters β, α, σ^2 in the simple linear regression process

$$\begin{aligned} y_t &= \alpha + \beta x_t + e_t, \quad t = 1, 2, \ldots, T \\ \mathrm{E}e_t &= 0, \mathrm{E}e_t e_s = 0 \text{ for } t \neq s, \mathrm{E}e_t^2 = \sigma^2 \end{aligned} \tag{1}$$

are given as

$$b = \Sigma\,(y_t - \overline{y})\,(x_t - \overline{x})/\Sigma\,(x_t - \overline{x})^2 \tag{2}$$

$$a = \overline{y} - b\overline{x} \tag{3}$$

$$s^2 = \frac{1}{T-2}\,\Sigma(y_t - a - bx_t)^2, \tag{4}$$

respectively, and the variance of b is estimated as

$$s_b^{\,2} = s^2/\Sigma\,(x_t - \overline{x})^2. \tag{5}$$

These are the best unbiased estimates of the parameters in the sense that the expected value of each of the estimates is equal to the corresponding parameter and the expected quadratic error attains the minimal value. In particular, when the beta coefficient of a stock is estimated by b, the following holds:

$$\mathrm{E}(b|\beta) = \beta \tag{6}$$

$$\mathrm{Var}\,(b|\beta) = \text{minimum over all estimates of } \beta \text{ satisfying (6).} \tag{7}$$

For these reasons, the sampling-theory estimation procedures are commonly applied to the estimation of the beta of a security. Yet, the criteria as represented by Eqs. (6) and (7) do not satisfactorily reflect the desired properties of a beta estimator. Eq. (6) describes an aspect of the distribution of the estimate assuming that the true value of the parameter is given. The actual situation is just the reverse: It is the sample coefficient that is known, and on the basis of this (and any prior or additional) information we want to infer about the distribution of the parameter.

To illustrate this point, assume that the estimated beta of a stock traded on the New York Stock Exchange is $b = .2$. In the absence of any additional information, this value is taken by sampling theory as being the best estimate of the true beta *because* any given true beta is equally likely to be overestimated as underestimated by the sample b. This, however, does not imply that given the sample estimate b, the true parameter is equally likely to be below or above the value .2. In fact, it is known from previous measurements that betas of stocks traded on the New York Stock Exchange are concentrated around unity, and most of them range in value between .5 and 1.5. Thus, an observed beta as low as 0.2 is more likely to be a result of underestimation than overestimation. The question of whether the estimate b is equally likely to lie below or above the true beta is irrelevant, since the true beta is not known. What is desired is an estimate such that given the sample information (which is available), the true beta will with equal probability lie below or above it.

To pursue this example further, assume that there are 1,000 stocks under consideration, the betas of which are known to be distributed approximately normally around 1.0 with standard deviation of .5. Each of these true betas is equally likely to be underestimated or overestimated by b. Therefore, there are 500 stocks with true beta higher than the observed estimate, and 500 with true beta lower than the estimate. If an estimate of $b = .2$ is observed, the stock might be any of the approximately $500 \times .945 = 473$ stocks with β larger than .2 and underestimated, or any of the approximately $500 \times .055 = 27$ stocks with β smaller than .2 and overestimated. Apparently, given the sample and our prior knowledge of beta distribution, the former is much more likely, and thus, it is not correct to take .2 for an unbiased estimate.

This has been recognized before in the special situation where portfolios were formed by ranking of sample estimates (cf. Wagner and Vasicek (1971)). The knowledge of the cross-sectional distribution of betas, however, can be used as prior information whenever a beta of a security is estimated. Also, as a referee pointed out to the author, a similar problem has been recently addressed by Bogue (1972). Following is a Bayesian analysis of the simple normal regression process with the cross-sectional prior information. For information about the principles and techniques of Bayesian statistical theory, the reader is referred to Raiffa and Schlaifer (1961).

BAYESIAN ESTIMATES

For computational convenience, reparametrize the regression process (1) as follows:

$$y_t = \eta + \beta\,(x_t - \overline{x}) + e_t, \qquad t = 1, 2, \ldots, T \tag{8}$$

where

$$\eta = \alpha + \beta\overline{x}.$$

Assuming normal distribution of the disturbances, the kernel $k(b, \bar{y}, s|v, \beta, \eta, \sigma)$ of the likelihood is proportional to (see Raiffa and Schlaifer (1961), p. 335)

$$\sigma^{-T} \exp[-(T-2)s^2/(2\sigma^2)] \times \exp\left[-\frac{1}{2\sigma^2}\left(T(\bar{y}-\eta)^2 + v\,(b-\beta)^2\right)\right] \quad (9)$$

where b, s^2 is given by Eqs. (2), (4),

$$\bar{y} = \frac{1}{T}\Sigma y_t,$$

and

$$v = \Sigma(x_t - \bar{x})^2.$$

Let the information available prior to sampling consist of knowledge of the cross-sectional distribution of betas. Assuming that the distribution is approximately normal with parameters b', s'_b, the marginal prior density of β is

$$f'(\beta) \propto \exp[-(\beta - b')^2/(2s'^2_b)]. \quad (10)$$

(In accordance with practice, the prior distributions and parameters are denoted by primed letters, the posterior by letters with double primes, and the sample information without superscripts.)

Unless some prior information is available on η, σ, it is assumed that the prior density of these parameters is assessed as

$$f'(\eta, \sigma) \propto \sigma^{-1} \quad (11)$$

and independent of $f'(\beta)$. The density (11) is an improper density function corresponding to the limiting case where the prior information on η, σ is totally negligible. The joint prior density of the parameters β, η, σ is then

$$f'(\beta, \eta, \sigma) \propto \sigma^{-1} \times \exp[-(\beta - b')^2/(2s'^2_b)]. \quad (12)$$

Note that the prior distribution (12) is not of the natural conjugate form (the bivariate normal-gamma distribution for the simple normal regression process). The reason why the natural conjugate density is not suitable here is that the conjugate prior expresses prior information in the form as if it were results of previous sampling from the same process, and it is not rich enough to give a good representation of the case when the prior information involves a cross-sectional relationship among several regression processes.

Given the prior density (12), the posterior density f'' of the parameters β, η, σ is evaluated using Bayes' theorem:

$$f''(\beta, \eta, \sigma \mid v, b, \bar{y}, s) = f'(\beta, \eta, \sigma)\, k\,(b, \bar{y}, s \mid v, \beta, \eta, \sigma)\, D^{-1}(b, \bar{y}, s) \qquad (13)$$

where

$$D(b, \bar{y}, s) = \int f'(\beta, \eta, \sigma) k\,(b, \bar{y}, s \mid v, \beta, \eta, \sigma)\, d\beta\, d\eta\, d\sigma.$$

The marginal posterior density of β is evaluated as

$$f''(\beta \mid v, b, \bar{y}, s) = \int f''(\beta, \eta, \sigma \mid v, b, \bar{y}, s)\, d\eta\, d\sigma.$$

After substitution, this yields

$$f''(\beta \mid v, b, \bar{y}, s) \propto \exp\,[-(\beta - b')^2/(2{s'_b}^2)].\ \left[T - 2 + \frac{v\,(\beta - b)^2}{s^2}\right]^{-\frac{1}{2}(T-1)}. \qquad (14)$$

When T is larger than 20, the posterior distribution of β is approximately normal with mean b'' and variance ${s''_b}^2$, where

$$b'' = \frac{b'/{s'_b}^2 + b/{s_b}^2}{1/{s'_b}^2 + 1/{s_b}^2} \qquad (15)$$

$${s''_b}^2 = \frac{1}{1/{s'_b}^2 + 1/{s_b}^2}. \qquad (16)$$

Here

$${s_b}^2 = s^2/v$$

is the estimated variance of b as given by Eq. (5). (In sampling-theory terminology, s_b is usually called the standard error of the estimate b.)

The marginal posterior density of β describes the knowledge about the distribution of the estimated parameter, given the information from the sample and the prior information. The choice of a point estimate of β depends on this posterior distribution as well as the utility function on the space of decisions (estimates). Under a quadratic terminal loss function (which is a Bayesian analogue to the sampling-theory concept of minimum variance estimates), the optimal estimate of β is the mean of the posterior distribution (14). For $T > 20$, the error of approximating the posterior mean by b'' does not exceed .01 and decreases approximately linearly with $1/T$. Since this error is small in comparison with the dispersion s''_b of the posterior distribution, no material loss is incurred when b'' is taken for the estimate that minimizes the expected quadratic opportunity loss.

DISCUSSION AND CONCLUSIONS

The Bayesian estimate b'' as given by Eq. (15) can be interpreted as an adjustment of the sample estimate b toward the best prior estimate b', the degree of adjustment being proportionate to the precision $h = 1/s_b{}^2, h' = 1/s'_b{}^2$ of the sample estimate and the prior distribution, respectively. Eq. (16) can be interpreted as stating that the precision $h'' = 1/s''_b{}^2$ of the posterior distribution is the sum of the precision of b and that of the prior distribution.

The choice of the parameters b', s'_b of the prior density $f'(\beta)$ depends on the prior information available. If nothing is known about a stock prior to sampling except that it comes from a certain population of stocks (e.g., from the population of all stocks traded on the New York Stock Exchange), an appropriate choice of the prior density is the cross-sectional distribution of betas observed for that population. For the New York Stock Exchange population, the prior parameters might be approximately $b' = 1, s'_b = .5$. In this case, the regression coefficient estimated from the sample is linearly adjusted toward unity, the degree of the adjustment depending on the standard error s_b of the estimate.

A somewhat similar procedure is used in the Security Risk Evaluation service by Merrill Lynch, Pierce, Fenner & Smith, Inc. Their simplified method utilizes a formula of the form

$$b'' = 1 + k(b - 1) \tag{17}$$

where k is a constant common for all stocks. This constant can be interpreted as the slope of the cross-sectional regression of beta estimates on those obtained over a prior nonoverlapping period. Comparison of Eq. (17) with Eq. (15) shows that this method assumes that the variance $s_b{}^2$ of the sample regression coefficient is the same for all securities. The effect of this procedure is thus to overadjust more accurate estimates and underadjust the less accurate ones.

In some cases, more can be known about a stock than that it comes from a certain population. Assume, for instance, that a stock is selected on the basis of an instrumental variable, which may be related to the true betas but not to the estimation error of the sample estimates b. In this case, a proper choice of the prior distribution is the distribution of betas implied by the knowledge of the instrumental variable. Thus, if a utility stock is considered, and it is known from previous measurements that betas of utilities are centered around .8 with a dispersion of .3, the estimate b is adjusted toward .8 by the formula (15) with $b' = .8, s'_b = .3$. In general, the degree and direction of the adjustment depend on the prior distribution $f'(\beta)$ as characterizing the information pertaining to β that is contained in the instrumental variable.

When estimating beta of a portfolio composed of N stocks, the sample estimate b is again adjusted through the formula (15). In this case, however, the value used for s'_b is the cross-sectional dispersion of betas of portfolios of size N. In most instances, a good approximation for this dispersion is obtained by assuming cross-sectional independence of the regression residuals (as in the diagonal model), and consequently using the cross-sectional dispersion of individual securities' betas reduced by the factor of $1/\sqrt{N}$.

In some cases, the prior information may contain information of another sample from the same process (as regression results over a previous period), but the two samples cannot be pooled. This situation arises, for example, when a portfolio is formed by ranking securities on the basis of their estimated betas, and then the portfolio's beta is estimated over the next period. In such cases, the estimation proceeds in two steps. First, the posterior distribution based on the first sample and the cross-sectional prior is obtained. Next, this posterior distribution is used as the prior density to utilize the information of the second sample. Thus, the sample estimate from the second sample is adjusted toward the adjusted first sample estimate.

In summary, the estimate of a security's beta that minimizes the expected squared estimation error is given by Eq. (15), where the parameters b', s'_b of the prior distribution are chosen to reflect *all* the information on beta available prior to sampling. The mean squared estimation error s''^2_b is given by Eq. (16).

The relative merit of this Bayesian estimation method as contrasted to procedures of sampling theory will now be briefly discussed. The main objection to the Bayesian estimation method is that the estimate b'' is not an unbiased estimate of β (in the sampling-theory sense), while b is unbiased,

$$\begin{aligned} &E(b''|\beta) \neq \beta, \\ &E(b|\beta) = \beta. \end{aligned} \tag{18}$$

To discuss this objection, it is useful to ask why unbiasedness in the sense of Eq. (18) is desirable. One can identify two reasons, the first of which is that, in virtue of the law of large numbers, an unbiased estimate converges in probability to the estimated parameter as the sample size increases,

$$\operatorname*{P\,lim}_{T\to\infty} b = \beta.$$

The same, however, is true for the estimate b'',

$$\operatorname*{Plim}_{T\to\infty} b'' = \beta,$$

since with increasing sample size $s_b{}^2 \to 0$ and the degree of the adjustment decreases. The second reason for requiring an unbiased estimate is that the mean quadratic error

$$E((\hat{\beta} - \beta)^2 \mid \beta) \tag{19}$$

is minimized in a class of estimates $\hat{\beta}$ of the same variance by an unbiased estimate. The expected value (19) is taken with respect to the conditional likelihood (9) of the sample. This, however, is not justified. Rather than minimizing the squared *sampling* error, what should be done is to minimize the squared *estimation* error. That is, minimize

$$E''\,(\hat{\beta} - \beta)^2, \tag{20}$$

the expectation being taken with respect to the posterior distribution of β. The estimate b'', not b, is the estimate $\hat{\beta}$ to minimize (20).

This is more than a mere philosophical point. If two persons, one using the estimate b and the other b'', were penalized proportionally to the squared difference of their respective estimates from the true parameter value β (or, for that matter, from the next-period sample estimate), the former would go broke first.

In conclusion, Bayesian estimates (15) are preferred to the classical sampling-theory estimates (2) for the following reasons: First, Bayesian procedures provide estimates that minimize the loss due to misestimation, while sampling-theory estimates minimize the error of sampling. This is because Bayesian theory deals with the distribution of the parameters given the available information, while sampling theory deals with the properties of sample statistics given the true value of the parameters. Secondly, Bayesian theory weights the expected losses by a prior distribution of the parameters, thus incorporating knowledge that is available in addition to the sample information. This is particularly important in the case of estimating betas of stocks, where the prior information is usually sizable.

REFERENCES

Bogue, M.C. (1972). "The Estimation and Behavior of Systematic Risk," unpublished dissertation, Graduate School of Business Administration, Stanford University.

Kalymon, B.A. (1971). "Estimation Risk in the Portfolio Selection Model." *Journal of Financial and Quantitative Analysis*, 6 (1) (January), 559–582.

Kantor, M. (1971). "Market Sensitivities." *Financial Analysts Journal*, 27 (1) (January), 64–68.

Lintner, J. (1965). "The Valuation of Risk Assets and the Selection of Risky Investments in Stock Portfolios and Capital Budgets." *Review of Economics and Statistics* (February).

Raiffa, H., and R. Schlaifer. (1961). *Applied Statistical Decision Theory*. Boston: Harvard University.

Sharpe, W.F. (1964). "Capital Asset Prices: A Theory of Market Equilibrium Under Conditions of Risk." *Journal of Finance* (September), 425–442.

Treynor, J.L.. (1961). "Toward a Theory of Market Value of Risky Assets," unpublished memorandum.

Wagner, W.H., and O.A. Vasicek (1971). "The Effect of Estimation Error of Beta on the Risk of Passive Portfolios," unpublished memorandum, Wells Fargo Bank (March).

CHAPTER 33

A Series Expansion for the Bivariate Normal Integral

ABSTRACT

An infinite series expansion is given for the bivariate normal cumulative distribution function. This expansion converges as a series of powers of $(1 - \rho^2)$, where ρ is the correlation coefficient, and thus represents a good alternative to the tetrachoric series when ρ is large in absolute value.

INTRODUCTION

The cumulative normal distribution function

$$N(x) = \int_{-\infty}^{x} n(u)du$$

with

$$n(u) = \frac{1}{\sqrt{2\pi}} \exp\left(-\frac{1}{2}u^2\right)$$

appears frequently in modern finance: Essentially all explicit equations of options pricing, starting with the Black-Scholes formula, involve this function in one form or another. Increasingly, however, there is also a need for the bivariate cumulative normal distribution function

$$N_2(x, y, \rho) = \int_{-\infty}^{x} \int_{-\infty}^{y} n_2(u, v, \rho)dudv \tag{1}$$

Journal of Computational Finance, 1 (4) (1998), 5–10.

where the bivariate normal density is given by

$$\mathrm{n}_2(u, v, \rho) = \frac{1}{2\pi}(1-\rho^2)^{-\frac{1}{2}} \exp\left(-\frac{1}{2}\left(u^2 - 2\rho uv + v^2\right)/(1-\rho^2)\right) \tag{2}$$

This need arises in at least the following areas:

1. *Pricing exotic options.* Options with payout depending on the prices of two lognormally distributed assets, or two normally distributed factors, involve the bivariate normal distribution function in the pricing formula. Examples include the so-called rainbow options (such as calls on maximum or minimum of two assets), extendible options, and spread and cross-country swaps.
2. *Correlations of derivatives.* While the instantaneous correlation of two derivatives is the same as the correlation of the underlying assets, calculation of the correlation over noninfinitesimal intervals often requires the bivariate normal function.
3. *Loan loss correlations.* If a loan default occurs when the borrower's assets fall below a certain point, the covariance of defaults on two loans is given by a bivariate normal formula. This covariance is needed when evaluating the variance of loan portfolio losses.

A standard procedure for calculating the bivariate normal distribution function is the tetrachoric series,

$$\mathrm{N}_2(x, y, \rho) = \mathrm{N}(x)\mathrm{N}(y) + \mathrm{n}(x)\mathrm{n}(y)\sum_{k=0}^{\infty} \frac{1}{(k+1)!}\mathrm{He}_k(x)\mathrm{He}_k(y)\rho^{k+1} \tag{3}$$

where

$$\mathrm{He}_k(x) = \sum_{i=0}^{[k/2]} \frac{k!}{i!(k-2i)!}(-1)^i 2^{-i} x^{k-2i}$$

are the Hermite polynomials. For a comprehensive review of the literature, see Gupta (1963).

The tetrachoric series (3) converges only slightly faster than a geometric series with quotient ρ, and it is therefore not very practical to use when ρ is large in absolute value. In this note, we give an alternative series that converges approximately as a geometric series with quotient $(1 - \rho^2)$.

THE EXPANSION

The starting point of this chapter is the formula

$$\frac{\mathrm{d}}{\mathrm{d}\rho}\mathrm{N}_2(x,y,\rho) = \mathrm{n}_2(x,y,\rho) \tag{4}$$

which is proven in the Appendix.

Because of the identity

$$\begin{aligned}\mathrm{N}_2(x,y,\rho) = {} & \mathrm{N}_2\left(x, 0, \frac{\rho x - y}{\sqrt{x^2 - 2\rho xy + y^2}}\operatorname{sgn} x\right) \\ & + \mathrm{N}_2\left(y, 0, \frac{\rho y - x}{\sqrt{x^2 - 2\rho xy + y^2}}\operatorname{sgn} y\right) \\ & - \begin{bmatrix} 0 \text{ if } xy > 0 \\ \frac{1}{2} \text{ if } xy < 0 \end{bmatrix}\end{aligned}$$

for $xy \neq 0$, we can limit ourselves to calculation of $\mathrm{N}_2(x,0,\rho)$. Suppose first that $\rho > 0$. Then by integrating Equation (4) with $y = 0$ from ρ to 1 we get

$$\mathrm{N}_2(x,0,\rho) = \min\left\{\mathrm{N}(x), \frac{1}{2}\right\} - Q \tag{5}$$

where

$$Q = \int_\rho^1 \mathrm{n}_2(x,0,r)\mathrm{d}r = \frac{1}{2\pi}\int_\rho^1 (1-r^2)^{-\frac{1}{2}} \exp\left(-\frac{1}{2}x^2/\left(1-r^2\right)\right)\mathrm{d}r.$$

To evaluate the integral, substitute

$$r = \sqrt{1-s}$$

to obtain

$$Q = \frac{1}{4\pi}\int_0^{1-\rho^2} (1-s)^{-\frac{1}{2}} s^{-\frac{1}{2}} \exp\left(-\frac{1}{2}x^2/s\right)\mathrm{d}s. \tag{6}$$

Using the expansion

$$(1-s)^{-\frac{1}{2}} = \sum_{k=0}^{\infty} \frac{(2k)!}{(k!)^2} 2^{-2k} s^k,$$

we get

$$Q = \frac{1}{4\pi} \int_0^{1-\rho^2} \sum_{k=0}^{\infty} \frac{(2k)!}{(k!)^2} 2^{-2k} s^{k-\frac{1}{2}} \exp\left(-\frac{1}{2}x^2/s\right) \mathrm{ds}. \tag{7}$$

Because

$$\frac{(2k)!}{(k!)^2} 2^{-2k} s^{k-\frac{1}{2}} \exp\left(-\frac{1}{2}x^2/s\right) \le s^{k-\frac{1}{2}} \le (1-\rho^2)^{k-\frac{1}{2}} \tag{8}$$

for $k > 0$ and $0 \le s \le 1-\rho^2$, the series in Equation (7) converges uniformly in the interval $[0, 1-\rho^2]$ and can be integrated term by term. It can be easily established that

$$\int_0^t s^{k-\frac{1}{2}} \exp\left(-\frac{1}{2}x^2/s\right) \mathrm{ds} = \frac{k!}{(2k+1)!}(-1)^k 2^{k+1} |x|^{2k+1}$$
$$\times \left[\exp\left(-\frac{1}{2}x^2/t\right) \sum_{i=0}^{k} \frac{(2i)!}{i!}(-1)^i 2^{-i} |x|^{-2i-1} t^{i+\frac{1}{2}} - \sqrt{2\pi}\mathrm{N}(-|x|/\sqrt{t})\right]$$

for $k \ge 0$. Substitution into (7) then gives

$$Q = \sum_{k=0}^{\infty} A_k \tag{9}$$

where

$$A_k = \frac{1}{k!(2k+1)}(-1)^k 2^{-k} |x|^{2k+1}$$
$$\times \left[\frac{1}{2\pi} \exp\left(-\frac{1}{2}x^2/(1-\rho^2)\right) \sum_{i=0}^{k} \frac{(2i)!}{i!}(-1)^i 2^{-i} |x|^{-2i-1} (1-\rho^2)^{i+\frac{1}{2}}\right.$$
$$\left. - \frac{1}{\sqrt{2\pi}} \mathrm{N}\left(-|x|/\sqrt{1-\rho^2}\right)\right]. \tag{10}$$

Equations (5), (9), and (10) give an infinite series expansion for $N_2(x, 0, \rho)$ with $\rho > 0$. When $\rho < 0$, integration of Equation (4) from -1 to ρ yields

$$N_2(x, 0, \rho) = \max\left\{ N(x) - \frac{1}{2}, 0 \right\} + Q \tag{11}$$

with Q still given by (9) and (10).

A convenient procedure for computing the terms in the expansion (9) is using the recursive relationships

$$A_k = -\frac{2k-1}{2k(2k+1)} x^2 A_{k-1} + B_k$$

$$B_k = \frac{(2k-1)^2}{2k(2k+1)} (1-\rho^2) B_{k-1}$$

with

$$B_0 = \frac{1}{2\pi}(1-\rho^2)^{\frac{1}{2}} \exp\left(-\frac{1}{2}x^2 / \left(1-\rho^2\right) \right)$$

$$A_0 = -\frac{1}{\sqrt{2\pi}} |x| N(-|x| / \sqrt{1-\rho^2}) + B_0$$

To determine the speed of convergence of (9), integrate the first half of inequality (8) from 0 to $1-\rho^2$. This results in the bound

$$0 < A_k \leq \frac{1}{4\pi\left(k+\frac{1}{2}\right)}(1-\rho^2)^{k+\frac{1}{2}}$$

for $k > 0$, and therefore the series (9) converges approximately as $\Sigma(1-\rho^2)^k/k$. As the tetrachoric series for $N_2(x, 0, \rho)$,

$$N_2(x, 0, \rho) = \frac{1}{2}N(x) + \frac{1}{\sqrt{2\pi}} n(x) \sum_{k=0}^{\infty} \frac{1}{k!(2k+1)} (-1)^k 2^{-k} He_{2k}(x) \rho^{2k+1} \tag{12}$$

converges approximately as $\Sigma\rho^{2k}/k$, a reasonable method for calculating $N_2(x, 0, \rho)$ is to use the tetrachoric series (12) when $\rho^2 \leq ½$ and expressions (5) and (11) with the series (9) when $\rho^2 > ½$.

The error in the calculation of $N_2(x, 0, \rho)$ resulting from using m terms in the expansion (9) is bound in absolute value by

$$\left|\sum_{k=m}^{\infty} A_k\right| \leq \frac{1}{4\pi\left(m+\frac{1}{2}\right)\rho^2}(1-\rho^2)^{m+\frac{1}{2}}.$$

NUMERICAL RESULTS

A comparison of the convergence of the tetrachoric series (12) and the alternative calculations (5) or (11) with the series (9) in calculating $N_2(x, 0, \rho)$ for high values of the correlation coefficient is given in Tables 33.1 and 33.2.

TABLE 33.1 Partial Sums of the Tetrachoric and Alternative Series

	$x = -1,\ \rho = .95$		$x = -1,\ \rho = .99$	
Number of Terms	Tetrachoric	Alternative	Tetrachoric	Alternative
1	.171033	.158632	.174894	.158655
2	.171033	.158631	.174894	.158655
3	.167298	.158631	.170304	.158655
5	.161764	.158631	.162651	.158655
10	.157961	.158631	.156068	.158655
20	.158466	.158631	.158068	.158655
30	.158660	.158631	.159374	.158655
50	.158632	.158631	. 158599	.158655
100	.158631	.158631	.158711	.158655
200	.158631	.158631	.158657	.158655
300	.158631	.158631	.158654	.158655
Exact	.158631		.158655	

TABLE 33.2 Number of Terms Necessary for Precision 10^{-4}

	$\rho = .8$	$\rho = .9$	$\rho = .95$	$\rho = .99$
Tetrachoric series				
$x = 0$	8	16	30	121
$x = \pm 1$	7	14	22	75
$x = \pm 2$	6	11	18	42
Alternative series				
$x = 0$	4	3	2	1
$x = \pm 1$	3	1	1	1
$x = \pm 2$	1	1	1	1

APPENDIX

We prove equation (4) by stating a slightly more general result. Let

$$\mathrm{n}_p(\boldsymbol{x}, \boldsymbol{\Sigma}) = (2\pi)^{-p/2}|\boldsymbol{\Sigma}|^{-\frac{1}{2}} \exp\left(-\frac{1}{2}\boldsymbol{x}'\boldsymbol{\Sigma}^{-1}\boldsymbol{x}\right)$$

and

$$\mathrm{N}_p(\boldsymbol{x}, \boldsymbol{\Sigma}) = \int_{-\infty}^{\mathrm{x}} \mathrm{n}_p(\boldsymbol{u}, \boldsymbol{\Sigma})\mathrm{d}\boldsymbol{u}$$

be the p-variate normal density function and cumulative distribution function, respectively, where $\boldsymbol{x} = [x_1, x_2, \dots, x_p]'$ is a $p \times 1$ vector and $\boldsymbol{\Sigma} = [\sigma_{\mathrm{ij}}]$ is a $p \times p$ symmetric positive-definite matrix. We now prove the following lemma:

Lemma. Let $p \geq 2$. Then for $i \neq j$

$$\begin{aligned}\frac{\partial}{\partial \sigma_{ij}}\mathrm{N}_p(\boldsymbol{x}, \boldsymbol{\Sigma}) &= \frac{\partial^2}{\partial x_i \partial x_j}\mathrm{N}_p(\boldsymbol{x}, \boldsymbol{\Sigma}) \\ &= \mathrm{n}_2(\boldsymbol{x}_{(1)}, \boldsymbol{\Sigma}_{(11)})\mathrm{N}_{p-2}(\boldsymbol{x}_{(2)} - \boldsymbol{\Sigma}_{(21)}\boldsymbol{\Sigma}_{(11)}^{-1}\boldsymbol{x}_{(1)}, \boldsymbol{\Sigma}_{(22)} - \boldsymbol{\Sigma}_{(21)}\boldsymbol{\Sigma}_{(11)}^{-1}\boldsymbol{\Sigma}_{(12)})\end{aligned}$$

Here $\boldsymbol{x}_{(1)} = [x_i, x_j]'$ is the 2×1 vector of x_i, x_j, $\boldsymbol{x}_{(2)}$ is the $(p-2) \times 1$ vector of the remaining components of $\boldsymbol{x}$, and $\boldsymbol{\Sigma}_{(11)}$, $\boldsymbol{\Sigma}_{(12)}$, $\boldsymbol{\Sigma}_{(21)}$, $\boldsymbol{\Sigma}_{(22)}$ are the 2×2, $2 \times (p-2)$, $(p-2) \times 2$, and $(p-2) \times (p-2)$ decompositions of $\boldsymbol{\Sigma}$ into the i-th and j-th row and column and the remaining rows and columns.

Proof. We have

$$\frac{\partial}{\partial \sigma_{ij}}\mathrm{n}_p(\boldsymbol{x}, \boldsymbol{\Sigma}) = \left(-\frac{1}{2}\mathrm{tr}\left(\boldsymbol{\Sigma}^{-1}\frac{\partial \boldsymbol{\Sigma}}{\partial \sigma_{ij}}\right) + \frac{1}{2}\boldsymbol{x}'\boldsymbol{\Sigma}^{-1}\frac{\partial \boldsymbol{\Sigma}}{\partial \sigma_{ij}}\boldsymbol{\Sigma}^{-1}\boldsymbol{x}\right)\mathrm{n}_p(\boldsymbol{x}, \boldsymbol{\Sigma})$$

Define $\boldsymbol{V} = [v_{ij}]$ by $\boldsymbol{V} = \boldsymbol{\Sigma}^{-1}$ and put $\boldsymbol{y} = [y_1, y_2, \dots, y_p]' = \boldsymbol{V}\boldsymbol{x}$. Since for $i \neq j$

$$\frac{\partial \boldsymbol{\Sigma}}{\partial \sigma_{ij}} = \boldsymbol{E}_{ij} + \boldsymbol{E}_{ji}$$

where $\boldsymbol{E}_{ij}$ is the matrix having unity for the (i,j)-th element and zeros elsewhere, we get on substitution

$$\frac{\partial}{\partial \sigma_{ij}}\mathrm{n}_p(\boldsymbol{x}, \boldsymbol{\Sigma}) = (-v_{ij} + y_i y_j)\mathrm{n}_p(\boldsymbol{x}, \boldsymbol{\Sigma}).$$

On the other hand,

$$\frac{\partial}{\partial x_i} \mathrm{n}_p(\boldsymbol{x}, \boldsymbol{\Sigma}) = -y_i \mathrm{n}_p(\boldsymbol{x}, \boldsymbol{\Sigma})$$

and

$$\frac{\partial^2}{\partial x_i \partial x_j} \mathrm{n}_p(\boldsymbol{x}, \boldsymbol{\Sigma}) = (-v_{ij} + y_i y_j) \mathrm{n}_p(\boldsymbol{x}, \boldsymbol{\Sigma})$$

and therefore

$$\frac{\partial}{\partial \sigma_{ij}} \mathrm{n}_p(\boldsymbol{x}, \boldsymbol{\Sigma}) = \frac{\partial^2}{\partial x_i \partial x_j} \mathrm{n}_p(\boldsymbol{x}, \boldsymbol{\Sigma}).$$

Integrating with respect to $\boldsymbol{x}$ and exchanging the order of integration and differentiation yields the first equality of the lemma. The second equality follows from the factorization

$$\mathrm{n}_p(\boldsymbol{x}, \boldsymbol{\Sigma}) = \mathrm{n}_2(\boldsymbol{x}_{(1)}, \boldsymbol{\Sigma}_{(11)}) \mathrm{n}_{p-2}(\boldsymbol{x}_{(2)} - \boldsymbol{\Sigma}_{(21)} \boldsymbol{\Sigma}_{(11)}^{-1} \boldsymbol{x}_{(1)}, \boldsymbol{\Sigma}_{(22)} - \boldsymbol{\Sigma}_{(21)} \boldsymbol{\Sigma}_{(11)}^{-1} \boldsymbol{\Sigma}_{(12)}).$$

REFERENCES

Gupta, S.S. (1963). "Probability Integrals of Multivariate Normal and Multivariate *t*." *Annals of Mathematical Statistics*, 34, 792–828.

Johnson, N.L., and S. Kotz. (1972). *Distributions in Statistics: Continuous Multivariate Distributions*. New York: John Wiley & Sons.

Vasicek, O.A. (1997). "The Loan Loss Distribution." Working paper, KMV Corporation.

CHAPTER 34

A Conditional Law of Large Numbers

ABSTRACT

It is shown that, when conditional on a set of given average values, the frequency distribution of a series of independent random variables with a common finite distribution converges in probability to the distribution which has the maximum relative entropy for the given mean values.

INTRODUCTION

In statistical mechanics and other areas of physics, empirical distributions in the phase space conform in many circumstances to the distribution maximizing the entropy of the system subject to its constraints. The constraints are typically in the form of specified mean values of some functions of phase. If $p = (p_1, p_2, \ldots, p_k)$ denotes the probability distribution over the state space, the constraints on p take the form

$$\sum_{i=1}^{k} a_{ji} p_i = c_j, \quad j = 1, 2, \cdots, r,$$

and the maximum entropy distribution is the one that maximizes the entropy function

$$-\sum_{i=1}^{k} p_i \ \log \ p_i$$

subject to the constraints.

Annals of Probability, 8(1) (1980), 142–147.

A principle stating that the empirical distribution possesses the maximum entropy within the restrictions of the system is due to Gibbs (1902). As a special case, he proposed the so-called canonical distribution as a description of systems subject to a single constraint that the average energy has a fixed value,

$$\sum_{i=1}^{k} a_i p_i = c,$$

where $a_1, a_2, \dots, a_k$ are the energy levels of each state. In this case, the maximum entropy distribution has the form

$$p_i = \exp(v + \lambda a_i), \quad i = 1, 2, \cdots, k,$$

which is the form that Gibbs called canonical.

Gibbs offered no justification for the canonical distribution, and the principle of maximum entropy in general. In spite of its apparent arbitrariness, however, the maximum entropy principle has since found a number of successful applications in a wide range of situations, and has led to many new developments in physics. For an informed discussion, see Jaynes (1967).

In a subsequent paper, Jaynes (1968) presented a demonstration that the distribution with the maximum entropy "can be realized experimentally in overwhelmingly more ways than can any other." Therefore, for large physical systems, the empirical distribution should, indeed, agree with the maximum entropy distribution.

In this chapter, a limit theorem is given that provides a foundation this physical principle in the same sense in which the law of large numbers justifies interpretation of limiting frequencies as probabilities. Informally stated, the theorem asserts that in the equiprobable case, the frequencies conditional on given constraints converge in probability to the distribution that has the maximum entropy subject to these constraints.

A generalization of this result is also given, which relaxes the assumption of all states being equally likely. In the general case, the frequencies conditional upon a set of conditions converge to the distribution that maximizes the entropy relative to the underlying distribution.

THE LIMIT THEOREMS

Let $\mathrm{X} = (x_1, x_2, \cdots, x_k)$ be a finite set of k elements and consider a series $X_1, X_2, \dots$ of independent identically distributed random variables with values on X, such that

$$P[X_1 = x_i] = 1/k, \quad i = 1, 2, \cdots, k. \tag{1}$$

Denote by $f_n = (f_{n1}, f_{n2}, \ldots, f_{nk}), n = 1, 2, \ldots$ the frequency distribution of $X_1, X_2, \ldots, X_n$,

$$f_{ni} = \frac{1}{n} \sum_{m=1}^{n} I[X_m = x_i], \quad i = 1, 2, \cdots, k,$$

where I is the characteristic function. Let (a_{ji}) be a given $r \times k$ matrix and $(c_1, c_2, \ldots\ c_r)$ a given vector. Put $p = (p_1, p_2, \ldots, p_k)$ and define

$$D_0 = \left[p : p \in S, \sum_{i=1}^{k} a_{ji} p_i = c_j, \quad j = 1, 2, \cdots, r \right] \tag{2}$$

where S is the set of probability distributions on $\mathbf{X}$,

$$S = \left[p : p_i \geq 0, i = 1, 2, \cdots, k, \sum_{i=1}^{k} p_i = 1 \right].$$

Assume that $D_0 \neq \emptyset$. Define the entropy of a distribution in S by

$$H(p) = - \sum_{i=1}^{k} p_i \ \log p_i, \ \ p \in S, \tag{3}$$

with the convention $0 \cdot \log 0 = 0$. Denote by $p_0 = (p_{01}, p_{02}, \ldots, p_{0k})$ the maximum point of H on D_0,

$$\max_{p \in D_0} H(p) = H(p_0). \tag{4}$$

Since H is continuous on S and D_0 is compact, the maximum exists. Moreover, it is unique by virtue of strict concavity of H on S and convexity of the set D_0.

Theorem 1. For every $\varepsilon > 0$, there exists $\delta(\varepsilon) > 0$ such that for every δ, $0 < \delta \leq \delta(\varepsilon)$,

$$P \left[|f_{ni} - p_{oi}| \leq \varepsilon, i = 1, 2, \cdots, k \,\middle|\, \left| \sum_{i=1}^{k} a_{ji} f_{ni} - c_j \right| \leq \delta, j = 1, 2, \cdots, r \right] \to 1 \tag{5}$$

as $n \to \infty$, where $p_0 = (p_{01}, p_{02}, \ldots, p_{0k})$ is the maximum entropy distribution, $\max_{p \in D_0} H(p) = H(p_0)$.

This theorem is a special case of the more general conditional law of large numbers, which will now be stated. Replace the assumption (1) of the equiprobable case by a general assumption that

$$P[X_1 = x_i] = q_i, \quad i = 1, 2, \cdots, k \tag{6}$$

where $q = (q_1, q_2, \ldots, q_k) \in S$ is a given distribution. Assume, without loss of generality, that $q_i > 0, i = 1, 2, \ldots, k$. Define the entropy H_q of a distribution in S relative to the distribution q by

$$H_q(p) = -\sum_{i=1}^{k} p_i \ \log(p_i/q_i), \quad p \in S. \tag{7}$$

Again let D_0 be the set in (2), $D_0 \neq \emptyset$, and replace the definition (4) of p_0 by the definition

$$\max_{p \in D_0} H_q(p) = H_q(p_0). \tag{8}$$

Again, the maximum relative entropy point p_0 exists and is unique.

Theorem 2. For every $\varepsilon > 0$, there exists $\delta(\varepsilon) > 0$ such that for every $\delta, 0 < \delta \leq \delta(\varepsilon)$,

$$P\left[|f_{ni} - p_{oi}| \leq \varepsilon, i = 1, 2, \cdots, k \,\middle|\, |\sum_{i=1}^{k} a_{ji} f_{ni} - c_j| \leq \delta, j = 1, 2, \cdots, r \right] \to 1 \tag{9}$$

as $n \to \infty$, where $p_0 = (p_{01}, p_{02}, \ldots, p_{0k})$ is the distribution with the maximum entropy relative to q,

$$\max_{p \in D_0} H_q(p) = H_q(p_0).$$

The maximum relative entropy distribution p_0 is easy to find. It is given by

$$p_{0i} = q_i \ \exp\left(v + \sum_{j=1}^{r} \lambda_j a_{ji} \right), \quad i = 1, 2, \cdots, k,$$

where the constants $v, \lambda_j, j = 1, 2, \ldots, r$ are determined by the condition $p_0 \in D_0$.

PROOF OF THE THEOREMS

Theorem 1 follows immediately from Theorem 2, since for $q = (1/k, 1/k, \ldots, 1/k)$

$$H_q(p) = H(p) - log\, k$$

so that the maximum points in Eqs. (4) and (8) coincide.

***Proof of Theorem* 2.** Let $\varepsilon > 0$ be fixed, and put

$$V = [p : p \in S, |p_i - p_{0i}| \leq \varepsilon, i = 1, 2, \cdots, k] \tag{10}$$

where p_0 is given by (8). For each $\delta > 0$, define

$$D_\delta = \left[p : p \in S, |\sum_{i=1}^{k} a_{ji} p_i - c_j| \leq \delta, j = 1, 2, \cdots, r \right]. \tag{11}$$

Define uniquely a point p_δ by

$$\max_{p \in D_\delta} H_q(p) = H_q(p_\delta). \tag{12}$$

Introduce a topology on S by the metric

$$\mathrm{d}(u, v) = \max_{1 \leq i \leq k} |u_i - v_i|, u, v \in S.$$

We will first prove that

$$\lim_{\delta \to 0+} p_\delta = p_0. \tag{13}$$

Let the set $\{p_\delta, \delta > 0\}$ be directed by the relation $\delta_1 \prec \delta_2$ if $\delta_1 \geq \delta_2$. Since S is compact, the directed set $\{p_\delta\}$ has at least one limit point. Let p^* be one such limit point. Choose an arbitrary $\delta > 0$ and put

$$\eta = \tfrac{1}{2}\delta / \sum_{j=1}^{r} \sum_{i=1}^{k} |a_{ji}|, \delta' = \tfrac{1}{2}\delta.$$

There exists $\delta'', 0 < \delta'' < \delta'$ such that

$$\max_{1 \leq i \leq k} |p_{\delta'' i} - p_i{}^*| \leq \eta.$$

Then

$$|\sum_{i=1}^{k} a_{ji}p_i^* - c_j| \le |\sum_{i=1}^{k} a_{ji}(p_i^* - p_{\delta''i})| + |\sum_{i=1}^{k} a_{ji}p_{\delta''i} - c_j|$$

$$\le \eta \sum_{i=1}^{k} |a_{ji}| + \delta'' \le \delta, \quad j = 1, \cdots, r$$

and therefore $p^* \in D_\delta$. Since this is true for every $\delta > 0$, it follows that

$$p^* \in D_0 = \cap_{\delta>0} D_\delta.$$

Now $H_q(p_\delta) \ge H_q(p_0)$ for every $\delta > 0$. Since H_q is a continuous function, the same is true for the limiting point,

$$H_q(p^*) \ge H_q(p_0).$$

But p_0 is the unique maximum point of H_q on D_0, and therefore $p^* = p_0$. Thus, p_0 is the only limit point of $\{p_\delta\}$, which proves Eq. (13).

It follows that there exists $\delta(\varepsilon) > 0$ such that for every δ, $0 \le \delta \le \delta(\varepsilon)$,

$$|p_{\delta i} - p_{0i}| \le \tfrac{1}{2}\varepsilon, \, i = 1, 2, \cdots, k. \tag{14}$$

Let δ be selected arbitrarily from $0 \le \delta \le \delta(\varepsilon)$ and fixed. Put $W = S - V$ where V is given by (10), and denote the adherence of W by $\overline{W}$. Put

$$h = \max_{p \in \overline{W} \cap D_\delta} H_q(p).$$

Since

$$\max_{p \in D_\delta} H_q(p) = H_q(p_\delta),$$

and $p_\delta \notin \overline{W}$ by virtue of Eq. (14), it follows that

$$h < H_q(p_\delta).$$

Put

$$h' = \tfrac{1}{2}(h + H_q(p_\delta))$$

so that

$$h < h', \tag{15}$$

and define

$$R = [p : p \in S, H_q(p) \geq h'].$$

Let

$$B = R \cap V \cap D_\delta.$$

We will now show that B contains an open set. Let $0 < \delta'' < \delta$ and put

$$s_\lambda = (1-\lambda)p_\delta + \lambda_{p_{\delta'}}, 0 < \lambda < 1.$$

The point s_λ is an interior point of D_δ for every $0 < \lambda < 1$. To prove that, choose

$$\eta = \lambda(\delta - \delta')/\sum_{j=1}^{r}\sum_{i=1}^{k} |a_{ji}|.$$

For every $p = (p_1, p_2, \ldots, p_k)$ such that

$$|p_i - s_{\lambda i}| \leq \eta, i = 1, 2, \cdots, k$$

it is true that

$$\left|\sum_{i=1}^{k} a_{ji}p_i - c_j\right| \leq \eta \sum_{i=1}^{k} |a_{ji}| + (1-\lambda)|\sum_{i=1}^{k} a_{ji}p_{\delta i} - c_j| + \lambda|\sum_{i=1}^{k} a_{ji}p_{\delta' i} - c_j|$$
$$\leq \lambda(\delta - \delta') + (1-\lambda)\delta + \lambda\delta' = \delta, j = 1, 2, \cdots, r$$

so that $p \in D_\delta$. Thus, s_λ belongs to the interior of D_δ for every $\lambda, 0 < \lambda < 1$. Since p_δ is an interior point of V and, by continuity of H_q, also of R, the point s_λ will be in the interior of both V and R if λ is sufficiently small. Thus, such s_λ is an interior point of B, and consequently B contains an open set, say C.

To summarize our results so far, we have proven that there exists an open set C such that

$$C \subset V \cap D_\delta,$$
$$H_q(p) \geq h' \quad \text{for every} \quad p \in C,$$

and

$$H_q(p) \leq h \leq h' \quad \text{for every} \quad p \in W \cap D_\delta.$$

Now

$$P\left[|f_{ni}-p_{oi}|\le\varepsilon, i=1,2,\cdots,k \,\middle|\, |\sum_{i=1}^{k} a_{ji}f_{ni}-c_j|\le\delta, j=1,2,\cdots,r\right]=\frac{1}{1+g_n}$$

where

$$g_n=\sum_{f_n\in W\cap D_\delta}\frac{n!}{(nf_{n1})!(nf_{n2})!\cdots(nf_{nk})!}q_1^{nf_{n1}}q_2^{nf_{n2}}\cdots q_k^{nf_{nk}}$$
$$/\sum_{f_n\in V\cap D_\delta}\frac{n!}{(nf_{n1})!(nf_{n2})!\cdots(nf_{nk})!}q_1^{nf_{n1}}q_2^{nf_{n2}}\cdots q_k^{nf_{nk}}.$$

We will make use of the inequality

$$n^n e^{-n}\le n!\le 3(n+1)^{\frac{1}{2}}n^n e^{-n} \tag{16}$$

valid for $n\ge 0$, where we define $0^0=1$ in agreement with the earlier convention $0\cdot\log\ 0=0$. The inequality (16) is easily established from the Stirling formula. Then

$$\begin{aligned}
g_n\le &\sum_{f_n\in W\cap D_\delta} 3(n+1)^{\frac{1}{2}}n^n(nf_{n1})^{-nf_{n1}}(nf_{n2})^{-nf_{n2}}\cdots(nf_{nk})^{-nf_{nk}}\\
&\cdot q_1^{nf_{n1}}q_2^{nf_{n2}}\cdots q_k^{nf_{nk}}\\
&/\sum_{f_n\in V\cap D_\delta} 3^{-k}(nf_{n1}+1)^{-\frac{1}{2}}(nf_{n2}+1)^{-\frac{1}{2}}\cdots(nf_{nk}+1)^{-\frac{1}{2}}\\
&\cdot n^n(nf_{n1})^{-nf_{n1}}(nf_{n2})^{-nf_{n2}}\cdots(nf_{nk})^{-nf_{nk}}q_1^{nf_{n1}}q_2^{nf_{n2}}\cdots q_k^{nf_{nk}}\\
\le\ & 3^{k+1}(n+1)^{(k+1)/2}\sum_{f_n\in W\cap D_\delta}\exp(nH_q(f_n))/\sum_{f_n\in V\cap D_\delta}\exp(nH_q(f_n))\\
\le\ & 3^{k+1}(n+1)^{(k+1)/2}\sum_{f_n\in W\cap D_\delta}\exp(nH_q(f_n))/\sum_{f_n\in C}\exp(nH_q(f_n))\\
\le\ & 3^{k+1}(n+1)^{(k+1)/2}\exp(-n(h'-h))\frac{\#[f_n : f_n\in W\cap D_\delta]}{\#[f_n : f_n\in C]},
\end{aligned}$$

and therefore

$$g_n\le 3^{k+1}(n+1)^{(k+1)/2}\exp(-n(h'-h))\frac{\#[f_n : f_n\in S]}{\#[f_n : f_n\in C]} \tag{17}$$

where #[Z] denotes the number of elements of a finite set Z. Now

$$\frac{\#[f_n : f_n \in S]}{\#[f_n : f_n \in C]}$$

converges with $n \to \infty$ to a finite limit $\mu(S)/\mu(C)$ where $\mu(S)$, $\mu(C)$ are the volumes of S, C, respectively, by $(k-1)$-dimensional Lebesgue measure, and $\mu(C) > 0$. Since $h' - h > 0$, the right-hand side of Eq. (17) converges to zero as $n \to \infty$, and consequently

$$P\left[|f_{ni} - p_{0i}| \leq \varepsilon, i = 1, 2, \cdots, k \,\middle|\, |\sum_{i=1}^{k} a_{ji} f_{ni} - c_j| \leq \delta, j = 1, 2, \cdots, r\right] \to 1,$$

which completes the proof.

REFERENCES

Gibbs, J.W. (1902). *Elementary Principles in Statistical Mechanics.* New Haven, CT: Yale University Press.

Jaynes, E.T. (1967). "Foundations of Probability Theory and Statistical Mechanics." In *Delaware Seminar in Foundation of Physics.* (Ed., M. Bunge). Berlin: Springer.

Jaynes, E.T. (1968). "Prior Probabilities." *IEEE Trans. System Science and Cybernetics*, 4, 227–241.

CHAPTER 35

A Test for Normality Based on Sample Entropy

ABSTRACT

This chapter introduces a test of the composite hypothesis of normality. The test is based on the property of the normal distribution that its entropy exceeds that of any other distribution with a density that has the same variance. The test statistic is based on a class of estimators of entropy constructed here. The test is shown to be a consistent test of the null hypothesis for all alternatives without a singular continuous part. The power of the test is estimated against several alternatives. It is observed that the test compares favorably with other tests for normality.

ENTROPY ESTIMATION

The entropy of a distribution F with a density function f is defined as

$$H(f) = -\int_{-\infty}^{\infty} f(x)\ \log f(x)\,dx. \tag{1}$$

Let $x_1, x_2, \dots, x_n, n \geq 3$, be a sample from the distribution F. Express (1) in the form

$$H(f) = \int_0^1 \log\left\{\frac{d}{dp}F^{-1}(p)\right\}\ dp. \tag{2}$$

An estimate of (2) can be constructed by replacing the distribution function F by the empirical distribution function F_n, and using a difference operator in place of the differential operator. The derivative of $F^{-1}(p)$ is then

J. Roy. Statist. Soc., Series B, 38 (1) (1976), 54–59.

estimated by $(x_{(i+m)} - x_{(i-m)})n/(2m)$ for $(i-1)/n < p \leq i/n, i = m+1, m+2, \ldots, n-m$, where $x_{(1)} \leq x_{(2)} \leq \ldots \leq x_{(n)}$ are the order statistics and m is a positive integer smaller than $n/2$. One-sided differences of the type $x_{(i+m)} - x_{(1)}$ or $x_{(n)} - x_{(i-m)}$ are used in place of $x_{(i+m)} - x_{(i-m)}$ when $p \leq m/n, p > (n-m)/n$, respectively. This produces an estimate H_{mn} of $H(f)$

$$H_{mn} = n^{-1} \sum_{i=1}^{n} \log \left\{ \frac{n}{2m} \left(x_{(i+m)} - x_{(i-m)} \right) \right\}, \tag{3}$$

where $x_{(i)} = x_{(1)}, i < 1$, and $x_{(i)} = x_{(n)}, i > n$.

To investigate the behavior of H_{mn}, it is useful to write it as a sum of three components,

$$H_{mn} = -n^{-1} \sum_{i=1}^{n} \log f(x_i) + V_{mn} + U_{mn}, \tag{4}$$

where

$$V_{mn} = n^{-1} \sum_{i=1}^{n} \log \left[\frac{F\left(x_{(i+m)}\right) - F(x_{(i-m)})}{f(x_{(i)}) \ \{x_{(i+m)} - x_{(i-m)}\}} \right].$$

$$U_{mn} = n^{-1} \sum_{i=1}^{n} \log \left[\frac{n}{2m} \left\{ F\left(x_{(i+m)}\right) - F(x_{(i-m)}) \right\} \right].$$

The first term in Eq. (4) does not depend on m and represents the sample mean estimate of $H(f) = E\{-\log f(x_i)\}$ assuming that the value of f at the points $x_1, x_2, \ldots, x_n$ is known. If the variance of $-\log f(x_i)$ is finite, it is the minimum variance unbiased estimate of $H(f)$ given the values of f at the sample points. The two remaining terms represent two sources of additional estimation error. The term V_{mn} is due to estimation of f by finite differences. For fixed n, its effect decreases with decreasing values of m. The term U_{mn} corresponds to the error due to estimating increments of F by increments of F_n. The increments are taken over intervals $(x_{(i-m)}, x_{(i+m)})$, whose length increases with m, and therefore the disturbance due to U_{mn} is the smaller the larger is the value of m.

As $n \to \infty$, simultaneous reduction of the effect of these two noise terms requires that $m \to \infty, m/n \to 0$. An optimal choice of m for a given n, however, depends on the (unknown) distribution F. In general, the smoother the density of F, the larger is such optimal value of m.

Since $F(x_{(1)}), F(x_{(2)}), \ldots, F(x_{(n)})$ are distributed as an ordered sample of size n from the uniform distribution on (0, 1), the distribution of U_{mn} does not depend on F. Its limiting behavior is given by the following lemma.

Lemma 1. The variable U_{mn} converges to zero in probability as $n \to \infty$, $m \to \infty$.

Proof. Put $y_{(i)} = F(x_{(i)})$, $1 - m \leq i \leq n + m$. Since the geometric mean does not exceed the arithmetic mean, it follows that $\exp(U_{mn}) \leq y_{(n)} - y_{(1)} \leq 1$. Therefore, U_{mn} is a nonpositive variable with the mean

$$EU_{mn} = \log n - \log(2m) + n^{-1} \sum_{i=1}^{n} E \ \log \ (y_{(i+m)} - y_{(i-m)}).$$

The variable $y_{(i+j)} - y_{(i)}$ has the beta distribution with parameters $j, n - j + 1$. The expected value of its logarithm is easily evaluated by differentiation of the generating function at zero as $E \ \log(y_{(i+j)} - y_{(i)}) = \psi(j) - \psi(n+1)$, where $\psi(x) = \Gamma'(x)/\Gamma(x)$ is the digamma function. Thus, after some algebra,

$$EU_{mn} = \log n - \log(2m) + \left(1 - \frac{2m}{n}\right) \psi(2m) - \psi(n+1)$$
$$+ \frac{2}{n} \sum_{i=1}^{m} \psi(i + m - 1). \tag{5}$$

The right-hand side of the last equality converges to zero with $n \to \infty$, $m \to \infty$. Thus, U_{mn} forms a series of nonpositive variables with expectations approaching zero, and consequently

$$U_{mn} \xrightarrow{P} 0.$$

Since the distribution of U_{mn} is independent of F, the bias due to the presence of U_{mn} in (4) can be eliminated by using

$$H'_{mn} = H_{mn} - EU_{mn}, \tag{6}$$

rather than H_{mn}, as an estimate of entropy. Here EU_{mn} is given by (5). The following theorem deals with consistency of H'_{mn} (and, by Lemma 1, also that of H_{mn}).

Theorem 1. Let $x_1, x_2, \ldots, x_n$ be a sample from a distribution F with a density f and a finite variance. Then

$$H'_{mn} \xrightarrow{P} H(f) \ \text{as} \quad n \to \infty, m \to \infty, m/n \to 0.$$

Proof. With some reorganization, H'_{mn} can be written

$$H'_{mn} = (2m)^{-1}\sum_{j=1}^{2m} S_j + U_{mn} - EU_{mn}, \tag{7}$$

where

$$S_j = -\sum_{\substack{i=1 \\ i \equiv j \ (\text{mod } 2m)}}^{n} \log\left[\frac{F\left(x_{(i+m)}\right) - F(x_{(i-m)})}{x_{(i+m)} - x_{(i-m)}}\right] \{F_n(x_{(i+m)}) - F_n(x_{(i-m)})\},$$

and F_n is the empirical distribution function. When $x_{(i-m)}, x_{(i+m)}$ belong to an interval in which $f(x)$ is positive and continuous, then there exists a value $x'_i \in (x_{(i-m)}, x_{(i+m)})$ such that

$$\frac{F(x_{(i+m)}) - F(x_{(i-m)})}{x_{(i+m)} - x_{(i-m)}} = f(x'_i).$$

Therefore, S_j is a Stieltjes sum of the function $-\log f(x)$ with respect to the measure F_n over the sum of intervals of continuity of f in which $f(x) > 0$. The contribution of terms in S_j that corresponds to intervals in which $f(x) = 0$ approaches zero with $n \to \infty$. Since in any interval in which $f(x)$ is positive, $x_{(i+m)} - x_{(i-m)} \to 0$ a.s. as $m/n \to 0$ and $F_n(x) \to F(x)$ a.s. uniformly over x, S_j converges a.s. to $H(f)$, which is either finite or $-\infty$ in virtue of finite variance of F. Moreover, this convergence is uniform over j. Consequently,

$$(2m)^{-1}\sum_{j=1}^{2m} S_i \to H(f) \quad \text{a.s.}$$

Since

$$U_{mn} - EU_{mn} \xrightarrow{P} 0 \quad \text{as} \quad n \to \infty, m \to \infty,$$

the statement of the theorem follows from (7).

TEST FOR NORMALITY

A well-known theorem of information theory (Shannon, 1949, p. 55) states that among all distributions that possess a density function f and have a given variance σ^2, the entropy $H(f)$ is maximized by the normal distribution.

The entropy of the normal distribution with variance σ^2 is log $\{\sqrt{(2\pi e)}\sigma\}$. The question arises as to whether a test of the composite hypothesis of normality can be based on this property. The estimate H_{mn} will be used for that purpose.

Definition. Let $x_1, x_2, \ldots, x_n$ be a sample from a distribution F and let $x_{(1)} \le x_{(2)} \le \ldots \le x_{(n)}$ be the order statistics. Let m be a positive integer smaller than $n/2$ and define $x_{(i)} = x_{(1)}$ for $i < 1, x_{(i)} = x_{(n)}$ for $i > n$. The K_m test of the composite hypothesis of normality is a test with critical region $K_{mn} \le K^*$, where

$$K_{mn} = \frac{n}{2ms} \left\{ \prod_{i=1}^{n} \left(x_{(i+m)} - x_{(i-m)} \right) \right\}^{1/n} \tag{8}$$

and

$$s^2 = n^{-1} \sum_{i=1}^{n} (x_i - \overline{x})^2.$$

Under the null hypothesis,

$$K_{mn} \xrightarrow{P} \sqrt{(2\pi e)} \quad \text{as } n \to \infty, m \to \infty, m/n \to 0.$$

Under an alternative distribution with density f and a finite variance σ^2,

$$K_{mn} \xrightarrow{P} \sigma^{-1} \exp \{H(f)\} < \sqrt{(2\pi e)}.$$

This means that the K test is consistent for such alternatives. There is no need, however, to restrict the use of the test to distributions with a density and a finite second moment, as will be established in Theorem 2. First, a lemma will be proven.

Lemma 2. Let F be a distribution with a density function f and without a finite second moment. Put

$$a_c = \int_{-c}^{c} f(x)\ dx.$$

For each c such that $a_c > 0$, define a density function f_c by

$$\left. \begin{aligned} f_c(x) &= f(x)/a_c, & |x| \le c, \\ &= 0, & |x| > c. \end{aligned} \right\}. \tag{9}$$

Denote the variance of f_c by σ_c^2. Then $H(f_c) - \log \sigma_c \to -\infty$ as $c \to \infty$.

Proof. Let d be such that $a_d > 0$. Then for $c > d$,

$$H(f_c) - \log \sigma_c = \log\ a_c - \frac{a_d}{a_c} \log a_d$$

$$+ \frac{a_d}{a_c} H(f_d) - a_c^{-1} \int_A f(x) \log f(x)\, dx - \log \sigma_c,$$

where $A = (-c, -d) \cup (d, c)$. According to an inequality in information theory (cf., for instance, Kullback, 1959, p. 15),

$$\int_A f(x) \log \{f(x)/g(x)\}\ dx \geq \int_A f(x)\ dx\ \log \left\{ \int_A f(x)\ dx \Big/ \int_A g(x)\, dx \right\} \tag{10}$$

for nonnegative functions f, g. Let g be the density of the normal distribution with the same mean and variance as f_c. An application of inequality (10) and the inequality $-\alpha \log \alpha \leq 1/e$ then yields

$$H(f_c) - \log\ \sigma_c \leq \frac{a_d}{a_c} H(f_d) + \frac{a_c - a_d}{a_c} \log\ \{\sqrt{(2\pi)}\} + \frac{1}{2} + \frac{2}{a_c}\frac{1}{e} - \frac{a_d}{a_c} \log\ \sigma_c.$$

For a fixed d and $c \to \infty$, the right-hand side of the last inequality approaches minus infinity, as was to be proven.

Theorem 2. The K_m test of any size $\alpha > 0$ is a consistent test, as $n \to \infty, m \to \infty, m/n \to 0$, for all alternatives without a singular continuous part.

Proof. Let $x_1, x_2, \ldots, x_n$ be a sample from a distribution F. If F has a density and a finite variance, the consistency of the test follows from Theorem 1. Assume that F has a density f but the second moment is infinite. Let f_c be the truncated density (9) with variance σ_c. Define a statistic K_{mnc} as

$$K_{mnc}(x_1, x_2, \ldots, x_n) = K_{mr}(x_{i_1}, x_{i_2}, \ldots, x_{i_r}),$$

where $(x_{i_1}, x_{i_2}, \ldots, x_{i_r})$ is the subsample of all x_i such that $|x_i| \leq c$. Since the subsample has the density f_c and $r \to \infty$ a.s. as $n \to \infty$, it follows that

$$K_{mnc} \xrightarrow{P} \sigma_c^{-1} \exp\ \{H(f_c)\}.$$

The difference $K_{mn} - K_{mnc}$ converges to zero in probability with $c \to \infty$ uniformly over n. Therefore,

$$K_{mn} \xrightarrow{P} \lim_{c \to \infty} \sigma_c^{-1} \exp\ \{H(f_c)\} = 0$$

in virtue of Lemma 2, which establishes consistency for that class of alternatives.

Finally, let F have an atom a with a weight $p > 0$. Then

$$P\{K_{mn} \neq 0\} \leq P\{\text{at most } 2m \text{ elements of } (x_1, x_2, \ldots, x_n) \text{ are equal to } a\}$$
$$= \sum_{i=0}^{2m} \binom{n}{i} p^i (1-p)^{n-i} \to 0$$

as $n \to \infty, m/n \to 0$. Thus,

$$K_{mn} \xrightarrow{P} 0$$

and the consistency of the test for alternatives with an atom follows. This completes the proof.

It can be shown that always

$$0 \leq K_{mn} < \sqrt{(2\pi e)} = 4.133 \ldots .$$

Except in the simplest case $n = 3, m = 1$, the distribution of K_{mn} under the null hypothesis has not been obtained analytically. To determine the percentage points $K^*_{mn}(\alpha)$, Monte Carlo simulations were employed. For each $n \leq 50, 5000$ samples of size n from the normal distribution were formed, using the congruence method of generating pseudo-random numbers and obtaining approximately normal deviates as sums of 12 uniform deviates. The statistic K_{mn} for several values of m was calculated from each sample, and percentage points of the distribution of K_{mn} were estimated by the corresponding order statistics. For each significance level and each value of m, the estimates were smoothed by fitting a polynomial in powers of $n^{-\frac{1}{2}}$. The lower-tail 5 percent significance points of K_{mn} for selected values of n, m are given in Table 35.1.[1]

The power of the test was estimated against several alternatives. The method was that of Monte Carlo simulation of the distribution of K_{mn} under alternative population distributions. For each alternative, 1,000 samples of sizes n = 10, 20, 50 were generated, and the test power was estimated by the frequency of the samples falling into the critical region. The continuous alternatives investigated were gamma (1) (exponential), gamma (2), beta (1,1) (uniform), beta (2,1), and Cauchy distributions.

[1]The full tables of percentage points of the statistic, together with the results of the power studies, have been deposited in the Society's Library.

TABLE 35.1 0.05 points for the K statistic

	$m = 1$	$m = 2$	$m = 3$	$m = 4$	$m = 5$
$n = 3$	0.99				
4	1.05				
5	1.19	1.70			
6	1.33	1.77			
7	1.46	1.87	1.97		
8	1.57	1.97	2.05		
9	1.67	2.06	2.13		
10	1.76	2.15	2.21		
12	1.90	2.31	2.36		
14	2.01	2.43	2.49		
16	2.11	2.54	2.60	2.57	
18	2.18	2.62	2.69	2.67	
20	2.25	2.69	2.77	2.76	
25		2.83	2.93	2.93	2.91
30		2.93	3.04	3.06	3.05
35		3.00	3.13	3.16	3.16
40			3.19	3.24	3.24
45			3.25	3.29	3.30
50			3.29	3.34	3.35

For these alternatives, the maximum power was typically attained by choosing $m = 2$ for $n = 10, m = 3$ for $n = 20$, and $m = 4$ for $n = 50$. With increasing n, an optimal choice of m also increases, while the ratio m/n tends to zero.

The power of the K test was compared to that of some other tests for normality against the same alternatives. The tests investigated by Stephens (1974) were considered. These are the Kolmogorov-Smirnov D, Cramér-von Mises W^2, Kuiper V, Watson U^2, Anderson-Darling A^2, and Shapiro-Wilk W tests. Of these, only the Shapiro-Wilk test is a test of the composite hypothesis of normality. The tests D, W^2, V, U^2, and A^2, based on the empirical distribution function (EDF), require a complete specification of the null hypothesis. When these tests are used to test the composite hypothesis, the parameters must be estimated from the sample. Critical values corresponding to such modification of the test statistics are then applicable.

Table 35.2 lists power estimates of .05 size tests with sample size $n =$ 20. These results have been obtained by Stephens (1974) for the EDF statistics against the exponential, uniform, and Cauchy alternatives; by Van Soest (1967) for D, W^2 against gamma (2); and by Shapiro and Wilk (1965) for W. The powers of V, U^2, and A^2 against gamma (2) and of the EDF statistics against beta (2,1) were estimated by the author from 2,000 samples, using

TABLE 35.2 Powers of .05 tests against some alternatives ($n = 20$)

Alternative	D	W^2	V	U^2	A^2	W	K_3
Exponential	.59	.74	.71	.70	.82	.84	.85
Gamma (2)	.33	.45	.33	.37	.48	.50	.45
Uniform	.12	.16	.17	.18	.21	.23	.44
Beta (2,1)	.17	.23	.20	.23	.28	.35	.43
Cauchy	.86	.88	.87	.88	.98	.88	.75

the critical values given in Stephens (1974). The standard error of the power estimates in Table 35.2 does not exceed .015.

It is apparent from Table 35.1 that none of the tests considered performs better than all other tests against all alternatives. Compared with any other test, however, the K test exhibits higher power against at least three of the five alternative distributions. For three of the alternatives, the power of the K test is uniformly the highest. Similar results hold for other sample sizes and sizes of the test.

These results, together with the relative simplicity of the K test (no tables of coefficients or function values are needed to calculate the test statistic) and its asymptotic properties against any alternative, suggest that the K test may be preferred in many situations.

ACKNOWLEDGMENT

This research was partly supported by Wells Fargo Bank, N.A. The author is indebted to Larry J. Cuneo for help with the computer simulations. The author wishes to express his thanks to the editor and referees of the *Journal* for their helpful suggestions.

REFERENCES

Kullback, S. (1959). *Information Theory and Statistics*. New York: John Wiley & Sons.

Shannon, C.E. (1949). *The Mathematical Theory of Communication*. Urbana: University of Illinois Press.

Shapiro, S.S., and Wilk, M.B. (1965). "An Analysis of Variance Test for Normality (Complete Samples)." *Biometrika*, 52, 591–611.

Stephens, M.A. (1974). "EDF Statistics for Goodness of Fit and Some Comparisons." *J. Amer. Statist. Ass.*, 69, 730–737.

Van Soest, J. (1967). "Some Empirical Results Concerning Tests of Normality." *Statist. Neerland.*, 21, 91–97.

CHAPTER 36

Monotone Measures of Ergodicity for Markov Chains

By Julian Keilson and Oldrich Vasicek

ABSTRACT

The following paper, first written in 1974, was never published other than as part of an internal research series. Its lack of publication is certainly unrelated to the merits of the paper since the paper is of current importance by virtue of its relation to relaxation time. This chapter provides a systematic discussion of the approach of a finite Markov chain to ergodicity by proving the monotonicity of an important set of norms, each a measure of ergodicity *whether or not time reversibility is present*. The paper is of particular interest because the discussion of the relaxation time of a finite Markov chain (Keilson 1979) has only been clean for time reversible chains, a small subset of the chains of interest. This restriction is not present here. Indeed, a new relaxation time quoted quantifies the relaxation time for all finite ergodic chains (cf. the discussion of $Q_1(t)$ below Eq. (7)). This relaxation time was developed by J. Keilson with A. Roy in his thesis (Roy 1996).

INTRODUCTION

Let $N(t)$ be a finite homogeneous Markov chain in continuous time on the state space $\mathbf{N} = \{1, 2, \ldots, K\}$, which is irreducible and hence ergodic.

Journal of Applied Mathematics and Stochastic Analysis, 11 (3) (1998), 283–288.

Let $\underline{p}^T(t) = (p_n(t))$ be the state probability vector at time t with $p_n(t) = P[N(t) = n]$. Let $\underline{e}^T = (e_n)$ be the ergodic vector $\underline{e}^T = \lim_{t\to\infty} \underline{p}^T(t)$.

Consider the norm function with probability weights $q_n > 0$,

$$h_\alpha(\underline{p},\underline{q}) = \left\{ \sum_n q_n \left(\frac{p_n}{q_n}\right)^\alpha \right\}^{\frac{1}{\alpha}}, -\infty < \alpha < \infty, \alpha \neq 0$$

$$h_0(\underline{p},\underline{q}) = \exp\left\{ \sum_n q_n \log \frac{p_n}{q_n} \right\} \tag{1}$$

defined for arbitrary probability vectors $\underline{p}, \underline{q}$ supported on $\mathbf{N}$. Of interest are the related functions of time

$$R_\alpha(t) = h_\alpha(\underline{p}(t), \underline{e}) = \left\{ \sum_n e_n \left(\frac{p_n(t)}{e_n}\right)^\alpha \right\}^{\frac{1}{\alpha}}, \alpha \neq 0$$

$$R_0(t) = \exp\left\{ \sum_n e_n \log \frac{p_n(t)}{e_n} \right\} \tag{2}$$

and

$$Q_\alpha(t) = \left\{ \sum_n p_n(t) \left(\frac{p_n(t)}{e_n}\right)^\alpha \right\}^{\frac{1}{\alpha}}, \alpha \neq 0$$

$$Q_0(t) = \exp\left\{ \sum_n p_n(t) \log \frac{p_n(t)}{e_n} \right\}. \tag{3}$$

The functions $h_\alpha(\underline{w}, \underline{e})$ are vector norms on $\mathbf{R}^K$, and $R_\alpha(t)$ then describes a time dependent norm function. The function $Q_\alpha(t)$ has related properties.

It will be shown (cf. Theorem 1) that $Q_\alpha(t)$ is strictly decreasing in t for $\alpha > -1$, and strictly increasing in t for $\alpha < -1$ when $\underline{p}_0 \neq \underline{e}$, that is, when the chain is not stationary. When $\alpha = -1, Q_{-1}(t) = 1$ for all t. A similar monotonicity of $R_\alpha(t)$ with t is demonstrated in Theorem 2. We note that lim $Q_\alpha(t) = 1$ for all α as $t \to \infty$. In particular,

$$Q_0(t) = \exp\{H(\underline{p}(t), \underline{e})\} \tag{4}$$

and

$$R_0(t) = \exp\{-H(\underline{e}, \underline{p}(t))\} \tag{5}$$

where (cf. Kullback (1968), Renyi (1970))

$$H(\underline{p}, \underline{q}) = \sum_n p_n \log \frac{p_n}{q_n} \tag{6}$$

is the divergence of the distribution $\underline{p}$ from the distribution $\underline{q}$, an entity closely related to entropy and other concepts in information theory. The monotonicity of $H(\underline{e}, \underline{p}(t))$ and $H(\underline{p}(t), \underline{e})$ for arbitrary chains has been known (Renyi 1970).

A value of α of special interest corresponding to weighted quadratic distance is $\alpha = 1$, for which

$$Q_1(t) = \sum_n \frac{p_n^2(t)}{e_n} \tag{7}$$

and this is strictly decreasing in t if the chain is not stationary.

In the time reversible case, the monotonicity of Eq. (7) is well known (see Keilson 1979; and Kendall 1959). Indeed, for this case, the quadratic distance to ergodicity

$$D(t) = \sqrt{\sum_n \frac{(p_n(t) - e_n)^2}{e_n}} = \sqrt{Q_1(t) - 1} \tag{8}$$

is strictly decreasing by virtue of the symmetry of $\underline{\underline{e}}_D^{1/2}[\underline{p}(t) - \underline{1}\underline{e}^T]\underline{\underline{e}}_D^{-1/2}$ and its associated spectral representation (cf. Keilson (1979)). That $Q_1(t)$ and $D(t)$ are monotone decreasing for *all* ergodic chains is striking. The function $D^2(t)$ decreases strictly to zero for *every* finite nonstationary homogeneous ergodic chain.

The monotonicity of the distance to ergodicity (8) does not appear to extend easily to the full family $R_\alpha(t)$ and $Q_\alpha(t)$.

It is shown in Roy (1996, Remark 3.2.2) that for any ergodic chain and initial distribution,

$$D(t) \leq D(0)\ \mathrm{e}^{-|\theta_1|t} = \sqrt{\sum_n \frac{(p_n(0) - e_n)^2}{e_n}}\ \mathrm{e}^{-|\theta_1|t} \tag{9}$$

where $-\theta_1$ is the smallest of the positive real singular values of $\underline{\underline{e}}_D^{1/2}\underline{\underline{Q}}\,\underline{\underline{e}}_D^{-1/2}$ (cf. Amir-Moez and Fass (1961)). When the chain is reversible in time, this agrees with the known result (Keilson 1979). Consequently, $T_{rel} = 1/|\theta_1|$ is a natural extension of the relaxation time for time reversible ergodic chains to all ergodic chains.

The distance $D(t)$ and the relaxation time also play a role in the covariance function $R_f(\tau) = \text{cov}[f_{J(t)}, f_{J(t+\tau)}]$ of any stationary ergodic chain $J(t)$. Here (cf. Keilson 1979),

$$R_f(\tau) = \underline{f}^T \underline{\underline{e}}_D[\underline{\underline{p}}(\tau) - \underline{1}\,\underline{e}^T]\underline{f} = \underline{f}^T \underline{\underline{e}}_D[\underline{\underline{p}}(\tau) - \underline{1}\,\underline{e}^T]\ \underline{\underline{e}}_D^{-1/2}\underline{\underline{e}}_D^{1/2}\underline{f} = \underline{g}^T(\tau)\ \underline{b}$$

where

$$\underline{g}^T(\tau) = \frac{1}{\underline{f}^T\underline{e}}\ \underline{f}^T \underline{\underline{e}}_D\,[\underline{\underline{p}}(\tau) - \underline{1}\,\underline{e}^T]\underline{\underline{e}}_D^{-1/2}, \quad \underline{b} = (\underline{f}^T\underline{e})\underline{\underline{e}}_D^{1/2}\underline{f}.$$

Since f may be made positive by adding a constant without altering $R_f(\tau)$, it follows that $\frac{1}{\underline{f}^T\underline{e}}\ \underline{f}^T\underline{\underline{e}}_D[\underline{\underline{p}}(\tau) - \underline{1}\,\underline{e}^T]$ is of the form $\underline{p}^T(t) - \underline{e}^T$ needed for Eq. (8) and that Eq. (9) is then relevant. One then has from the Schwartz inequality

$$|R_f(\tau)| \le \sqrt{\underline{g}^T(\tau)\underline{g}(\tau)}\ \sqrt{\underline{b}^T\underline{b}} \le \sqrt{\underline{g}^T(0)\underline{g}(0)}\ \sqrt{\underline{b}^T\underline{b}}\ \mathrm{e}^{-|\theta_1|t}. \tag{10}$$

Note that for the Frobenius norm of $\underline{\underline{r}}(t) = \underline{\underline{e}}_D^{1/2}[\underline{\underline{p}}(t) - \underline{1}\,\underline{e}^T]\underline{\underline{e}}_D^{-1/2}$,

$$||r(t)||^2_{FROB} = \text{Trace}[\underline{\underline{r}}(t)\underline{\underline{r}}^T(t)] = \sum_{m,n} e_m \frac{(p_{mn}(t) - e_n)^2}{e_n}$$

and this is strictly decreasing in time. This follows from Eq. (7) with $p_n(0) = \delta_{mn}$, weighting by e_m, and summation over m. Indeed,

$$\begin{aligned}
\sum_{m,n} e_m \frac{(p_{mn}(t) - e_n)^2}{e_n} &= \sum_m e_m D_m^2(t) \\
&\le \sum_m e_m D_m^2(0)\ e^{-2|\theta_1|t} \\
&= e^{-2|\theta_1|t}\ \text{Trace}[\underline{\underline{e}}_D[\underline{\underline{I}} - \underline{1}\ \underline{e}^T]\underline{\underline{e}}_D^{-1}[\underline{\underline{I}} - \underline{e}\,\underline{1}^T]]
\end{aligned}$$

and

$$||r(t)||_{FROB} \le e^{-|\theta_1|t}\ \sqrt{K-1}.$$

When $\alpha = \pm\infty$,

$$Q_\infty(t) = \max_n \frac{p_n(t)}{e_n} \tag{11}$$

is a decreasing function of t, and

$$Q_{-\infty}(t) = \min_n \frac{p_n(t)}{e_n} \tag{12}$$

is an increasing function of t.

SOME BASIC LEMMAS

Lemma 1. For $y > 0$, let

$$g_\alpha(y) = \frac{1}{\alpha+1}\, y^{\alpha+1} - \frac{1}{\alpha} y^\alpha + \frac{1}{\alpha(\alpha+1)}$$

$$g_0(y) = y - 1 - \log\ y; \quad g_{-1}(y) = y^{-1} - 1 + \log\ y. \tag{13}$$

Then for all real α and all $y > 0$,

$$g_\alpha(y) \geq 0 \tag{14}$$

with equality if and only if $y = 1$.

Proof.

$$g_\alpha(y) = \int_1^y z^\alpha\ (1 - z^{-1})\ dz, y > 1$$

$$g_\alpha(y) = \int_y^1 z^\alpha\ (z^{-1} - 1)\ dz, 0 < y < 1$$

Consequently, $g_\alpha(y) \geq 0$. Moreover, strict inequality holds for $y \neq 1$.

Lemma 2. Let $\underline{\underline{R}} = (r_{mn})$ be a doubly conservative matrix, that is,

$$r_{mn} \geq 0, m \neq n, \sum_m r_{mn} = \sum_n r_{mn} = 0.$$

Then, for all real $\alpha \neq 0$ and all $x_n > 0, n = 1, 2, .., K$

$$\frac{1}{\alpha} \sum_m \sum_n x_m\ r_{mn}\ x_n^\alpha \leq 0 \tag{15}$$

and

$$\sum_m \sum_n x_m \; r_{mn}(1 + \log x_n) \leq 0. \tag{16}$$

Moreover, equality holds if and only if $x_m = x_n$ whenever $r_{mn} > 0, m, n = 1, 2, \ldots, K$.

Proof. Let $\alpha \neq 0, -1$. Then form simple algebra with $y_{mn} = \frac{x_n}{x_m}$:

$$\frac{1}{\alpha} \sum_m \sum_n x_m \; r_{mn} \; x_n^\alpha = -\sum_m \sum_{n \neq m} r_{mn} \; x_m^{\alpha+1} g_\alpha(y_{mn}). \tag{17}$$

By taking $\alpha \to 0$, Eq. (17) yields

$$\begin{aligned}
\sum_m \sum_n x_m \; r_{mn}(1 + \log \; x_n) &= \lim_{\alpha \to 0} \sum_m \sum_n x_m r_{mn} \; \left(1 + \frac{x_n^\alpha - 1}{\alpha}\right) \\
&= \lim_{\alpha \to 0} \frac{1}{\alpha} \sum_m \sum_n x_m r_{mn} \; x_n^\alpha \\
&= -\sum_m \sum_{n \neq m} r_{mn} \; x_m g_0(y_{mn})
\end{aligned} \tag{18}$$

Lemma 2 then follows from Lemma 1.

Remark 1. Note that for special value $\alpha = 1$,

$$\sum_m \sum_n x_m r_{mn} \; x_n \leq 0$$

for all real $\underline{x}$, because

$$\begin{aligned}
\sum_m \sum_n x_m \; r_{mn} \; x_n = &-\tfrac{1}{2} \sum_m \sum_n r_{mn} \; (x_m - x_n)^2 \\
&+ \tfrac{1}{2} \sum_m \sum_n r_{mn} x_m^2 + \tfrac{1}{2} \sum_m \sum_n r_{mn} x_n^2
\end{aligned}$$

and the last two terms are zero.

THE MAIN RESULT

Theorem 1. For a finite ergodic chain in continuous time, let

$$Q_\alpha(t) = \left\{ \sum_n p_n(t) \; \left(\frac{p_n(t)}{e_n}\right)^\alpha \right\}^{\frac{1}{\alpha}}, Q_0(t) = \left\{ \sum_n p_n(t) \; \log\left(\frac{p_n(t)}{e_n}\right) \right\}.$$

If the chain is not stationary, $Q_\alpha(t)$ is a strictly decreasing function of t on $[0,\infty)$ when $\alpha > -1$ and a strictly increasing function of t on $[0,\infty)$ when $\alpha < -1$.

Proof. Since $p_n(t)$ is differentiable, $Q_\alpha(t)$ is also differentiable. Then for $\alpha \neq 0$

$$\frac{d}{dt}\ Q_\alpha(t) = \frac{\alpha+1}{\alpha}\ (Q_\alpha(t))^{1-\alpha}\left\{\sum_n p'_n(t)\left(\frac{p_n(t)}{e_n}\right)^\alpha\right\}. \tag{19}$$

Let $\underline{\underline{p}}(t) = (p_{mn}(t))$ be the transition matrix for the chain $N(t)$, so that $\underline{\underline{p}}(t) = \exp\{\underline{\underline{S}}\ t\}$ where $\underline{\underline{S}} = (s_{mn})$ is the infinitesimal generator of the chain. Let $r_{mn} = e_m s_{mn}$. Then $\underline{\underline{r}} = (r_{mn})$ is doubly conservative in the sense of Lemma 2. Let $x_m(t) = p_m(t)/e_m$. Then

$$\begin{aligned}\frac{1}{\alpha}\left\{\sum_n p'_n(t)\left(\frac{p_n(t)}{e_n}\right)^\alpha\right\} &= \frac{1}{\alpha}\sum_n\sum_m\ p_m(t)\ s_{mn}\ \left(\frac{p_n(t)}{e_n}\right)^\alpha. \\ &= \frac{1}{\alpha}\sum_m\sum_n\ x_m(t) r_{mn} x_n^\alpha(t) \end{aligned}\tag{20}$$

The expression $x_m(t) > 0$ for $t > 0$ is a property of ergodic chains in continuous time. By Lemma 2, the expression (20) is always nonpositive for $t > 0$. From (19) it follows that $\frac{d}{dt}\ Q_\alpha(t)$ is nonpositive for $\alpha + 1 > 0, \alpha \neq 0$, and nonnegative for $\alpha + 1 < 0$. It attains the value 0 iff $s_{mn} > 0$ implies $x_m(t) = p_m(t)/e_m = x_n(t) = p_n(t)/e_n$. For chains with positive transition rates between all pairs of states, this is possible only if $p_n(t) = e_n$ for all n, that is, if the chain is stationary. The result then follows for all ergodic chains. When $\alpha = 0$,

$$\frac{d}{dt}\ Q_0(t) = Q_0(t)\sum_m\sum_n\ x_m(t) r_{mn}(1 + \log\ x_n(t)) \leq 0$$

with equality iff the chain is stationary.

Similar monotonicity properties hold for the family $R_\alpha(t)$. From (2) and (3) we have

$$R_\alpha(t) = [Q_{\alpha-1}(t)]^{(\alpha-1)/\alpha}. \tag{21}$$

When $\alpha > 1$ or $\alpha < 0$, $R_\alpha(t)$ and $Q_{\alpha-1}(t)$ have the same monotonicity properties with t. When $0 < \alpha < 1$, $R_\alpha(t)$ increases when $Q_{\alpha-1}(t)$ decreases. When $\alpha = 0$, we have $\frac{d}{dt}\ R_0(t) = -R_0(t)\ \sum_n p'_n(t)\frac{e_n}{p_n(t)}$, which for nonstationary chains is strictly positive for any $t > 0$ by virtue of Eq. (20) and Lemma 1. This yields the following theorem.

Theorem 2. Under the conditions of Theorem 1, $R_\alpha(t)$ is strictly decreasing in t for $\alpha > 1$, strictly increasing in t for $\alpha < 1$, and $R_1(t) = 1$.

ERGODIC CHAINS IN DISCRETE TIME

The results of the previous section apply also to discrete time finite Markov chains with the strict monotonicity replaced by weak monotonicity. Since the state probabilities $p_n(t)$ can be zero, we will restrict ourselves to the case $\alpha \geq 0$ only. In keeping with this convention, $p \log p$ will be defined to be zero whenever $p = 0$.

Theorem 3a. Let $\alpha \geq 0$. For a finite ergodic Markov chain, the sequence $Q_\alpha(t), t = 0, 1, 2, \ldots$ is a nonincreasing sequence.

Theorem 3b. If the elements of the one-step transition matrix are positive and the chain is not stationary, then $Q_\alpha(t)$ is strictly monotone in t.

The details of the proofs are similar to that for the continuous time case and are somewhat tedious. They will not be given here.

REFERENCES

Amir-Moez, A.R., and Fass, A.I. (1961). *Elements of Linear Spaces*. Ann Arbor, MI: Edwards Bros.

Keilson, J. (1979). *Markov Chain Models—Rarity and Exponentiality*. New York: Springer-Verlag, Applied Mathematical Sciences Series 28.

Kendall, D.G. (1959). "Unitary Dilations of Markov Transition Operators and the Corresponding Integral Representations for Transition Probability Matrices" (edited by U. Grenander), *Probability and Statistics*. Stockholm: Almqvist and Wiksell.

Kullback, S. (1968). *Information Theory and Statistics*. New York: Dover Publications Inc.

Renyi, A. (1970). *Foundations of Probability*, San Francisco: Holden-Day.

Roy, A. (1996). *Transient Analysis of Queuing Systems*, Ph.D. Thesis. Ann Arbor, MI: University of Rochester. This is available from UMI, Ann Arbor.

CHAPTER 37

An Inequality for the Variance of Waiting Time under a General Queueing Discipline

ABSTRACT

We show that the expected value of any convex function of the waiting time (such as the variance) in a general queuing system under any queuing discipline independent of the service times does not exceed that under the last-come-first-served discipline, and is not less than that under the first-come-first-served discipline.

INTRODUCTION

It has been noted (see, for instance, Cohen (1969), Riordan (1962), Vaulot (1954)) that the variance of the waiting time in the $M/M/1$ and $M/G/1$ queuing systems under the last-come-first-served (LCFS) discipline exceeds that under service in the order of arrivals, first-come-first-served (FCFS). This observation has been made by comparison of explicit expressions for the variance. Moreover, in the cases when the waiting-time variance has been determined under service in random order (SIRO), it was found to attain an intermediate value (see Riordan 1962). The expected waiting times in all three cases are, of course, equal.

This has led to an interpretation of the FCFS discipline as more "fair" than either the SIRO or LCFS: While the expected waiting time of a given customer is not influenced, the total waiting time of all customers is more equally divided under FCFS than under SIRO, while the LCFS discipline is the least "egalitarian" of the three.

Operations Research, 25 (5) (1977), 879–884.

Vasicek (1965) has shown that in the $M/M/1$ system the variance of the waiting time actually attains its minimum and maximum for the FCFS and LCFS disciplines, respectively, within the following class of queueing disciplines: Let $r_{kn}, k = 1, \ldots, n; n = 1, 2, \ldots$ be given nonnegative numbers such that $r_{1n} + \cdots + r_{nn} = 1, n = 1, 2, \ldots$. If the queue length at the instant of completion of service is n and the waiting customers are enumerated in the order of their arrivals, then the k-th customer is selected for service with probability r_{kn}. Obviously, the three previously mentioned queuing disciplines are special cases of this scheme. The proof of the proposition was specific for the Markov character of the system.

In this paper, we give a proof of a general statement that similar inequalities hold in any queuing system with an arbitrary arrival process and any service time distribution, as long as the service times are independent of each other and of the process of arrivals. The queuing discipline can be any rule of selection among the customers present in the system at that moment that is independent of their (future) service times. Such a rule can, however, depend on the past experience of the system. Actually, a more general result is proven, establishing inequalities for the expectation of any convex function of the waiting times.

ASSUMPTIONS AND DEFINITIONS

Consider a $G/G/c$ system, $c \geq 1$, with a queuing capacity. The arrival process is arbitrary. It could be temporally and spatially nonhomogeneous, and the interarrival times need not be independent. Group arrivals are possible. The queuing capacity can be limited or unlimited, and balking based on queue length is permitted. It is assumed that the service times are independent identically distributed variables that are independent of the arrival process. We assume further that each period of nonempty queue ("queue" meaning the customers in the system that are not in service) is finite with probability 1. The symbol $GI/G/c$ will be used to denote a system with a homogeneous renewal process of arrivals and independent identically distributed service times.

We will restrict the use of the term *queuing discipline* to any rule of selection for service from the queue that is independent of the service times of the customers in queue at the instant of selection. In other words, it is required that the selection rule does not anticipate the service times. Such a rule may, however, depend on any other aspect of the system, such as the arrival times of the customers in the queue.

The disciplines FCFS and LCFS (as well as SIRO) are obviously admissible under the definition. On the other hand, consider a system with several classes of customers, each class having a different service time distribution but independent Poisson arrivals. Such a system can be viewed as a single-class $M/G/c$ system with a service time distribution that is a mixture of the distributions for individual classes. A priority assignment to the classes will not constitute a queuing discipline in the previous sense.

THE MAIN RESULTS

Theorem 1. Let D be a queuing discipline in a $G/G/c$ system. Let the number of customers entering service during a period of nonempty queue be n, and denote by $W_k, k = 1, \dots, n$ the waiting times under the discipline D. Let $W_k{}'$ and $W_k{}'', k = 1, \dots, n$ be the waiting times under the FCFS and LCFS disciplines, respectively. Then for any convex function f on $[0, \infty)$,

$$\sum_{k=1}^{n} Ef(W_k') \leq \sum_{k=1}^{n} Ef(W_k) \leq \sum_{k=1}^{n} Ef(W_k''). \tag{1}$$

Moreover, the quantity $\sum_{k=1}^{n} EW_k$ does not depend on the queuing discipline.

The proof of the theorem is based on the following lemma:

Lemma. Let $t_1 \leq \cdots \leq t_n$, $s_1 \leq \cdots \leq s_n$ be two series of numbers such that $t_k \leq s_k, k = 1, \dots, n$. Let $R = (R(1), \dots, R(n))$ be any permutation of $(1, \dots, n)$ such that

$$t_{R(k)} \leq s_k, k = 1, \cdots, n. \tag{2}$$

Put $R' = (1, \dots, n)$, $R'' = (R''(1), \dots, R''(n))$, where $R''(k) = \max\,[i : i \neq R''(j), j = 1, \dots, k-1;\ t_i \leq s_k]$, $k = 1, \dots, n$. Let f be a convex function on $[0, \infty)$, and define $V(R) = \sum_{k=1}^{n} f(s_k - t_{R(k)})$. Then $V(R') \leq V(R) \leq V(R'')$.

Proof. Let R be a permutation of $(1, \dots, n)$ such that (2) holds. If $R = R''$, then $V(R) = V(R'')$. Suppose then that $R \neq R''$. Then there exist i, j such that $i < j, R(i) < R(j)$, $t_{R(j)} \leq s_i$. Define a permutation R^* by $R^*(k) = R(k), k \neq i, j, R^*(i) = R(j)$, $R^*(j) = R(i)$. Obviously, $t_{R^*(k)} \leq s_k$, $k = 1, \dots, n$. Then

$$V(R^*) - V(R) = f(s_i - t_{R(j)}) + f(s_j - t_{R(i)}) - f(s_i - t_{R(i)}) - f(s_j - t_{R(j)}). \tag{3}$$

If $t_{R(i)} = t_{R(j)}$, then $V(R^*) - V(R) = 0$. Let $t_{R(i)} < t_{R(j)}$, and put $\alpha = [t_{R(j)} - t_{R(i)}]/[s_j - s_i + t_{R(j)} - t_{R(i)}]$. Write (3) as

$$V(R^*) - V(R) = \alpha f(s_i - t_{R(j)}) + (1-\alpha) f(s_j - t_{R(i)}) - f(s_j - t_{R(j)}) \\ + (1-\alpha) f(s_i - t_{R(j)}) + \alpha f(s_j - t_{R(i)}) - f(s_i - t_{R(i)}). \quad (4)$$

Since $0 \leq \alpha \leq 1$, it follows from the convexity of f that the right-hand side of (4) is nonnegative, and consequently $V(R) \leq V(R^*)$.

If $R^* = R''$, then $V(R) \leq V(R'')$. If $R^* \neq R''$, then there must exist i, j such that $i < j, R^*(i) < R^*(j), t_{R^*(j)} \leq s_i$. In that case, a new permutation can be defined by interchanging $R^*(i)$ and $R^*(j)$ with the value of V not smaller than $V(R^*)$. This process can be repeated until permutation R'' is reached. This will happen in a finite number of steps because each new permutation contains more inversions than the previous one, so that they are all distinct. This establishes the inequality $V(R) \leq V(R'')$.

Again, let R be a permutation such that (2) holds. If $R = R'$, then $V(R) = V(R')$. Assume that $R \neq R'$. Then there exist i, j such that $i < j, R(i) > R(j)$. Define a permutation R^{**} by $R^{**}(k) = R(k), k \neq i, j$, $R^{**}(i) = R(j)$, $R^{**}(j) = R(i)$. Clearly, $t_{R^{**}(k)} \leq s_k$, $k = 1, \dots, n$. But R is obtained from R^{**} by an operation that has been shown not to decrease the value of V, and consequently $V(R^{**}) \leq V(R)$. Repeated construction of new permutations by interchanging inversions leads in a finite number of steps to R', and therefore $V(R') \leq V(R)$. This completes the proof of the lemma.

Proof of Theorem 1. Let $t_1 \leq \cdots \leq t_n$ be the arrival times of the n customers entering service during a period of nonempty queue, and let $s_1 \leq \cdots \leq s_n$ be the epochs of commencement of service under a queuing discipline D. Let $s'_1 \leq \cdots \leq s'_n$, $s''_1 \leq \cdots \leq s''_n$ be the epochs of commencement of service under the disciplines FCFS and LCFS, respectively. Since the selection from the queue under a queuing discipline is independent of the service times of the customers in queue, the distributions of $(s_1, \dots, s_n), (s_1', \dots, s_n')$, and $(s_1'', \dots, s_n'')$ are all the same.

Let $R = (R(1), \dots, R(n))$ be the order in which the customers are served under the discipline D; that is, the customer selected for the k-th service is the $R(k)$-th arrived. Obviously, R is a permutation of $(1, \dots, n)$, and $t_{R(k)} \leq s_k$, $k = 1, \dots, n$. By the lemma

$$\sum_{k=1}^{n} f(s_k - t_{R'(k)}) \leq \sum_{k=1}^{n} f(s_k - t_{R(k)}) \leq \sum_{k=1}^{n} f(s_k - t_{R''(k)}),$$

where $R'(k) = k$ and $R''(k) = \max\,[i : i \neq R''(j), j = 1, \dots, k-1; t_i \leq s_k]$ for $k = 1, \dots, n$.

But R', R'' are the orders of service under the FCFS and LCFS disciplines, respectively, given that the service commencement times are $s_1, \ldots, s_n$. The quantities $W_k = s_k - t_{R(k)}, s_k - t_{R'(k)}, s_k - t_{R''(k)}, k = 1, \ldots, n$ are the corresponding waiting times under D, FCFS, and LCFS, respectively. Since $(s_1', \ldots, s_n')$ has the same distribution as $(s_1, \ldots, s_n)$, the actual waiting times $W_k' = s_k' - t_{R'(k)}, k = 1, \ldots, n$ under FCFS have the same joint distribution as $s_k - t_{R'(k)}, k = 1, \ldots, n$, and $\sum_{k=1}^{n} Ef(W_k') = \sum_{k=1}^{n} Ef(s_k - t_{R'(k)}) \leq \sum_{k=1}^{n} Ef(W_k)$. Similarly, the actual waiting times $W_k'', k = 1, \ldots, n$ under LCFS have the same distribution as $s_k - t_{R''(k)}, k = 1, \ldots, n$ (here R'' is not necessarily the actual order of service), and $\sum_{k=1}^{n} Ef(W_k'') = \sum_{k=1}^{n} Ef(s_k - t_{R''(k)}) \geq \sum_{k=1}^{n} Ef(W_k)$. This proves the inequalities (1). Now, since both $f(x) = x$ and $f(x) = -x$ are convex functions, it follows that $\sum_{k=1}^{n} EW_k' = \sum_{k=1}^{n} EW_k = \sum_{k=1}^{n} EW_k''$. Consequently, the sum of expected waiting times in a period of nonempty queue is independent of the queuing discipline. This completes the proof of Theorem 1.

The proof of Theorem 1 did not in fact require that the service times be independent identically distributed variables. All that was necessary was that the epochs of commencement of service had the same joint distribution under any queuing discipline. Thus the inequalities (1) will hold as long as the distribution of the service time does not depend on the particular customer served. If a barber doubles his speed when the queue is long, the FCFS and LCFS disciplines still distribute the total waiting time in the most equitable and least equitable fashion, respectively. On the other hand, the theorem does not hold when customers are selected for service based on the knowledge of their service times. If that customer is served first whose service time is the shortest among those waiting (the shortest remaining processing time rule), the total waiting time over a period of nonempty queue in fact decreases (see Schrage 1968).

In the special case when the waiting times are identically distributed we have

Theorem 2. Let D be a queuing discipline in a stationary $GI/G/c$ system, and denote by W, W', W'' the waiting times under D, FCFS, and LCFS, respectively. Then for any convex function f on $[0, \infty)$,

$$Ef(W') \leq Ef(W) \leq Ef(W''). \tag{5}$$

Moreover

$$EW' = EW = EW''. \tag{6}$$

Proof. Let W be the waiting time of a given customer. If the customer arrives while at least one service line is idle, then $W = 0$ independently of the queuing discipline. Assume that the customer arrives while all service lines are busy. Because the system is stationary, such a customer is equally likely to be any of the (say) n customers entering service during that period of nonempty queue. If $W_1, \dots, W_n$ are the waiting times of these n customers, then $Ef(W) = (1/n) \sum_{k=1}^{n} Ef(W_k)$, where the expectation on the left is conditional on n. Theorem 1 then implies the relations (5) and (6) conditionally on n. Since this is true for any n, the theorem follows.

By choosing $f(x) = (x - a)^2$ where $a = EW$, we obtain:

Corollary 1. In a stationary $GI/G/c$ system

$$\text{Var } W' \leq \text{Var } W \leq \text{Var } W''. \tag{7}$$

The variance has been singled out for historical reasons. Obviously, inequalities similar to (7) hold for any moment of order at least 1, and for any absolute moment around the mean of order at least 1 (such as the mean absolute deviation). Another special case is given by

Corollary 2. Let ϕ, ϕ', ϕ'' be the Laplace transforms of the waiting times in a stationary $GI/G/c$ system under an arbitrary queuing discipline and under the FCFS, LCFS disciplines, respectively. Then for any $u \geq 0$, $\phi'(u) \leq \phi(u) \leq \phi''(u)$.

REFERENCES

Cohen, J. (1969). *The Single Server Queue*. Amsterdam: North-Holland, 1969.

Riordan, J. (1962). *Stochastic Service Systems*. New York: John Wiley & Sons.

Schrage, L. (1968). "A Proof of the Optimality of the Shortest Remaining Service Time Discipline." *Opns. Res.*, 16, 687–690.

Vasicek, O. (1965). "Poznámka k čekací disciplíně v systémech hromadné obsluhy." *Aplikace Matematiky*, 10, 423–427.

Vaulot, E. (1954). "Delais d'attente des appels telephoniques dans l'ordre inverse de leur arrivee." *C. R. Acad. Sci. Paris*, 238, 1188–1189.

About the Author

Dr. **Oldrich Alfons Vasicek** works in mathematical finance, particularly on development of quantitative models of firms, financial instruments, and financial markets. He was a founding partner of KMV Corporation, a firm pioneering the use of structural models for credit valuation. Earlier in his career, he was a vice president in the Management Science Department of Wells Fargo Bank, a consultant to Gifford Fong Associates, and a special adviser to Moody's KMV. His academic appointments included five years of teaching graduate finance at the University of Rochester, the University of California at Berkeley, and at Ecole Supérieure des Sciences Economiques et Commerciales (ESSEC) in France.

A native of the Czech Republic, he holds a PhD in probability theory from Charles University in Prague. He has published over 35 articles in financial and mathematical journals and has received a number of honors, including the Graham and Dodd Award, the Roger F. Murray Prize, the Award of the Institute for Quantitative Research in Finance, the IAFE Financial Engineer of the Year Award, and the Risk Magazine Lifetime Achievement Award. He has been inducted into the Derivatives Strategy Hall of Fame, the Fixed Income Analysts Society Hall of Fame, and the Risk Magazine Hall of Fame. His theory of the term structure of interest rates is generally recognized as a genesis of that field in finance.

Index

Printed and bound by CPI Group (UK) Ltd, Croydon, CR0 4YY
23/04/2025
14660999-0003